1830 Citizens
of Texas

Gifford White

EAKIN PRESS Fort Worth, Texas
www.EakinPress.com

Copyright © 1999
By Gifford White
Published By Eakin Press
An Imprint of Wild Horse Media Group
P.O. Box 331779
Fort Worth, Texas 76163
1-817-344-7036
www.EakinPress.com
ALL RIGHTS RESERVED
1 2 3 4 5 6 7 8 9
ISBN-10: 1-68179-131-9
ISBN-13: 978-1-68179-131-5

TABLE OF CONTENTS

	Foreword	v
	Preface	vii
I	Austin's "Register of Families"	1
	Volume I	1
	Volume II	43
II	Titles in DeWitt's Colony	63
III	1830 Census of San Antonio	77
IV	1830 Census of Nacogdoches	113
V	General Land Office Records	133
VI	Clerk's Returns and Reports	181
VII	Registered Voters of 1867	215
	Appendix	239
	A Population Statistics For Texas	239
	B Land Laws	240
	Bibliography	242
	Index	243

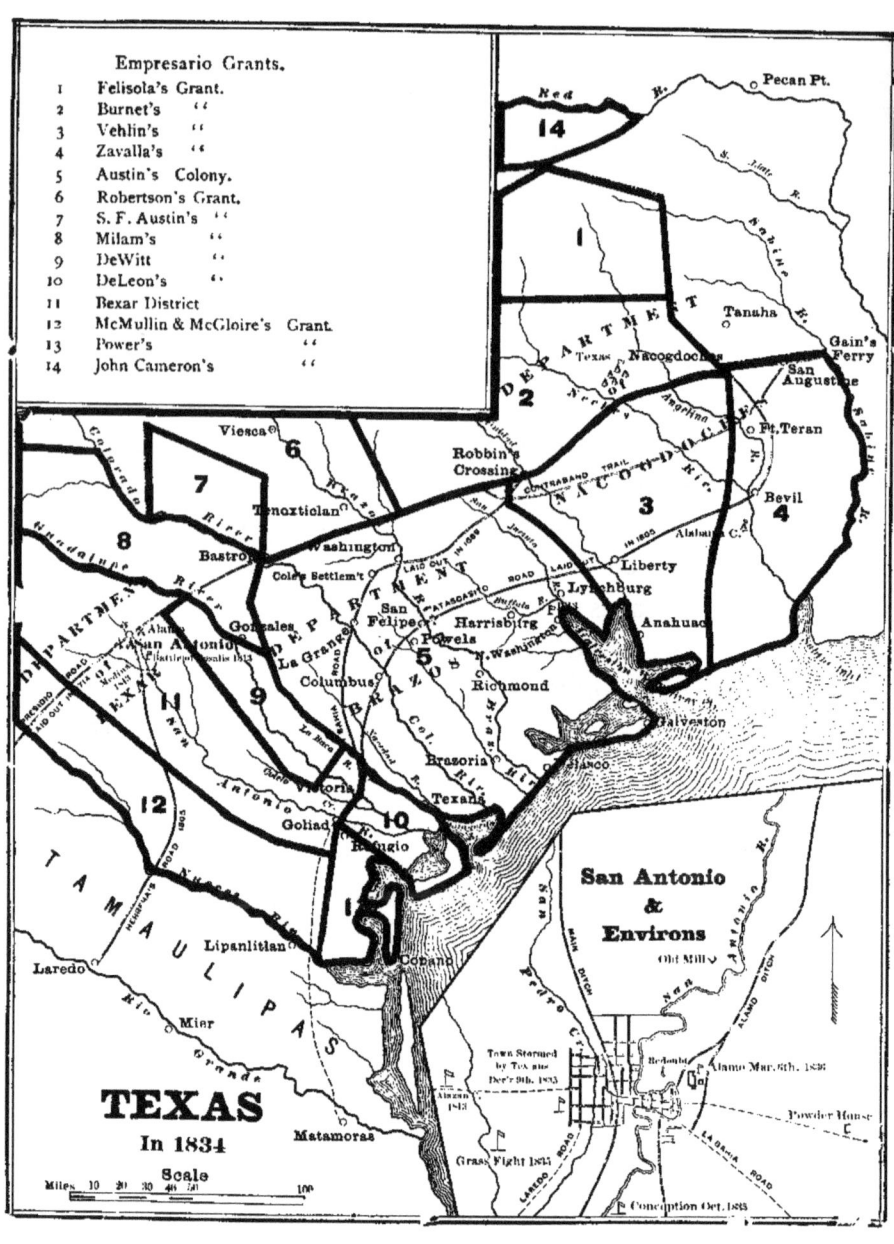

From A PICTORIAL HISTORY OF TEXAS
by Rev. Homer S. Thrall, A.M.
St. Louis, Mo. 1879
N. D. Thompson & Co.

FOREWORD

Some 152 years ago, in 1830, census takers trudged door to door in San Antonio de Bejar and Nacogdoches gathering data on the inhabitants. Either they got no farther, or else their other returns have been lost. Whichever, in *1830 Citizens of Texas*, Gifford White has finished the work they began.

Herein are reproduced every major contemporary public list of persons in, or sworn to be in, Texas in 1830. The result is a document as close as possible to a census of Texas contemporary with the decennial United States census. Better than that, Gifford White often provides more information than the U.S. census takers gathered. Indeed, several of the lists he includes yield more data on the individuals named than the Mexican enumerators sought. Among the lists here one can find the names of wives, dates of immigration, country or state of nativity or previous residence, and occupation.

In a reference book such as this, most readers will begin at the back consulting the index for the name(s) they seek. Beware. Eager, indiscriminate haste can make real waste and disappointment. The names in the index are as they appear on the original lists. Texas in 1830, it must always be remembered, was a part of Mexico. Recorders of official information spoke and wrote Spanish, not English. As with Americans and their English of the period, the Spanish that the recorders wrote often was phonetic, not dictionary Spanish. Deciphering an English phonetic spelling of an English name many times is chore enough. But to fathom (or is it "phazom"?) how the unfamiliar English name sounded to the Spanish scribe and was then written phonetically, or even translated into Spanish, takes an extra measure of sagacity. "Santiago Buy," for instance, is actually "James Bowie." Adolfo Estern is Adolphus Stern. Claque is Clark; Esmite on one roll and Hesmite on another both are Smith; and Quese likely is Case. For the contemporary lists in this book, an ear for Spanish and a knowledge of Spanish names are essential.

Over the last fifteen years, Gifford White has produced nearly a

RUINS OF THE SAN JOSE MISSION
A Pictorial History of Texas, Homer S. Thrall, St. Louis 1879

dozen works, primarily for genealogists: several volumes of minutes and certificates of land distribution in Austin, Fannin, Harris, Harrison, Liberty, and Shelby counties; first settlers of Red River County; the 1840 census of Texas; and the massive *Texas Scholastics, 1854-55*, with its supplement. The *1830 Citizens of Texas* is his most ambitious undertaking to date, and will be his most welcomed as well. It brings together scattered documents few researchers would take the time, or have the expertise, to review in the original. In addition, the work can significantly advance our understanding of Mexican Texas by making possible accurate collective study of the inhabitants. In *1830 Citizens of Texas*, Gifford White has provided us a most important, useful new tool for research.

David B. Gracy II
Texas State Archives

PREFACE

Genealogical research in Texas has been handicapped because early census schedules are not complete and do not coordinate with the decennial census of the eastern states. The gap has been partially filled by publication of the early Mexican census returns and poll and property tax rolls from the Republic. Reference should be made to the Bibliography. The 1840 ad valorem tax rolls make an alternate for the 1840 census, but nothing has been gathered into one compilation that covers 1830. Although a Mexican census must have been taken in all of Texas in 1830, only partial schedules can be found in the archives, and even these have not been published. This book is an attempt to gather together a useful substitute.

The records presented in abstract here are of several kinds. The extant census schedules for 1830 need no description, but they list only about one-eighth of the population. The section from Austin's "Register of Families" contains those who applied for land in 1830 and it gives the same information as a census. Other names are taken from records made after 1830 in which citizens swore to immigration before 1830, for example. Names with these "bridging dates" have been taken from the General Land Office records of applications for land in 1838-39.

Special mention should be made of the 1867 Register of Voters, created by the military government after the Civil War. This very large register of over 100,000 names is the first record of many minority population members. From this register have been taken the names of men who swore that they had been in Texas for thirty-seven years or more, proving them to have been citizens in 1830.

Important information from each source has been copied although the book is thereby swelled. The value of having all the basic facts summarized in one place justifies the space. The consultation of original sources in a rapid research is inconvenient and consumes much time. Explicit locations are given for each archive so that copies of the original may be obtained.

Names were not culled from personal narrative and local history because of the varying credibility of dates in accounts usually made long after the occurrence. All the sources used were originally made under oath, or at least under the force of a law that compelled true answers. Equally important, the information was given in 1830 or not long afterward.

There is some duplication of names from the different sources but no attempt has been made to associate them as the same (or different) persons.

An Appendix discusses the population records of Texas and arrives at a non-Indian population of about 17,000 in 1830. Of these, perhaps 3,000 are blacks, leaving 14,000 Anglo-Europeans and Mexican nationals. This book must then contain a substantial fraction of the adult males. A lesser part of the names of women and minors will appear.

One of the books on the land system of Texas should be read because the history of Texas land is much too complex to summarize. The lists of names will be much more significant when the laws that led to the compilation of these records are understood.

The usual caveats that preface transcriptions of handwritten sources should be remembered. Early spellings of names were often phonetic and the writing of each scribe had a personal bias. Moreover, the archival document that appears to be the original was often a COPY of a now vanished working record. Errors multiplied at each transcription. Ingenuity in the search for the name of a person will be essential.

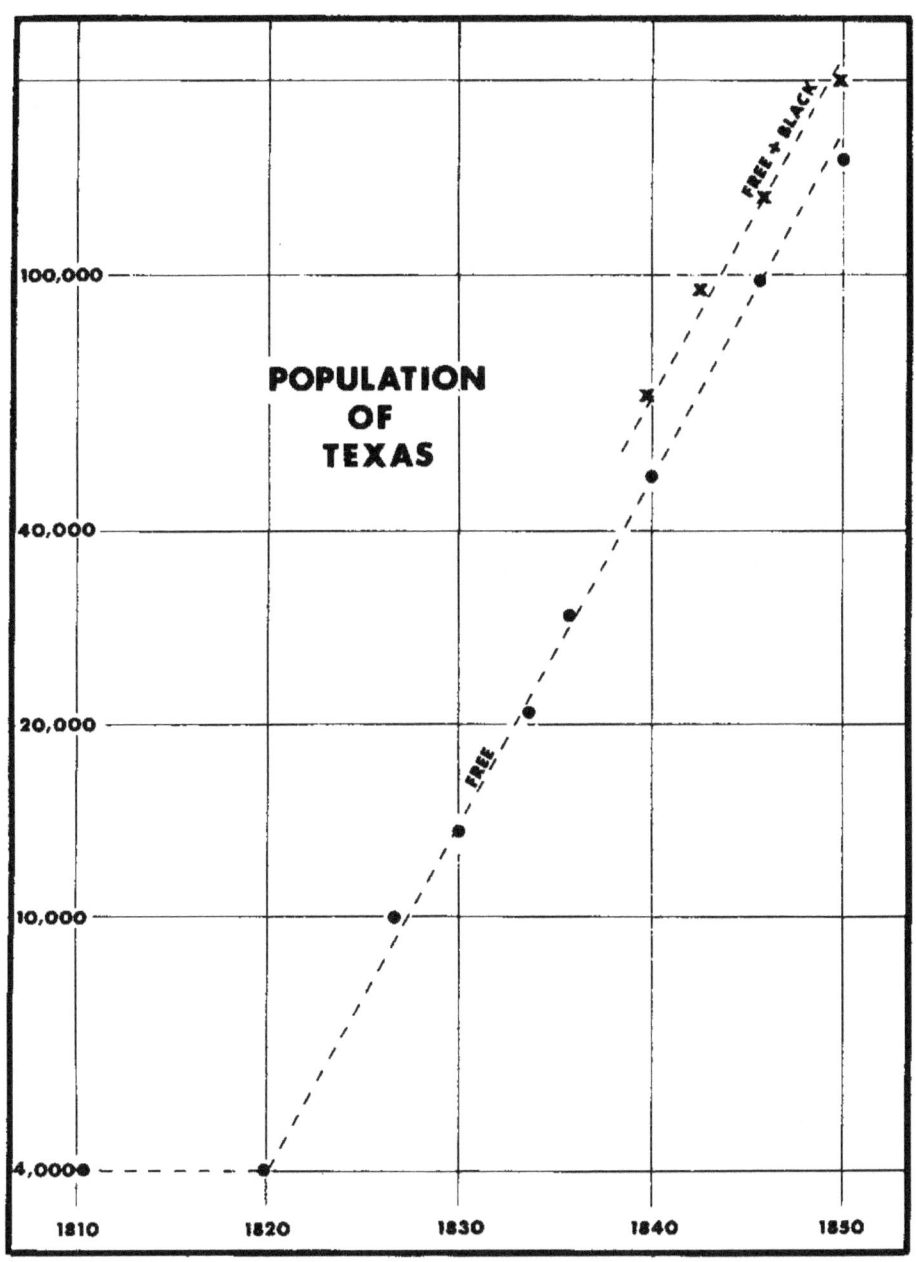

Refer to Appendix A, Page 239

STEPHEN FULLER AUSTIN
History of Texas, John Henry Brown, St. Louis 1892

AUSTIN'S "REGISTER OF FAMILIES"

Stephen F. Austin was the first contractor with the new Republic of Mexico who undertook to bring colonists into the thinly populated area of Texas. As Empresario, he began granting land to Anglo-American immigrants in 1823. Under a new Colonization Law passed in 1825, he was required to record detailed personal information on every new entrant. This information was written into the "Register." Most of the actual recording was done in Spanish by Secretary Samuel M. Williams. The "Register" now consists of two bound manuscript volumes in the Spanish Archives of the General Land Office in Austin.

Information on settlers that shows them in Texas in 1830 has been taken from these two volumes. Page numbers in ( ) are the original manuscript page numbers. Everything added by the editor has been enclosed [ ].

In translating from Spanish, English equivalents for most place names have been used, but personal names have been copied exactly as written within the limits of legibility.

Entries were made on two facing pages in the originals. The right hand page was usually used for a description of the land chosen, and a few other notes. Notes of genealogical interest that could be read in the sometimes very fine handwriting have been copied under the entries originally on the left hand page.

Frequent use is made of id, idem, do and ". They all mean "repeat the above."

EVENTS THAT AFFECTED THE MAKING OF THE "REGISTER OF FAMILIES"

1821 Mexico became independent of Spain, and the Austin plan for colonization of Texas was delayed. Anglo-American immigrants bound for the new colony began arriving in Texas.

1823 April. Stephen F. Austin finally obtained approval for his colonization contract in Mexico City, and returned to Texas to deliver land titles to "The Old Three Hundred" settlers waiting for him.

1824 May. Samuel May Williams arrived in Texas and assumed the duties of secretary and business manager for Austin, a position he held for the next eleven years. He was the principal keeper of the "Register."

1825 March 24. The Colonization Law that mandated the keeping of personal records on land claimants was passed.

1835 October 17. Revolution was beginning in Texas and the new Permanent Council ordered all land offices to be closed.

1836 March 2. Independence from Mexico was declared.

LAND TERMS

Vara. A Spanish linear measure of varying value; Texas finally settled on 33-1/3 inches. Also a square vara.

League. A linear measure of 5000 varas. Also a measure of land equal to a plot one league square, equal to 4428.4 acres.

Labor of land. 1,000,000 square varas, or 177.1 acres, considered the amount of tillable land for one farmer.

Sitio. One square league as needed for a ranching operation.

Hacienda. Five or more square leagues.

Augmentation. The amount of land due a settler because of a change in his status (marriage, for example), to be added to his previous allotment.

PLACE NAMES

Place names no longer in popular use may have the following modern equivalents.

Francisco. Probably San Francisco de Béxar, to be equated with San Antonio.

Aises. Probably the same as Ayish, a bayou between the Sabine and Neches Rivers, and a settlement of the same name.

Palogacho. Possibly Palo Gaucho Bayou in now San Augustine County, and a settlement of the same name.

Atacapas. In early Louisiana, a district and then a county. Not now in use, it covered Lafayette and St. Martin and other nearby Parishes.

Opelousas. An early Louisiana settlement around the present town of the same name.

SAMUEL MAY WILLIAMS

. . . born on October 4, 1795, in Providence, Rhode Island . . . Williams arrived in San Felipe, the Capital of Austin's colony, in May, 1824, and immediately assumed the duties that Austin had outlined for a recorder. For the next eleven years he served . . . Besides English,

Williams wrote and spoke both Spanish and French fluently; he wrote a fine Spencerian hand and had charge of all maps, charts and clerical work of Austin's colonies.

The Handbook of Texas, The Texas State Historical Assoc., Austin 1952. II-915.

LAW OF COLONIZATION OF THE STATE OF COAHUILA AND TEXAS

Art. 3. Whatever foreigner at present resident in Coahuila and Texas, may determine on settling there, shall make a declaration to that effect, addressed to the municipal authorities of the town in which he is desirous of fixing his residence. The municipal authorities then shall bind him by oath, which he shall make, to abide by and obey the general Constitution, and that of the State; to observe the Religion as stipulated by the former; and in a book (the register of foreigners) which shall be kept for that purpose, his name and those of the members of his family, if he has any, shall be set down; noting the country from whence he comes, whether married or single, his employment . . .

Art. 5. . . . new settlers . . . must prove, by certificate from the authorities of the place from whence they came, that they are Christians, and also the morality and propriety of their conduct.

Art. 7. . . . no settlement be made within twenty leagues of the boundaries of the United States of North America, and ten leagues along the coast of the Gulf of Mexico . . .

Art. 14. To each of the families included in a project of colonization, whose sole occupation is the cultivation of the land, one division of land shall be given [one labor]; should it also breed cattle . . . quantity to complete one lot [league].

Art. 15. . . . those who are alone . . . must content themselves with one-fourth part of the above.

Saltillo, 24th March, 1825
Rafael Ramos y Valdez
President

The Laws of Texas, H.P.N. Gammel, Austin 1898. I-99

EXCERPTS FROM AUSTIN'S "REGISTER OF FAMILIES"

(10)

Robert A. Burney, single, arrived 25 Decr 1828, will bring one servant and others. Took the oath 18 Novbr 1829. Issued the certificate the same day.

Certificate issued to William Collins of Opelousas, is to emigrate within five months, family and his wife, son, daughter, 8 servants, 1 orphan dependent, 13 souls. The sitio above and adjoining with that of Isaac Lee on Cummins Creek. 5 December 1829.

Mathew Duty for the minor heirs of Solomon Duty, wants to take the land for them adjoining and above his situated on the east bank of the Colorado River above the Bexar Road.

Joseph Duty wants to take his land in augmentation on the Colorado River bank on the right side three miles above the Bexar Road between the land of Winslow Turner and the road on a plain that is there.

Mr. George Ewing for Mr. Davis wants to take a sitio on the east bank above the junction of the Navidad and Sandy Creek between a sitio of Crozier and Scott, to have the location or in case not, west bank of the Navidad in front of Crozier.

M. Cummins wants land near the Bexar Road west of the Brazos adjoining the land between Spears and land of John Williams.

21 Dec 1829. Mr. Thomas J. Chambers wants to settle in this Colony

(11)

on the Navasota River course to the east of the Brazos, begining at the place called Rocky Shoals, and the same east to the point and to the south and to the east and north to the point to compensate for quantity.

21 Decr 1829. Today have issued certificates to the following men who have returned to bring their families, and have been given a term of sixteen months beginning after the 1st of next January to verify their moving here. They are:

Anthony Winston	William O. Winston
Isaac Winston	John T. Dillard
Benjamin A. Jones	Gibson Wooldridge
William J. Adair	Milton Winston
William Winston	George Carrol
Joel W. Winston	Richard S. Jones

Which gentlemen have designated their land on the Navidad River and Lavaca.

(12)   [1830]

24 January. Today issued certificates to the following gentlemen of the State of Alabama who have the term of 16 months after the first of this month to verify the removal of their families into this Colony, and are

Austin's "Register of Families"

George Sutherland
John Sutherland
William Manifee
Thomas Manifee
William H. Heard
Joseph Rector
William Pride
Jessey White
Benjamin White
Samuel Rogers

Robert G. Crosier
William Haskins
Pulaskey Dudley
James N. Smith
Mary Smith
Richard R. Royall
Thacker Winter
John Caldwell
Washington J. Cockrill

These gentlemen have designated their land on the Arroyo Karankahuas and Arroyo Navidad.

24 January. Today have issued a certificate to Mr. Joseph Davis and given the term to the 1st of May of the year 1831 to bring his family and has chosen his land on the right bank of the Navidad River.

I have issued certificates to the following gentlemen of the State of Missouri and given a term to the 15 of June of the following year of 1831 to bring their families.

Stephen F. Danklin
William W Hunter

George Hammond
Henry Bates

[Marginal note]: Not in Texas

(13)

Today issue a certificate to T. McQueen and gave a term for moving here until the 20 of Feby of the following year.

Today have issued certificates to the following gentlemen and gave the term to 24 Feb 1831:

James Wright
Simon Calkins

Rensalleer W. Lee
Henry Thorpe

Today issued certificates to Messers. Alexr H. Morton and James G. Boughan and gave a term until 15 April of next year of 1831 to bring their families.

Today issued certificates to the following gentlemen, gave until 1st Feby of 1831 to bring their families from Missouri:

John Jones
John Hawkins

Myers F. Jones

Today have issued certificate to the following gentlemen gave a term until the 1st of March 1831 for bringing their families from Mississippi.

Hugh McDonald Senior
Daniel McDonald

Hugh McDonald
Roderick Nicholson

1st March 1830. Today issued certificates to Messrs. Santiago [James] Bowie and Isaac Donoho who were received and took the proper oath this day 20 of Feby.

(14)

21 June. Jn H. Moore left bank of the Colorado above Thompson and above the Labahia Road to join Thompson.

2d August. Issued 15 passports with the term of 18 months.

6 August. Knight and White a site on the bank of the Colorado above and joining with that of Jenkins.

14 Sept. J. H. Bell by virtue of the commissions made by the Government of the State dated 22 of May of the past year has issued one of the sites of land as follows, that is the sitio allowed to R. C. Crosier on Lavaca, or the site at the junction of the creek "Mustang Creek" and the Navidad. The first in case that George Sutherland does not take that promised Crosier, and in case that he takes it, Bell is to give the site in the junction.

1 Novbr. David Grammer wants a quarter which was reserved for Panky and abandoned, joining Gates and Widow Panky, is some of the election of land made by H. Chriesman, also Grammer is to present recommendations.

8 Novbr. Have issued certificates to Messrs. J. W. and Benjamin F. Hughes with the term of 6 months from this date.

18 Novr. To Charles Donoho, Elijah Conklin, Alexander Oden gave a term of three months.

18 Novr. To Mr. George Ewing have given the site in front of that reserved for Crosier on the east bank of the Navidad River and which was chosen by Davis, in case that Mr. Davis does not come.

18 Novr. Mr. Saml P. Browne has the choice of the sites on Navidad and Lavaca saved for the Alabamans if they do not come for the same. The site chosen by Richard Ellis is reserved for Mr. Browne in the case that Ellis does not come.

(15)

December 7. Have issued a pass port to John Flanders — six months.

December 10, 1830. James R. Phillips goes to the north. 16 passports for others as many families who must emigrate from Alabama in one year.

Decr 12. The tract between John Austin and John D. Taylor on Buffalo Bayou is entered for Wm T. Austin, another of John Austin.

P. W. Grason has applied for a tract on the east fork of Karankawy and is to have a preference there, if the Alabamans who selected land there should fail. S. F. Austin

Thomas Barnet has requested the sitio on the west bank of the Brazos River above and joining the sitio of Joel Lakey which was conceded to John Elam in the First Colony of the Empresario Estevan F. Austin and abandoned by John Elam and the title lapsed. The said Barnet is to have the preference of said sitio over whichever other, the first which I can give, and for being a man of the highest quality and much merit, and an old colonist. San Felipe de Austin

17 December 1830   Estevan F. Austin

Samuel Chance wants the choice of land joining with Joseph San Pierre on the east bank of the Navidad in front of Hardy and Alley.

Mr. R. R. Royall wants the sitio at the junction of Carancuhuay and Colorado which was entered by Mr. Smith in case he does not come.

(21)   [June 1831]

Abednigo Biddy 33 years of age, born in S. Carolina. Cold. Patsy 26. 3 Male 1 female children. Moved from Alabama and arrived in this Colony in Decr 1830.

John Talbott 45 years of age. Susanna my wife 32 years old. One male 2 female children. 23d June took the oath. Moved from Arkansas and arrived 23 Decr 1830.

Thomas Toulson, single, 40 years of age, of the State of Virginia. Arrived in June 1830, wants his land in the contract of 100 families. Took the oath today 25 June 1831. (Lives with Rosseau).

John Kerley, 36 years of age, arrived in Feb. 1830, single, took the oath June 25, 1831.

Isaac Harris 25 years of age. Martha my wife 18 years of age. One male child. Mr. Harris has been living on the Trinity for about 7 years and being desirous to move into the Colony wishes to obtain a place on Cypress Bayou. He has a large stock of cattle. He also has a brother married and a single brother anxious to move here. The place he wants is about 4 to 6 miles from the mouth of Cypress Bayou on the west side, and is promised the place on the first vacancy.

John Hubbell 24 years of age, born in Upper Louisiana and came to the province about 4 years came to the Colony in Augt 1830.

John Mahuna 30 years of age native of Ireland and arrived in this country in 1824 unmarried, took the oath and obtained a certificate July 18.

(23)   [July 1831]

William M. Alley, single, 29 years of age, of Missouri, arrived in 1828. West bank of the Navidad adjoining, above Hardy.

Robert Mills, single, of Kentucky, arrived in 1830. Took the oath and recived certificate. Living in Brazoria.

Wm H. Cox, single, of England, arrived in 1830.

Lemuel Dickinson 37 years of age, widower, 2 female children. Moved from Louisiana and arrived in this Colony in 1825.

(24)

Jesse M. Evans 29 years of age, unmarried, moved from Tennessee and arrived in this Colony October 1830. Surveyor & farmer.

(25)

John Yorke 31 years of age. Zutitia his wife 27 years of age. 3 Male 2 female children. Arrived in this Colony in 1822. Issued certificate 22 Novr 1831.

William Eaton 23 years of age from Ohio and arrived in this Colony in February 1827, entered as a colonist in the Coast Colony 27, February 1831. Issued a certificate and recd his note, took the oath under the State Constitution.

(26)   [1832]

William Eckle single man arrived in this Colony in 1830 took the oath & has a certificate of admission in the Coast Colony.

(31)   [Dec 1832]

James J. Dewitt 50 years of age, widower. 2 Male 1 female children. Been in the country 7 years. Made a petition for his title.

(33)

Radford Berry 32 years of age single from the State of Mississippi. Has eight years of residence in Texas. Wants his land on the east of the Brazos near Navasota.

(34)

Reuben D. Wood 23 years of age. Martha his wife 22 years of age. One female child. From Tennessee, moved into Texas in 1827. Took the oath.

(37)   [February 1833]

James Crawford 23. Sarah his wife 22. 1 Male 1 female [children]. Arrived in this country from Tennessee in 1830.

Austin's "Register of Families"

(43)

Municipality of Austin

Register of the families introduced by the Citizen Empresario Estevan F. Austin by virtue of . . . the Colonization Law of the State of Coahuila and Texas dated 25 March 1825

Author's abbreviations used for professions: Carpenter - Carpen; Schoolmaster - Schlmst; Shoemaker - Shoemkr; Blacksmith - Blcksmth

No.	Name	Age	St.	Children	Dep.	Profes.	Orig.	Arrived	Took Oath [1829]	Total Souls
1	George B. McKinstry	27	S			Trader	GA	4/20/29	5/19	1
2	Luis DeMoss	26	M	1F		Farmer	MO	yr 1823		3
	Catherine his wife	20								
3	Abraham Roberts	56	W	1M	9	Farmer	LA	1/2/27	Nov	11
4	Robert Burney		S		1	Farmer	LA	11/1828	11/18	2
5	Robert Pebles	30	M	1M	5	Doctor	LA	9/10/29	10/27	8
	Pamelia his wife	25								
6	John Peterson	23	S			Farmer	LA	11/1824	12/1	1
7	James B. Miller	29	S			Doctor	KY	5/10/29	12/1	1
8	Henry Chever	30	S			Trader	LA	7/1826	12/1	1
9	Thomas J. Gasley	31	M	2M	1	Doctor	OH	11/16/28	1/12	5
	Eliza	29								
10	G. B. Cotten	38	S			Printer	LA	8/10/29	12/2	1
11	Joseph McGeorge	25	S			Trader	LA	7/26	12/2	1
12	Thos F. Converse	32	S			Printer	LA	8/10	12/2	1
13	Horatio H. Hickoke	22	S			Printer	AL	10/ 7	12/2	1
14	William Robinson	39	W	2F	10	Farmer	AR	8/1827	12/2	13
15	James Stephenson	39	M	3M	2F	Farmer	GA	3/1826	12/3	7
	Amelia his wife	30								
16	E. Alexander J. Blair	21	S			Trader	LA	7/13/29	12/5	1
17	Edward Lang	22	S			Trader	LA	7/13/29	12/5	1

1830 Citizens of Texas

#	Name	Age	Status			Occupation	Origin	Date	Date2	#
18	Charles Bury	36	S			Trader	LA	7/13/29		1
19	William Munson	39	W		1F	Farmer	AR	7/29/24		2
20	Thomas Bell	35	M			Farmer	GA	yr 1824		2
	Abigail his wife	21								
21	Florence Stack	30	S			Carpen	Ire.	yr 1825		1
22	Joshua Fletcher	47	S			Trader	LA	7/18/29		1
23	Thomas Cox	37	M		1F	Farmer	AL	3/1822	12/5	3
	Cynthia his wife	28								
24	Patrick Scott	54	W	5M	3F	Farmer	AL	2/1829		11
25	Henry W. Munson	36	M	3M		Farmer	LA	yr 1828		24
	Ann B. his wife									
26	Jefferson George	22	S			Farmer	LA	yr 1828		1
				(45)					[1829]	
27	Robert Hodges	26	M	1M		Farmer	LA	3/1829	12/10	4
	Susan his wife	20								
28	Henry Scott	38	M	5M	3F	Farmer	AL	2/1829	12/10	10
	Patsey his wife	33								
29	Thomas J. Pilgrim	24	S		1F	Schlmst	NY	1/1829	12/10	1
30	Nestor Clay	31	M	2M		Farmer	KY	12/1827	12/7	10
	Nancy his wife	22								
31	John Little	31	M		1F	Farmer	OH	6/22/25	12/10	3
	Winniford his wife	21								
32	James Moore	32	M	4M	2F	Farmer	TN	2/1824	12/10	18
	Olive his wife	29								
33	Job Williams	45	M	2M	4F	Farmer	MO	12/1825	12/10	8
	Nancy his wife	45	Enters his obligation to S. P. Browne							
34	Isaac McGary	27	S			Farmer	MS	3/1825	12/11	1
35	Fredk J. Calvit	42	S			Farmer	LA	6/1828	12/11	1
36	John Partin	27	M		1F	Farmer	TN	6/1826	10/12	
	Nancy Partin his wife	26								
37	James Small	34	S		2	Farmer	LA	5/1825	10/8	3

Austin's "Register of Families" 11

#	Name	Age	S/M/W	Males	Females	Slaves	Occupation	State	Date	Date2	No.
38	Moses Cummins	44	W	1M	3F	2	Schlmst	KY	2/1829	10/14	7
39	John Williams	41	M	2M	4F	12	Farmer	AR	in 1823	10/14	20
	Rebecca his wife	28									
40	Johnson Hensley	22	M		2F		Farmer	AR	11/8/28	10/17	11
	Sarah his wife	22									
41	Daniel Etherton	26	S				Farmer	LA	4/1825		1
42	William D. Finley	29	M	2M	1F		Doctor	OH	1/18/29		5
	Lydia V. his wife	27									
43	Edwd N. Cullum	29	S				Carpen	LA	10/1826	10/15	1
44	Rice F. Murray	22	S				Farmer	KY	3/1826	10/18	1
45	Luke Lesassier	38	M		1F	6	Farmer	LA	12/1829	10/19	9
	Eliza his wife	30									
46	John S. Evans	31	M	2M	4F		Farmer	LA	12/1829	10/19	8
	Sarah his wife	29									
47	John W. Moore	31	S				Trader	TN	7/1828	10/20	1
48	William Hensley	29	S				Farmer	AR	11/1828	10/20	1
49	Robt M. Williamson	23	S				Lawyer	AL	6/13/27	10/20	1
50	Wm Dunlap	52	M	5M	2F		Trader	GA	4/25/28	10/20	9
	Dolly his wife	40									
51	Anthony Winston	45	M	4M	3F	85	Farmer	AL	11/1829	12/19	96
	Sally Anne his wife	39			(47)						
52	George Sutherland	42	M	3M	2F	6	Farmer	AL	11/1829	12/19	13
	Frances his wife	40									
53	Jessie White	46	M	4M	2F	3	Farmer	AL	11/1829	10/19	11
	Mary his wife	27									
54	James N. Smith	22	M	1M	1F	25	Farmer	AL	11/1829	12/19	
	Sarah Anne his wife	24									
55	R. C. Crozier	20	M			5	Farmer	AL	11/1829	12/16	7
	Sarah H. his wife	38									
56	George Ewing		S				Farmer	AL	11/1829	12/19	1

12 1830 Citizens of Texas

#	Name	Age				Occupation	From	Date		#
57	—— Haney	36	M	2M	3F	Farmer	AL	11/1829	12/19	1
58	William Hardy	27				Farmer	TN	12/1822	12/19	9
	Margaret his wife									
59	Samuel C. Hiroms	43	S [sic]		2F	Carpen	Atacapas	1/1826		4
	Nancy W. his wife	29								
60	Sylvanus Hatch	48	M	4M	1F	Farmer	LA	8/15/29	10/21	10
	Pamelia his wife	39								
61	James D. Allcorn	30	S			Farmer	AR	in 1824		1
62	Warren D. Hall	34	S	1M		Farmer	LA	11/12/28	12/21	16
	Julietta his wife	29								
63	Matthew Dury	36	S			Farmer	LA	7/15/29	12/21	1
64	Elizabeth Powell	30	W	2M	2F	Farmer	LA	11/1828	12/21	5
65	Nelson Smith	25	M	1M		Farmer	AR	3/1829	12/21	3
	Darkay his wife	23								
66	John W. Little	55	M	2M	2F	Farmer	LA	11/1829	12/21	6
	Edith his wife	48								
67	William Barret	30	M			Farmer				
	Elizabeth his wife	25								
68	Bryant Dottery	32	M	3M	1F	Farmer	LA	12/1829	12/22	8
	Anne his wife	29								
69	Andrew Miller	44	M	3M	1F	Farmer	LA	12/1829	12/22	11
	Celia his wife	32								
70	Elisha Roberts	54	M	3M	3F	Farmer	LA	12/1829	12/22	38
	Patsey his wife	50			(49)	30				
71	Aaron Colvin	33	M	1M	2F	Farmer	LA	12/1829	12/22	5
	Margaret his wife	30	His family in district of Nacogs & coming very quickly							
72	John W. Noble	29	M	2M	1F	Farmer	MI	12/1829	12/22	9
	Fanny his wife	35	His family is coming in two months							
									[1829]	
73	David Selkriggs	18	S	Orphan		Farmer	MS	1825	12/22	1
74	Edmund R. Miller	25	M	1M	1F	Farmer	AR	1824	12/23	4

Austin's "Register of Families" 13

#	Name	Age	M/S			Occupation	From	Year	Date	#
	Lucinda his wife	19								
75	Simon Miller	22	S			Farmer	AR	1824	12/23	1
76	James Thompson	36	M	6M		Farmer	TN	1827	12/23	8
	Agnes Dinning his wife	34								
77	Anthy R. Clarke	55	S			Farmer	NY	1824	12/23	1
78	Wm Chase	37	M	2M		Farmer	MA	1826	12/23	4
	Eliza his wife	40								
79	Isaace House	49	M	2M	1F	Farmer	LA	1823	12/23	6
	Kizia his wife	23								
80	Widow of G.B. Hall and the heirs				1					
81	Alexander Hodge for the heirs of his son									
82	Henry Harrison	32	S		Blacksmith &	Farmer	LA	1825	12/23	1
83	Henry L. Baire	22	M			Farmer	LA	1824		
	Louisa Hamey wife	17								
84	Thomas Jefferson Pryor	23	S			Farmer	AL	1824	12/25	
85	William Hunter	51	M	4M	4F	Farmer	MS		12/25	28
	Nancy his wife	49			18					
86	Peyron R. Splane	32	W		1F	Farmer	LA		10/25	8
					6					
87	Levi Bostic	51	M	2M	3F	Farmer	TN	1829	12/25	16
	Patsey his wife	47			9					
88	Joseph Davis	48	M			Farmer	AR	1829	12/26	2
	Rachael his wife	44								
89	John Whiteside	30	M		1F	Farmer	MO	1826	12/26	3
	Elizabeth his wife	18								
90	James Wallace	56	M			Farmer	GA	1826	12/26	2
	Patsey his wife	50								
91	Jonathan Newman	30	M	1M	1F	Farmer	MO	1826	12/26	4
	Polley his wife	20								
92	Elish Jackson	23	S			Farmer	IL	1827	12/26	1
93	Mary Ann Pankey	44	W	2M	5F	Farmer	LA	1824	12/26	8
	Widow of M. Early									
94	James Pankey	46	S			Farmer	LA	1827	12/26	1

14   1830 Citizens of Texas

No.	Name	Age	Status	Males	Females		Occupation	From	Year	Date	
95	John F. Edwards	22	S				Farmer	AL	1822		
96	Isaac Jackson	32	M		(51)						
	Samantha his wife	30			3F		Farmer	OH	1827	[1829]	5
97	James Bell	38	S				Farmer	GA	1824	12/26	1
98	Jacob Stevens	24	M	1M	1F		Farmer	MO	1826	12/26	4
	Nancy his wife	20									
99	Archie Hodge	39	M	3M	2F		Farmer	AR	1826	12/26	7
	Charlotte his wife	37									
100	James Pevyhouse	25	M	3M	2F		Farmer	AR	1826	12/26	7
	Mary his wife	25									
101	Alexr E. Hodge	29	S				Farmer	AR	1826	12/26	1
102	Richd R. Royall	31	M	3M	2F	20	Farmer	AL	1829	12/26	27
	Anne R. his wife	29									
103	E. P. Myrick	24	M				Farmer	AL	1826	12/26	3
	Nicma his wife	22									
104	David Harris	33	S	4M	3F		Trader	LA	1828	12/26	1
105	Benjn Osborn	60	W	4M			Farmer	MS	1826	12/26	8
106	John Brown	33	M	2M			Farmer	MO	1829	12/26	4
	Nancy his wife	23									
107	John Keller		W	2M	3F		Farmer & Carpen	KY	1829	12/27	5
108	Patrick Greene	35	M	3M							
	Elizabeth his wife	25									
109	Allen Larrison	32	S		1F		Artisan	OH	1825	12/27	1
110	Samuel Love	38	M	2M		5	Farmer	LA	1825		10
	Nancy his wife	35									
111	Abraham Darst	43	M	7M	3F		Farmer	MO	1829	12/28	12
	Jemimah his wife	32									
112	Jn W. Mitchell	52	S				Farmer	GA	1822		1
113	Edwd Baty	24	W	1M			Farmer	AR	1822	12/28	2
114	Thos S. Saul	34	M		1F		Farmer	LA	1829	12/28	3

Austin's "Register of Families" — 15

#	Name	Age	Status	M	F	(?)	Occupation	From	Year	Date	#
	Melissa M. his wife	23									8
115	James Stephens	35	M	4M	2F		Farmer	MO	1829	12/28	
	Mary his wife	34									7
116	Sarah Parker	40	W	1M	5F			MO	1827		2
117	George Dennett	38	M				Artisan	KY	1828	12/29	
	Sarah his wife	31									
118	John Denton	29	S				Farmer	TN	1827	12/7	1
					(53)						
119	Francis Keller	50	M	2M	2F	4	Farmer	MS	1829		10
	Anne his wife	34									
120	Heirs of Cassy	)	16								
	Steward two children	)	14								2
121	Elijah Curtis	22	S				Farmer	AL	1823		
122	Adolphus Hope	22	S				Farmer	AL	1823		1
123	Washington Curtis	25	S				Farmer	LA	1827		1
124	Prosper Hope	26	S				Farmer	AL	1823		1
125	Daniel Arnold	48	M	2M	2F	5	Farmer	LA	1825		
	Rachael his wife	43					Farmer	MS	1826	12/29	11
126	James Gilliland	30	M	1M	2F		Farmer	AR	1828	12/29	5
	Dianah his wife	25									
127	ThosJ. Williams	22	S				Farmer	AR	1822	12/29	1
128	Nicholas George	36	M	2M	3F	12	Farmer	LA	1829	12/29	19
	Nancy his wife	25									
129	Alexr McCoy	37	S				Carpen	PA	1823		1
130	Samuel Pharr	28	S				Farmer	LA	1823		1
131	John Hodge	24	M	3M	3F	2	Farmer	AR	1824		8
	Polley his wife	32									
132	Leander Woods	21	S				Farmer	MO	1824		1
133	John H. Edwards	31	M	1M	1F		Farmer	LA	1827		6
	Sarah Anne	23									
134	Robert Brown	34	S				Shoemkr	PA	1826		1

#	Name	Age			Occupation	State	Year	Date	
135	Amos Edwards	53	M	4M	10 Farmer	KY	1829		16
	Penelope his wife	43	Took the oath in Nacogdoches						
136	Darius Gregg	25	S		Farmer	KY	1829	12/31	1
137	Jonathan Vess	50	M	2M	4F Farmer	MO	1829	12/31	8
138	Moses Rousseau	37	W	1M	2F 3 Farmer	AL	1828	12/31	7
139	John H. Allcorn	25	S		Farmer	AR	1823		1
140	Wm E. Allcorn	24	M		Farmer	AR	1823		2
	Sarah his wife	16							
141	Sylvester Bowen	38	M		1F Farmer	R.I.	1827		3
	Almira	20							
142	Thomas Jefferson Allcorn	21	S		Farmer	AR	1823		1
143	Ts Peyton Kuykendall	21	S		Farmer	AR	1825		1
	read Thornton P.K.			(55)				1829	
144	James Kegans	27	M	2M	Farmer	MO	1826	12/31	4
	Nancy his wife	24						1830	
145	Hugh Kilgore)								
	Delila Armstrong)	32	W	4M	1F Farmer	LA	7/1829	1/1	6
146	George Grimes	46	M	4M	5F Farmer	TN	1827	1/1	11
	Disey his wife	43							
147	Robert Ray	29	M		Farmer	NY	1824	1/1	2
	Margaret his wife	14							
148	Fredk Grimes	22	S		Farmer	TN	1827	1/1	1
149	Leonard W. Groce		S		Farmer	AL	1822		1
	[all the above entry was crossed out]								
149	James Bennett		S			OH			
150	Leonard W. Groce		S		Farmer	AL			
151	Harman Hensley	50	M	2M	2F Farmer	AR			
	Betsey his wife	54							
152	James Clark	40	M	6M	1F Farmer	MO	1828	1/2	9
	Rhoda his wife	33							

Austin's "Register of Families" 17

#	Name	Age	S/M	M	F		Occupation	From	Date	Frac	#
153	William Burney	31	M	2M	1F		Farmer	Opelousas	1828		5
	Susan his wife	24									
154	James Holland	21	S				Farmer	OH	1824		1
155	Joseph Miller	37	M	3M	2F	1	Farmer	MO	1829		8
	Hannah his wife	34									
156	Nathaniel Hutcheson	40	M	1M	3F		Farmer	MO	1829	1/3	6
	Mary his wife	28									
157	Josiah Wilbarger	29	M	1M			Farmer	MO	1827	1/3	3
	Margarette his wife	19									
158	Abijah Highsmith	34	M	3M	3F		Farmer	MO	1/1828	1/4	8
	Debora his wife	35									
159	Thomas Garretson	17	S				Farmer	AL	1828	1/4	1
160	William Barton	47	M	2M	3F	5	Farmer	AL	1828	1/4	12
	Stacy his wife										
161	Edward Jinkins	34	M	2M	1F		Farmer	AL	1829	1/4	5
	Sarah his wife	30									
162	Montraville Woods	23	M		1F		Farmer	MO	1824		3
	Isabelle his wife	17									
163	J. D. Morris	42	S				Farmer	MO	1828		1
164	Stephen Cottle	43	M	4M	6F		Farmer	MO	1828		12
	Sally his wife	42			(57)						
165	John Cocke	29	M	1M	1F		Farmer	AR	1825	1/4	3
	Anna his wife	29									
166	Thos Powell	37	S				Farmer	IL	1829	1/4	1
167	Nicholas Lynch	41	M	4M			Farmer	AL	3/22/28	1/4	6
	Nancy his wife	45									
168	Louis Geffray	41	M	3M	1F		Farmer	LA	8/1829	1/5	6
	Irene his wife	28									
169	Francis W. Johnson	30	S				Farmer	MO	9/1829	1/5	1

18 1830 Citizens of Texas

#	Name	Age	M/S	M	F	Occupation	From	Date	Col	#
170	Elisha Hall	30	M	1M		Farmer	AR	11/1829	1/5	3
	Jemima his wife	21	W							
171	Elizabeth Campbell	45	W	3M	2F	Farmer	AR	1829	1/5	6
172	Isaac Lee	60	M		1F	Farmer	AR	1829	1/5	3
	Patsey his wife	54							[1830]	
173	Sandford Woodward	30	M	1M	3F	Farmer	AR	1829	1/5	6
	Nancy his wife	26								
174	Hiram Lee	23	S			Farmer	AR	1829	1/5	1
175	Davis Chandler	30	M	1M	1F	Farmer	AR	1829	1/5	4
	Prissa his wife	23								
176	Frances Bland	60	W	4M	4F	Farmer	IL			
177	Alvin B. Clark	31	M	1M		1 Farmer	MS	1829		4
	Elizabeth his wife	24								
178	Lewis Hearst	40	W	4M		Farmer	AR	1826		5
179	Adam Stafford	25	S			Farmer	TN	1824		1
180	Elisha W. Barten	39	M	3M	2F	1 Farmer	AL	1/1/30	1/6	8
	Susana his wife	39								
181	Francis J. Haskins	35	S		VOID returned note		NY	12/14/29		1
182	Thos Alley	25	S			Farmer	MO	1826	1/6	1
183	W. B. White	27	S			Farmer	MO	9/1826		1
184	Jesse B. McNeily	27	M	1M		Farmer	LA	12/1829	1/7	3
	Elizabeth his wife	18								
185	Sarah Kennedy	36	W	3M	3F	8 Farmer	LA	1/1829		15
186	Franklin Lewis	28	S			Farmer	AL	1827		1
187	William McFarlane	54	M			Farmer	KY	1827		4
	Martha his wife	50								
188	Paschal P. Borden	23	S			Blcksmth	IN	12/18/29		1
189	Henry T. Armstrong	20	S			Farmer	IN	12/18/29		1
190	Gail Borden	52	W	1M		Tanner & Farmer	IN	12/18/29		

(59)

Austin's "Register of Families"   19

#	Name	Age	Status	Family	Occupation	Origin	Date		
191	William Deaver	25	S		Farmer	MO	1827		1
192	Lemon Barker	43	W	1F	Farmer	MO	1827	1/9	2
193	John B. Walters	29	S		Farmer	MO	1825		1
194	John F. Webber	35	S		Farmer	MO	1825		1
195	Wm Murphee	53	S		Farmer	TN	1826		1
196	Jos K. Looney	28	S		Farmer	KY	1828		1
197	William New	32	S		Farmer	KY	12/1829		1
198	Charles McLaughlin	32	S	6	Farmer	LA	12/1829		7
199	Peter Bertrand	38	M	3M 1F	1	Farmer	TN	1/1830	1/12	7
	Anne W his wife	30							
200	Gail Borden Jr	28	M	1F	1	Farmer	MS	12/1829	1/12	4
	Penelope his wife	18							
201	Eli Mercer	40	M	3M 2F	10	Farmer	MS	11/1829	1/12	17
	Nancy his wife	33							
202	James McCoy	30	M	2M		Farmer	PA	11/1829		4
	Matilda his wife	17							
203	Amasa Ives	49	S		Farmer	LA	12/1829		1
	Married after receiving his certificate								
204	Ezekiel Clampit	24	M	1M		Farmer	LA	12/1825		3
	Catherine his wife	17							
205	Caliste de Jesus Solis	17		Orphan		Farmer	Bexar			1
206	John T. Berry	29	M		Farmer	AR	1828		2
	Nep..cy his wife	19							
207	John B. Taylor	30	M	1M		Carpen	NY	1830	1/14	3
	Mary his wife	26							
208	Charles W. Ewing	31	M	1F		Lawyer	MI	1830	1/14	3
	Abbie B his wife	20	His family is still in the U. States						
209	Louisiana Kenney	39			Farmer	LA	1822		1
210	Susannah Clampit	44	W	2M		Farmer	LA	1825		3
211	Andrew L. Castleman	21	S			MO	1825		
	Devolved to his brother because of his death								
212	Francis Moore	41	M	2M 3F		Farmer	TN	1830	1/20	7

1830 Citizens of Texas

#	Name	Age	M/S	M	F	Occupation	From	Date1	Date2	#
	Sarah his wife	33								
213	Barnabas Wickson	55	M	6M	5F	Farmer	OH	1827	1/20	13
	Hutrah his wife	43								
214	Asa Holdridge	27	S			Doctor	LA	1830	1/21	1
215	Martin Wells	55	M	5M	3F	Farmer	AL	1/1830	1/22	10
	Sarah his wife	40								
216	Robert Bullock	24	S		(61)		AL	1/1830	1/22	1
									1830	
217	John Landrum	29	M	1M	1F	2 Farmer	AL	1/20	1/22	6
	Mary his wife	22								
218	William Landrum	26	M	1M		2 Farmer	AL	1/20	1/22	5
	Nancy his wife	22								
219	William Alkins	29	M	2M	2F	Farmer	LA	12/1829	1/22	6
	Phoebe his wife	36								
220	Evan Corner	23	S			Farmer	LA	12/1829	1/22	1
221	Abijah W. Draughan	26	S			Farmer	LA	12/1829	1/22	1
222	Asa Wickson	26	S		1F	Farmer	OH	12/1827	1/24	1
223	Reuben R. Russel	23	M			Farmer	AR	1/2/30	1/26	3
	Luisiana his wife	20								
224	Elisha Moore	40	M	3M	2F	Farmer	MO	3/1827		7
	Jane his wife	28								
225	M. Sandefur	28	M			Farmer	AR	1828	1/27	2
	Elisabeth his wife	28								
226	John D. Ziekanski	30	S			Farmer	VA	1824		1
227	James Schrier	24	M	2M	1F	Farmer	LA	11/1829	1/29	5
	Sarah his wife	22								
228	Laughlin McLaughlin	45	S			Farmer	MS	12/1829	1/29	1
229	Peter White	29	M	1M	1F	Farmer	MO	1827	1/20	4
	Nancy his wife	25								
230	John Corner	28	M			Farmer	LA	12/1829	1/30	2
	Prussia his wife	19								

Austin's "Register of Families" 21

No.	Name	Age	M/S			Occupation	From	Date	Date2	#
231	Thos Corner	22	S			Farmer	LA	12/1829	1/30	1
232	Silas Clark	46	S			Carpen	LA	12/1829	2/1	1
233	Miguel Micoless	36	S			Trader	LA	1828	2/2	1
234	Nichs Whitehead	35	S			Farmer	LA	1825	2/2	1
235	Alexr Thompson	31	M			Farmer	GA	1823	2/2	2
	Asena his wife	19								
236	Wm K. Wilson	31	S			Trader	MD	1828	2/2	1
237	Phinneas Gleason	52	M	2M	3F	Farmer	OH	1822	2/4	7
	Cynthia his wife	30	His family is in Ohio wants land before bringing							
238	Philo Fairchild	34	M	1M		Farmer	IL	1826		3
	Mahaley his wife	23								
239	Jefferson Singleton	23	S			Farmer	LA	1/1830	2/6	7
240	Wesley Singleton	20	S			Farmer	LA	1/1830	2/6	1
			(63)							
241	Thomas Thompson	25	S			Farmer	AR	1825	2/8	1
	William Perkins	40	M			Mariner	LA	8/1829	2/4	2
	Leonora his wife	30								
242	Arter Crownover	20	M			Farmer	AR	8/1829	2/8 [1830]	2
	Clarissa his wife	17								
243	Andrew Robinson Jr	21	M			Farmer	AR	11/1821	2/8	2
	Mary his wife	21								
244	B. Barton	44	S			Farmer	AL	12/1829	2/9	1
245	James Trammel	30	S			Farmer	AL	7/1829	2/9	1
247	James Beardslee	50	M	3M	3F	Farmer	NJ	2/1830	2/16	8
	Hester his wife	32								
	[The original has numbering errors]									
248	John M. Hensley	24	M			Farmer	AR	1828	2/20	2
	Mary his wife	24								
249	Obadiah Hudson	32	W	1M		Farmer	AR	2/1830	2/20	2
250	John Clark	68	W	1M		Farmer	LA	1828	2/20	2
251	Saml Fulton	39	M		4F	Farmer	LA	12/1829	2/23	6

22 1830 Citizens of Texas

#	Name	Age	S				Occupation	From	Arrived	Date	#
	Elisabeth his wife	31									
252	Adam Lawrence	25	S			1	Farmer	AR	1824	2/23	2
253	Saml Lawrence	25	S				Farmer	AR	1829	2/23	1
254	David Lawrence	27	M	1M			Farmer	AR	1/1830	2/23	3
	Jenny his wife	22									
255	Young Coleman	25	M		1F		Farmer	TN	12/1829	2/8	3
	Lucy his wife	22									
256	Peter Aldrich	43	S				Farmer	NH	12/1829	2/5	1
257	Chauncey Treat	31	M				Trader	NY	2/1830	2/24	2
	Mary his wife	31	His wife is in New York								
258	Mary Owens	50	W				Farmer	LA	1826	2/25	1
259	Joseph B. Chance	30	M	3M	1F		Farmer	TN	1/7	2/27	6
	Nancy his wife	29									
260	Thos Jefferson Hall	21	M				Farmer	LA	1824	3/7	2
	Nancy his wife	20									
261	Margaret Wightman	26	S				Farmer	NY	12/1828	3/6	1
262	John Hinkson	32	S				Farmer	MO	10/1826	3/3	1
263	John E. Bacchus	42	M		3F		Farmer	LA	4/1829	3/7	5
	Mary his wife	24									
264	James L. Loving	21	S				Farmer	OH	2/1830	3/10	1
265	Isaac Jackson	40	M	3M	2F		Farmer	AL	2/1830	3/10	7
	Tilly his wife	40			(65)						
266	Thos P. Helm	24	S				Farmer	KY	7/1828	3/14	1
267	Samuel Bruff	45	W		1F		Farmer	TN	2/1830	3/13	2
268	Joseph Rees	46	M	4M	2F	9	Farmer	TN	2/1830	3/15	17
	Margaret his wife	41									
269	Christopher G. Cox	27	M	1M		1	Doctor	TN	2/1830	3/15	4
	Harriet H. Cox	24									
270	Abraham Bowman	44	S				Farmer	TN	2/1830	3/15	1
271	Thomas Cayce	34	M	5M	3F	5	Farmer	TN	2/1830	3/15	15

Austin's "Register of Families"

#	Name	Age					Occupation	From	Date	Date	#
	Hannah his wife	34									
272	Mary Corner	53	W	3M			Farmer	LA	12/1829	3/19	4
273	Benjamin Rigby	26	M	1M			Farmer	LA	12/1829	3/19	3
	Cathrine his wife	19									
274	Alexander McCulloch	30	M	3M	2F		Farmer	LA	12/1829	3/19	7
	Mariam his wife	32									
275	Mastin Holden	22	S		annulled		Farmer	LA	12/1829	3/19	1
276	Horace Gorden	22	S				Farmer	MS	8/1829	3/19	1
277	William Isaacs	35	S				Farmer	TN	1829	3/19	1
278	George M. Cash	29	S				Tanner	PA	1829	3/24	1
279	Abraham Dillard	25	S				Farmer	MO	1827	3/24	1
280	Charles Gates	34	M	1M			Farmer	AR	1822		3
	Minerva his wife	25									
281	S. Rhoads Fisher	35	M	2M	1F		Trader	Phil	2/1830	3/26	5
	Anne his wife	35									
282	Robt Wilson	36	W	2M			Artisan	LA	1/1830	3/26	3
283	James Braberry	27	S				Farmer	LA	1/1829	3/26	1
284	Robert Clokey	25	M				Farmer	PA	3/1830	3/26	2
	Anne his wife	22									
285	Thomas Moore	25	M				Farmer	AR	10/1829	3/27	2
	Nancy his wife	20									
286	Benjn F. Jaques	33	M	1M	2F	1	Farmer	MO	3/1830	3/27	6
	Adeline his wife	24									
287	Alext Farmer	32	S				Artisan	LA	1829	3/27	1
288	Stephen Jones	53	M	3M	2F		Farmer	AR	12/1828	3/27	7
	Susannah his wife	53									
289	James McCain	35	M	2M			Farmer	TN	12/1828	3/28	4
	Sarah his wife	27									
290	Moses A. Foster	31	S			2	Farmer	LA	3/1830	3/28	3
					(67)						
291	Nathl Lewis	23	S				Mariner	MA	8/1829	3/28	1

1830 Citizens of Texas

#	Name	Age	S/M			Occupation	From	Date1	Date2	#
292	Henry Tierwester	33	S			Farmer	OH	1828	3/28	1
293	Noah Griffeth	44	M	4M	1F	Farmer	NY	1/1829	3/29	7
	Estet his wife	42								
294	Levina Hubbs	25	S	[female]			MS	1825		1
295	Demis Maria Pierce	19	S	[female]			NY	1/1829	3/14	1
296	Edward S. Carrell	23	S			Farmer	LA	1/1830	3/14	1
297	Alfonse Courseaux	26	S			Farmer	LA	1/1830	3/14	1
298	Benjn C. Reeder	45	M	2M	1F	Farmer	MS	1827	3/18	5
	Mary his wife	45								
299	Joseph D. Harrison	50	M	4M	3F	Farmer	AL	1/1830	3/21	9
	Rachael F his wife	46								
300	Eliza Hubbs	23	S	[female]				1825		1
301	Samuel B. Ormsbee	21	S			Trader	VT	2/1830	3/30	1
302	Matthew Moss	24	S			Farmer	AR	11/1829	3/30	1
303	Louis C. Moore	21	S			Farmer	LA	3/1830	3/31	1
304	Lewis L. Veeder	38	S			Farmer	MO	2/1830	3/31	1
305	Robert Matthews	32	S			Farmer	LA	2/1830	3/31	1
306	John Cole	25	M	1M	2F	Farmer	MO	1/1830	4/1	5
	Polly his wife	25								
307	Albert Cone	30	S			Trader	CT	2/1830	4/1	1
308	John G. King	36	M	3M	4F	Farmer	LA	4/1830	4/3	9
	Pamelia his wife	28		Annulled. Has returned documents of interest						
309	Richard Allen	37	S	VOID Turned over certificate			LA	12/1827	4/5	1
310	Cornelius H. Vandewier	31	M	3M		Carpen	LA	2/1830	4/5	5
	Anne his wife	21								
311	Samuel Hinch	26	M			Farmer	KY	2/1827	4/6	2
	Leah Anne his wife	18								
312	Laurence Martin	25	S			Farmer	AL	3/31	4/6	1
313	Wm E. Dundass	39	S			Farmer	MS	1829	4/7	1
314	Wm J. Russell	28	S			Mariner	LA	1828	4/7	1
315	Alexr Bailey	30	S			Farmer	OH	1827	4/8	1
316	Arrabella Harrington	58	W				AR	1826	4/9	1

Austin's "Register of Families" 25

#	Name	Age	Status	M	F	Other	Occupation	State	Year	Date	Last
317	Nancy Frailey	32		2M	2F			AL	1824	4/10	5
318	Emilins Savage	38	M	1M			Farmer	NY	1829		
	Mary his wife										
319	John Shaw	30	M	2M	2F		Farmer	AR	1828	4/10	6
	Polly his wife					(69)					
320	William Wroe	40	M			2	Farmer	LA	1825	4/12	4
	Nancy his wife	43									
321	Caleb Kemp	38	W	4M	3F		Farmer	LA	3/1829	4/12	8
322	Patrick Dolan	41	M	2M			Tailor	LA	2/1830	4/12	4
	Anne his wife	45									
323	R. L. Dunn	30	M	1M		7	Farmer	LA	4/1830	4/12	10
	Eliza his wife	30									
324	Rhody Kennedy		[Written over]: Returned the note					MO	1828	4/12	1
325	Francis Adams	38	S				Farmer	SC	1822		1
326	William Spence	32	S				Farmer	LA	1824	4/14	1
327	Elliot M. Millican	23	M				Farmer	AR	1822	4/14	2
	Elizabeth his wife	18									
328	Leroy Stafford	47	M	5M	2F	80	Farmer	LA	4/1830	4/14	89
	Elizabeth his wife	30									
329	Hugh McDonald	50	M	4M	5F	28	Farmer	MS	1830		39
	Catherine his wife	44									
330	Dennis Sullivan	21	S					LA	2/1830	4/14	1
331	James R. Phillips	26	S			8		AL	1828	4/14	9
332	Elizabeth Gordon	46	W	1M	1F			LA	8/1829	4/14	3
333	Jesse Grimes	42	M	5M	2F		Farmer	AL	1827	4/19	9
	Rosanna his wife	28									
334	William McIntire	23	S				Farmer	LA	1825	4/19	1
335	Margaret McIntire	38	W	1M			Farmer	LA	1825	4/19	2
336	Mary Caruthers	50	M				Farmer	AL	1/1830	4/19	1
337	John M. Burton	24	S				Farmer	GA	3/1830	4/20	1

1830 Citizens of Texas

#	Name	Age	S/M	Children	Occupation	State	Date	Date2	#
338	Jn W. Mayo	28	S		Farmer	LA	2/1830	4/21	1
339	Mark McCausland	23	S		Farmer	LA	3/1830	4/22	1
340	Charles Edwards	25	M		Farmer	NY	1/1829	4/26	3
	Polly Anne his wife	18		1F					
341	Daniel Yeamans	22	S		Farmer	NY	1/1829	4/26	1
342	Joseph Yeamans	21	S		Farmer	NY	1/1829	4/26	1
343	Jeremiah J. Robinson	23	S		Farmer	MS	1830	4/16	1
344	Bartholmew McClure	24	S		Farmer	KY	1830	4/16	2
	Sarah Anne his wife	18							
345	James Lindsey	30	S		Farmer	KY	12/1827	4/26	1
346	William Burnett	28	M	2M	3F	Farmer	LA	3/1830	4/29	7
	Nancy his wife	28							
347	Josiah Lester	37	M	4M		Farmer	LA	12/1829	4/29	6
	Solita his wife	33							
				(71)					
348	William Fitzgibbons	46	M	2M	1F	Farmer	LA	1822		5
	Nancy his wife	50							
349	William Whitaker	28	M	2M		Farmer	LA	1822		4
	Nancy his wife	24							
350	John Cartwright	43	M	5M	2F	11	Farmer	MS	1830	5/3	18
	Mary his wife	42							
351	John Marshall	48	M	5M	1F		Farmer	AR	1/1830	5/4	8
	Leah his wife	44							
352	Jesse Cliffi	31	M	1M		Blcksmt	LA	2/1830	4/4	2
	Mary his wife	16							
353	Francis G. Keller	29	M	1M		Farmer	MS	1825	5/8	3
	Levina his wife	23	[written over]: Annulled						
354	Gross Welsh	55	M	3M	6F	Farmer	LA	5/1830	5/11	1
355	Jesse Leftwich	42				Farmer	TN	4/1830	5/13	11
	Sarah his wife								
356	E. M. Connelly	34	S			Mariner	LA	4/1830	5/13	1

Austin's "Register of Families" 27

No.	Name	Age	Status	M	F		Occupation	From	Date		
357	Wm Sutherland	30	M				Farmer	LA	4/1830	5/15	2
	Susan his wife	30									
358	Asa Yeamans	57	M	3M	1F		Farmer	NY	1/1829	5/15	6
	Jerusha his wife	52									
359	Margaret Kennedy	37	W	1M	1F		Farmer	LA	1824		3
360	Annulled [entry not legible]										
361	Wm H. Taylor	41	W	1M	4F		Farmer	LA	1829		6
362	Henry Morse	34	M	2M	1F	3	Farmer	MS	4/1830	5/17	8
	Eliza his wife	28									
363	Phinneas Jones	23	S				Farmer	TN	3/1830	5/17	1
364	S.J. Moseley	27	S				Doctor	TN	3/1830	5/17	1
365	Theophalus Eddings	56	M	4M	3F		Farmer	AL	4/1830	5/17	9
	Nancy his wife	40									
366	Henry Q. Wright	40	M	1M	4F		Farmer	OH	4	5/17	7
	Anne his wife	39									
367	John Sullivan	38	M	3M	2F		Farmer	OH	2/1830		7
	Eunice his wife	37									
368	Harlem Hatch	23	M		1F		Farmer	OH	2/1830		3
	Mary his wife	19									
369	Robert J. Moseley	24	S			1	Farmer	TN	3/1830		2
370	Hugh McDonald Jr	28	M		(73)		Farmer	MS	3		2
	Mary his wife	22									
371	Daniel McDonald	32	M	1M	2F		Farmer	MS	3		5
	Mary Ann his wife	29									
372	Roderick Nicholson	28	M	1M	1F		Farmer	MS	3		4
	Mary Anne his wife	18									
373	James Norton	38	S				Farmer	LA	1826		1
374	Dugald McFarlane	33	M	1M	1F			AL	4/[1830]		4
	Eliza his wife	27									
375	Norman Woods	25	S				Farmer	MO	1826		1

28 1830 Citizens of Texas

#	Name	Age	Status			Occupation	From	Date	#
376	Jorge Fisher		M	3M		Trader	MS		12
	Elizabeth his wife								
					7				
377	J. H. Bostic	23	S			Farmer	TN	3	1
378	Abram Eddings	22	S			Farmer	AL	3	1
379	William Sexton	24	S			Farmer	LA	1/1830	1
380	Henry K. Lewis	37	S			Farmer	KY	2/1829	1
381	Isaac Jamieson	31	M	2M	1F	Farmer	TN	4/10	5
	Margaret his wife	28							
382	Saml P. Browne	35	M	3M	1F	Farmer	MO	4/10	6
	Susan his wife	27							
383	John Jones	38	M	4M	1F	Farmer	MO	4/10	13
	Mary his wife	30							
					6				
384	James Stuart	29	M		2F	Farmer	MS	11/1829	4
	Zillah Anne his wife	22							
385	Levi Killen	18	Orphan			Farmer	LA	4/2	1
386	Hughes Witt	30	S			Farmer	FL	4	1
387	Amos Gates	29	M			Farmer	AR	1822	2
	Lydia his wife	20							
388	George A. Bell	47	S			Farmer	LA	1828	1
389	Archibald S. White	49	M	4M	3F	Farmer	AL	2/1830	
	Margaret his wife	53							
390	Toliver Martin	36	M				Car	2/1830	
	Elizabeth his wife	37							
391	Joshua Nelson	39	S			Schlmstr	NY	1/1829	1
392	M. Hubert	34	M		2F	Farmer	AL	1/1830	4
	Frances his wife	32							
393	Wm M. Rankin	43	M	2M	2F	Farmer	AL	1/1830	6
	Sarah his wife	33							
394	Zacariah Landrum	64	M			Farmer	AL	1/1830	2
	Lettuce his wife	54							

Austin's "Register of Families"   29

#	Name	Age			(75)	Occupation	State	Date	
395	William Rankin	21	S			Farmer	AL	1/1830	1
396	Crawford Burnett	24	M	1M	1F	Farmer	LA	12/1829	1
	Anne his wife	22							
397	James Copeland	28	S			Farmer	GA	8/1827	1
398	Thomas Cope	28	S			Farmer	LA	7/1829	1
399	John Owen	21	M			Farmer	LA	1822	1
	Christina his wife								
400	Elisha Flack	31	M			Farmer	KY	2/1830	1
401	Reuben Hornsby	37	M	5M	1F	Farmer	MS	2/1830	8
	Sarah his wife	35							
402	David Kneeland	45	M		1F	Farmer	LA	5/1830	3
	Silence his wife	41							
403	James H. Skinner	35	S			Farmer	LA	5/1830	1
404	Henry Linney	50	W	2M	1F	Farmer	KY	5/1830	
405	James F. Perry	39	M	4M	2F	Farmer	MO	4/1	8
	Emily M his wife	34							
406	Alexr H. Morton	29	M		1F	Farmer	NY	5/1	3
	Elenor his wife	25							
407	Thomas Gay	25	S			Farmer	GA	5/1830	1
408	John G. Holtham	29	S			Lawyer	LA	11/1829	1
409	Samuel Gordon	23	S			Farmer	LA	8/1827	1
410	James Smith	25	S			Farmer	LA	1826	1
411	James Rankin	22	S			Farmer	LA	1827	1
412	Mary Smith		W				LA	1829	4
413	Augt Hotchkiss	30	M	2M	1F	Farmer	LA	1830	5
	Anne my wife								
414	Talbot Chambers	35	S			Farmer	PA	1827	1
415	James Foster	26	S			Farmer	LA	1830	1
416	Wm D. Mayes	24	S			Farmer	MS	1830	1
417	Lewis Endt	27	M			Farmer	MS	1830	2
	Mary my wife	15							

#	Name	Age					Occupation	From	Date	#
418	John Gates									
419	Edwd Burleson	33	M	3M	1F		Farmer	TN	1830	6
	Sarah my wife	35								
420	Edw Shipman	26	S					AR	1823	1
421	Saml Hoit	44	W			4		MS	1830	5
422	John Lawrence	50	W					LA	1827	1
423	D. S. Ford	26	S					TN	2/1830	1
					(77)					
424	Elizabeth Smith	64	W	1M	1F		Farmer	LA	5/1/30	3
425	James North Cross	28	S				Farmer	AL	8/1829	1
426	Timothy Davis	50	S					NC	1827	1
427	J. C. Tannehill	32	M	1M	1F		Farmer	TN	4/1828	4
	Jane his wife	26								
428	Heirs of Pace			5M	3F					8
429	William Smith	28					Farmer	GA	4/1/30	1
430	Wm H. Jack	25	M		1F		Farmer	AL	6/2/30	
	Laura H his wife	17								
431	Richard Andrews	30	S				Farmer	GA	1827	
432	George Kimball	22	S				Farmer	LA	1830	
433	Ira Ingram	40	W				Farmer	LA	1825	
434	James Hall	55	M	2M		1	Farmer	IL	6/3/30	5
	Winneford his wife	54								
435	John Moore	27	W	1M	2F		Farmer	LA	4/1830	4
436	L. Smither	27	S					AL	4/1826	1
437	John Smith	37	M	2M	2F		Farmer	OH	1/1830	6
	Sarah his wife	26	His family is in Ohio							
438	Nichs Lockridge	53	M	5M	5F	1	Farmer	LA	4/1830	13
	Alsey his wife	45								
439	Rosalie Hammer	24		1M		4	Farmer	LA	4/1830	6
	Abandoned woman									
440	G. Manent	26	S					France	6/1830	2

Austin's "Register of Families" 31

#	Name	Age	S/M	M	F	Occupation	State	Date	#
441	J. Manent	24	S			Farmer	&LA		1
442	Gains Bailey	25	S			Farmer	LA	1822	1
443	John Kincaid	33	S			Farmer	KY	1826	1
444	Noah Smithwick	22	S			Farmer	TN	1827	1
445	V. Pepin	49	—	2M	2F	Farmer	LA	6/1830	5
446	John McClaren	36	S			Farmer	VA	1825	1
447	James Cochran	30	S			Farmer	AL	7/1829	1
448	John Dinsmore	40	S			Farmer	NH	1829	1
449	Saml Lockhart	45	M	1M		Farmer	LA	6/1830	3
	Conicy his wife	34							
450	David Stoddard	35	S			Farmer	LA	8/1829	1
451	Richard Morris	39	M	1M	4F	Farmer	NY	5/1830	7
	Cathrine his wife	34			(79)				
452	William P. Harris	31	S			Artisan	LA	7/1830	1
453	Andrew L. Phinney	30	S			Farmer	LA	11/1829	1
454	S. W. Peebles	28	S			Tailor	AL	5/1830	1
455	Alfred Metcalf	36	S			Farmer	MS	7/1830	1
456	Henry Smith	40	M	3M	4F	Farmer	MO	3/1827	9
	Elizabeth his wife	30							
457	S. C. Bundick	21	S			Farmer	LA	1/1830	1
458	J. R. Jefferson	24	S			Farmer	TN	7/1829	1
459	Jeremiah Brown	30	S			Mariner	RI	2/1830	1
460	Perkins Lovejoy	38	M			Mariner	LA	7/1830	1
	Caroline his wife	23							
461	William Williamson	42	M			Carpen	OH	7/1830	1
	Mary T his wife	18							
462	William Busby	21	S			Carpen	LA	3/1830	1
463	William Birch	26	S			Farmer	MO	7/1830	1
464	Antonio Mancha	48	M	4M	3F	Farmer	Bexar		9
	Maria Canado	46							

32   1830 Citizens of Texas

#	Name	Age				Occupation	State	Date	
465	George Tennell	58	M	2M	2F	Farmer	MO	1826	6
	Sally his wife	34							
466	William C. Clark	30	M	3M	1F	Farmer	LA	1/1830	6
	Rebecca his wife	28							
467	Nathl Townsend	26	M			Trader	MS	7/1830	2
	Maria his wife	25							
468	Daniel E. Colton	28	S			Trader	NY	7/1830	1
469	Henry T. Walker	24	M		1F	Farmer	AL	6/1830	3
	Prudence his wife	20							
470	Thos Choate	51	M		6F	Farmer	LA	6/1830	8
	Jane his wife	37							
471	John Anderson	27	M		1F	Mariner	LA	8/1830	3
	Anne his wife	36							
472	Henry Harter	25	S			Farmer	OH	6/1830	
473	James Bell	29	M	1M	3F	Farmer	TN	6/1830	1
	Winsey his wife	29							
474	Thomas Bird	25	M	1M	2F	Farmer	TN	6/1830	
	Nancy his wife	23							
475	Ephraim Fuqua	40	M	3M	2F	Farmer	AL	4/1828	
	Martha his wife	36							
	(81)								
476	Wily B.D. Smith	25	S			Farmer	AL	1827	
477	James Day (orphan)	19	S			Farmer	LA	3/1829	
478	Humphrey N. Gores	34	S			Farmer	LA	4/1830	
479	Daniel Gilleland	35	M	2M	3F	Farmer	AR	7/1830	
	Priscilla his wife	26							
480	Michael Scanlon	21	S			Trader	LA	8/1830	
481	John Bowman	50	M	1M	1F	Farmer	AR	8/1830	
	Margaret his wife	29							
482	Patrick Dunn	25	S			Mariner	LA	8/1829	
483	B. A. Porter	25	S			Farmer	KY	3/1830	

Austin's "Register of Families" 33

484	Thos H. Mays	27	S			Farmer	TN	5/1830
485	Michael Young	27	M	2M		Farmer	AL	3/1829
	Rachael his wife	24						
486	A. J. James	25	S			Farmer	AL	3/1829
487	Jeremiah Dwyer	42	M	1F	2	Farmer	TN	6/1830
	Eliza his wife	25						
488	Jesse Wilson	39	M	Free men of color		Farmer	LA	5/1830
	Jane his wife	24						
489	Robt Spears	22	Orphan			Farmer	AL	3/1828
490	Anne White	30	W	4M	1F	Farmer	AL	4/1830
491	James D. Grey	30	M	1M	1F	Farmer	AL	2/1830
	Levina his wife	25						
492	Daniel McDonald	31	M	2M	1F	Farmer	Canada	8/1830
	Hannah his wife	28						
493	John H. Scott	34	S			Farmer	AL	1828
494	Ephraim Anderson	49	W	3M	4F	1	Farmer	AL	4/1830
495	Milton J. Anderson	25	S			Farmer	AL	4/1830
496	Henry Austin	50	M					
497	John H. Connell	30	M			Farmer	PA	9/1830
	Matilda his wife	22						
498	Ira Strickland	30	S			Farmer	MS	4/1830
499	Abraham Peck	32	S			Farmer		1828
500	Philip Coonce	24	S			Blcksmt	LA	1828
501	William Laughlin		S				KY	1824
502	John Morris	40	M			Farmer	TN	1830
	Nancy his wife	32						
503	Franklin J. Greenwood	26	M			Farmer	AR	10/1830
	Mary Jane his wife	22						
				(83)				
504	Robert Martin	40	S		40	Farmer	LA	1829
505	William Burnett	28	S		5	Farmer	KY	1828

34 1830 Citizens of Texas

#	Name	Age	M/S	Children	Occupation	Origin	Date
506	John Burdgess	37	M		Farmer	Scot	7/1830
	Margaret C. his wife	37					
507	William Clapp	27	S		Farmer	AR	7/1830
508	David Grammer	28	S		Farmer	TN	2/1830
509	Chs. S. P. Johnstone	26	S		Farmer	FL	1/1830
510	Andw Montgomery	30	S		Farmer	AL	10/1830
511	James Stephenson	40	M	2M 1F	Farmer	Canada	10/1830
	Dimanes his wife	37					
512	C. C. Wyatt	27	S		Farmer	LA	5/1830
512	C. B. Stewart	26	S		Trader	SC	6/1830
513	Burrel Perry	58	M	1M 4F	Farmer	LA	11/1830
	Jane his wife	37					
514	James Rion	21	S		Farmer		11/1830
515	Henry Griffith	40	W	2M 2F	Farmer	NY	12/1828
516	B. B. Pool	30	M	2M 1F	Farmer	AR	10/1830
	Sarah his wife	31		His family in Orleans; has nine months to 23 Novr [1831] to bring			
517	Michael Gill	32	M	1M 1F	Farmer	Ire	6/1830
	Mary his wife	29					
518	Edward Dickenson	26	S		Farmer	Eng	3/1824
519	Susan Vince	33	S		Farmer	MS	1822
520	Chs H. Bennet	23	S		Farmer	NY	1/1830
521	Elizabeth Standeford	35	W	2M 1F	Farmer	AL	3/1829
522	James Standeford	21	M	1F	Farmer	AL	3/1829
	Sarah his wife	19					
523	Heirs of Gillet		4		Farmer	MO	3/1827
524	John F. Brush	25	S		Farmer	NY	7/1830
525	Charles K. Reese	20	S		Farmer	TN	2/1830
526	H. B. Stringer	39	W	1F	Farmer	VA	8/1830
527	Jabez Barney	30	M	3F	Farmer	R.I.	7/1830
	Anne Eliza his wife	30					
528	Howard McElroy	26	M	1M 1F	Farmer	AR	11/1830

Austin's "Register of Families"   35

#	Name	Age	Status	M	F	Notes	Occupation	From	Date
	Betsey his wife	20							
529	John Smith	22					Farmer		
530	Samuel Kinman	34	M	2M	2F		Farmer	IN	
	Carey his wife	27							
					(85)				
531	Edwd Hogan	45	M	2M	2F		Farmer	LA	12/1830
	Hannah his wife	35				Native of Ireland. Has until 1 June 1831 to bring his family.			
532	Francis Lowen	25	S				Farmer	KY	12/1830
533	John S. Black	40	M	3M	2F		Farmer	TN	1830
	Mary his wife	32							
534	Joseph Johnson	51	S				Farmer	LA	11/1830
535	John Flanders	32	S				Farmer	NH	12/1830
	Flanders is to be included as a colonist although he takes no land								
536	Perry B. Iles	29	M	1M			Farmer	KY	8/1830
	Nancy his wife	27							
537	Pleasant B. Riggs	25	S				Farmer	TN	8/1830
538	George M. Patrick	29	S				Farmer	KY	1/1828
539	James Walker Moore	33	M	2M			Farmer	AR	12/1830
	Matilda his wife	21							
540	Wallis Stanley	28	M	1M	1F		Farmer	AR	12/1830
	Betsey his wife	23							
541	J.W.E. Wallace	31	W	1M			Farmer	LA	2/1830
542	Francis F. Mayes	35	M		3F	1	Farmer	MS	12/1830
	Betty his wife	25							
543	Garret Low	28	S				Farmer	MS	12/1830
544	Abner Lee	30	W	1M			Farmer	AR	8/1830
	Jonathan Wodwort								
	John McHenry	32	M	1M			Farmer	LA	1828
	[blank]	28							
545	Robert Taylor Jr	24	S				Farmer	LA	11/1830
546	Edmund Andrews	34	M	1M			Farmer	Car	12/1830

36 1830 Citizens of Texas

#	Name	Age	M/S	Males	Females	Occupation	Origin	Date
	Isabella his wife	24						
547	A. Brigham	41	M	2M		Farmer	LA	4/1830
	Elizabeth S his wife	41						
548	Samuel H. Barlow	30	M	2M		Farmer	VT	12/1830
	Rebecca J his wife	24						
549	James Morgan	43	M	2M	2F	Farmer	Car	12/1830
	Celia his wife	30						
550	Henry Dibble	24	S			Farmer	NY	12/1830
	G. F. Richardson	26	S			Farmer	IL	3/1830
551	William Dupuy	39	S			Farmer	KY	3/1830
	Francis W. Dempsey	67	M	1M		Farmer	OH	12/1830
	Maria his wife	45			(87)			
552	Thos P. Crosby	26	M	1M	1F	Farmer	Phil	
	Clementina his wife	20		Family in Phila				
	Sidney Whitehead	18		Orphan				
553	James Perry	41	M	3M	3F	Farmer	MS	12/1830
	Elisabeth his wife	36						
554	Joel Wheaton	42	M	4M	1F	Blcksmt	MS	12/1830
	Elisabeth his wife	26						
	John T. Vince	25	S					1822
555	Allen T. Milburn	30	M	1M			LA	12/1830
556	Phinneas Smith	45	M	1M	1F	Farmer	NY	12/1830
	Sophia his wife	43						
	Colbert Baker	37	M	1M		1 Farmer	AR	12/1830
	Anne his wife	26						
557	Benjamin Bowles	43	M	2M	5F	Farmer	MO	3/1827
	Betsey his wife	36						
558	Daniel Perry	39	M	1M		3 Farmer	MS	12/1830
	Eliza his wife	26						
559	Moses H. Boyden	33	M		2F	Farmer	MS	12/1830

Austin's "Register of Families"   37

		Age				Occupation	From	Date
	Clarissa W his wife	19		1M			AR	11/1830
560	Joel Greenwood	28	M			Farmer		
	Anne his wife	18					IN	1825
563	Isaac Maden	20	S			Farmer	IN	1825
564	J. San Pierre	56	M	2M		Farmer		
	Margaret his wife	45						
565	William D. Lacey	22				Farmer	TN	
566	William Hardin	49	M	2M	4F		KY	12/1830
	Caroline his wife	29						
567	Josiah F. Hamilton	32	M	2M		Farmer	MO	5/1830
	Fanny his wife	21						
568	Daniel Monroe	27	M	1M	1F	Farmer	LA	10/1830
	Sally his wife	22						
569	Samuel Woody	26	M		1F	Farmer	AL	1/1830
	. . . his wife	26						
	John H. Money	35						[1831]
571	George Gailbreth	30	S			Farmer	SC	10/1830
572	James Miles	31	M	1M	3F	Farmer	AR	1/1830
	Sarah his wife	30						
573	James Hodge	28	M	1M		Farmer	AR	in 1824
	--liena his wife	16						
574	Joseph House	60	M	1M	4F	Farmer	LA	12/1830
	Mary his wife	50						
	Joseph House	26	S			Farmer	LA	12/1830
575	Felix P. Earnest	27	S			Farmer	TN	4/1827
582	Wm Montgomery	58	W		1F	Farmer	TN	9/1830
583	Elisabeth Hensen	36	W	3M	1F	Farmer	TN	9/1830
584	Joshua W. Martin	28	S			Farmer	ME	1/1830
586	John Bird	36	M		2F	Farmer 2	TN	6/1830
	Sally his wife	31						

1830 Citizens of Texas

ID	Name	Age	Status	Children		Occupation	Origin	Date
587	Alexr Brown	32	M		1F	1 Farmer	AR	11/1830
	Sally his wife	24						
589	Coleman Hays	22	[S]			Farmer	AR	11/1830
590	Levi Taylor	26	M		1F	Farmer	AR	11/1830
591	Mary Clarisa	21						
592	John Harris	23	S			Farmer	AR	11/1830
593	Hannah Cornaugh	62	W			3 Farmer	MO	12/1829
594	James Hollingsworth	38	S			Farmer	AR	6/1829
595	Wm W. Ford	27	S			Farmer	AL	in 1828
				(91)				[1831]
599	Thomas McCaslen	30	S			Farmer	PA	3/1830
600	Dudley J. White	27	M			Farmer	GA	2/1827
	Bethis his wife	24						
603	John Byrne	37	M			Farmer	Ire	4/1829
	Pamelia his wife	30						
604	Obadiah Pitts	37	M	3M	4F	Farmer	AR	[blank]
	Polly his wife	28						
605	Levi B. Jones	50	M	2M	1F	Farmer	MS	12/1829
	Sarah his wife	35	Free man of color					
62	Thomas Bray	43	M		1F	Farmer	Eng	8/1830
	Cynthia Anne	23						
613	James Cox	26	M			Farmer	AR	8/1830
	Sarah his wife	20						
615	John A. Schutte	26	S			Farmer	AL	4/1829
617	Holdon Evans	25	M		1F	Farmer	AL	2/1830
	Charlotte his wife	25	Returned to the United States of the North					
				(93)				[1831]
620	Benj Fuqua	36	S			Farmer	AL	3/1828
621	John Shannon	36	M	5M	3F	Farmer	AR	10/1830
	Charlotte his wife	30						

Austin's "Register of Families"   39

No.	Name	Age					Occupation	Origin	Date
622	Owen Shannon	70	M				Farmer	AR	10/1830
	Margaret his wife	60							
624	Matthew Boren	28	M	3M			Farmer	AR	12/1830
	Nancy his wife	20							
625	A. C. Reynolds	45	M	1M	3F		Farmer	NY	2/1830
	Harriet his wife	40							
626	William R. Hunt	50	M	3M	1F		Farmer	AL	2/1830
	Rhody his wife	49							
627	Thomas Hanson	40	S				Farmer	LA	2/1830
628	Lydia Allen	26	W	1F		1	Farmer	MO	5/1830
630	James Hislop	33		Left the Country			Farmer	Scot	10/1829
631	John Brown	21	S				Farmer	LA	3/1830
634	David Hanson	29	S				Farmer	LA	1/1830
635	Marcus L. Black	26	S				Farmer	AL	12/1830
637	John Hall	24	S				Farmer	IL	6/1830
				(95)					
	[A numbering error was made here]								
545	John Matthews	33	S			20	Farmer	AL	12/1830
547	Raleigh Rogers	37	M	1M	3F		Farmer	LA	12/1830
	Polly Anne his wife	24							
549	Abraham M. Clare	29	M				Farmer	MO	1822
	Sarah his wife	16							
550	Stephen G. Letcher	39	W	1M	1F		Farmer	AL	12/1830
553	Francis Courteaux	37	W	1M	2F		Farmer	MO	4/1830
556	Samuel Kennelly	36	M	1M			Farmer	Eng	4/1829
	Jane his wife	36							
559	John Logan	26	S				Farmer	VA	7/1830
				(97)					
	Andrew Ray	50	S				Farmer	Aises	2/1830
565	Tandy Walker	62	M	2M		6	Farmer	Palo-	6/1830

1830 Citizens of Texas

#	Name	Age	M/S	M	F	Occupation	Origin	Date
	Mary his wife	55					gacho	1831
568	Edward Dwyer	23	S			Farmer	Ire	12/1830
570	Joseph Powell	25	S			Farmer	LA	12/1830
572	John Crownover	56	M		1F	Farmer	AR	1830
	Elizabeth his wife	52						
574	Archolaus Dodson	23	S			Farmer	MO	1827
575	James Murphy	32	S			Farmer	Ire	1830
581	Samuel McCarley	55	M	5M	5F	Farmer	Nacog.	12/1830
	Celia his wife	32						
582	Jacob Walker	31	M		1F	Farmer	LA	12/1830
	Sarah Anne his wife	19						
					(99)			
586	Thomas J. Reed	21	M		1F	Farmer	AL	12/1830
	Martha his wife	18						
588	William C. Manifee	35	M	4M	2F	Farmer	AL	12/1830
	Agnes his wife	36						
589	David Clarke	35	M	1M		Farmer	LA	12/1830
	Bershela his wife	26						
593	James McLaughlin	32	W		1F	Farmer	LA	3/1829
597	Francis Christie	55	S			Farmer	TN	11/1830
598	John Tumlinson	26	M	1M		Farmer		1821
	Laura his wife	20						
599	Kesiah Crier	33	W	2M	1F		AR	12/1830
604	James Price	41	M	3M	3F	Farmer	AR	8/1830
	Margaret his wife	41						
605	Joseph Smith	23	S			Farmer	NY	4/1829
					(101)			[1831]
609	Pendleton Rector	25	S			Farmer	AL	1/1830
610	Claiborne Rector	27	S			Farmer	AL	1/1830
612	William Heard	30	M		2F	Farmer	AL	12/1830

Austin's "Register of Families"

#	Name	Age	Status	M	F	Occupation	State	Date
	America his wife	21	W	4M	3F	Farmer	AL	12/1830
613	Thomas Manifee	51	S			Farmer	LA	12/1829
622	Mills McDowell	21	M	2M	2F	Farmer	AR	11/1830
626	Jacob Shannon	28						
	Catherene his wife	28						
627	Kinchen W. Davis	39	M	2M	3F	Farmer	AL	1/1830
	Fanny his wife	30						
					(103)			[1831]
630	Burk Trammell	26	S			Farmer	AL	1/1828
633	Lewis Barksdale	26	S			Farmer	TN	2/1828
635	Nathaniel Moore	52	M			Farmer	AR	11/1830
	Rebecca his wife	43						
636	Elizabeth McConnell	21	W			Farmer	MS	10/1828
637	Augustus Williams	21	M			Farmer	AR	1825
645	Stephen Burnham	23	S			Farmer	MS	1822
646	John M. Allen	25	S			Farmer		2/1830
					(105)			
	Samuel Fuller	37	M	1M	2F	Farmer	MA	10/1830
	Hannah his wife	39						
	William T. Austin	22	M		1F	Farmer	CT	11/1830
	Joanna his wife	20						
	Henry Louis	43	M	6M	1F	Farmer	AL	1/1830
	Sarah his wife	34						
	Joshua Abbott	51	M	2M	3F	Farmer	AR	12/1830
	Elizabeth his wife	37						
	Joseph T. Bell	31	M	2M	2F	Farmer	TN	1/1830
	Jane his wife	24				1		
					(107)			
	Winston S. McDaniel	28	M		1F	Farmer	TN	11/1830

1830 Citizens of Texas

Name	Age				Occupation	Origin	Date
Lydia his wife	24						
Joseph Urban	35	M			Mer	Fran	1/1826
Uabetia fire	36						
William Scott	23	S	3M	4F	Farmer	AL	3/1829
James Taylor	37	M		2F	Farmer	NY	6/1830
Rachael his wife	39						
Thomas McQueen	35	S			Mer	LA	1/1830
W.W. Thompson	31	M	3M	2F	Farmer	AL	6/1830
Fanny Nixon his wife	27						
Benjamin Jewell	32	S			Farmer	LA	6/1830
William Malcolm	30	S			Farmer	LA	7/1830
Silas Jones	40	M	2M	1F	Farmer	AL	3/1829
Milly his wife	28						
Thomas Husham	27	S			Farmer	Ire	1/1831
Spencer A. Pugh	36	M	3M	1F	Farmer	VA	5/1830
Susan his wife	36						
Mathew T. Hines	31	S			Farmer	VA	7/1829
J. W. Mason	27	M		3F	Farmer	VA	1/1831
Malinda his wife							
				(109)			
John Nicholls	33	M	2M	2F	Farmer	Sabine	1827
Fanny his wife	31						
Henry Klonne	58	S			Farmer	Ger	7/1829
John H. Jones	28	S			Farmer	MS	2/1829
				(114)			

Waters, single, came in 1828.
Elemeleck Sweatinger, wife and one child, came in 1830.

AUSTIN'S REGISTER OF FAMILIES
VOLUME II

6 Apl 1835. Asahel C. Holmes, Georgia. [Arrived] Apl 1824. Merchant. His family in Geo. Dont intend to bring his family. Applies for ¼ league of land. Wants land between the Brazos & ____ surveys above Bell.

9 Apl 1835. John Chever, Alabama. [Arrived] Feb 1830. Single. Farmer. Wants land. By W. Seale.

12 Apl 1835. Dan Etherton, England. [Arrived] some 8 or 10 years ago. Family. Farmer. Applies for League No. 3 on Trespalacios side, per S. R. Fisher.

27 Apl 1835. Jose Franco Mancha, Mexican citizen, 24 years old. Malina his wife. Authorized to select land. Mr. John H. Alcorn did so, paid Commissioner as per receipt.

Steward, heirs of. Steward from Missouri [Arrived] 1830. 2 Males, 1 Female. Decd in this Colony. J. D. Allcorn, Step Father [Arrived] 1830.

Green Webb, Tenn., [Arrived] 1829, 22 years [of age] his wife 19 years [of age]

15 May 1835. Thos. O. Berry, Tennessee. [Arrived] 1828. 30 years old. Lucinda his wife 18 years old. 1 Male [child]. Farmer. Applies for a league of land on the divide between Buckners Creek and the Labahia Road on a road leading to Hopkins mustang pens.

15 May 1835. Noah Carns, Tenn. [Arrived] 1830. 34 years of age. Farmer, his wife 25 years of age. 2 Male, 2 Female children. Wants land in the same place. This is where Greens have taken land, all unsurveyed.

13 May 1835. James Panky, Tenn. [Arrived] Long time ago. 53 years old. Mary his wife 40 years old. 1 Male, 3 Female children, Farmer.

William Lewis, Tenn. [Arrived] 1830. 30 years old. Farmer. Applies for League 3 on west side Colorado below.

25 May 1835. John Crownover, Arkansas. [Arrived] 1830. 69 years old. His wife 58 years old. Farmer. Applies for League H Navasota new survey.

26 May 1835. Robt J. Moseley, Tennessee. [Arrived] 1830. 29 years. Susan Ann his wife 21 years. Farmer. 1 Son. Applies for a league of land unsurveyed on the west Bernard in the road leading from this place to Moseleys including a Spring on the road. Land to run northerly and westerly.

Jared E. Groce Jr. Applies for land (1 league) west of McKinney's & Charles Donoho north of the Bernard tract & Whiteside's league East of C---

23 May 1835. Mortimer Donoho, Missouri. [Arrived] Feb 18, 1830. Single Brickman. Applies for one fourth league of land joining T. Stevens, Bell & Bracy East of ---.

24 June [1835]. Thomas Shadoin, Tennessee, arrived in 1829. Married Mahely (Chadoin) 3 children. Farmer. Wants one of the leagues of land on Labacca surveyed by Hensley below the Gonzales Road the north league.

Peter Kinzy. Resident. [Arrived] 1830. 35 years Carpenter. Married. Sarah former wife of Robt Kuykendall. 1 female child. No. 16 on Matagorda Bay West side of Colorado.

28 July 1835. Thomas M. Blake, Kentucky. [Arrived] 6 Jul 1830. 25 years Single. Blacksmith. Applies for ¼ league No. 3 head of Bay Prairy.

Jonathan Kemp, Louisiana. [Arrived] 1830. 22 years old. Charlotte his wife 18 years old. 1 Female child. Farmer. J. George, Agent. Applies for a league of land on Bay Prairy back of Bowman.

4 August [1835]. John L. Sleight, N. York. [Arrived] 24 Dec 1830. 26 years. Single. Merchant. Has a certificate (old). Applies for a quarter on Dry Creek NW Nicholas.

15 Sep 1835. Richd Smith, Alabama. [Arrived] March 1830. 70 years. Margaret his wife, 53 years. 2 Male, 4 female children. Farmer. Applies for a league of land.

Dolores Arrista, Mexican. Family applies for league No. G.

Jesse Richards, Penn. [Arrived] 1825. Family. See pg. 45. Applies for a league on Pin O. Cr. No. 3 previously applied for by Gage.

John Cherny, Missouri. [Arrived] 1830. Family. Applies.

Phinneas Smith. N.York. [Arrived] 1830. Family. Certificate 556. H. Austin, Agent. Application made 1st May 1835. Selects League I on Yegua, C's New Survey.

27 Sept [1835]. Matthew Sparks, Arkansas. Family. Betsey his wife.

Patrick Dunn [Arrived] 1829. Single. See Remembrances

29 Sept [1835]. John L. Marshall, Arkansas [Arrived] 1830. 24

years. Eliza his wife, 20 years. 2 Female children. Blacksmith. Applies for No. 14 on Lake Creek.

Ponton with his wife and family. [Arrived] 1830. Farmer. Applies for a league on west side Navidad next below Mrs L.

12 Oct [1835]. John W. Williamson. Resident. March 1824. 35 years. Single Farmer. Applies for land on the east side Navidad above Whites survey.

Charles S. Smith, Missouri. [Arrived] 1828. 28 years old. Narcissa his wife 22 years old. Farmer. Takes League No. 17 east of Col. back of Knight & White new survey.

16 Oct. 1835. Jesse T. Davis, Missouri. [Arrived] 1828. 30 years old Family. Applies for ¾ league on Bayou Floris No. 1 east side.

CHARACTER CERTIFICATES
AND CERTIFICATES OF RECEPTION

In the Spanish Archives Division of the General Land Office is a file that contains Certificates of Character, letters of application, Certificates of Reception, a few passports and other personal documents relating to entrance into one of the colonies of Texas. They are filed in alphabetical order, according to the name of the applicant.

The Mexican colonization laws required that entrants be of good character and reputation. Some immigrants brought statements of good character from officials of their home state. Others already in Texas for some time, and who now intended to take up land, obtained them from their municipality of residence. A large number are from Nacogdoches and San Augustine where the year of 1835 saw a flurry of activity.

The Certificates of Reception were given by the empresarios when an entrant applied for inclusion in the colony and was accepted. Austin's "Register of Families" has many entries noting that certificates were issued. The Certificate of Reception gave the applicant time to select land and bring in his family or otherwise arrange his personal affairs before paying land fees.

Many short letters of application to Austin are in the file. They contain personal and family information as required by the land laws.

Certificates of Reception issued for the DeWitt Colony were gathered with all other documents relating to land in the DeWitt Colony and bound into three volumes in the Spanish Archives of the GLO. They appear in a separate section of this work.

Information from this Spanish Archives file has been abstracted with exceptions. Some appear in Austin's "Register" and are not repeated. Most of the Nacogdoches certificates are omitted because information from them has already been published in *Nacogdoches — Gateway to Texas* by Carolyn Reeves Ericson. Information from all the others was copied if it proved or implied residence in Texas in 1830.

CHARACTER CERTIFICATES AND CERTIFICATES OF RECEPTION
Spanish Archives, General Land Office

San Augustine, August 18, 1835. **Bailey Anderson Snr** — native of Virginia, family of five children, emigrated to Texas in the year 1822.

San Augustine, August 18, 1835. **Bailey Anderson Jr.** — native of S. Carolina, wife and ten children, emigrated to Texas in 1821.

San Augustine, May 18, 1835. **Benjamin Anderson** — native of South Carolina, wife and twenty-one children [no date of emigration]

San Augustine, August 18, 1835. **Hazzard Anderson** [also C. H. Anderson] — native of Indiana, wife and one child, emigrated to Texas in 1821.

San Augustine, August 18, 1835. **Holland Anderson** — native of Kentucky, wife and two children, emigrated to Texas in 1830.

San Augustine, August 17, 1835. **Jonathan Anderson** — native of Kentucky, wife and six children, emigrated to Texas in 1819.

San Augustine, 29 August 1835. **Frederick Anthony** — native of Tennessee, emigrated in 1830.

San Augustine, August 18, 1835. **John Applegate** — wife and two children, emigrated in 1829.

San Augustine, August 17, 1835. **Henry Ashabranner** — native of No. Carolina, family of 10 persons, emigrated in 1830.

San Augustine, August 17, 1835. **Alanson Barr** — native of Vermont, wife and 5 children, emigrated in 1821.

Austins Colony, April 1831. We have known **Thomas Barron** two years on Red River and one year in this colony, 1822   Walter Sutherland, William Cooper, Abner Kuykendall

Bejar, 8 December 1832. To: Austin & Williams. I am a Mexican by birth. My name is **Pedro Sanciro de la Baume**, native of Nacogdoches, single, 25 years old.

San Augustine, 17 Sept 1835. **James Bennett** — native of Virginia, family of four persons, emigrated in 1830.

Nacogdoches, September 12, 1835. **Milly Berry** is a widow with family, resident in this Department since 1830.

San Augustine, August 18, 1835. **Jonathan Bittick** — native of Tennessee, family of seven persons, emigrated to Country in 1830.

Jurisdiction of Liberty, June 30, 1835. **Wm Bloodgood** — native of New Jersey, wife and three children, emigrated in 1824.

Precinct of Tannahaw, September 21, 1835. **Hiram Blossom** — native of Vermont, family of two persons emigrated in 1829.

San Augustine, September 1, 1835. **Minor Blossom** — native of New York, single man, emigrated in 1830.

San Augustine, 18 August 1835. **Benjamine Bostic** — citizen of this municipality, native of North America, family of 4 persons, emigrated about 1821.

Town of Austin, 20 May 1832. To: S.F. Austin. **James H. Bostic** from Tennessee, unmarried. Arrived March 22, 1830.   J.H. Bostick [signed]

Town of Austin, 19 Feby 1831. To: S.F. Austin. **Stephen Bowie** — 31 years of age, unmarried, farmer, moved from Louisiana, arrived 26 November 1830.

San Augustine, August 18, 1835. **James Bowlin** — native of Tennessee, family of wife and one child, emigrated in 1826.

San Augustine, August 18, 1835. **Jeremiah Bowlin** — native of Virginia, wife and 2 children, emigrated in 1826.

San Augustine, August 31, 1835. **Mary Ann Bowlin** — native of Tennessee, emigrated April 1826, had family of two in number.

To: Estevan F. Austin & Samuel M. Williams: "I am European by birth, married to a Mexican in the City of Bejar" desire to be admitted in Colony. "My name is **Juan Francisco Buchetti**, native of the Canton of Falais in Switzerland, 48 years of age. My wife Da Gertrudis de la Baume y Buchetti, native of Nacogdoches and of age 18 years" Bejar, 13 Dec 1832. Juan Francisco Buchetti

San Augustine, August 18, 1835. **Terry Buckley** — native of Mississippi, single, emigrated in 1822.

San Augustine, 29 August 1835. **John C. Burk** — native of South Carolina, family of 7, emigrated to this Country in 1820.

San Augustine, 17 day Sept 1835. **William Burnett** — a native of Virginia, emigrated 1830, man of a family of three persons.

Nacogdoches, 15 Novr 1834. **Thomas Burrus** — living in this Department 10 years, widower with family.

San Augustine, August 17, 1835. **Ahira Butler** — single, native of Tennessee, emigrated 1828.

Nacogdoches, 6 April 1835. **Maria de Cantu'** — citizen of this Municipality for many years. Widow with family.

Nacogdoches, 9 Sept 1835. **Manuel Carmonales** — citizen of the Department since 1822, married with family.

Nacogdoches, 9 Sept 1835. **Maria Gertrudis Carmona** — widow with family, citizen of this Municipality since 1820.

San Augustine, August 21, 1835. **Isaac Caradine** — native of Mississippi, wife and one child. Emigrated 1827.

San Augustine, August 31/35. **Robert P. Caradine** — native of Mississippi, single man. Emigrated 1827.

San Augustine, Sept 1, 1835. **Agaton Carr** [also Argratone Carr] — native citizen; family 6 persons.

San Augustine, Sept 1, 1835. **Anastacea Carr** — native citizen, single.

San Augustine, 6 Sept 1835. **Elizabeth Carrol**, native of South Carolina, woman of family of two persons. Emigrated to Texas 1827.

Sabine District [no date]. **George Carter**—a native of North Carolina, has a family, emigrated in 1824. B. Holt Comm.

Town of Austin, May 1830. "I have visited your Colony . . . settlement in it for my family that are now residing in the District of Aises . . ." **John Cartwright**, 43 years old, Five male children. Mary my wife, 42 years old. Two female children. Occupation farmer, moved from Mississippi. Jno Cartwright [signed]

District of Sabine, April 7, 1835. **Robert G. Cartwright** — has resided in the District of Ayish since March 1826, a young man . . .

San Augustine, Sept 22, 1835. **Jose Cervantes** — native citizen, family of eight persons.

San Augustine, August 20, 1835. **Sarah Chappell** — native of Tennessee, widow woman of a family of two persons, emigrated 1828.

Villa de Austin, 23 December 1829. **William Chase** — arrived month of November in the year 1823, married, 4 persons.

San Augustine, September 1st, 1835. **David Cherry** — native of South Carolina, family of six persons, emigrated in 1830.

San Augustine, September 1st, 1835. **Smith R. Cherry** — native of No. Carolina, single, emigrated 1830.

District of Bevil, August 29, 1835. **Daniel Chessher** — native of Georgia, emigrated 1829, family of 3 persons.

District of Bevil, August 29, 1835. **James Chessher** — native of Georgia, emigrated 1824, family of 8 persons.

San Augustine, 18 September 1835. **Elijah Clark** — from Mississippi, emigrated 1824, family 2 persons.

Villa de Austin, 23 Dec 1829. **Anthony R. Clarke** — is a Colonist, arrived Novr 1824, single, one person.

Nacogdoches, 15 Sept 1835. **Isaac Clover** — married with family, citizen of this Department since 1823.

Town of Austin, 13 May 1830. I have emigrated to this Colony . . . **Elijah M. Connly** — 34 years of age, single. Mariner. From Louisiana, arrived April 1830.   Elijah M. Connelly [signed]

Precinct of Tannehaw, Sept first 1835. **William Cornwall** — native of Caintuckey, family of 3 persons. Emigrated 1829.

Austin, February 4, 1830. I have emigrated to this Colony . . . **Leonard W. Cottle**, I am 21 years of age, I removed from Missouri. I arrived here February 1828.

Nacogdoches, Oct 6, 1835. **John Cotton** married with family, citizen of this Department since 1821.

Nacogdoches, 4 December 1835. **William Creager** married with family, citizen of this Department since 1822.

Austin's "Register of Families" 49

Sabine District, Sept 6, 1835. **Redmond Dayly** has a family, has resided District of Ayish since 1829.

Precinct of Tannehaw, Sept 17, 1835. **Alfred B. Davis**—native of South Carolina, family of 3 persons. Emigrated 1828.

San Augustine, August 18, 1835. **Nathan Davis Senr**—native of South Carolina, family of wife and six children, emigrated in 1822.

District of Sabine, 2 Sept 1835. **William Defee [Deffee]** — native of South Carolina, family of four persons. Emigrated 1830.

San Augustine, August 10, 1835. **John B. Dillard**—native of North Carolina, family of wife and seven children. Emigrated 1830.

Austin, May 24, 1832. I have emigrated to this Colony . . . **Thomas Dillard**, 34 years of age. Occupation Physician. Unmarried. Moved from Alabama and arrived Novemr 1830.

San Augustine, Sept 23, 1835. **Daniel Dry**—native of Germany, family of 4 persons, emigrated 1830.

John Dry—native of Germany, family of 5 persons, emigrated 1830.

John F. Dry—native of Germany, family of 3 persons, emigrated 1830.

Paul Dry — native of Germany, family of 2 persons, emigrated 1830.

District of Sabine, 20 August 1835. **Matthew Earl**—native of Louisiana, resided in District since 1824, family of five persons.

District of Sabine, August 20, 1835. **William Earl**—native of Louisiana, resided in the District since 1824.

San Augustine, 7 April 1835. **Nicholas Elliott**—native of the U.S., family of 4 persons, emigrated in 1825.

Town of Austin, 17 June 1830. I have emigrated to this Colony . . . **Lewis Enett**—27 years old, married. Occupation, farmer. Mary my wife 15 years old. Moved from Mississippi, arrived this Colony June 1830.

San Augustine, August 17, 1835. **James English** — native of Tennessee, single, emigrated 1829.

San Augustine, August 18, 1835. **James English** — native of North Carolina, family of wife and seven children, emigrated to Texas 1827.

San Augustine, May 24, 1835. **John English** — native of South Carolina, family of wife and five children, emigrated 1825.

San Augustine, August 17, 1835. **Jonas English** — native of Tennessee, family of wife, emigrated 1824.

San Augustine, August, 1835. **Joseph English** — native of Tennessee, family of wife and two children, emigrated in 1823.

San Augustine, August 18, 1835. **Joshua English**— native of Tennessee, family of wife, no children, emigrated 1826.

San Augustine, September 1st, 1835. **Richard B. English**—native of Tennessee, single, emigrated 1827.

San Augustine, August 17, 1835. **Stephen English [Inglish]** — native of Tennessee, family of four persons, emigrated in 1825.

San Augustine, August 17, 1835. **Thomas English**—native of Tennessee, family of wife and eight children, emigrated 1825.

50   1830 Citizens of Texas

Ayish District, 2 Decr 1830. This is to certify that we have known **Holden Evans** for the last year . . . John Cartwright, Jacob Garrett, Alcalde

State of Alabama, Perry County, 17 July 1830. **Jesse J. Evans** — of State and County . . . removing to Texas . . . we certify that we know . . . [with signatures of 2 Justices of Peace and friends]

San Augustine, October 12, 1835. **Huott Farmer** — native of Tennessee, family of three persons emigrated 1829.

San Augustine, Octr 5, 1835. **Joseph Fish** — native of Georgia, family of four persons, emigrated 1829.

Nacogdoches, 11 December 1835. **Isaac H. Fishback** — married with family, citizen this Dept. since 1827.

Town of Austin, 1st May 1830. I have emigrated . . . **William Fitzgerald**, 46 years old, married. Occupation farmer. Nancy my wife, 50 years old. Two male children, one female. Moved from Louisiana and arrived in this Colony in 1822.

San Augustine, September 1, 1835. **Robert F. Foot** — native of South Carolina, single man. Emigrated 1830.

Town of Austin, 19 June 1830. I have emigrated to this Colony . . . **Drury S. Ford**, 26 years old, unmarried. Moved from Tennessee, arrived Feby 1830.

San Augustine, August 19, 1835. **James Forsythe** — native of Kentucky, man of family, wife and three children. Emigrated in 1821 and his wife is a Mexican citizen.

San Augustine, August 19, 1835. **John Forsythe** — native of Kentucky, family of wife and three children. Emigrated in 1822.

To: Mr. S. F. Austin. I have emigrated to this Colony . . . **John Foster** 26 years old, unmarried. Moved from Carolina and arrived Feby 1830.

Precinct of Tannahaw, Sept 7, 1835. **Sebastian Francis** — a native of South Carolina, family of two persons, emigrated 1830.

San Augustine, Sept 17, 1835. **Isaac Freeland** — native of Kentucky, family of two persons. Emigrated 1830.

San Augustine, Sept 1st 1835. **Choyl Freeland** — native of Louisiana, family of three persons. Emigrated 1827.

San Augustine, 27 September 1835. **Daniel Fuller** — native of South Carolina, emigrated 1830. Family of six persons.

State of Alabama, County of Perry, October 18, 1830. **Daniel R. Gandy** has made known . . . going immediately to the Province of Texas that he may obtain land . . . [Signatures of a J.P. and friends]

San Augustine, August 18, 1835. **Charles Gates** — native of Kentucky, family of wife and four children, emigrated 1821.

San Augustine, August 18, 1835. **Andrew W. Goodwin** — native of Tennessee, family of three persons. Emigrated 1830.

To: Mr. S.F. Austin. I have emigrated to this Colony . . . Single man aged 23, farmer, removed from Louisiana. Arrived 5 August 1829. **Samuel Gordon** [signed]

Nacogdoches, 11 December 1835. **John Gragg** married with family, citizen of this Dept. since 1820.

Austin's "Register of Families" 51

San Augustine, August 19, 1835. **Phillip Groves** — native of Tennessee, single man, emigrated 1824.

Town of Austin, 5 June 1830. **Thomas Gary [Gay]** — 25 years unmarried, moved from Georgia. Arrived May 1830.

Nacogdoches, 20 October 1835. **Clery Grillet** — married with family, citizen of this Dept. since 1825.

San Augustine, August 20, 1835. **Christian Gross** — native of North Carolina, family of 3 persons. Emigrated 1828.

San Augustine, August 20, 1835. **George Grounds** — native of Missouri, family of 5 persons. Emigrated 1828.

San Augustine, August 18, 1835. **Allen Haley** — single, native of Tennessee, emigrated 1822.

San Augustine, October 10, 1835. **Charles Haley** — native of Louisiana, single man, emigrated 1821.

San Augustine, August 19, 1835. **John Haley** — native of South Carolina, family of wife and ten children, emigrated 1822.

San Augustine, August 19, 1835. **Mark Haley** — native of Alabama, wife and one child, emigrated 1825.

San Augustine, August 18, 1835. **Mary Ann Haley** — native of Georgia, family of four persons. Emigrated 1828.

San Augustine, August 29, 1835. **R. B. Haley** — native of Tennessee, family of 2 persons. Emigrated 1822.

San Augustine, August 17, 1835. **Richard Haley** — native of North Carolina, wife and eight children. Emigrated 1822.

San Augustine, August 18, 1835. **Thomas Haley** — single man, native of Alabama. Emigrated 1822.

District of Sabine, September 15, 1835. **Burgess G. Hall** — old settler, emigrated from North Caroliona in 1828.

San Augustine, 29 August 1835. **Harvay Hall** — native of Tennessee, emigrated 1829.

To: Mr. S. F. Austin. I have emigrated to this Colony . . . **Cauaohas K. Ham**, 28 years of age, unmarried, arrived Feby 1830.

San Augustine, September 29, 1835. **Francis Hamelton** — native of Missouri, family of twelve persons. Emigrated 1827.

San Felipe de Austin, 6 July 1830. I have removed to this Colony . . . **Rosalie Hamner**, 24 years, one male child. Acting for myself, my husband having abandoned me in Louisiana. Four servants. Removed from Louisiana, arrived April last [1830].

Nacogdoches, November 13, 1835. **Lawrence G. Hampton** — has lived in this Country seven years or more, married, 5 children.

Nacogdoches, October 5, 1835. **Samuel G. Hanks** — native of Indiana, no family. Emigrated 1827.

Precinct of Tannahaw, October 7, 1835. **John Hardison** — native of Caintuckey, married man of family. Emigrated in 1830.

San Augustine, October 5, 1835. **Nathan Hardwick** — native of Georgia, family of seven persons. Emigrated in 1830.

District of Tenehaw, August 12, 1835. **William Harkins** — native of Virginia, family of seven persons. Emigrated 1830.

San Augustine, October 7, 1835. **Henry Harper** — native of Virginia, family of 8 persons. Emigrated 1826.

San Augustine, October 5, 1835. **James Harris** — native of Alabama, family of two persons. Emigrated 1830.

San Augustine, September 1, 1835. **Almond Harrison** — native of New York, single. Emigrated 1830.

San Augustine, August 17, 1835. **Jonas Harrison** — native of New Jersey, wife and seven children. Emigrated January 1821.

San Augustine, September 7, 1835. **Seth Hazel** — native of South Carolina, family of five persons. Emigrated 1830.

San Augustine, August 18, 1835. **Edwin Hancock** — native of Kentucky, wife and 2 children. Came to Texas in 1824.

San Augustine, August 17, 1835. **Henry Hendrick** — native of Virginia, single man, emigrated 1824.

San Augustine, September 1st 1835. **Obideah Hendrick** — native of Kentucky, single, emigrated 1826.

District of Sabine, 25 August 1835. **Albert Hines** — native of Georgia. Has resided Dist. of Sabine last ten years. Family of six persons.

District of Sabine, 17 June 1835. **Allen Hines** — has resided in Dist. eleven years. Family 3 persons.

San Augustine, September 1st 1835. **William Hines** — native of Georgia, family of 7 persons. Emigrated in 1823.

Precinct of Tannahaw, October 12, 1835. **John B. Hixon** — native of Virginia, married, family of 5 persons. Emigrated in 1828.

State of Tennessee, Davidson County, 21 November 1825. Know ye that Joses Holdy a citizen of this County . . . is about to emigrate and settle . . . in Texas . . . Robert Weakley, a Justice of P

San Augustine, February 22, 1835. Power of Attorney to M. Cartwright from Joses Holdey.

Nacogdoches, 19 September 1835. **Henry H. Hobson** married with family, citizen of this Dept. since 1822.

Nacogdoches, 13 October 1835. **David Hufman** — married with family, citizen of this Dept. since 1829.

San Augustine, August 17, 1835. **Caleb Holloway** — native of Mississippi, single, emigrated 1821.

San Augustine, August 18, 1835. **Daniel Holloway** — native of South Carolina, single, emigrated 1821.

Nacogdoches, 13 August 1835. **Lewis Holoway** — married with family, citizen of this Dist. since 1821.

San Augustine, August 17, 1835. **Simpson Holloway** — native of South Carolina, family of 3 persons. Emigrated 1821.

Precinct of Tennahaw, September 17, 1835. **Samuel Holmes** — native of

Caintuckey, family of two persons. Emigrated 1829.

San Augustine, August 18, 1835. **Benjamin Holt** — native of Mississippi, family of wife and six children. Emigrated 1825.

Nacogdoches, 11 December 1835. **James E. Hopkins** — married with family, citizen of this Dept. since 1824.

To: Mr. S.F. Austin. January 10, 1832. I have emigrated to . . . **George House**, 45 years, Married. Sally my wife, 35 years. 3 Male 2 female children. Moved from Louisiana and arrived this Colony Decemr 1830.

San Augustine, August 20, 1835. **Hartwell Howard** — native of Virginia, family of 5 persons. Emigrated 1823.

San Augustine, September 1st 1835. **Joseph Howe** — native of Ohio, single, emigrated 1827.

To: Mr. S.F. Austin. May 27, 1830. I have emigrated to . . . **Matthew Hubert**, 34 years. Married. Frances my wife 32 years. 2 Female children. Moved from Alabama, arrived 20 Jany 1830.

District of Sabine, August 1st 1835. **James T.P. Irvine** — native of Tennessee, man of family. Emigrated 1830.

San Augustine, August 18, 1835. **William A. Irvine** — native of Virginia, man of family of two persons. Emigrated 1822.

San Augustine, 10 June 1835. **William Jacobs** — native of the U.S., family of 3 persons. Emigrated 1830.

San Augustine, 30 August 1835. **Winney Jewel** — native of North Carolina, woman of family of five persons. Emigrated 1830.

Nacogdoches, 19 November 1834. **Alvey R. Johnson** — has 5 years in this country, married with a family.

Nacogdoches. 12 Sept 1835. **John Johnson** — married with family, citizen of this Dept. since 1828.

San Augustine, October 5, 1835. **Crawford Jones** — native of South Carolina, family of 3 persons. Emigrated in 1830.

San Augustine, September 22, 1835. **Lewis Jones** — a native citizen of this country, family of four persons.

Nacogdoches, October 3, 1835. **William Jordan** — native of South Carolina, emigrated in 1825 family of 6 persons.

To: Mr. S.F. Austin, March 1830. I have emigrated to . . . My age is 29 years. My wife Lavenia aged 28 years, oldest child female Lucinda aged 16 months. I was born in Ohio, came to Texas 1825, have been a resident of your Colony since 12 Nov 1829. **Francis G. Keller**

Town of Austin, May 24, 1830. I have emigrated to . . . I am single, 18 years of age. Farmer by occupation. Removed from Louisiana, arrived in this Colony 2 April 1830. [Note] An orphan. **Levi Kellen**

"A memorandum from Mrs. Kenedy. **Margaret Kennidy** age thirty seven moved to this Colony in June 1824, from Atacapas, one son and daughter." [no date]

San Augustine, August 25, 1835. **Samuel Kimbro** — native of Tennessee with wife and 2 children. Emigrated 1830.

San Augustine, August 18, 1835. **William King**—native of Georgia with wife and 4 children. Emigrated 1830.

Town of Austin, 8 July 1830. I have emigrated to . . . **John Kinkead** [signed] 33 years old. from Kentucky. Occupation farmer, arrived Jany 1826.

I hereby certify that **Thomas H. Kinley** a native of Mississippi man of a family of two persons, emigrated in 1830 [No date or place] Nathan Davis, Commasaryo

Town of Augustine, 3 June 1830. I have emigrated to . . . **David Kneeland**, 45 years old, married. Silence my wife, 41. One female child. Moved from Opelousas, arrived May 1830.

Esteban F. Austin y Samuel M. Williams, 21 Dec 1832. I am European by birth and married in Nacogdoches [wants to be admitted]. My name is **Josep de la Baume** born in Montpelier, France. Married . . . have five children, 3 male and two female. My spouse is Maria Louisa Couturier native of new Orleans, of age 50 years . . .

San Augustine, August 19, 1835. **Garrett M. Lankford**—native of Tennessee, family of eight persons. Emigrated 1829.

San Augustine, August 19, 1835. **John Latham**—native of North Carolina, family of wife and seven children. Emigrated in 18_04_.

Tennaha, Oct 10, 1835. **Ross Law**—native of Virginia, family of 5 persons. Emigrated in 1827.

Town of Austin. I have emigrated to . . . **Jesse Leftwich** 55 years of age, married. Merchant. Sarah my wife, 42 years. Three male, six female children. Moved from Tennessee, Maury Co. Arrived April 1830.

District of Ayish, 12 Jany 1833. **John L. Lewis**—late of Louisiana who removed to this neighborhood Jany 1830.

State of Tennessee, Henry County, 28 Jany 1827 . . . certify that . . . Joseph Lindly, man of good character [signed by three J.P.'s]
[Note added in Texas]: Wife & 4 children
    At the place he has improved = Vehlein-Rankin

San Augustine, 6 Sept 1835. **Charles Lindsey**—native of South Carolina, family of 7 persons, emigrated in 1824.

Town of Austin, 26 April 1830. I have emigrated to . . . **James Lindsey**, 30 years old, unmarried. Occupation carpenter & farmer. Moved from Kentucky. Arrived Dec_r_ 1827. James Lindsay [signed]

San Augustine, 6 Sept 1835. **Micajer Linsey**—native of South Carolina, family 2 persons. Emigrated 1824. Micagah Lindsey [signed]

San Augustine, 6 Sept 1835. **Pennington Lindsey**—native of South Carolina, family 2 persons. Emigrated 1824.

Ayish Bayou, September 17, 1835. **Thos Lindsey**—native of Louisiana, family 2 persons. Emigrated 1824.

Town of Austin, 5 June 1830. I have emigrated . . . **Hugh Linney**, 50 years of age, widower. Occupation farmer. 2 Male children 1 female. Moved from the State of Kentucky. Arrived this country in 1823 and this Colony May 1830.

Austin's "Register of Families"   55

San Augustine, August 18, 1835. **William M. Lloyd** — native of Tennessee, single. Emigrated 1828.

San Augustine, October 10, 1835. **John Lock** — native of Tennessee, family of 5 persons. Emigrated 1829.

San Felipe de Austin, July 14, 1830. I have emigrated . . . My name is **Samuel Lockhart** aged 45 years. My wife Winey aged 34. One male child. Moved from Louisiana. Occupation farmer. Arrived this Colony in June 1830.

San Felipe de Austin, 6 July 1830. I have emigrated . . . My name is **Nicholas Lockridge**, aged 53 years. My wife Alsey aged 45 years. Five male children, five female. One servant. Removed from Louisiana, arrived this Colony April last [1830]. [Recommendation from Clinton, La. Nov. 17, 1829]

State of Tennessee, McNairy County, 25 May 1828. Removing from friends [to go to Texas] **Isaac Low**

Sabine District, 26 April 1830. **Isaac Low** — from Tennessee emigrated with family to this Dist. in August 1828.

San Augustine, Tunahaw District, Sept 26, 1835. **John Lowry** — native of Louisiana, single, emigrated 1821.

Nacogdoches, 8 Sept 1835. **Stephen Lynch** — widower with family, resident of this Dept. since 1825.

San Augustine, August 19, 1835. **Felipe Madregol** — man of family with 3 children, native Mexican.

San Augustine, August 1835. **Timothy Mahan** — native of Kentucky, man of family with 2 children. Came to Texas in 1824.

San Augustine, August 19, 1835. **W. T. Malone** — native of Mississippi, family of wife and 2 children. Emigrated 1812.

Town of Austin, 6 July 1830. I have emigrated . . . **Gabriel Manent** — native of France, 26 years of age, unmarried arrived this Colony June 1830. Moved from France.

Jacque Manent — native of France, 24 years old, unmarried. Moved from France, arrived in June 1830.

District of Sabine, 27 May 1832. **Henry Martin** — emigrated to this district with his family from Alabama in March 1822, wishes to move to Austin's Colony. [Added note]: Wife and 5 children. Three Cabin Bayou abt 15 miles from Coast. David G. Burnet Grant

Town of Austin, 26 May 1830. I have emigrated . . . **Tolliver Martin** — 36 years old, married. Elizabeth my wife. Moved from South Carolina and arrived in Feby 1830.

San Augustine, September 2, 1835. **James Mason** — native of South Carolina, family of wife and four children. Emigrated in 1830.

San Augustine, October 6, 1835. **James Y. Mason** — native of Virginia, family of 3 persons. Emigrated in 1829.

San Augustine, 27 September 1835. **John Mason** — native of South Carolina, emigrated in 1830. Family of 8 persons.

San Augustine, August 20, 1835. **Morris May** — native of Georgia, family of 3 people, emigrated 1828.

San Augustine, October 6, 1835. **Alfred Mayfield** — native of Missouri, family of five people. Emigrated in 1830.

San Felipe de Austin, February 26, 1830. Col. Austin: We have been acquainted for some time with **Mr. John W. Mayo** . . . Joshua Fletcher, J. White

San Augustine, August 19, 1835. **Edward A. Merchant** — native of South Carolina, man of family of 6 persons. Emigrated 1829.

San Augustine, September 23, 1835. **Jacob Messenhama** — native of Germany, family of 8 persons. Emigrated 1830.

John Mesenhama — native of Germany, family of 2 persons. Emigrated 1830.

San Augustine, 15 May 1835. **J. F. Middleton** — native of the U.S., family of 5 persons. Emigrated 1829.

San Augustine, September 1st 1835. **Elizabeth Melton** — native of Georgia, widow woman with a family of three persons, emigrated in 1824.

San Augustine, October 10, 1835. **William Melton** — native of Alabama, family of two persons, emigrated in 1830.

San Augustine, September 1, 1835. **Elizabeth Mitchell** — native of Virginia, widow with a family of two persons, emigrated in 1830.

District of Sabine, September 15, 1835. **Narcissa Monett** — native of Louisiana, emigrated in 1829, has a family of 3 persons.

San Augustine, April 23, 1835. **D. S. D. Moon** — was a citizen as early as 1826.

District of Tenehaw, September 3, 1835. **Richard Mooney** — native of Mississippi, family of four persons, emigrated in 1830.

Town of Austin, 3 July 1830. I have emigrated to . . . **John Moore** 54 years of age, widower, occupation farmer. 2 Male 1 female children. Moved from Louisiana, arrived this Colony Apr 1830.

San Augustine, August 29, 1835. **Henry Morgan** — native of New York, single, emigrated 1829.

District of Bevil, February 7, 1835. **Edmund Morrisson** — native of Maryland, family of 6 persons, emigrated January 1825.

Town of Austin, 17 May 1830. I have emigrated . . . **Henry Moore** aged 34 years married. Elisa W my wife, 28. Two male, one female children, three dependents. Moved from Mississippi, arrived this Colony April 1830.

To: S. F. Austin. I have emigrated to . . . **Socrates S. Moseley** 27 years of age, unmarried. Occupation physician, moved from Tennessee and arrived this Colony April 1830.

San Augustine, August 30, 1835. **Cyreny McCrery** — native of Kentucky, woman of family of 5 persons, emigrated in 1822.

San Augustine, August 19, 1835. **Jonathan McFaden** — native of Louisiana, single, emigrated 1822.

San Augustine, August 19, 1835. **Samuel McFaden** — native of Kentucky, man of family of seven persons. Emigrated 1822.

San Augustine, September 1st 1835. **Elizabeth McIntyre**, widow, native of Virginia, nine persons in family, emigrated 1829.

Austin's "Register of Families" 57

San Augustine, September 1st 1835. Thomas McIntyre — native of Tennessee, single man, emigrated 1829.

San Augustine, September 1st 1835. Hezekiah McKelvy — native of Tennessee, family of six persons emigrated 1824.

San Augustine, August 18, 1835. James McCelvey — native of Tennessee, family of wife, no children. Emigrated 1824.

San Augustine, August 17, 1835. Jesse McCelvey — native of Tennessee, single, emigrated 1825.

San Augustine, September 1st 1835. Susannah McCelvey [McKelvey] — native of Virginia, widow with a family of 3 persons, emigrated 1824.

Nacogdoches, 14 Decr 1835. James McKenny — married with family, citizen this Department since 1824.

Nacogdoches, 14 Decr 1835. Wm C. McKinny — married with family, citizen of this Department since 1824.

Town of Austin, 12 July 1830. I have emigrated . . . John McClaren, 36 years old, single, moved from Virginia and arrived in Feby 1825. John McLaren [signed]

Nacogdoches, 14 Septr 1835. James McLean — married with family, citizen of this Department since 1830.

San Augustine, Sept 1st 1835. Polly McVay — native of Tennessee, widow of family of 2 persons, emigrated 1829.

San Felipe, May 26, 1830. Having been in this Colony since 20 January 1829 . . . I have no family . . . native of New York, age 39 years. Occupation school teacher. Joshua Nelson

Nacogdoches, District of Bevil, October 3, 1835. William Nichols — emigrated in 1826 from Louisiana, family of six persons.

San Augustine, September 1st 1835. John Norris — is a native of the country and man of family of six persons.

San Augustine, September 1st 1835. Sarah H. Norris — a native citizen, widow with a family of 4 persons.

San Augustine, September 1st 1835. Thomas Norris — native of Maryland, man of family of six persons, emigrated 1803.

Town of Austin, 19 June 1830. I have emigrated . . . James Northcross 28 years old, unmarried, farmer. Moved from Alabama arrived August 1829.

To: Mr. S. F. Austin. I have emigrated . . . James Norton age 28 years. Emigrated from New Orleans in the State of Louisiana and arrived in this colony in October 1827.

Nacogdoches, 1 September 1835. Quintius Cincinnatus Nujent — of Mississippi, married with family, citizen of this Municipality since 1825.

San Augustine, October 1st 1835. Thomas Oban — native of South Carolina, family of nine persons, emigrated 1822.

San Augustine, Septr 1st 1835. Benjamin Odle — native of Tennessee, with family. Emigrated 1825.

San Augustine, September 1st 1835. Washington Orsment — native of Massachusetts, single, emigrated in 1830.

Town of Austin, 2 June 1830. I have emigrated . . . **John Owen**, 21 years old, occupation farmer. Christina my wife 21 years. Moved from Louisiana and arrived this Colony in 1822.

Town of Austin, 24 June 1830. Mr. Austin: **James Robert Pace, William Carrol Pace**, minors and 14 years of age and **Albert Gallatin, Wesley Walker, Patsey Jones, Dempsey Council, Mary Ann Elizabeth & Gideon**, minors under 14 years of age of the late Gideon Pace, want to be admitted under your contract . . . James R. Pace for himself & brothers & sisters

District of Sabine, September 8, 1835. **William Pace**, family of eight, resident this district nine years, emigrated from Louisiana in 1826.

San Augustine, [1835?]. **Johnson Parmer Junior** — native of the U.S., man of family of 4 persons, emigrated in 1828.

I hereby certify that I have known **John C. Partin** from the time he landed in the Country to the present day . . . 8th Dec_r_ 1829.

    Thos M. Duke   Lewis Demoss
    William Duty   Peter Demsy?
    John Demoss   William Demoss
    Ralph Wright

San Augustine, 17 August 1835. **G. H. Patterson** — native of Virginia, family of wife and six children, emigrated to Texas in 1824.

San Augustine, 9 October 1835. **John Patterson** — single, no family, resident since 1830.

San Augustine, August 17, 1835. **John C. Payne** — native of Tennessee, single, emigrated 1825.

Town of Austin, 12 July 1830. I have emigrated . . . My name is **Victor Pepin** 49 years of age. My family consists of 2 sons and 2 daughters that are now in the U.S.

San Augustine, August 20, 1835. **James Perkins** — native of Virginia, family of wife and one child. Emigrated in 1830.

Nacogdoches, 30 September 1835. **William Peyton** — single, citizen since 1829.

San Augustine, September 1st 1835. **John Polvadore** — native of France, family of seven persons, emigrated about 50 years since.

San Augustine, September 1st 1835. **Atruis Procell** [Gertrude Procelo on reverse] is a native citizen, widow woman of family of six persons.

San Augustine, September 1st 1835. **Henry M. Quirk** — native citizen, married, two in family.

District of Tenahaw, July 21, 1835. **Samuel Raimond** — native of Tennessee, family of five persons emigrated 1830.

Austin, June 2d 1832. I have emigrated . . . **John Raney** 50 years of age, native of England. Nancy 51 years of age. 2 Female children. Arrived this Country in April 1830.

San Felipe de Austin, June 10, 1830. I have emigrated . . . My name is **James Rankin** age 22 years, single. My father is dead. No parent in this country. Removed from Alabama, arrived this Colony 1827. Occupation, farmer. James Rankin Jr. [signed]

Austin's "Register of Families" 59

To: S. F. Austin [June 10, 1830]. I have emigrated . . . **William Rankin** 21 years old, unmarried, an orphan. Moved from Alabama and arrived this Colony in 20 Jany 1830.

District of Tenahaw. August 20, 1835. **John Raydon** — native of Georgia, family of 3 persons, emigrated 1830.

San Augustine, September 1, 1835. **Green Reaves** — native of Kentucky, family of 5 persons, emigrated 1830.

District of Sabine, [1834?]. **David Renfro** — has family of 5 persons, citizen of this place since 1827.

District of Sabine, [1834?]. Certify **Isaac Renfro**, native of Missouri, has a family emigrated 1825.

San Augustine, August 18, 1835. **Clinton Rice** — native of Tennessee, family of 3 persons, emigrated 1826.

San Augustine, August 20, 1835. **Joseph Rice** — native of Tennessee, family of 5 persons, emigrated 1826.

San Augustine, August 1835. **Noel Roberts** — native of Louisiana, family of 3 persons, emigrated in 1824.

To: Mr. S. F. Austin. I have emigrated to . . . **Jeremiah S. Robinson**. My age is 23 years, born in the State of Mississippi and emigrated from that state and arrived in this Colony in 1830, am unmarried. Farmer and stock raiser.

San Augustine, Octr 5, 1835. **John E. Ross** — native of Tennessee, family of 5 persons, emigrated in 1826.

San Augustine, September 17, 1835. **Johnson Runnels** — native of Kentucky, emigrated 1812.

San Augustine, September 1, 1835. **Hosa Francisco Sanches** — a native citizen, single man.

San Augustine, August 19, 1835. **Jose Santos** — native of Spain, family of wife and four children. Came to this Country when a child.

San Augustine, August 17, 1835. **Henry Sentehfield** [Reverse side: Schritchfield] native of Louisiana, single, emigrated in 1822.

Town of Austin, May 21, 1830. I have emigrated . . . **William Sexton** — 24 years old, unmarried. Occupation farmer. Moved from Louisiana and arrived in this Colony 5 Jany 1830. Three dependents.

San Augustine, August 29, 1835. **William H. Sewall** — native of Georgia, family of two persons emigrated in 1826.

State of Alabama, Perry County, August 2d 1830. **William Shepherd** — intends moving to Texas. [Signed by two J.P.'s and friends]

San Augustine, September 1st 1835. **William Sinclair** — native of South Carolina, family of ten persons, emigrated 1830.

San Augustine, October 10, 1835. **George Slaughter** — native of Mississippi, single, emigrated in 1826.

San Augustine, October 10, 1835. **Samuel Slaughter** — native of Mississippi, single, emigrated in 1826.

Recommendation to Depart of Bexar, December 6, 1829. We the undersigned citizens of the Jurisdiction of Austin, certify . . . **James Small** . . . head of family, two dependents, both female, one twenty four years of age named Rhody, and the other six years of age and called Emeline. He is 34 years of age, occupation farmer . . . pray that he be given land . . .

   James Whiteside   Walter C. White
   Oliver Jones   Thomas ---
   John York

  San Augustine, August 18, 1835. **Archibald Smith** — native of Louisiana, family of wife and three children, emigrated in 1822.

  Town of Austin, July 31, 1830. I have emigrated . . . **John W. Smith** 37 years of age, farmer. Sarah my wife 26. 2 Male 2 female children. Arrived this Colony in Jany 1830. Wife and family in Ohio expected to arrive soon.

  District of Sabine, October 12, 1835. **Joseph Smith** — native of South Carolina, has family, emigrated 1830.

  San Felipe de Austin, 10 June 1835. I have emigrated . . . My name is **Mary Smith** widow, one male child, two female. Removed to this colony in Novr 1829 from Louisiana. Occupation stock raising.

  San Augustine, August 17, 1835. **Menan Smith** — native of Louisiana, family of 4 persons. Emigrated in 1822.

  San Augustine, September 1st 1835. **Nimrod Smith** — native of Kentucky, family of 3 persons. Emigrated in 1826.

  San Augustine, September 29, 1835. **William Smith** — native of Tennessee, family of wife and two children. Emigrated in 1830.

  Town of Austin, 7 August 1830. I have emigrated . . . **Lancelott Smith** 27 years of age, unmarried, farmer. Moved from Alabama, arrived in this Colony April 1828.

  Town of Austin, 9 July 1830. I have emigrated . . . **Noah Smithwick** 22 years of age, moved from Tennessee, arrived in this Colony in 1827. Occupation Gunsmith.

  Nacogdoches, 11 December 1835. **Jacob Stallins** — married with family, citizen of this Department since 1819.

  San Augustine, October 10, 1835. **Amos Stephens** — native of Virginia, family of 8 persons. Emigrated in 1829.

  Town of Austin, 19 February 1831. I have emigrated . . . **A. B. Sterrett** 33 years of age. Occupation farmer. Martha my wife 22 years of age. 2 Male children. Moved from Louisiana and arrived 1 Decr 1830.

  San Augustine, August 20, 1835. **Peter Stockman** — native of Louisiana, family of 3 persons. Emigrated 1810.

  Town of Austin, 16 July 1830. I have emigrated . . . **David Stoddard** 35 years of age unmarried, from Massachusetts. Arrived this Colony in August 1829.

  San Augustine, August 19, 1835. **William Stout** — native of Tennessee, widower, no children. Emigrated in 1827.

  San Augustine, Octr 5, 1835. **John Strange** — native of North Carolina, family of 8 persons. Emigrated in 1827.

  San Augustine, August 20, 1835. **Samuel Strickland** — native of Kentucky, family of wife and three children. Emigrated in 1821.

Precinct of Tenahaw, [1835]. **Williston P. Talbot** — native of Virginia, family of two persons. Emigrated in 1828.

Town of Austin, 22 June 1830. I have emigrated . . . **Jesse C. Tannehill** 32 married. Occupation farmer. Jane my wife 26. One male, one female children. Moved from Tennessee and arrived in this Colony April 1828.

Nacogdoches, October 5, 1835. **Owin Taylor** — native of Georgia, emigrated in 1829, family of six persons.

Town of Austin, 7 May 1830. I have emigrated . . . **William H. Taylor** 41 years old, widower. One male and four female children. Moved from Louisiana and arrived in Texas in 1821 and in this Colony in April 1829.

San Augustine, August 19, 1835. **Edward Teal** — native of Maryland, family of three children. Emigrated in 1824.

San Augustine, August 19, 1835. **Samuel Thompson** — native of North Carolina, family of two persons. Emigrated in 1826.

San Augustine, August 24, 1835. **Alexander C. Thornburgh** — native of North Carolina, family of five persons. Emigrated in 1829.

Nacogdoches, 29 August 1835. **Theresa Tomlinson** — of Louisiana, widow with a family of five children, citizen of this Municipality since 1824.

San Augustine, August 20, 1835. **Clement Tutt** — native of South Carolina, family of nine persons. Emigrated in 1827.

Tenahaw, August 19, 1835. **Mason Van** — native of South Carolina, family of eight persons. Emigrated in 1822.

Nacogdoches, 19 September 1835. **Wiley Waldrope**, married, citizen of this Department since 1827.

Nacogdoches, 3 October 1835. **Hardy Ware** — widower with family, citizen of this Department since 1824.

Jurisdiction of Liberty, June 30, 1835. **Chas C. Welch** — native of South Carolina, emigrated in 1829. Wife and two children. Acting Comisario of the Precinct of Cedar Bayou.

Town of Austin, 11 May 1830. I have emigrated . . . **Gross Welsh** — 27 years old, single, occupation farmer. Moved from Louisiana and arrived May 1830.

Town of Austin, 17 May 1830. I have emigrated . . . **Henry P. Welsh** — 23 years old, unmarried. Moved from Louisiana and arrived in this Colony 15 May 1830.

District of Bevil, October 4, 1835. **Gade West** — came this province in December 1829, native of Mississippi, family of eight persons.

To: S.F. Austin [not dated, after 1829]. **William H. Wharton** — 25 years of age. Sarah Anne my wife 22 years of age. One child male. Moved from Tennessee and arrived this Colony Novemr 1827.

Town of Austin, 27 May 1834. **Archibald S. White** — 59 years old, married. Margaret my wife 53 years old. Four male, three female children. Moved from Tennessee and arrived in this Colony Feby 1830.

District of Sabine, August 20, 1835. **Benjamin White** — native of Louisiana, emigrated in 1823.

District of Sabine, August 20, 1835. **Elizabeth White**—native of Louisiana, emigrated this place in 1823, family of 5 persons.

To: S.F. Austin. **Saml A. White** 26 years of age unmarried. Moved from Tennessee and arrived in this Colony 20 Feby 1830.

San Augustine, August 10, 1835. **Henry Whiteside**—native of Kentucky, family of wife and two children. Lived in Texas six years commencing in 1824.

San Augustine, August 17, 1835. **Harbor L. Wiggins**—native of North Carolina, family of wife and one child. Emigrated in 1830.

Nacogdoches, 18 August 1835. **David Wilkerson**—native of South Carolina, family of eight persons. Emigrated in 1822.

San Augustine, October 10, 1835. **James Williams**—native of Tennessee, family of six persons. Emigrated in 1829.

Austin, Feby 15, 1832. **Parker Williams**—unmarried 43 years old. Moved from Virginia and arrived in this Colony Augt 1830.

District of Bevil, August 27, 1835. **Richard Williams**—native of Louisiana. Emigrated 1829. Family of two persons.

San Augustine, August 18, 1835. **Richard Williams**—native of Georgia, single. Emigrated 1821.

District of Sabine, September 17, 1835. **William Williams**—native of Louisiana, family of three persons. Emigrated in 1830.

San Augustine, October 5, 1835. **William A. Williams**—native of North Carolina, family of three persons. Emigrated in 1829.

San Augustine, September 1st 1835. **Arthur Willis**—native of Tennessee family of five persons. Emigrated in 1823.

San Augustine, August 29, 1835. **John Win**—native of Georgia, family of two persons. Emigrated in 1830.

Villa de Austin, Certificate of Reception, 15 Dec 1830. **Jonathan Woodworth**—arrived December 1830, married with a family of 14 persons. His family is in Connecticut and he has a period of two years to bring them.

San Augustine, August 18, 1835. **Moses Wootan**—native of North Carolina, family of wife and six children. Emigrated in 1822.

San Augustine, August 22, 1835. **Robert Wyres**—native of Virginia, family of 2 persons. Emigrated in 1830.

TITLES IN DeWITT'S COLONY

Green DeWitt as an Empresario made a contract with the Mexican government to establish a colony west of the Austin Colony and centered around Gonzales. It was active in settlement in 1830-31. In Vol. VIII-2, October 1904 of the Quarterly of the Texas State Historical Society will be found a history of DeWitt's Colony by Ethel Zively Rather. One section is a census of the inhabitants of Gonzales presumed to have been taken in 1828, although at least one family in it arrived in January 1829.

In Volumes 12 and 13 of the Spanish Archives of the General Land Office entitled "Titles in DeWitt's Colony" are bound all the documents relating to the early grantees. Settlers arriving in 1829 and later were given Certificates of Reception that stated important personal information. Subsequently, the settler applied for land of his choice in a Petition that contained further personal facts. Both documents have been abstracted here. The grant documents and records of survey usually do not give additional genealogical information.

These same documents were used by Rather for the 1904 history, but they have been consulted again to obtain the maximum genealogical data. Some of the arrivals were in 1831, although the person may already have been in Texas for some time. The complete list was copied.

Most of the records were signed at Gonzales by Green DeWitt or his surveyor Byrd Lockhart. Name spellings vary, but when the applicant signed, his own spelling is used.

The first listing is the abstract of the Certificate of Reception and the second is from the Petition for land.

Abstracts from "TITLES IN DeWITT'S COLONY"

2 March 1830. JONATHAN COTTLE arrived this colony 6 July 1829, married, family of 3 persons.

29 April 1831. JONATHAN COTTLE native of the U.S., married, one son.

1 April 1831. CHURCHILL FULLSHEAR arrived 31 March 1831, married, family of 3 persons.

24 April 1831. BENJAMIN FULSHEAR native of the U.S. [applies for] brother CHURCHILL FULLSHEAR who is married, one male child.

22 May 1830. JOHN McCOY SR arrived 9 March 1827, married, family of 4 persons.

24 April 1831. JOHN McCOY, native of the U.S., married, 2 children, 1 of them male.

17 Dec 1830. JAMES THOMPSON arrived 1 Dec 1830, married, family of 9 persons.

24 April 1831. JAMES THOMPSON native of the U.S., married, with seven children of which 6 are males.

4 March 1831. SIMEON BATEMAN arrived 20 Feb 1831, married, family of 38 persons.

22 April 1831. SIMEON BATEMAN native of the U.S., married, 5 children of which 3 are males, more than 24 dependents.

25 May 1830. JOHN G. KING arrived 15 May 1830, married, family of 9 persons.

22 April 1831. JOHN G. KING native of the U.S., married, 7 children of which 3 are male.

5 Feb 1830. GRAVES FULSHEAR arrived 20 Jan 1829, single.

22 April 1831. GRAVES FULSHEAR native of the U.S., single.

8 May 1831. BENJAMIN FULSHEAR arrived 19 Dec 1826, single.

22 April 1831. BENJAMIN FULSHEAR native of the U.S., single.

16 Jan 1831. JACOB C. DARST arrived 10 Jan 1831, married, 4 persons.

22 April 1831. JACOB DARST native of the U.S., 4 children, 1 a male.

14 Feb 1830. JESSE McCOY arrived 9 March 1827, 1 person.

22 April 1831. JESSE McCOY native of the U.S., single.

22 March 1830. BYRD LOCKHART arrived 20 March 1826, widower, 5 persons.

15 April 1831. BYRD LOCKHART native of the U.S. Large family, including his mother, sister and 2 children of his dead wife.

22 July 1830. STEPHEN SMITH arrived 25 March 1830, married, 4 persons.

14 April 1831. STEPHEN SMITH native of the U.S., married, two daughters.

2 March 1831. CLAIBORNE STINNETT arrived 30 May 1830, single.

14 April 1831. CLAIBORNE STINNETT native of the U.S., single.

28 Jan 1830. WINSLOW TURNER arrived 4 Dec 1829, married, 8 persons.

14 April 1831. WINSLOW TURNER native of the U.S., married, six children, four of them boys.

22 May 1830. THOMAS HAMILTON arrived 19 Jan 1830, married, two persons.

14 April 1831. ELIZA DeWITT native of the U.S. "Came to the Colony with my spouse THOMAS HAMILTON who was admitted in the contract of my father the Empresario Green DeWitt . . . who died."

26 Feb 1830. JAMES HINDS arrived 24 Feb 1830, married, five persons.

24 May 1831. JAMES HINDS native of the U.S., married, three children, two of them sons.

3 May 1830. BYRD B. LOCKHART arrived Feb 1829, single.
24 May 1831. BYRD B. LOCKHART native of the U.S., single.
3 Feb 1830. PETER TEAL arrived 24 April 1829 ____ persons.
23 May 1831. PETER TEAL native of the U.S., single.
22 Feb 1831. SPENCER MORRIS arrived 20 Feb 1831, 5 persons.
23 May 1831. SPENCER MORRIS native of the U.S., married, three sons.
9 Feb 1830. RICHARD HEATH arrived 24 Oct 1828, single, one person.
23 May 1831. RICHARD HEATH native of the U.S., single.
22 Feb 1831. JOHN A. NEILL arrived 20 Feb 1831, married, three persons.
18 May 1831. JOHN A. NEILL native of the U.S., married, one son.
14 Feb 1830. FRANCIS BERRY arrived 12 May 1825, married, six persons.
15 May 1831. FRANCIS BERRY native of the U.S., arrived 12 May 1825, married, four children, two of them sons.
26 Nov 1830. ISAAC HOUSE arrived 6 Nov 1830, married, five persons.
14 May 1831. ESTHER BERRY origin the U.S., family of three male children. Her spouse ISAAC HOUSE died after a little time.
26 Feb 1830. GERREN HINDS arrived 13 April 1825, married, two persons.
9 May 1831. GERREN HINDS native of the U.S., married.
CHARLES LOCKHART arrived 2 March 1829, six persons, married.
9 May 1831. CHARLES LOCKHART native of the U.S., married, three children, two of them boys.
28 March 1830. CALEB BROCK arrived 26 Feb 1830, married, fifteen persons.
4 May 1831. CALEB BROCK native of the U.S., married, five children, one a male.
22 Feb 1831. ROBERT SMITH arrived 20 Feb 1831, married, five persons.
4 May 1831. ROBERT SMITH native of the U.S., married, three daughters.
22 Feb 1831. ALMERION DICKINSON arrived 20 Feb 1831, married, two persons.
4 May 1831. ALMERION DICKINSON, married.
28 May 1830. CALEB P. ALEXANDER arrived 26 Feb 1830, twenty-five persons.
14 May 1831. CALEB P. ALEXANDER native of the U.S., married, two sons.
18 April 1830. WILLIAM A. MATTHEWS arrived 12 Feb 1830.
4 May 1831. WILLIAM A. MATTHEWS native of the U.S., single.
5 Sept 1830. SAMUEL SHUPE arrived 27 March 1827, single, one person.
4 May 1831. SAMUEL SHUPE native of the U.S., single.
20 April 1830. JOHN McCOY arrived 9 March 1827, married, four persons.

4 May 1831. JOHN McCOY the younger, married, is son of John McCoy, native of the U.S. Married, two daughters.

22 Feb 1831. JOHN E. GARVIN arrived 20 Feb 1831.

4 May 1831. JOHN E. GARVIN native of the U.S., single.

25 Feb 1830. JESSE ROBINSON arrived 10 Sept 1827, single.

4 May 1831. JESSE ROBINSON native of the U.S., single.

22 Aug 1830. WILLIAM COBBEY arrived 22 Aug 1830 single.

4 May 1831. WILLIAM COBBEY native of the U.S., single.

22 Feb 1831. JOHN HENRY arrived 20 Feb 1831, married, seven persons.

4 May 1831. JOHN HENRY native of the U.S., married, five children, two of them male.

10 Feb 1830. ELIJAH TATE arrived Feb 1829, single, one person.

4 May 1831. ELIJAH TATE native of the U.S., single.

17 Feb 1830. JOHN OLIVER arrived 20 May 1835, married, two persons.

1 May 1831. JOHN OLIVER native of the U.S., married, no children.

27 Jan 1830. ANDREW TUMLINSON arrived 12 Nov 1827, married, three persons.

1 May 1831. HARRIET COTTLE native of the U.S. having recently arrived with her spouse Andrew Tumlinson . . . one child.

17 April 1830. GEORGE F. MANAGHAN arrived 25 March 1830, single.

1 May 1831. GEORGE F. MANAGHAN native of the U.S., single.

24 May 1830. JOSEPH McCOY arrived 29 Jan 1829, married, seven persons.

1 May 1831. JOSEPH McCOY native of the U.S., married, six children, four of them males.

22 Jan 1831. PHINEAS JAMES arrived 7 Jan 1831, married, two persons.

10 May 1831. PHINEAS JAMES native of the U.S., married, without offspring.

27 Jan 1830. SAMUEL HIGHSMITH arrived 4 Sept 1829, three persons.

1 May 1831. SAMUEL HIGHSMITH native of the U.S., arrived this colony 4 Sept 1829, married, two sons.

26 Jan 1830. BYRUM WICKSON arrived 13 Mar 1829, single.

1 May 1831. BYRUM WICKSON native of the U.S., single.

This land relinquished to the Republic in 1843.

28 Jan 1830. THOMAS JACKSON arrived 6 July 1829, married, four persons.

1 May 1831. THOMAS JACKSON native of the U.S., arrived 6 July 1829, married, three children, two of them males.

25 Jan 1830. IRA NASH arrived 29 May 1829, married, six persons.

1 May 1831. IRA NASH native of the U.S., married, four children, two of them males.

1 May 1831. WINSLOW TURNER native of the U.S., single.
[Certificate of Reception missing]. [Signed]: Junc

Titles in DeWitt's Colony   67

1 may 1831. FELIX TAYLOR native of the U.S., married, three children, two of them males.
[Certificate of Reception missing].
15 Feb 1830. EZEKIEL WILLIAMS arrived Jan 1829, single, one persons.
1 May 1831. EZEKIEL WILLIAMS native of the U.S., single.
5 March 1831. DANIEL DAVIS arrived 20 Feb 1831, married, three persons.
1 May 1831. DANIEL DAVIS native of the U.S., married, one son.
1 June 1831. BENJAMIN FULSHEAR origin U.S., married, two children, of which one is male.
[No Certificate of Reception here]
1 April 1831. GEORGE ALLEN arrived 31 Mar 1831, married, four persons.
2 June 1831. GEORGE ALLEN first arrived at Gonzales.
22 Feb 1831. SOLOMON SEAL arrived 20 Feb 1831, married, two persons.
30 June 1831. SOLOMON SEAL origin U.S., married.
6 Sept 1830. ISAAC WELDON arrived 25 July 1828, single, one person.
28 June 1831. ISAAC WELDON native of the U.S., single.
20 March 1830. JAMES C. DAVIS arrived 28 March 1829, single, one person.
28 June 1831. JAMES D. DAVIS native of the U.S., single.
22 Feb 1831. JAMES F. WOOD arrived 20 Feb 1831, married, eight persons.
21 June 1831. JAMES F. WOOD native of the U.S., married, six children, of which three males.
10 Feb 1830. JOHN J. TUMLINSON arrived 1829, married, two persons.
14 June 1831. JOHN J. TUMLINSON native of the U.S., married.
22 Feb 1831. MOSES BAKER arrived 20 Feb 1831, married, five persons.
23 June 1831. MOSES BAKER native of the U.S., married, three children, of which two are male.
2 Aug 1830. ANDREW KENT arrived 12 June 1830, married, ten persons.
28 June 1831. ANDREW KENT native of the U.S., married, eight children, of which three male.
9 Feb 1830. BENJAMIN DUNCAN arrived 16 Oct 1828, single, one person.
26 June 1831. BENJAMIN DUNCAN native of the U.S., single.
4 March 1830. JAMES GEORGE arrived 20 Feb 1830, married, five persons.
28 June 1831. JAMES GEORGE native of the U.S., married, three daughters.
3 June 1830. WILLIAM A. SOWELL arrived 31 May 1830, single, one person.
20 June 1831. WILLIM A. SOWELL native of the U.S., single.

22 Feb 1831. STEPHEN B. MORRISON arrived 20 Feb 1831, married, eight persons.

22 June 1831. STEPHEN B. MORRISON native of the U.S., married, six children, one a male.

22 Feb 1831. MATTHEW CALDWELL arrived 20 Feb 1831, married, five persons.

21 June 1831. MATTHEW CALDWELL native of the U.S., married, three sons.

22 Feb 1831. MICHAEL GILLEN arrived 20 Feb 1831, married, five persons.

21 June 1831. MICHAEL GILLEN native of the U.S., married, six children, one a male.

22 Feb 1831. SILAS M. MORRIS arrived 20 Feb 1831, married, eight persons.

21 June 1831. SILAS M. MORRIS native of the U.S., married, six children, three of them males.

4 May 1831. JOHN SOWELL arrived 3 May 1831, married, six persons.

4 May 1831. JOHN SOWELL native of the U.S., married, six children, four of them males.

22 Feb 1831. ALEXANDER PORTER arrived 20 Feb 1831, married, two persons.

21 June 1831. ALEXANDER PORTER native of the U.S., married.

4 May 1830. LEWIS D. SOWELL arrived 3 May [blank], single.

22 June 1831. LEWIS D. SOWELL native of the U.S., single.

18 Feb 1831. EBEN HAVEN arrived 13 July 1827, married, two persons.

22 June 1831. EBEN HAVEN native of the U.S., married.

24 Jan 1831. GEORGE FOLEY arrived 20 Nov 1827, widower, alone.

9 July 1831. GEORGE FOLEY native of the U.S., widower.

26 Jan 1830. JOHN JONES arrived 14 Sept 1825, single, one person.

9 July 1831. JOHN JONES native of the U.S., single.

29 Jan 1831. JONATHAN SCOTT arrived 20 Aug 1830, single, one person.

9 July 1831. JONATHAN SCOTT native of the U.S., single.

4 May 1830. SQUIRE BURNS arrived 15 Aug 1826, single, one person.

9 July 1831. SQUIRE BURNS origin U.S., single.

4 March 1830. WILLIAM P. STAPP arrived 20 Feb 1830, single, one persons.

9 July 1831. WILLIAM P. STAPP native of the U.S., single.

25 November 1830. DARWIN M. STAPP arrived 4 June 1828, single, one person.

19 July 1831. DARWIN M. STAPP native of the U.S., single.

7 March 1831. ZACHARIAH DAVIS arrived 20 Feb 1831, married, six persons.

18 July 1831. ZACHARIAH DAVIS origin U.S., married, four children, one a male.

18 May 1830. ABRAHAM O. McCLURE arrived 10 May 1830, single, one person.

5 July 1831. ABRAHAM O. McCLURE origin U.S., single.

5 Feb 1830 ARTHUR BURNS arrived 1 Aug 1826 married, seven persons.

8 July 1831. ARTHUR BURNS origin U.S., married, four children, two of them males.

8 Sept 1830. SAMUEL LOCKHART arrived 29 July 1830, married, three persons.

8 July 1831. SAMUEL LOCKHART native of the U.S., married, one male child.

20 May 1830. SAMUEL McCOY arrived 4 Jan 1829, single, one person.

6 May 1831. JOSEPH McCOY for his brother SAMUEL McCOY, native of the U.S., single.

4 March 1830. JOHN M. ASHBY arrived 20 Feb 1830, married, seven persons.

17 July 1831. JOHN M. ASHBY origin U.S., married, five children, three of them male.

8 March 1830. RUSSEL WARD arrived 5 March 1830, single, one person.

19 July 1831. RUSSEL WARD origin U.S., single.

12 July 1831. ALMOND COTTLE origin U.S., single.
[No Certificate of Reception]

22 March 1830. ELIJAH STAPP arrived 20 March 1830, married, eight persons.

16 July 1831. ELIJAH STAPP origin U.S., married, six children, 5 of them males.

25 November 1830. WILLIAM HOUSE arrived 17 November 1830, single, one person.

5 July 1831. WILLIAM HOUSE origin U.S., single.

1 Feb 1830. PATRICK DOWLEARN arrived 24 June 1827, single, one person.

25 July 1831. PATRICK DOWLEARN origin U.S., applies as a single man now.

28 May 1830. JOSIAH TAYLOR arrived 16 Jan 1829, married.

23 July 1831. HEPZIBETH TAYLOR native of the U.S., has lost her husband; as fruit of their marriage has nine children, of whom six are males. [signed]: Hepzibeth Taylor Widow of Josiah Taylor.

28 March 1830. JOHN McCRABB arrived 20 March 1830, single, one person.

12 July 1831. JOHN McCRABB origin U.S., single.

8 Feb 1830. KIMBER W. BARTON arrived 15 March 1829, married, three persons.

10 July 1831. KIMBER W. BARTON native of U.S., married, two daughters.

30 April 1830. JOSEPH CAMPBELL arrived 22 March 1827, married, seven persons.

23 Aug 1831. CYRUS CAMPBELL for self and in the name of his siblings HILL CAMPBELL, JOSEPH CAMPBELL, RUFUS CAMPBELL, JUAN CAMPBELL and RACHAEL CAMPBELL who arrived in this country in the year 27 brought by our deceased father JOSEPH CAMPBELL.

10 April 1830. MILES G. DIKES arrived 28 Dec 1829, single, one person.

21 Aug 1831. MILES G. DIKES origin the U.S., single.

25 June 1830. WILLIAM PAGE arrived 15 June 1828, single.

22 Aug 1831. WILLIAM PAGE origin U.S., single.

27 Jan 1830. WILLIAM H. TAYLOR arrived 28 Jan 1828, married, three persons.

6 Aug 1831. WILLIAM TAYLOR origin the U.S., married, one son.

10 June 1830. WILLIAM HILL arrived 10 June 1830, married, eight persons.

10 Aug 1831. WILLIAM HILL origin the U.S., married, six children, four of them males.

26 Feb 1830. WILLIAM CHASE arrived 30 Aug 1826, married, 3 persons.

15 Aug 1831. WILLIAM CHASE origin the U.S., married, one son.

21 July 1830. ABRAHAM ZUMWALT arrived June 1830, married, three persons.

11 Aug 1831. ABRAHAM ZUMWALT origin the U.S., married, one daughter.

28 May 1830. JOSEPH TUMLINSON arrived Feb 1829, single, one person.

6 Aug 1831. JOSEPH TUMLINSON origin the U.S., single.

15 June 1830. WASHINGTON LOCKHART arrived 25 March 1829, single, one person.

8 Sept 1831. GEORGE WASHINGTON LOCKHART origin U.S., single.

14 Feb 1830. SAMUEL P. MIDDLETON arrived 30 December 1829, single, one person.

10 Sept 1831. SAMUEL P. MIDDLETON origin U.S., single.

25 April 1830. ROBERT MILLS arrived 23 April 1830, single, one person.

10 Sept 1831. ROBERT MILLS origin U.S., single.

16 Feb 1830. RICHARD H. CHISHOLM arrived Jan 1829, married, four persons.

6 Sept 1831. RICHARD H. CHISHOLM origin U.S., married, two children, one a male.

26 Jan 1830. JAMES B. PATRICK arrived 27 March 1829, married, two persons.

2 Sept 1831. JAMES B. PATRICK origin U.S., married, one son born in the last three months.

16 May 1830. BARTHOLOMEW D. McCLURE arrived 10 May 1830, married, two persons.

6 Sept 1831. BARTHOLOMEW D. McCLURE origin U.S., married.

10 Mar 1831. GEORGE W. DAVIS arrived 20 March 1831 [error?] married, six persons.

4 Sept 1831. GEORGE W. DAVIS origin U.S., married, four children, three of them males.

17 Feb 1830. ANDREW LOCKHART arrived 25 March 1829, married, nine persons.

11 Sept 1831. ANDREW LOCKHART origin U.S., married, seven children, 2 of them males.

15 Oct 1830. THOMAS R. MILLER arrived 16 June 1830, single, one person.

15 Sept 1831. THOMAS R. MILLER origin U.S., single.

25 Oct 1830. EDWIN RICHESON arrived 15 April 1830, married, three persons.

10 Sept 1831. EDWIN RICHESON origin U.S., married, one daughter.

25 May 1830. JOHN DAVIS arrived 16 Feb 1830, single.

25 Oct 1831. JOHN DAVIS origin U.S., single.

3 May 1830. JOHN B. LOCKHART arrived 24 Feb 1829, single.

25 Oct 1831. JOHN B. LOCKHART origin U.S., single.

22 Mar 1830. WILLIAM DEARDUFF arrived 20 Mar 1830, single, one person.

1 Oct 1831. WILLIAM DEARDUFF origin U.S., single. [Signed]: William Der duff

15 Feb 1830. JOSEPH D. CLEMENTS arrived 25 Dec 1829, married, seven persons.

25 Oct 1831. JOSEPH D. CLEMENTS origin U.S., married, six children, four of them males.

28 March 1830. STEPHEN F. SANDERS arrived 26 March 1830, single.

25 Nov 1831. STEPHEN F. SANDERS origin U.S., single.

9 Feb 1830. GEORGE BLAIR arrived 10 Feb 1829, seven persons.

26 Nov 1831. GEORGE BLAIR origin U.S., married, five children, two of them male.

25 Sept 1830. MALKIJAH WILLIAMS arrived 1 Aug 1830, single, one person.

12 Nov 1831. MALKIJAH WILLIAMS origin U.S., single.

28 Jan 1830. ADAM ZUMWALT arrived 20 May 1829, married, nine persons.

10 Aug 1831. ADAM ZUMWALT origin U.S., married, seven children, two of them males.

4 May 1830. GEORGE C. KIMBALL arrived 5 March 1825, single, one person.

15 Nov 1831. GEORGE C. KIMBALL origin U.S., single.

16 May 1830. DAVID W. BRAND arrived 20 April 1830, single, one person.

13 Nov 1831. DAVID W. BRAND origin U.S., single.

3 June 1830. UMPHRIES BRANCH arrived 29 May 1830, married, four persons.

4 Nov 1831. UMPHRIES BRANCH origin U.S., married, two children, one a male.

12 May 1830. EDWARD DICKINSON arrived 25 April 1825, single, one person.

25 Nov 1831. EDWARD DICKINSON origin U.S.

22 Jan 1831. ELIHU MOSS arrived Jan 1831, married, five persons.

15 Nov 1831. ELIHU MOSS origin U.S., married, three children, one a male.

_____. VALENTINE BENNET arrived 1 April 1831, single, one person.

1 Nov 1831. VALENTINE BENNET origin U.S., single.

17 May 1830. ALLAN B. WILLIAMS arrived 16 May 1830, married, ten persons.

3 May 1832. ALLAN B. WILLIAMS origin U.S., married, eight children, three of them males.

26 August 1830. DAVID BURKET arrived 1 June 1830, married, six persons.

20 Nov 1831. DAVID BURKET origin U.S., married, four children, two of them males.

29 Jan 1830. JOHN SMOTHERS arrived September 1828, widower, four persons.

2 May 1832. JOHN SMOTHERS origin U.S., here with family since 1827, having the misfortune to lose his spouse a little after. Three children, two of them males.

20 Feb 1831. TOBIAS WENTWORTH arrived 24 June 1828, single, one person.

14 May 1832. TOBIAS WENTWORTH origin U.S., single.

9 Feb 1830. ABRAHAM DENTON arrived 16 July 1825, single, one person.

8 May 1832. ABRAHAM DENTON origin U.S., single.

3 Oct 1830. JESSE K. DAVIS arrived 29 Sept 1830, single.

16 May 1832. JESSE K. DAVIS Origin U.S., single.

22 Feb 1831. CHRISTOPHER WILLIAMS arrived 20 Feb 1831, single, one person.

6 May 1832. CHRISTOPHER WILLIAMS origin U.S., single.

24 May 1830. ADAM ZUMWALT 2d arrived 22 May 1830, married, nine persons.

2 May 1832. ADAM ZUMWALT origin U.S., married, seven children, five of them males.

28 May 1830. PHILANDER PRIESTLY arrived 24 May 1830, single, one person.

4 Dec 1831. PHILANDER PRIESTLY origin U.S., single.

4 May 1830. JAMES TUMLINSON JR. arrived December 1828, single, one person.

2 Dec 1831. JAMES TUMLINSON origin U.S., single.

Titles in DeWitt's Colony 73

13 May 1830. LITTLETON F. TUMLINSON arrived Nov 1828, single, one person.

2 Dec 1831. LITTLETON TUMLINSON origin U.S., single.

[Signed]:   L. F. Tumlinson

17 March 1831. DAVID C. TUMLINSON arrived 15 Dec 1831 [1830?] single.

8 Dec 1831. DAVID C. TUMLINSON origin U.S., single.

3 June 1832. WILLIAM ST. JOHN origin U.S., single.

[Petition not signed, and no Certificate of Reception]

10 Nov 1830. SAMUEL WILLIAMS arrived 9 Nov 1830, single, one person.

8 June 1832. SAMUEL WILLIAMS origin U.S., single.

17 Dec 1830. EDWARD HUGHART arrived 20 June 1830, single, one person.

15 July 1832. EDWARD HUGHART origin U.S., single.

27 Jan 1830. JOSEPH KENT arrived 20 July 1827, single, one person.

4 June 1832. JOSEPH KENT origin U.S., single.

16 Feb 1831. JAMES HUGHES arrived 15 Feb 1831, single, one person.

4 June 1832. JAMES HUGHES origin U.S., single.

19 Oct [?] 1830. JOSE' RAMON BEDFORD arrived 20 Sept 1830, single, one person.

1 June 1832. JOSE' RAMON BEDFORD origin U.S., single.

22 Feb 1831. BETHEL MORRIS arrived 20 Feb 1831, single, one person.

20 June 1832. BETHEL MORRIS origin U.S., single.

17 March 1830. JAMES PERRY arrived January 1829, single, one person.

June 1832. JAMES PERRY origin U.S., single.

22 March 1830. AMBROSE FINNEY arrived 20 March 1830, married, four persons.

14 June 1832. AMBROSE FINNEY origin U.S., married, two male children.

20 April 1830. BENJAMIN FUQUA arrived 6 March 1830, single, one person.

8 June 1832. BENJAMIN FUQUA origin U.S., male.

15 Aug 1830. ISAAC BAKER arrived 13 Aug 1830, single, one person.

8 June 1832. ISAAC BAKER origin U.S., single.

18 Sept 1830. JAMES GIBSON arrived 1 August 1830, married, two persons.

10 Aug 1831. JAMES GIBSON origin U.S., married.

29 Jan 1830. ANDREW PONTON arrived 17 Dec 1829, single, one person.

2 June 1832. ANDREW PONTON origin U.S., single.

23 July 1830. WILLIAM LEACH arrived 19 July 1830, single, one person.

4 June 1832. WILLIAM LEACH origin U.S., single.

4 March 1831. JAMES SHAW arrived 20 Feb 1831, single, one person.

10 June 1832. JAMES SHAW origin U.S., single.

25 March 1830. DANIEL McCOY arrived 20 March 1830, married, two persons.
12 June 1832. DANIEL McCOY origin U.S., married.
15 May 1830. SILAS FUQUA arrived 11 May 1830, married, six persons.
10 June 1832. SILAS FUQUA origin U.S., married, five children, two of which are males.
4 March 1830. DAVID G. MILLS arrived 20 Feb 1830, single, one person.
8 June 1832. DAVID G. MILLS origin U.S., single.
15 Feb 1831. WILLIAM W. ARRINGTON arrived 15 Feb 1831, single, one person.
11 June 1832. WILLIAM ARRINGTON origin U.S., single.
7 June 1832. WILLIAM STRODE origin U.S., married.
[No Certificate of Reception].
24 March 1830. JOSEPH McCOY arrived 20 March 1830, single, one person.
7 July 1832. JOSEPH McCOY origin U.S.
23 March 1830. FREDERICK KISTLER arrived 20 March 1830, married, seven persons.
7 July 1832. FREDERICK KISTLER origin U.S., married, five children, two of them males.
16 Feb 1830. JOHN ROE arrived 25 April 1827, single, one person.
2 July 1832. JOHN ROE origin U.S., single.
1 Feb 1830. ISAAC COTTLE arrived 15 Jan 1830, married, nine persons.
8 Sept 1832. ISAAC COTTLE origin U.S., emigrated with a large family, two daughters one son, in the month of Jan 1830.
20 June 1830. JOHN FENNELL arrived 5 June 1830, single.
4 Sept 1832. JOHN FENNELL origin U.S., single.
22 Feb 1831. JOSEPH P. LAWLOR arrived 20 Feb 1831, single, one person.
5 Sept 1832. JOSEPH P. LAWLOR Origin U.S., single.
22 May 1830. GEORGE W. COTTLE arrived 6 July 1829, married, two persons.
4 Sept 1832. GEORGE W. COTTLE origin U.S., married.
1 May 1830. WILLIAM B. LOCKHART arrived 15 March 1829, single, one person.
10 Sept 1832. WILLIAM B. LOCKHART origin U.S., single.
22 Feb 1831. JOHN MORRIS arrived 20 Feb 1831, single, one person.
8 Sept 1832. JOHN MORRIS origin U.S., single.

SPECIAL GRANTS BY JOSE' ANTONIO NAVARRO AND GREEN DeWITT IN DeWITT'S COLONY

1—William Pettus, old settler of the first contract of Stephen F. Austin. [applies] for Colonist Eduardo Pettus. Gonzs 15 May 1831

4—Eduardo Pettus, son of the deceased Freeman Pettus who emigrated to this country in 1822 and died in 1827 . . . [Certificate of Character] Villa de Austin   7 Dec 1830   Eduardo de Pettus is a young man of very good . . . [Received]   10 Dec 1830   Green DeWitt

9—Jesus Canto resident of Bejar . . . land on the Guadalupe. 1 Nov 1830

18—Eligio Gortari origin San Fernando de Bejar   16 Aug 1831

31—Sarah Seely spouse of Green DeWitt, with a family of 6 children; arrived in 1826 with family from Missouri
[asks for land in her own name]   Sarah Seely

36—William Pettis, origin U.S., one of the first colonists of Stephen F. Austin.

37—William Pettus . . . emigrated to this country in 1822

42—Byrd Lockhart, origin U.S., widower, emigrated to this country with his family in 1825

71—Benjamin Fulcher & Graves Fulcher, origin U.S.   1 June 1831   Graves Fulshear   Benn Fulshear [signed]

72 — Benjamin Fulchear & Graves Fulchear, sons of majority [age] of Churchill Fulchear, came with their father in 1822, are 25 years of age, served 7 years in the militia.   Villa de Austin   1 Dec 1830

77 — James Kerr, origin U.S., one of the first emigrant Colonists to Austin   5 July 1831   Santiago Kerr

78—Santiago Kerr, came 24 March 1825   [Certificate]   Villa de Austin 1 Dec 1830

84—Marjila Chirino, spouse of retired Lt. Don Jose' Salinas.   1 March 1832   By Jose' Ramon Bedford

85 — Margila Chirino, widow of the deceased C. Jose' Salinas, both citizens . . .

97—Anastacio Mansolo origin San Fernando de Bejar, resident here after this date.   16 August 1831   Jose' Maria Salinas

98—Anastacio Mansolo, 42 years 3 months 7 days old   13 April 1831

133—Joseph de la Baume, here since 1816, in San Fernando de Bejar 6 June 1832   Concession 22 Jan 1826

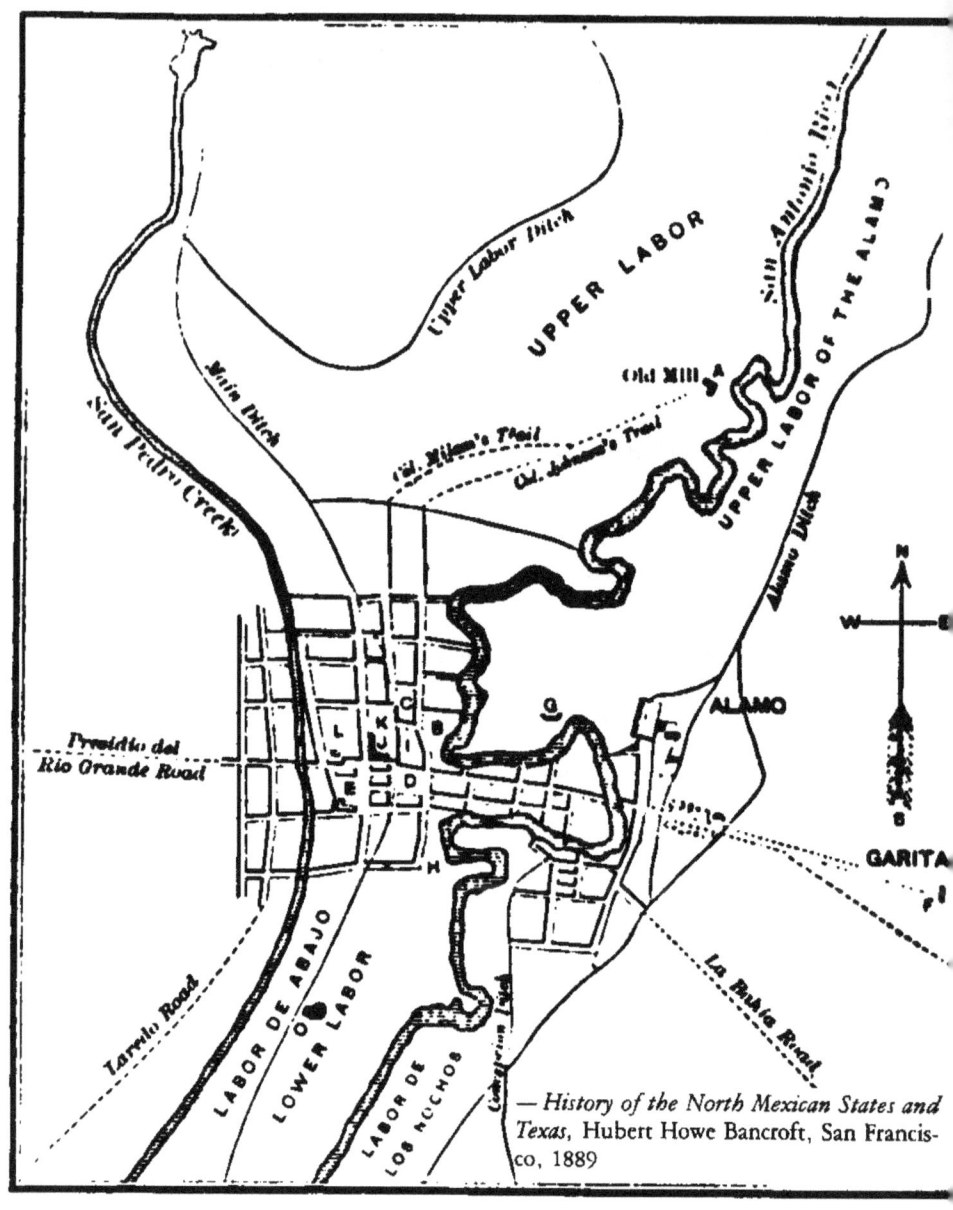

SAN ANTONIO AND ENVIRONS

A. Old Mill.
B. House of Veramendi.
C. House of Garza.
D. Main Square, or Plaza de la Constitucion.
E. Military Plaza.
F. Powder house, or Garita.
G. Redoubt.
H. Quinta.
I. Priest's House.
J. House of Antonio Navarro.
K. Zambrano Row.
L. Mexican Redoubt.

THE 1830 CENSUS OF SAN ANTONIO

The manuscript schedules of the 1830 and 1831 census of the Department of San Antonio de Béjar are in the Bexar Archives, mixed into two document groups. They have been microfilmed and this transcription was made from the microfilm edition. Roll and Frame numbers are cited so that prints may be ordered. The microfilm and originals are in the Archives Division of the University of Texas Library, Austin, Texas.

By using marginal notations, physical oddities of the leaves, and internal evidence from the family groups, the two years of records can be separated. They have been so separated here.

A statistical report for San Fernando de Béjar (which may be equated with modern San Antonio) for 1830 is found in the Archives of the Texas State Library. It shows 1621 souls were counted in the Department in 1830. The surviving rolls contain about 1360 names, so that about 260 names have not been found.

The originals have columns to check off sex under each marital status, and to place the age number in various age groups. The summary displays this original division of the data. In transcription, this was simplified to save space, without loss of information.

All persons shown to have a profession also had a tabulation of their property, particularly ranch stock and draft animals. These were not copied because they give minimal genealogical information.

It must be emphasized that these documents were written in a cramped hand in phonetic Spanish. Errors of copy cannot be avoided. There appear to be no Anglo-American names on the rolls. This may be an illusion. Juan Esmite is probably John Smith. In 1831, James Bowie was there as Santiago Buy. There are no doubt others.

Roll 142 of the Bexar Archives microfilm, covering part of June into July 1831, has a "List of citizens who have not paid . . ." an assessment. It lists the following divisions (barrios) of San Antonio de Béjar:

    Barrio del Norte   [North]
    Barrio del Sur   [South]
    Barrio de Alamo y Villita [Valero]

1830 Citizens of Texas

Mission de la Espada   [surrounding]
Mission de San Jose'

The 1831 census contains the schedule for San Jose', which is missing for 1830. The 1831 schedule is included as a replacement.

CENSUS AND STATISTICS
STATE OF COAHUILA AND TEXAS
DEPARTMENT OF THE CITY OF SAN FERNANDO DE BÉJAR

	Single		Married		Widowed		Total Souls
	M	F	M	F	M	F	
Under 7	171	148	0	0	0	0	319
7 to 16	163	151	0	16	0	0	330
16 to 25	87	72	51	73	0	11	294
25 to 40	37	37	116	131	12	43	373
40 to 50	11	7	46	34	9	27	134
50 up	16	2	43	31	30	46	168
Totals	485	417	256	285	51	127	1621

Béjar Archives
Texas State Archives
Austin

1830 CENSUS OF SAN ANTONIO

Barrio de Valero

[Letters underscored were raised and underlined in the original to indicate abbreviation]

Name	Sex	Status	Age	Occupation
449 Roll 132				
D. Vicente Gortari	M	Married	58	Farmer
Da Maria Estrada	F	Married	60	
Jose' Ontero	M	Single	35	Laborer
Gertrudis Menchaca	F	Widow	35	
Jesusa Martines			6	
Da Concepcion Charle'	F	Widow	30	
Juana Losoya	F	Single	1-	
Juan Losoya			7	
Jesus Cantu	M	Married	43	Farmer
Alexandro Gortari	M	Widower	62	Farmer
Santa Gortari	F	Married	26	
Jesusa Cantu			12	
Lucia Cantu			10	
Miguel Cantu			8	
Jesus Cantu			6	
Juana Travieso	F	Widow	40	
Matilde Gamboa	F	Widow	64	
D. Pedro del Toro	M	Married	47	
Ma Alvina Charle	F	Married	27	
Martin del Toro			5	
Ponciano Muños	M	Married	40	Farmer
Ma Gertrudis delos Stos	F	Married	30	
Fecundo Ortega	M	Single	16	Farmer
Disidora Ortega			11	
Eugenio Muños			8	
Jose' Maria Muños			7	
Franco Muños			5	
Ma Rosa Muños			1	
Jose' Anto de la Garza	M	Married	50	Farmer
Gertrudis de la Garza	F	Married	46	
Clemente Mansolo	M	Married	52	Farmer
--delaria Rios	F	Married	35	
Josefa Padilla			3	
Bautsa Padilla	F	Single	18	Laborer
450	Valero			

80 1830 Citizens of Texas

Name	Sex	Status	Age	Occupation
Nepomucena Hernandes	F	Widow	22	
Franco Valdes			7	
Josefa Castillo			3	
Da Juana Leal	F	Widow	32	
Vicente Farin	M	Single	16	Farmer
Juan Maria Farin			12	
Joaquin			8	
Macario			6	
Juan Ygo Texeda	M	Married	50	Farmer
Maria Josefa Flores	F	Married	45	
Maria Anta del Rio	F	Single	25	
Juan Jose' Texeda	M	Single	15	Farmer
Mariano Texeda			14	
Pedro Texeda			10	
Paula Texeda			6	
Gavino Texeda			1	
Felipe Loa	M	Married	47	Farmer
Ana Maria Oxtolan	F	Married	44	
Juana Loa	F	Single	23	
Anastacia Loa	F	Single	18	
Demetria Loa	F	Single	17	
Romalda Loa	F	Single	15	
Maria Rosalia de los [blank]	F	Widow	45	
Franco de Salas	M	Single	23	Farmer
Doroteo Pacheco	M	Single	17	Farmer-Laborer
Teodoro Rodrigz			7	
Ma del Carmel			1	
D. Jose' Labome	M	Married	59	Farmer
Jose' Labome	M	Single	24	Farmer
Gertrudis Labome	F	Single	19	
D. Alexandro Vidal	M	Married	38	Merchant
Da Vitorina Labome	F	Married	25	
Alexandro Vidal			1	
Vicente Leal	M	Married	24	Farmer
Carmel Ramos	F	Married	30	
Maria de Jesus Leal			4	
451	Valero			
D. Jose' de la Garza	M	Married	45	Farmer
Da Consolacion Leal	F	Married	34	
Da Yga Arocha	F	Widow	26	
Miguel Sandoval			8	
Salome Sandoval			5	
Juan Jose' de los Reyes	M	Married	30	Laborer
Nepomucena Servantes	F	Married	28	
Anto de los Reyes			9	
Maria de Jesus de los Reyes			8	
Franca de los Reyes			5	

1830 Census of San Antonio 81

Adanto de la Serda	M	Married	40	Farmer
Juana Servantes	F	Married	30	
Guadalupe de la Serda			4	
Dolores de la Serda			3	
Nicolasa de la Serda			1	
Fernando Cabrera	M	Married	35	Artisan
Maria Ynes Medina	F	Married	37	
Juan Jose' Cabrera	M	Single	18	
Luciano Cabrera			8	
Graviel Martines	M	Married	35	Farmer
Perfecta Alcantar	F	Married	25	
Louisa Martines			11	
Tomasa Martines			8	
Jesusa Martines			1	
Maria Manla Mansolo	F	Single	28	
Manuel de Torres			3	
Anastacio Mansolo	M	Married	35	Farmer
Josefa Robles	F	Married	38	
Pablo Mansolo			5	
Decidenia Padilla			8	
D. Manuel Arciniega	M	Married	37	Farmer
Da Alejandra Losoya	F	Married	23	
Jose' Miguel Arciniega			8	
Petra Arciniega			6	
Maria de Jesus Arciniega			4	
Gregorio Arciniega			1	
Senovia Peres	F	Single	32	Laborer
Juan de Leon			11	Laborer
Gertrudis Flores	F	Widow	52	
Juliana Arciniega	F	Widow	58	
D. Crecencio Leal	M	Married	26	Farmer
Dolores Arciniega	F	Married	16	
452				
Ygnacio Ortis	M	Married	21	Farmer
Teresa Lopes	F	Married	17	
Perfecta Luna	F	Widow	56	
Maria Josefa Ximenes	F	Widow	36	
Petra Leal	F	Single	16	
Juan Casanova	M	Married	40	Farmer
Ma de Jesus Leal	F	Married	32	
Remigio Casanova			11	
Estevan Casanova			10	
Anto Casanova			5	
Simon Casanova			8	
Anto Casanova 2d			1	
Ma Rafaela Martines	F	Widow	48	
Ma Josefa Garcia	F	Widow	30	

82   1830 Citizens of Texas

Ma de Jesus Lara			6	
Ma Eugenia Lara			5	
Luis Gallardo	M	Married	60	Farmer
Ma Alvina Martines	F	Married	27	
Manl Gallardo			15	
Pedro Gallardo	M	Married	36	Farmer
Franca Amador	F	Married	18	
Jesusa Gallardo			1	
Jorge Franco Salazar	M	Married	41	Artisan
Ma Juana Vidal	F	Married	27	
Jose' Basilio Salazar			5	
Jose' Joaquin Salazar			2	
Ma Trinidad Salazar			1	
Maria de Jesus Martines	F	Widow	40	
Nicolas de los Stos			12	
Jose' Ma Gil	M	Married	34	Laborer
Juana Ma de los Stos	F	Married	24	
Concepsion Gil			5	
Manl Gil			1	
Manl Herrera	M	Married	22	Farmer
Concepn de los Stos	F	Married	19	
Ma Gertrudis Herrera			2	
Roman Herrera			1	
Jesus del Toro	M	Married	62	Farmer
Ma Josefa Gonsales	F	Married	55	
Ana Ma Baca	F	Widow	60	
Jose' Gil Rodrigues			12	
453				
Polonio Tapia	M	Married	40	Artisan
Mariana Navarrer	F	Married	30	
Rosa Tapia	F	Single	14	
Pilar Tapia			9	
Merced Tapia			8	
Ramon Tapia			7	
Eugenio Tapia			3	
Josefa Tapia			2	
Manl Tapia			1	
Teresa de los Santos			60	
Andres Arenaser	M	Single	22	Laborer
Jose' Ma Errera	M	Married	50	Laborer
Dolores Tapia	F	Married	19	
Victor de Errera	M	Single	14	
Anto Errera			12	
Ma Anto			1	
Rafael Herrera	M	Married	20	Farmer
Vicenta Curbier	F	Married	16	
Manl Herrera			1	

1830 Census of San Antonio 83

Manl Menchaca	M	Widower	57	Farmer
Manl Menchaca	M	Single	18	
Encarnacion Pulido	M	Widow	50	
Jose' Pacheco	M	Single	20	Farmer
Franco Pacheco	M	Single	18	Farmer
Anto Pacheco	M	Single	16	Farmer
Wenceslao Pacheco	M	Single	15	Farmer
Luciana Pacheco			11	
Mariquita Barrera	F	Widow	30	
Melchora Truegas	F	Single	12	
Estevan Truegas			10	
Anto Delgado	M	Married	30	Farmer
Refugio de la Serda	F	Married	22	
Pedro de la Serda	M	Widower	48	Farmer
Ma Juliana Hernandes	F	Widow	39	
Jose' Andres Nava	M	Single	18	Farmer
Ma del Carmel Nava	F	Single	13	
Doroteo Nava			8	
Anto Rodrigues	M	Married	40	Farmer
Josefa Farias	F	Married	38	
Juana Guedes	F	Widow	62	
Victor Herrera	M	Single	15	Farmer
Anto Herrera			12	
454				
Santos Salanveda	M	Married	65	Farmer
Ma Lucia Torres	F	Married	50	
Jose' Franco	M	Single	22	Farmer
Jose' Alameda	M	Single	15	Farmer
Maria Rita	F	Single	14	
Juliana Bosque	F	Widow	50	
Pedro Cabrera	M	Single	14	Farmer
Jeraido Hernandes	M	Married	38	Farmer
Juana Bustillo	F	Married	55	
Ma Ynes de los Stos	F	Widow	60	
Polonia Cabasos	F	Single	14	
Dolores Ocon	M	Married	35	Farmer
Sebastian Vela	F	Married	19	
Encarnacion Ocon			1	
Ana Petra de la Peña	F	Widow	55	
Graviel Arriola	M	Single	3-	Farmer
Simon Arriola	M	Single	21	
Leandro Arriola	M	Married	23	Farmer
Polonia Fuentes	F	Married	18	
Teresa Arriola			2	
Dionicio Martines	M	Married	50	Farmer
Ma Josefa Nuñes	F	Married	40	

1830 Citizens of Texas

Jose' Ma Martes	M	Single	21	Farmer
Graviel Martines	M	Single	18	Farmer
Anicolo Marts	M	Single	15	
Gerarda Marts	F	Single	13	
Isabel Losoya	F	Widow	55	
Ma Josefa de la Garza	F	Widow	62	
Ma Josefa Sandoval	F	Widow	60	
Ma Ocon	F	Widow	20	
Salome Peres			3	
Ma Franco Peres			1	
Laureano Granados	M	Married	26	Farmer
Ma de Jesus de la Pena	F	Married	24	
Carlota Granados			4	
Fernando Granados			2	
Ma de la Luz Granados			1	
Catarina Flores	F	Married	36	
Jose' Maria Arocha	M	Married	44	Farmer
Matias Curbier	M	Single	14	
Fernando Curbier	M	Single	12	

455

Franco Farias	M	Married	62	Farmer
Encarnacion Rosales	F	Married	56	
Ma Josefa Farias	F	Single	13	
Manl Zepeda	M	Married	32	Artisan
Anta Rodrigs	F	Married	24	
Maria del Carmel Zepeda			5	
Jose' Miguel Zepeda			3	
Juan Jose'			1	
Jose' Ma Monfaras	M	Married	26	Laborer
Concepn Ruis	F	Married	26	
Gertrudis Dias	F	Widow	45	
Carmel Fuentes			11	
Loreta Fuentes			9	
Martina Fuentes			7	
Jose' Anto Farias	M	Married	39	Farmer
Manla Flores	F	Married	34	
Ma de Jesus Farias	F	Single	12	
Pablo Farias			10	
Trinidad Farias			7	
Micaela Farias			5	
Franco Farias			1	

456 [Blank page]

457   Valero

Dolores Alderete	F	Widow	40	
Cornelio Gil	M	Married	18	Farmer
Pabla Ximenes	F	Married	12	
Jose' Graviel Rodrigs			8	

1830 Census of San Antonio

Agustin Rodrigs			7	
Andres Rodrigs			4	
Regina Peres	F	Widow	34	
Jose' Ma Martines	M	Married	44	Farmer
Ysidra Montoya	F	Married	32	
Ma Paula --rcia Marts	F	Single	14	
Ma Dolores Marts			10	
Jesusa Marts			3	
Jose' Maria Marts			4	
Ursula Martines			1	
Felix Dimite	M	Married	35	Merchant
Ma Luisa Laso	F	Married	30	
Santiago Dimite			4	
Napolean Dimite			2	
Josefa Dimite			1	
Ma Concepn Sanches	F	Single	15	Laborer
Juan Jose Muños	M	Single	14	Laborer
Pablo Villalpando	M	Married	55	Farmer
Ma Anta Mancha	F	Married	32	Farmer
Ma de Jesus Villalpando			10	
Ma Lina			4	
Ma Josefa			1	
Juan Jose' Flores	M	Married	22	Farmer
Ma Ufemia de Villalpando	F	Married	15	
Pablo Mancha	M	Widow	72	
Alifonso Mancha			11	
Ygo Casas	M	Married	60	Farmer
Concepn Gonss	F	Married	40	
Manl Casas	M	Single	25	Farmer
Luis Casas			10	
Franco Casas			8	
Yga Casas			7	
Estevan Casas			5	
Joaquin Casas			14	
Agator Quiñones	M	Married	23	Farmer
Ma de los Stos	F	Married	20	
Antonio Quiñones			5	
Ma Dorotea Quiñones			3	

        Bejar   July 7, 1830   Bustillo
        [Barrio del] Sur

[* The original shows confusion in the use of the M-F columns on the first two pages.]

484   Roll 132

Panteolona Gomes		Single	26
Josepa Ernandes		Single	4
Josepa delos Santos		Single	80

CATHEDRAL DE SAN FERNANDO
A Pictorial History of Texas, Homer S. Thrall, St. Louis 1879

1830 Census of San Antonio

Maria Paubla delos Santos	Widow	35	
Juana Montes	Single	14	
Fernando delos Santos	Married	29	Artisan
Juliana Gimenes	Married	23	
Margarita delos Santos	Single	5	
Antonio delos Santos	Single	3	
Manuel Arenales	Single	40	
Juliana Bosque	Widow	28	
Pedro Cabrera	Single	14	
Juan Esteban Sotelo	Married	30	
Maria Trinidad Longoria	Married	28	
Baltasar Sotelo	Single	12	
Maria --- Sotelo	Single	14	
Ylaliario Montolla	Married	25	4 Artisans
Disodora Peres		20	
Martin Montolla	Single	5	
Antonia Montolla	Single	1	
Pomneseno Montolla	Married	24	Artisan
Getrudes Gimenes	Married	19	
Anastacio Montolla	Single	3	
Dolores Montolla	Single	1	
Francisco Drogeides	Married	33	Artisan
Maria Gualupe Guez--	Married	20	
Maria Gabriela Rodrigz	Single	14	
Concision Rodrigz	Single	12	
Maria Ynacia Rodrigz	Single	11	
Andrella Rodrigz	Single	2	
Juana Getrudes Gomes	Widow	44	
Maria Luisa Rondonda	Single	14	
Maria Josipa Redonda	Widow	30	
Agustin Barera	Married	25	Artisan
Antonia Salinas	Married	19	
Dolores Barera	Single	2	
Agustin Barera	Single	1	
Petra Rodrigz	Single	12	
Petra Rodrigz	Widow	30	
Josefa Rodrigz	Single	1	
485			
Juan Andres Leal	Single	26	Farmer
Francica Gimenes	Widow	60	
Josepa Leal	Widow	23	
Carl-- Casanaba	Single	15	
Francico Langabilla	Single	11	
Juana Leal	Single	11	
Maria Leal	Single	8	
Getrudis Gimenes	Widow	80	
Getrudes Flores	Single	11	
Dolores Ortis	Single	--	
Domingo Bustillos	Single	50	Farmer

88   1830 Citizens of Texas

Maria Calisma Bustillos	F	Widow	60	
Teresa Galona	F	Single	25	
Policarpa Peres	F	Single	60	
Bruno Martines	M	Single	20	
Francisca Agilar	F	Single	17	
Jose' Perez	M	Single	80	
Maria Josepa Flores	F	Married	38	
Juan Esmite	M	Married	37	Artisan
Maria de Jesus Curbelo	F	Married	16	
Teresa Trebiño	F	Single	14	
Toribo Astrigo	M	Single	16	
Anamand Fuentes	M	Widower	60	
Carlos Peres	M	Married	54	Laborer
Sapopa Dias	F	Married	45	
Antonio Peres	M	Single	1	
Juan Andres Curbelo	M	Married	40	
Juana Dela Garza	F	Married	25	
Miguela Curbela	F	Single	3	
Maria Luisa Curbela	F	Single	1	
N--- Curbela	F	Widow	38	
Jesus Calderon	M	Single	21	
Maria de Jesus Calderon	F	Single	23	
Jose' deLeon Calderon	M	Single	19	
Juan Francisco Calderon	M	Single	16	
Antonio Calderon	M	Single	13	
Candelario Ybarbo	M	Single	10	
Josepa Curbela	F	Widow	60	
Francisco Birado	M	Married	30	Laborer
Maria Josepa Garsilla	F	Married	20	
Manuel Birado	M	Single	4	
Francisco Birado	M	Single	2	
487				
Antonio Dias	M	Married	61	Artisan
Jucepa Nabaseta	F	Married	40	
Gulupe Dias	F	Single	17	
Paliono Dias	M	Single	14	
Rafael Dias	M	Single	13	
Margarita Dias	F	Single	6	
Juan Jose' Dias	M	Single	3	
Pablo Salinas	M	Married	30	
Fiodora Dias	F	Married	20	
Luz Gro	F	Widow	50	
Carmel Menchaca	F	Single	16	
Jose' Menchaca	M	Single	10	
Honor Menchaca	F	Widow	26	
Refugio Menchaca	F	Single	1	
Francisco Flores	M	Married	50	Farmer
Pedro Flores	M	Single	22	
Manuel Flores	M	Single	20	

1830 Census of San Antonio

Clarita Flores	F	Single	18	
Jose' Flores	M	Single	16	
Eguardo Flores	M	Single	13	
Antonio Flores	M	Single	8	
Tonides Flores	F	Single	4	
Concion Flores	F	Single	2	
Santiaga Delores	F	Single	20	
Ynacio Guagardo	M	Married	38	
Agustina Miranda	F	Married	25	
Ynacio Trabiero	M	Married	26	
Encarnacion Gomes	F	Married	23	
Andres Trabiero	M	Single	4	
Francisco Trabiero	M	Single	2	
Juan Gomes	M	Married	30	
Juana Casillas	F	Married	24	
Antonio Gomes	M	Single	6	

486

Juan Loned	M	Married	30	
Juana Flores	F	Married	20	
Juan Loned	M	Single	6	
Tomas Loned	M	Single	4	
Jesus Garza	M	Married	40	
Antonio Arocha	M	Single	26	
Felipe Musquis	M	Widower	25	
Ucebio de la Garza	M	Married		
Maria de los Angeles Gomez	F	Married	30	
Juana Peña	F	Single	16	
Francisco de la Garza	M	Single	15	
Martin Raba	M	Married	41	
Maria Cenona	F	Married	35	
Manuel Raba	M	Single	6	
Maria Rosa Raba	F	Single	4	
Jesusa Raba	F	Single	2	
Vicente Espinosa	M	Married	50	
C--- Menchaca	F	Married	40	
Maria Jesus Espinosa	F	Single	18	
Franco Menchaca	M	Single	5	
Franco Flores	M	Single	25	
Lonjino Vidal	M	Widower	35	
Franco Gonzalez	M	Single	45	Artisan
D. Erasmo Seguin	M	Married	48	Merchant
Da Josefa Becerra	F	Married	36	
Da Ma Leonides Seguin	F	Single	19	
Ma del Pilar Rojo	F	Single	5	
Ma Concepn Rojo	F	Single	3	
Trinidad Saucedo	F	Single	16	
Juana Almquis	F	Single	11	
Eugenio Herns	M	Single	12	
Domingo Dias	M	Married	22	

90   1830 Citizens of Texas

Name	Sex	Status	Age	Occupation
Maria Delgado	F	Married	18	
488		Sur		
Juana Dias	F	Single	2	
Franca Dias	F	Single	1	
Apolonia Delgado	M	Married	28	
Mariana de la Cruz	F	Married	25	
Silbestra Delgado	F	Single	19	
Antonio Delgado	M	Single	3	
Jose' Delgado	M	Single	2	
Juana Delgado	F	Single	1	
Ygno Aguirre	M	Married	30	
Feliciana Aguirre	F	Married	20	
Am--- Aguirre	F	Single	8	
--- Aguirre	F	Single	5	
Cipriano ---	M	Single	20	
Patricia Frayle	F	Widow	40	
Jose' Maria Garzia	M	Married	56	Farmer
Maria Rodrigz	F	Married	41	
Geronimo Leal	M	Single	26	Laborer
Franco Leal	M	Single	16	
Maria del Carmel Leal	F	Single	14	
Plaval Leal	F	Single	10	
Consepsion Leal	F	Single	7	
Jose' Ma Leal	M	Single	4	
Jose' Ma Moraida	M	Married	40	
Dolores Bergana	F	Married	21	
Santos Moraida	M	Single	10	
Biscorte Moraida	M	Single	6	
Getudis P-iñones	F	Widow	40	
Josefa Arauza	F	Single	27	
Manl Flores	M	Married	25	Farmer
Getudis Salinas	F	Married	24	
Cosme Collantes	M	Single	12	
Consepion Agilar	F	Widow	21	
D. Clemento Delgado	M	Married	60	Farmer
Maria Sausedo	F	Married	42	
Josefa Delgado	F	Married	20	
Manuela Delgado	F	Single	7	
Alvina Otona	F	Married	44	
Felisiana Coronado	F	Single	22	
Carmel Alderete	F	Single	9	
Pilar Tores	F	Single	2	
Maria Anta Tores	F	Single	1	
Jose' Casiano	M	Married	39	Merchant
Getrudis Ponces	F	Married	37	
Jose' Ygnasio Casiano	M	Single	1	
489				
Concision Cordero	F	Single	16	

1830 Census of San Antonio

Petra Sandovala	F	Single	20	
Gualupe de la Cruz	F	Married	40	
Dolores Escalera	F	Single	21	
Jusefa Travieso	F	Married	25	
Maria de Jesus Travieso	F	Single	16	
Franco Dias	M	Married	39	Artisan
Ygnacia del Rio	F	Married	16	
Jose' Sanches	M	Widower	56	Laborer
Barvara Sanches	F	Widow	41	
Manuela Cordova	F	Widow	46	
Ygnacio Spinosa	M	Single	18	
Ginomena Servantes	F	Single	5	
Birenta Cordova	F	Single	1	
Jose' Ma Espinosa	M	Married	23	
Franca Bergara	F	Married	18	
Margarita Espinosa	F	Single	1	
Antonia Rodrigz	F	Widow	55	
Franco Bustillos	M	Single	38	Artisan
Getrudis Rodrigz	F	Married	14	
Fernando Sandoval	M	Single	7	
Carlos Sandoval	M	Single	5	
Bonifasio Bustillos	M	Single	10	
Alvino Gonsales	M	Single	18	
Jusefa Garzia	F	Single	20	
Jesusa Badio	F	Single	18	
Encarnasion del Rio	F	Widow	48	
Jose' Maria Morales	M	Married	32	Artisan
Anta Jaimes	F	Married	26	
Corones Morales	F	Single	7	
Gualupe Morales	M	Single	6	
Trinida Morales	F	Single	3	
Grutiudis Morales	F	Single	2	
Jose' Ma Morales	M	Single	1	
Martina Morales	F	Single	36	
Franco Flores	M	Single	19	Artisan
Franca Flores	F	Single	17	
Pedro Flores	M	Single	15	
Petinario Gil	M	Married	47	Laborer
Barvara de los Santos	F	Married	26	
Anselmo Muños	M	Single	18	
Maria Ugenia Gil	F	Single	3	
Josefa Gomes	F	Single	48	
Jose' Guadalupe de los Santos	M	Single	16	Laborer
490				
Rafael de los Santos	M	Single	32	Laborer
Jose' Ma Ureña	M	Married	30	Farmer
Anta Farias	F	Married	24	
Jose' de Jesus Ureña	M	Single	1	
Juliana Fuertes	F	Widow	58	

1830 Citizens of Texas

Franca Ureña	F	Single	12	
Coleta Galvana	F	Widow	46	
Sension Navaro	F	Widow	41	
Anto Conde	M	Married	26	
Maria Marcia Juares	F	Married	27	
Felipe Conde	M	Single	15	
Maria Anta Conde	F	Single	13	
Jose' Ano Conde	M	Single	9	
Ramona Conde	F	Single	8	
Polonia Conde	F	Single	7	
Pascual Conde	M	Single	3	
Manl Gintero	M	Married	41	
Leandra Peres	F	Married	28	
Maria Peres	F	Widow	56	
Lusiano Montolla	M	Single	25	
Galupe Ramos	F	Widow	55	
Jose' de Sosa	M	Married	52	Merchant
Getrudes de la Serdo	F	Married	48	
Nemesio de la Serda	M	Single	22	
Margarita de Sosa	F	Single	15	
Brigida de Sosa	F	Single	9	
Juan Caravajala	M	Single	40	Merchant
Juan Angl Seguin	M	Single	..	
Juan Nepno Seguin	M	Married	23	Merchant
Gertrudis Flores	F	Married	20	
Antonia Seguin	F	Single	3	
Teresa Seguin	F	Single	2	
Erasmo Seguin	M	Single	1	
Refugio Tovar	F	Single	25	
Concesion Perez	F	Single	11	
Ramon Arocha	M	Married	40	Laborer
Ananazia Cantura	F	Married	36	
Manl Arocha	M	Single	2	
Jose' Maria Arocha	M	Single	18	
D. Anto Saucedo	M	Widower	58	
Franco Salinas	M	Single	8	
Manuel Salinas	M	Single	3	
Anta Ramires	F	Married	60	
Petra --	F	Widow	52	

491

Ygnacio Juanseca	M	Married	54	Farmer
Gualupes de los Santos	F	Married	34	
Maria Luisa Peres	F	Single	15	
Refugia Juanseca	F	Single	9	
Franco Juanseca	M	Single	2	
Maria Ginovesa Maloas	F	Single	30	
Florensia Oldivas	F	Single	5	
Pedro Flores	M	Widower	80	
Jose Ma Rios	M	Married	37	

1830 Census of San Antonio

Catarina Rolen	F	Married	33	
Hermengilda Rios			10	
Ygno Castillo	M	Married	--	
Ma de Jesus Menchaca	F	Married	18	
Jose Nestor Castillo			1	
Migl Barrera	M	Married	40	
Guadalupe	F	Married	20	
Manl Monfarar	M	Married	45	Farmer
Ma Josefa Leal	F	Married	24	
Carmel Monfarar			5	
Remijio Monfarar			4	
Manuela Monfarar			2	
Anta Curvier	F	Widow	39	
Ambrozio Rodrigs	M	Married	24	Farmer
Teresa Olibarri	F	Married	17	
Jose Ma Rodrigs			1	
Jose Ma Cardenas	M	Married	30	Merchant
Ma Erlinda Curvier	F	Married	25	
Ma Anta Cardenas			6	
Jose Cardenas			4	
Adriano Cardenas			2	
Jesus Cardenas			1	
Ma Micaela Alcantar			13	
Manl Ximenes	M	Married	54	Farmer
Alexandra Curvier	F	Married	46	
Ypolito Zotelo	M	Married	25	
Dolores Flores	F	Married	28	
Elijio Gortari	M	Married	32	Farmer
Josefa Curvier	F	Married	34	
Ma de los Angeles Gortari			16	
Baltasar Calvo	M	Married	40	Farmer
Ma del Rosario Zoto	F	Married	33	
Vitor Delgado	M	Single	18	
Magdalena Gerra	F	Widow	60	
Anto Rivas	M	Married	30	Farmer
Ma Josefa Seguin	F	Married	31	
Ma de Jesus			9	
Jose' Flores	M	Married	54	
Jose' Maria Anta Rodrigz	F	Married	50	
Jose' Maria Flores	M	Single	20	
Salvador Flores	M	Single	18	
Ygnacio Flores	M	Single	16	
Ponusena Flores	M	Single	15	
Carlos Flores	M	Single	13	
Manl Estrada	M	Single	18	
Loreta Estrada	F	Single	16	
Trinida Estrada	F	Single	14	

94   1830 Citizens of Texas

Fiodora Montes	F	Widow	70
Jusefa Tigerina	F	Widow	53
Juana Franca Hernandes	F	Single	30
Anta Peres	F	Widow	24
Desiderio de la Garza	M	Single	12
Enselmo Bergara	M	Married	58	Laborer
Margarita Castro	F	Married	48
Maria del Carmel Bergara	F	Single	17
Franco Bergara	M	Single	14
Dolores Bergara	F	Single	12
Jose' Antonio Ogoda	M	Single	8
Ma Menchaca	F	Single	20
Manl Menchaca	M	Single	16
Trinida Benites	F	Widow	30
Getrudis Toscana	F	Widow	28
Jesus Ernandes	M	Single	16	Laborer
Juan Hernandes	F	Single	14
Manuel Hernandes	M	Single	13
Miguel Castillo	M	Single	7
Jose' Anto de la Garza	M	Widower	78
Anto Butieres	M	Married	22	Farmer
Jusefa Montolla	F	Married	23
Anta Butieres	F	Single	2
Manl Savala	M	Married	30
Maria Getrudis Santos	F	Married	23
Santiago Savala	M	Single	8
Manuel Flores	M	Widower	63	Artisan
Anta Flores	F	Widow	27

492

Antonio Peres	M	Married	27	Laborer
Maria Josefa Gimenes	F	Married	18
Rafela Peres	F	Single	1
Jose' Antonio Camaño	M	Single	80
Jesusa Peres	F	Widow	28
Ambrosio Peres	M	Single	4
Jose' Lino Peres	M	Single	3
Jose' Maria Peres	M	Single	1
Jose' Laso	M	Widower	50
Dolor Delaso	F	Widow	20
-- Laso	F	Single	16
Jose' Maria C--	M	Single	3
Catarina Peres	F	Widow	40
Maria Josepa Drogeides	F	Single	16
Jose' Antonio Drogeides	M	Single	2
Francisca Salasar	F	Single	40
Marua Luisa Salasar	F	Single	4
Jose' Antonio del Castillo	M	Married	73

1830 Census of San Antonio 95

Maria Calmel Balderas	F	Married	37	
Maria de Jesus Morales	F	Single	17	
Miguel Morales	M	Single	9	
---ano Castillo	M	Single	7	
Maria del Rosario Castillo	F	Single	6	
Jose' Francisco Castillo	M	Single	3	
Clestonia Ramos	F	Widow	25	
Juana Drogeides	F	Single	8	
Rosaria Peres	F	Single	3	
Margarita Bargas	F	Widow	25	
Maria Manuela delos Santos	F	Widow	80	
Juan Maldonado	M	Single	22	

493

Ramon Musques	M	Married	33	Merchant
Francica de Castañeda	F	Married	22	
Francica Castañeda	F	Single	5	
Ramos Musques	M	Single	1	
Apolima Prado	F	Single	14	
Ynacia Gimenes	F	Married	36	
Dolores Castañeda	F	Single	13	
Jose' Frias	M	Single	24	Artisan
Camilio Musques	M	Single	23	Merchant
Bisente Flasolla	F	Married	40	Artisan
Antonio Segura	F	Married	40	
Dolores Duran	F	Single	16	
Gualupe Tores	F	Single	30	
Francica Podilla	M	Single	16	
Ynacio Erera	M	Married	27	
Maria Antonia Orivalin	F	Married	26	
Maria Antonia Erera	M	Single	3	
Francica Garsilla	F	Single	25	
Felis Sosa	M	Married	40	
Dolores Olibaria	F	Married	30	
Gillermo Sosa	F	Single	8	
Juan Jose' Sosa			4	
Esteban Gonsalos	M	Married	30	Artisan
Ynacia Maldonada	F	Married	29	
Andres Gonsalos	M	Single	10	
Juana Gonsalos	F	Single	5	
Migel Gonsalos	M	Single	3	
Antonio Gonsalos	M	Single	1	
Juana Desoto	F	Widow	80	
Mariano Bidales	M	Single	14	
Puceno Bidales	M	Single	12	

494

Ignasio Peres	M	Married	41	Farmer
Jusefa Cortines	F	Married	38	
Jesus Peres	M	Single	16	

96   1830 Citizens of Texas

Name	Sex	Status	Age	Occupation
Trinida Peres	F	Single	14	
Seguro Peres	M	Single	8	
Jusefa Peres	F	Single	6	
Jose' Ygnasio Peres	M	Single	2	
Polinario Arcealeado	M	Married	46	
Jusefa Pena	F	Married	30	
Salvador de los Prelles	M	Widower	42	
Rafael Basques	M	Married	32	
Maria G--go	F	Married	30	
Maria de Jesus Basques	F	Single	12	
Antolino Basques	M	Single	11	
Jesus Basques	M	Single	8	
Encarnacion Basques	F	Single	4	
Cristoval Basques	M	Single	1	
Franco Aldape	M	Single	45	
Manl de Castro	M	Married	30	
Maria Antonia Lopes	F	Married	30	
Maria Agapita de Castro	F	Single	3	
Ydurige Basques	F	Single	21	
Manl Quinto	M	Married	25	Laborer
Maria del Rosario Dominiques	F	Married	20	
Domingo Losolla	M	Married	45	Laborer
Maria Domingues	F	Married	30	
Felipa Domingues	F	Single	8	
Diego Domingues	M	Married	50	

[End of tabulation, with totals. No signature]

[Roll 142 of the microfilm edition of the Bexar Archives contains two manuscript groups calendared for 1831. The marginal notations and physical marks on the paper show one of them to be the 1830 census of Barrio del Norte. It is transcribed on the pages that follow.]

232   Roll 142   [Barrio del] Norte   10
Ciud<u>nos</u>   [Citizens]

Name	Sex	Status	Age	Occupation
Ignacio Chaves	M	Married	39	Farmer
Ma Leonarda Montes	F	Married	34	
Margarita Chaves			18	
Zomara Chaves			14	
Juana Franca Chaves			12	
Agustin Chaves			10	
Jose Ma Chaves			7	
Juan Anto Chaves			3	
Pilar Chaves			1	
Ed--ige Recuedo			20	
233				
Rafael Rivas			8	
Gertrudis Sanches	F	Widow	46	

1830 Census of San Antonio 97

Jose Ma Carbajal	M	Single	20	
Manl Carvajal	M	Single	14	
Jose Luis Carvajal	M	Married	24	Farmer
Ma de Jesus Flores	F	Married	18	
Juana Franca Sanches	F	Widow	50	
Ancelmo Galban	M	Single	12	
Mariano Seguin	M	Married	34	Farmer
Ma de Jesus Rodrigs	F	Married	37	
Simona de la Rodrigs			20	
Juan Rodrigs			14	
Jesus Rodrigs			12	
Angela Seguin			8	
Anto Seguin			6	
Carmel Seguin			3	
Escandon	M	Widower	--	
Numerio	M	Single	25	
Prudencio	M	Married	37	
Candelaria	F	Married	36	
Jose Ma Salinas	M	Married	34	Merchant
Teresa Arreola	F	Married	29	
Ma Anta Arebalo			14	
Clara Arebalo			12	
Pedro Arebalo			6	
Gertruds Salinas			2	
Jose Ma Salinas			1	
Pedro Lafuente	M	Married	40	
Ynes Rodrigs	F	Married	30	
Ma Lafuente			3	
Jose Lafuente	M	Single	15	
Franco Miranda	M	Married	26	
Loreta Gonsava	F	Married	30	
Julian Loya	M	Married	40	
Franca de Loya	F	Married	35	
Ma de Loya			3	
Loreta Arañaga	F	Single	25	
Juan Franco Bueno	M	Married	37	Farmer
Ma Josefa Torres	F	Married	24	
Ma Elena Bueno			2	
Gertrudis Ramires			8	
Juana Balderas	F	Single	14	
Claudio	M	Single	25	
Juana	F	Married	40	
George Anto	M	Single	35	Merchant
Manuela Montalbo	F	Widow	30	
234	**Norte**			**20**
Evaristo Cordova	M	Married	38	Artisan
Anta Gonzals	F	Married	38	

Ana Ma Gonzales	F	Single	36	
Jesus Flores	M	Single	14	
Carmel Alderete			10	
Candido Foche			3	
Domingo Peres	M	Married	40	Farmer
Anta Arocha			39	
Ma de Jesus Peres			19	
Gertrudis Peres			15	
Jose Anto Peres			10	
Concepcion Peres			4	
Ma Anta Peres			2	
Trenidad Peres			1	
Franco Peres			45	
Geronimo Lial	M	Married	25	Farmer
Ma Luisa Carvajal	F	Married	22	
Jose Ma Lial			5	
Manuela Montes de Oca	F	Widow	80	
Manl Arocha	M	Single	56	Farmer
Jose Ximenes	M	Married	45	Farmer
Santa Manchagua	F	Married	36	
Anto Ximenes			11	
Melchor Ximenes			6	
Franco Ximenes			3	
Ma Josefa Arocha	F	Widow	50	
Juan Martin de Beramendi	M	Married	51	Merchant
Josefa Navarro	F	Married	34	
Ursula Frutosa Beramendi			18	
Juana Gertrudis Beramendi			16	
Marco Anto Beramendi			12	
Ma Josefa Beramendi			9	
Juan Martin Beramendi			7	
Jose Primo Beramendi			6	
Ma Anta Beramendi			3	
Eufemia Beramendi			1	
Teresa de los Angeles			1	
Anestacio de los Rios	M	Married	38	
Alexandra Gonzales	F	Married	39	
Concepcion de los Rios			8	
Lorenzo Garzia	M	Married	34	
Gertrudis Romero	F	Married	27	
Ynacia Garzia			1	
Manl Flores	M	Married	37	

235

Monica de Flores	F	Married	35	
Ma Gertrudis Flores			10	
Franca Flores			8	
Crisanta Flores			5	
Mauricio Rodrigs	M	Widower	47	

1830 Census of San Antonio 99

Tomas Villegas	M	Widower	44	
Franco Ruvio	M	Single	36	
Vizente Saucedo	M	Married	50	
Juan Anto Flores	M	Married	28	
Juana Ma Flores	F	Married	25	
Ma Ygna Sanches	F	Married	47	
Manl Barrera	M	Married	50	Merchant
Jose Domingo Barrera			11	
Juan Manl Barrera			7	
Guadalupe Barrera			5	
Gerusa Vidal	F	Widow	40	
Martin de los Santos Coy			12	
Perfecta Dias	F	Widow	50	
Torivio Herrera	M	Single	16	
Jose Herrera	M	Single	14	
Macedonia Miranda			6	
Trenidad Ximenes			11	
Catarina Ximenes	F	Widow	96	
Maria Trenidad			15	
Ma de Jesus Garzia	F	Single	32	
Migl Garzia			3	
Dionicio Garzia			2	
Bisente Zoto	M	Married	40	Artisan
Casilda Gerra	F	Married	30	
Juan Zoto			4	
Franco Manl Zoto			1	
Juan Zoto	M	Widower	60	Artisan
Marselino Lopes	M	Married	25	Laborer
Timotea Hortis	F	Married	30	
Maria Luisa Hortis	F	Married	36	
Rosalia Peres	F	Widow	60	
Ma Castro	F	Single	34	
Catarina Zepeda	F	Widow	35	
Ramon Treviño	M	Single	17	Farmer
Ma de Jesus Treviño			14	
Jose de Jesus Treviño			12	
Polinaria Treviño			8	
Concepcion Treviño			7	
Franco Treviño			5	
236				30
Justo Tratiero	M	Widower	70	
Jose Ma Martins	M	Single	--	
Jose Anto Sais	M	Married	34	Artisan
Ma Guadalupe Villegas	F	Married	20	
Pedro Sais			10	
Ma Josefa Sais			8	

1830 Citizens of Texas

Name	Sex	Status	Age	Occupation
Vicente Sais			6	
Polonia Sais			3	
Anto Sais			1	
Santiago Lerma			15	
Juaquin Flores	M	Married	70	
Josefa Martins	F	Widow	47	
Jose Anto Ruis	M	Married	40	Farmer
Ysabel Seguin	F	Married	38	
Franco Ruis	M	Single	17	
Ma Sinforosa Ruis			15	
Jose Ruis			10	
Jose Anto Ruis			7	
Eduvije Ruis			4	
Ma Luisa Ruis			1	
Manl Seguin	M	Single	41	Farmer
Gertrudis Chirino	F	Widow	26	
Manl Lopes			12	
Alexandra Lopes			6	
Anto Hernands	M	Married	30	Farmer
Manuela Zapata	F	Married	35	
Margarita Giral			16	
Feliciana Hernands			5	
Anto Hernands			2	
Juan Delgado	M	Married	45	Farmer
Concepcion Zepeda	F	Married	41	
Ygno Delgado	M	Single	20	
Pablo Delgado			15	
Jose Delgado			11	
Trenidad Delgado			10	
Caledonio Delgado			7	
Rita Delgado			7	
Margarita Delgado			2	
Migl Delgado	M	Married	50	Farmer
Felipe Gaime	M	Married	25	Laborer
Juana Rodrigs			15	
Jose Xaime			7	
Josefa Xaime			5	
237				1
Marcos Xaime			1	
Petra Nabarsete	F	Widow	32	
Carlos Ybarra			1	
Josefa Ximemes	F	Widow	35	
Anto Arocha	M	Single	18	
Lino Arocha	M	Single	13	
Canuta Ramon	F	Widow	70	
Manl Menchaca	M	Single	20	

1830 Census of San Antonio 101

Name	Sex	Status	Age	Occupation
Vicente Duran	M	Married	60	Farmer
Beralda de los Stos Coy	F	Married	35	
Nicolos Duran	M	Single	17	
Dolores de los Stos Coy			5	
Refugia Ramon	F	Widow	80	
Alejos Bustillos	M	Married	50	Merchant
Josefa de la Garza	F	Married	40	
Josefa Bustillos			19	
Clemente Bustillos	M	Single	16	
Anto Menchaca	M	Married	26	Laborer
Teresa Ramon	F	Married	27	
Juaquina Menchaca			3	
Ma de Jesus Menchaca			1	
Rosario Ramon	M	Married	33	
Mariana Leal	F	Married	19	
Concepcion Ramon			2	
Ma Seledina Menchaca	F	Widow	65	
Fernando Enriques	M	Single	24	
Juan Resendos	M	Single	17	
Anto Carbajal			2	
Barbara de la Serda	F	Widow	60	
Margarita Zamora			12	
Mariana Zamora			5	
Juan Carbajal	M	Married	70	
Dolores Gil	F	Married	60	
Gertrudis Gil	F	Widow	70	
Jose Ma Briseño	M	Single	--	Laborer
Franco Carbajal	M	Married	28	Artisan
Teresa Berban			16	
Juan Franco Carbajal			1	
Luis Carbajal	M	Widower	58	
Justo Gil	M	Single	18	
Ma Josefa Martins	F	Widow	30	
Gertrudis Mireles	F	Widow	70	
238				40
Juaquin Ramon	M	Married	40	Artisan
Luz Navarrete	F	Married	42	
Teresa Ramon			7	
Martin Ramon			1	
Silvestre Camaguas [?]	F	Widow	28	
Ancelmo Balberde	M	Single	15	
Lugarda Martins	F	Widow	37	
Jose Martins	M	Single	16	
Migl Sanches			8	
Feliciana Venavids	F	Single	25	
Juan Manl Rivas	M	Married	24	Farmer
Gertrudis Menchaca	F	Married	23	

102   1830 Citizens of Texas

Name	Sex	Status	Age	Occupation
Jose Luis Rivs			5	
Franco Rivs			1	
Josefa Recio	F	Single	27	
Luisa Flores			7	
Margarita del Toro	F	Single	50	
Juan Montes	M	Married	32	Farmer
Gertrudis Chavez	F	Married	35	
Anto Montes			11	
Jose Ma Montes			9	
Alejo Montes			6	
Juanita Montes			3	
Carmel Montes			1	
Jose Ma Vecerra	M	Widower	60	
Franco Flores	M	Single	23	
Paula Vecerra	F	Widow	40	
Ysidra Seguin			12	
Anta Vecera			5	
Anto de la Garza	M	Married	54	Farmer
Josefa Menchaca	F	Married	--	
Carmel Garza			16	
Vicente Garza	M	Single	14	
Rafael Garza			12	
Reducinda Garza			4	
Anto Garza			1	
Jesus Garza			1	
Margarita Garza			1	
Juana Rainules			14	
Leonardo Gonzales			13	
Gertrudis Padron	F	Widow	65	
Anestacia Garzia	F	Married	16	
239				
Matias Silva	M	Married	22	
Luzio Enriques	M	Single	17	
Juaquin Menchaca	M	Single	62	
Rafael Padilla	M	Married	44	
Segunda Sanches	F	Married	40	
Juana Padilla			16	
Jose Padilla			9	
Xabiel Uriegas	M	Married	41	
Anta Torres	F	Married	39	
Juan Manl Uriegs	M	Single	26	
Ugenia Uriegs			2	[?]
Rafael Alcantar	M	Married	38	
Dolores Martins	F	Married	13	
Juan Coronado	M	Married	37	
Josefa Ornos	F	Married	29	

1830 Census of San Antonio   103

Name	Sex	Status	Age	Occupation
Jose Padilla	M	Widower	45	
Sabino Billa Sor	M	Married	26	
Franca Hernands	F	Married	30	
Migl Billa Sor			8	
Encarnacion Sanchez	M	Married	40	
Felipa Valdez	F	Married	39	
Jose Ortiz	M	Single	22	
Juana Ortiz			12	
Jose Dolores Garzia	M	Married	21	
Feliciana Martins	F	Married	25	
Jose Ma Dias	M	Married	50	
Josefa de Dias	F	Married	37	
Jose Dias	M	Single	11	
Balentin Dias			7	
Eduardo Ramires	M	Single	19	
Jose Luis Cuellar	M	Married	38	
Maria de Cuellar	F	Married	24	
Jose Ma Rosas	M	Single	16	
Pedro Martins	M	Married	37	Artisan
Gertrudis	F	Married	34	
Ferman Martins			12	
Juan Martins			8	
Manuel Martins			7	
Petra Livas	F	Widow	50	
Gregorio Esparza	M	Married	19	
Ana Esparza	F	Married	18	
Ma de Jesus Castro			4	
240				50
Enriques Esparza			2	
Trenidad Garzia	F	Widow	70	
Leonarda Vasques	F	Married	50	
Dolores Vasques			14	
Gaspar Flores	M	Married	49	Farmer
Petra Sambrano	F	Married	39	
Rita flores			19	
Manuela Flores			16	
Juan Bautista Flores			11	
Ma de Jerina	F	Married	40	
Andres Filano	M	Single	25	
Masimo Garzia	M	Single	30	
Nicolas Flores	M	Married	24	Farmer
Teresa Baldes	F	Married	21	
Ma Josefa Flores			1	
Manl Yturri Castillo	M	Married	39	Merchant
Josefa Rodrigz	F	Married	28	

1830 Citizens of Texas

Blasa de Yturri			13
Jose Ma Pineda			11
Concepcion Echavaria			10
Catarina Gutierres			3
Dolores Dias			8
Ma Utliaga	F	Widow	36
Jesusa			14
Feliciano Servantes	M	Married	30
Ma de Servantes	F	Married	25
Felipe Longoria	M	Married	45
Formosa Rodrigs	F	Married	40
Josefa Longoria			8
Jose Soto	M	Married	30
Josefa Rodrigs	F	Married	28
Jose Ma Garzia	M	Single	35
Leonardo de la Cruz	M	Single	30
Manl Olgin	M	Married	25
Pabla Soto	F	Married	25
El Sor Cura Refugio Garza			55
Nieves Garcia	F	Single	16
Jose de Jesus Garcia			6
Felipe Benites	M	Widower	80
Ylario Errera	M	Single	75
Jose Ma Ramon	M	Widower	53

241

Felipe de la Garza	M	Married	22
Concepcion Martins	F	Married	19
Anto de la Garza			2
Faustino Flores	M	Married	43
Nicolosa Hernands	F	Married	24
George Flores			7
Concepcion Flores			3
Anto Chapa	M	Married	25
Juana Granados	F	Married	17
Gregoria Chapa			2
Diego del Toro	M	Single	35
Fabian Carrera	M	Single	14
Franco Carrera	M	Single	17
Manl Gonsales	M	Married	44
Juliana de la Garza	F	Married	45
Enriques de los Reyes			7
Estefana de la Garza	F	Widow	27
Esclava Anta Rodrigs *	F	Single	35
Paula Dias	F	Widow	46
--- Sanches			15

1830 Census of San Antonio

Jose de Jesus Flores			2	
Josefa Ruiz	F	Widow	64	
Jose Angl Navarro	M	Single	42	Merchant
Anto Navarro	M	Single	33	Merchant
Manuela de Peña	F	Widow	86	
Gertrudis Ruiz			11	
Juana de la Garza	F	Widow	47	
Ygno de Leon	M	Married	54	Farmer
Manuela de la Garza	F	Married	48	
Anto de Leon	M	Single	22	
Semon Leon	M	Single	16	
Josefa de Leon			14	
Concepcion Escalera			3	
Jose Ma Balmaceda	M	Married	39	Merchant
Mariana de Leon	F	Married	20	
Vicente Balmaceda			2	
Petra Balmaceda			1	
Bitoriano Pacheco	M	Married	40	
Petra de Pacheco Cedilla	F	Married	24	

* Esclava = Female slave

243 [Microfilmed out of order] 60

Casiana Sambrano	F	Married	30	
Concepcion Sambrano			10	
Melchora Sambrano			7	
Benicia Sambrano			5	
Susana Sambrano			2	
Luciano Navarro	M	Married	30	Artisan
Teodora Carbajal	F	Married	26	
Agela Navarro			6	
Cecilia Navarro			4	
Josefa Navarro			2	
Luciano Navarro			1	
Anestacia de Anda	F	Widow	30	
Ramon Argullo	M	Single	34	
Manuel Carbajal	M	Single	13	
Guadalupe Ruiz	F	Married	30	
Luisa Risa			40	
Ma de la Merse Risa			16	
Xabiera Flores			60	
Margarita de la Garza	F	Single	33	
Ma del Carmel Navarro			13	
Jose Anto Navarro			12	
Gertrudis Navarro			8	
Angl Navarro			3	
Franca Montalvo			16	
Franco Gallardo	M	Single	17	
Jose Gomez	M	Married	50	Farmer

1830 Citizens of Texas

Ma Luisa de la Garza	F	Married	40	
Juan Jose Gomez	M	Single	25	
Vitoriana Pragedis			10	
Juaquin de la Garza			50	
Juana Gomez	F	Widow	36	
Ma del Carmel Martins			17	
Ma Anta Martins			14	
Juan Martins			11	
Jesusa Martins			7	
Trenidad Martins			4	
Teresa Ureña	F	Widow	30	
Migl Pechea			30	Farmer
Santiago Cobarubia	M	Single	40	
Josefa Castro	F	Widow	46	
Franco Hernands	M	Married	51	Farmer
Polonia Olivar	F	Married	40	
Manl Hernands	M	Single	22	
242				
Gregorio Hernands	M	Single	17	
Gertrudis Hernands			9	
Franco Herrera	M	Married	50	Artisan
Encarnacion Delgado	F	Married	45	
Jose Montes	M	Single	21	
Carmel Carabajal			11	
Jose Menchaca	M	Married	67	
Ma Esparea	F	Widow	40	
Margarita Ce--ana			7	
Juana Peres			1	
Josefa Ximenes	F	Single	32	
Jose Felipe de Luna	M	Single	15	
Matias Carrillo	M	Married	25	Farmer
Teodora Mireles	F	Married	17	
Isabel Carrillo			1	
Barbara Lopes	F	Widow	50	
Anto Arocha	M	Married	50	Farmer
Hermenegilda Flores	F	Married	39	
Gertrudis Arocha			16	
Jesusa Arocha			14	
Macedonio Arocha			3	
Benigno Arocha			1	
Carmel Ramon	F	Widow	60	
Juan Lombraña	M	Single	22	
Anto Lombraña	M	Single	20	
Rafaela Cuellar	F	Widow	38	
Anto Salinas	M	Single	50	Farmer
Margila Chirino	F	Widow	50	
Margl Salins	M	Single	18	

1830 Census of San Antonio

Anto Morfaras			12	
Trenidad Salins			10	
Luis Salins			6	
Teresa Bernal	F	Single	38	
Juana Treviño			13	
Franco Sais			6	
Franca Seana			1	
Anto Rodrigs	M	Married	25	Farmer
Franca Arocha	F	Married	21	
Anta Rodrigs			2	
Bitoriana Valdes	F	Widow	51	
Juan Rodrigs	M	Married	30	Farmer
Juana Delgado	F	Married	16	
Juan Manl Rodrigs			1	
244				70
Franco Rodrigs	M	Single	30	Laborer
Ma Anta Contrerra	F	Widow	30	
Ramon Rutia	M	Single	21	Artisan
Nepomucena Rutia			14	
Melchor de la Garza	M	Married	39	Farmer
Feliciana Montoya	F	Married	36	
Soledad Garza			14	
Guadalupe Garza			12	
Jose Miguel Garza			10	
Jose Anto Garza			7	
Concepcion Garza			4	
Ma Franca Garza			2	
Ana Ma Musquiz	F	Widow	50	
Anto Benites			15	
Rumalda Benites			12	
Jose Migl Benites			10	
Manl Martins	M	Married	29	Farmer
Encarnacion Hernands			16	
Manl Martins			2	
Manl Chaves	M	Married	30	Farmer
Josefa Calrillo	F	Married	25	
Anglestina Ruda	F	Widow	48	
Jose Hernands	M	Married	46	Laborer
Anta Rosas	F	Married	28	
Sencion Martins	F	Single	19	
Franco de la Garza	M	Married	30	Farmer
Ynez Saucedo	F	Married	25	
Margarita de la Garza			4	
Anto Garza			3	
Juana Gerra	F	Widow	70	
Franco Ximenes	M	Married	45	
Ylaria Rosales	F	Married	38	

1830 Citizens of Texas

Juan Ximenes	M	Single	18
Gil Ximenes			12
Sinforiana Ximenes			2
Franca Soleto	F	Widow	40
Franco Cortins	M	Single	18
Franco Rivas	M	Married	55	Farmer
Josefa de los Stos	F	Married	45
Calletano Rivas	M	Single	19
Eduardo Rivas	M	Single	14
Jose Rivas			11
Guadalupe de la Garza	F	Single	30
Juan Sambrano	M	Single	19
Jose Sambrano			7

245

Trenidad Gerrero	F	Widow	45
Ma Yfinea Ximenes	F	Single	19
Ponciano Ximenes	M	Single	17
Casiano Ximenes			11
Crestina Menchaca			7
Alexandro Ximenes			3
Jose Ma Ximenes	M	Married	22
Maria Luisa Ma--dos	F	Married	18
Jose Manl de la Garza	M	Married	55	Farmer
Mansioia Flores	F	Married	36
Luisa Fuentes	F	Widow	73
Pedro Cararillo	M	Single	22
Gregorio Bega	M	Married	50
Maria de Bega	F	Married	30
Rafael Morales	M	Single	16
Jesus Balderas	M	Married	39	Artisan
Eugenia Arredondo	F	Married	25
Trenidad Balderas			9
Manuel Balderas			7
Jesus Balderas			3
Juan Balderas			1
Franco Balderas			1
Manl Nuñez	M	Married	56	Farmer
Brigida Treviño	F	Married	40
Polonia Baldes			8
Ysabel Gonzales	F	Widow	60
Ma de Jesus Treviño	F	Single	23
Ygno Arocha	M	Married	24
Juana Garcia	F	Married	24
Tomas de Arocha			5
Refugio Arocha			3
Jose Anto Arocha			2
Manuela Arocha			1

1830 Census of San Antonio

Name	Sex	Status	Age	Occupation
Magdalena Ramirez	F	Single	19	
Ma Anta Ramirez	F	Widow	50	
Paula Arocha			19	
Nepomuceno Arocha	M	Married	42	Farmer
Encarnacion Rodrigs	F	Widow	40	
Rosa del Balle	F	Single	25	
Jesus Serra			6	
Juan Anto Garza			3	
Candelaria Martins			2	
Trenidad Gonsales			5	
Jesus Gonsales			3	

[In margin]   7-1-1830

[Internal evidence and the number "80" show that this sheet is a continuation of the 1830 schedules filmed on roll 142 and calendared for 1831]

Name	Sex	Status	Age	Occupation
496 Roll 132				80
Blas de la Lerna	M	Married	30	Artisan
Marian Martins	F	Married	16	
Jose Delgado	M	Married	58	Farmer
Franca Peres	F	Married	38	
Andrea Delgado			14	
Neo-- Delgado			11	
Anta Delgado			5	
Ma de la Luz Delgado			2	
Serafina Menchaca			80	
Anto del Rio	M	Married	32	Artisan
Manuela Sanchez	F	Married	21	
Manuel del Rio			6	
Ygno del Rio			3	
Anto Sanchez	M	Married	25	
Victoria Ortis	F	Married	18	
Marcos Sanchez			1	
Gasinto Nava	F	Married	30	
Pedro de la Garza	M	Married	70	Farmer
Ygna Carillo	F	Married	67	
Ma del Carmen Galban			11	
Julio Cordova	M	Married	39	Artisan
Gregorio Martins	F	Married	29	
Ygno Cordova			6	
Merel Tapia			9	
Anto Baca	M	Single	39	
Franco Padilla	M	Widower	80	Farmer
Jose Ma Hernands	M	Married	28	Farmer
Josefa Padilla	F	Married	25	
Crecencio Hernands	M	Single	2	
Anto Salasar	M	Single	16	

110   1830 Citizens of Texas

Bernal Hernands	M	Single	20	
Franco de Leon	M	Married	50	
Luisa Martins	F	Married	37	
Josefa de Leon	F	Single	17	
Refugio de Leon			3	
Carmel de Leon			1	
Bizenta Zepeda	M	Married	60	Farmer
Mariana	F	Married	50	
Refugio Rodrigs	M	Married	24	Farmer
Dolores Ruiz	M	Married	19	
Margarita Rodrigs			1	
Manl Cadena	M	Married	34	Farmer
Anta Montes	F	Married	24	
Anta Cadena			3	
Juan Manl Cadena			2	
Jesus Cadena			1	
Juan Ortes	M	Married	24	
Fernanda Gutierres	F	Married	16	
--- Ortes			2	
Dionicio Ortes			1	

497

Manl Montalbo	M	Single	45	
Jose Ma Sambrano	M	Widower	64	Farmer
Anastacia Sambrano	F	Widow	76	
Anto Sambrano	M	Single	15	
Esclava Regina Rodrigs *	F	Married	46	[Slave]
Casimira la Biña			9	
Manl Zoto	M	Widower	69	
Mariano Salasar	M	Married	30	
Fermin Solis	M	Single	20	
Jose Ma Rodrigs	M	Married	27	
Juan Rodrigs	M	Single	20	
Manl Garza	M	Married	45	
Jose Ma Menchaca	M	Single	20	
Juana de Dios Nieto	F	Widow	51	
Luciano Balverde	M	Single	15	
Ma Luisa Flores			2	
Franca Salins	F	Married	18	
Melchor Leal	M	Married	50	Artisan
Rosalia Zepeda	F	Married	46	
Franca Leal	F	Single	21	
Concepcion Leal			12	
Jose Esperidion Leal			10	
Ma Josefa Leal			7	
Manl Zepeda	M	Married	48	Farmer
Antona Padilla	F	Married	23	
Juan Franco Zepeda			7	

1830 Census of San Antonio 111

Josefa Zepeda			3	
Frutosa Borgas	F	Single	25	
Franco Bolen	M	Married	32	Laborer
Eugenia de Castro	F	Married	32	
Beriana Sandobal	F	Single	34	
Jose Ma Montez	M	Single	14	
Juan Bervan			7	
Manuela Bervan			4	
Pascual Bervan			1	
Jose Bervan	M	Married	38	
Juana Calbello	F	Widow	70	
Josefa Romano	F	Widow	44	
Domasio Romano	M	Single	17	
Damian Treviño	M	Married	48	Laborer
Guadalupe Servantes	F	Married	30	
Jose Ma Castillo	M	Married	48	Laborer
Juana Lopez	F	Married	40	
Lino Castello	M	Single	14	
Simon Castello			4	

* Esclava = female slave

Bexar   9 July 1830   Ygno Chaves

1831 CENSUS OF MISSION DE SAN JOSE'

230   Roll 142

Tomas de Leon	M	Widower	4-	Farmer
Juan de Leon	M	Single	19	
Teresa de Leon			8	
Benita de Leon			7	
Rosalia Sartuche	F	Widow	67	
Pilar Garcia	F	Single	14	
Tomas Cortes	M	Married	37	Farmer
Margarita del Toro	F	Married	40	
Juan Jose de la Cruz	M	Single	22	
Melchora de la Cruz	F	Single	21	
Petra de la Cruz	F	Single	19	
Paula de la Cruz	F	Single	18	
Catarina Cortes	F	Single	16	
Dolores Cortes	M	Single	18	
Melchora Cortes			6	
Jesus Castañon	M	Married	32	
Guadalupe Sartuche	F	Married	29	Artisan
Pedro Castañon	M	Single	11	
Luis Castañon	M	Single	5	
Jesusa Castañon	F	Single	4	
Dolores Castañon	F	Single	1	
Julian Cierra	M	Married	36	Farmer

Ygnacia Almansa	F	Married	30	
Noviesto Cierra	M	Single	9	
Jose Maria Cierra	M	Single	7	
Anto Cierra	M	Single	4	
Juan Cierra	M	Single	2	
Josefa Franco	F	Widow	55	
Anto Huizar	M	Married	48	Farmer
Teodora Guerrero	F	Married	44	
Domingo Huizar	M	Single	16	
Franca Huizar	F	Single	12	
Graviclas Huizar	F	Single	8	
Pablo Huizar	M	Single	6	
Anto Huizar	M	Single	4	
Lasaro Huizar	M	Single	2	
Ygnacio Ruis	M	Married	22	Farmer
Maria Rivera	F	Married	20	
Maria Ygnacia Roble	F	Widow	77	
Bernardino Ruis	M	Single	26	Farmer
Lino Ruis	M	Single	20	Farmer
Esmereguido Ruis	M	Single	18	Farmer
Franco Ruis	M	Single	24	Farmer
Jose Maria Ruis	M	Married	35	Farmer
Trenidad Fuentes	F	Married	16	
Guillermo Lara	M	Single	35	Farmer
Juan Jose Solis	M	Married	73	Farmer
Maria Gertrudis Cortinas	F	Married	70	
Juan Palacio	M	Single	25	

231

Anto Garcia	M	Married	3-	Farmer
Anestacia Reyes	F	Married	2-	
Juana Vueno	F	Single	3-	
Manl Vueno	M	Single	25	Farmer
Maugricia Vueno	F	Single	10	
Luis Romero	M	Married	45	Farmer
Bonifacia Arocha	F	Married	43	
Pilar Romero	F	Single	20	
Teresa Romero	F	Single	18	
Franco Romero	M	Single	3	
Candelario Romero	M	Single	2	
Estevan Romero	M	Married	26	Laborer
Juana Pantaleon	F	Married	20	
Melchora Romero	F	Single	3	
Maria de Jesus Romero	F	Single	2	

San Jose'   23 June 1831   Tomas de Leon

1830 CENSUS OF NACOGDOCHES

The Nacogdoches Archives are now in the Texas State Archives at Austin. In them will be found the surviving records of Mexican census records taken between 1826 and 1835. The original manuscript for 1830 is now only about two-thirds complete when compared with the R. B. Blake transcripts, of which the Texas State Archives also has a copy. Both have been consulted in making this translation.

The few Spanish words in the census schedules have been translated, except that no non-Spanish equivalents for names have been attempted. In the Blake transcripts will be found a list of Ango-American names thought to be equal and identical with some of these names. The names have been copied exactly as written within the limits of legibility. The original has a column for religion, but since everyone prudently professed to be a "Catholic Apostolic," it was not copied.

When the age column has a blank, copied as "-", this seems to indicate a child not yet one year old.

Aggregated (Agregados) indicates persons living with the family but not direct family members.

1830 CENSUS OF NACOGDOCHES

Census which contains the number of souls in the Pueblo of Nacogdoches, taken by the Constitutional Alcalde of said Pueblo on this date from Atoyaque to the Trinidad [Rivers]

Nacogs   June 30, 1830

	Status	Occupation	Age
Vicente Cordova	Married	Farmer	32
His wife Ma Anta Cordova			22
His children Ramon Cordova	Child		5
Jose' Dario Cordova	Child		2
Franco Prosela	Married	Farmer	29
His wife Ma Getrudes Martines			28
His children Felipe Santiago Prosela	Child		5
Maria Remigia			4
Franco Guerrero	Single	Blacksmith	59
Aggregated with Ma Getrudes Medina	Widow		36
Her daughter Ma Macaria			7

OLD STONE FORT, NACOGDOCHES
— *Courtesy Carolyn Reeves Ericson*

1830 Census of Nacogdoches   115

Ma Niebes free negro			42
Her son Tomas Guerrero	Single	Farmer	26
Ygnacio Sartucho	Widower	Farmer	55
His son Jose' Candelario Sartucho	Child		5
Juan Ma Lazarin	Married	Farmer	34
His wife Ma Josefa de la Bega			26
His children Jose' Anto Lazarin	Single		10
Franco Lazarin	Single		8
Maria Teodora	Child		3
Jose' Eugenio	Child		1
His slaves Maria Ynocencia			18
Maria Secilia	Child		3
Juan Bautista Chirino	Married	Farmer	43
His wife Ma Mersed Sanches			31
His children Jose' Angel	Single	Farmer	24
Ma Maurisia			10
Baberio Labaume	Married	Farmer	38
His wife Ma Ursina David			30
His children Maria Ursina Labaume			6
Jose' Benigno	Child		3
Ma Constancia	Child		1
Aggregated Pedro Labaume	Single	Farmer	24
Jose' Rovinson	Single	Carpenter	42
Jose' Severano Cordova	Married	Farmer	30
His wife Ma Vicenta Prosela			19
His son Pedro Jose	Child		2
Aggregated Ma Josefa Cordova	Widow		60
Anastacio Ybarvo	Married	Farmer	38
His wife Ma Manuela Sanches			30
His children Maria Tomaza			8
Maria Petra			6
Maria Encarnacion			4
Maria Gregoria	Child		2
Jose' Desiderio	Child		1
Jose' Ygnacio Ybarvo	Widower	Farmer	53
His children Juan Anto Ybarvo	Single	Farmer	23
Manl Marian Ybarvo	Single	Farmer	22
Marcimiliano Ybarvo	Single	Farmer	10
Maria Teresa Ybarvo	Child		6
Juan Mora	Married	Tailor	30
His wife Maria Carmel Ybarvo			18
Benigno Ybarvo	Married	Farmer	23
His wife Ma Olaya Cruz			18
His children Leonardo Ybarvo	Child		2
Maria Mariana	Child		-
Pedro Jose' Caro	Married	Farmer	60
His wife Maria Miguela Ex.			57

116   1830 Citizens of Texas

His children Juan Caro	Single	Farmer	26
Feliciano Caro	Single	Farmer	22
Ma Anta			17
Jose' Sebastian	Single	Farmer	19
Maria Cleta			14
Jose' Trivio	Youth		12
Aggregated Maria de Jesus			8
Tomas Caro	Married	Farmer	43
His wife Ma Getrudes Tejeda			37
His children Ma Bacilia			14
Maria Leonicia			10
Jose' Justo	Child		7
Maria Marcelina	Child		5
Jose' Encarnacion	Child		2
Aggregated Jose' Alejandro			7
Jose' Ybarvo	Married	Farmer	46
His wife Maria Luciana Caro			33
His children Jose' Anto de Jesus	Single	Farmer	15
Jose' Franco	Single	Farmer	13
Vicente Ysiderio	Child		7
Jose' Leonicio	Child		5
Ma Petra	Child		3
Bentura Tejeda	Single	Farmer	30
Aggregated Ma Yasenta Shamar			29
Her children Jose' Ysidro	Single	Farmer	13
Jose' Miguel	Child		2
Aggregated Ma Francisca			14
Anto Caro	Married	Farmer	37
His wife Maria Celeste Rogas			25
His children Jose' Anastacio	Youth		12
Maria Ysabel			11
Jose' Anto Marselo	Child		6
Maria Olaya	Child		7
Maria Eulogia	Child		4
Jose' Encarnacion	Child		2
Maria Gavina	Child		-
Jose' Agaton Caro	Single	Farmer	35
Aggregated Ma Norin Palbado			33
Her children Candida Rosa	Child		4
Maria Luiza	Child		3
Maria Bitorina	Child		-
Damian Cordova	Married	Tailor	42
His child Maria Dolores			11
Juan Flores	Married	Farmer	24
His wife Maria Josefa Cordova			19
His child Ma Bitoriana	Child		1
Martin Ybarvo	Married	Farmer	64
His wife Ma Josefa Arriola			66

His children Concepcion Ybarvo	Single		28
Aggregated Juan Bautista Ybarvo			5
Maria Anta Ybarvo			3
Maria Dolores Sanches	Widow		53
Jose' Mariano Acosta	Married	Farmer	39
His wife Maria Josefa Delgado			35
His children Maria Anta			19
Franco Deciderio	Youth		11
Juana Franca			9
Juan Jose' de la Cruz	Youth		7
Maria de los Angeles	Child		5
Maria Getrudes			2
Juan Ysidro Acosta	Married	Farmer	36
His wife Ma Encarnacion de Soto			29
Ma Dominga			10
Maria Luiza			8
Jose' Nicolas			6
Jose' Maria del Pilar	Child		4
Maria Concpion	Child		1
Jose' Anto Sepulbeda	Married	Farmer	50
His wife Maria Guadalupe Chavana			25
His children Jose' Seguimundo	Youth		11
Maria Anta			9
Mari Bernabe			7
Mari Torivia	Child		5
Maria Juana	Child		3
Jose' Esiquio	Child		1
Bartolo Escovedo	Single	Farmer	34
Maria Guadalupe Leyva	Widow		47
Her son Franco de Castro	Single	Farmer	26
Batis Andre Bacoqui	Married	Farmer	34
His wife Maria Faustina Chirino			29
His children Maria Madalena			9
Maria Eme	Child		5
Marcemiliano	Child		-
Slaves Jacobo	Male		34
Aseli	Female		35
Eusevio Ysur	Married	Farmer	28
His wife Maria Eme Bascoqui			28
His children Maria Agli			8
Maria Crisantos	Child		4
Slave Franco	Male		70
Batis David	Married	Farmer	28
His wife Feliciana de Castro			24
His children David	Child		6
Tiofilo David	Child		4
Maria Selestina	Child		2

Anto Menchaca	Married	Tailor	35
His wife Ma Feliciana de los Santos Sanches			22
His children Mari Concepcion	Child		3
Maria Rafaela	Child		2
Cuñados Nepomaceno Sanches	Single	Tailor	15
Jose' Anto Sanches	Youth		13
Maria Olaya Sanches			11
Dolores Ramon	Married		46
His son Jose' Anto de los Santos Coy	Single	Farmer	19
Maria Bifida Nancaro			45
Mariana Obidia	Widow		27
Her children Guadalupe Bitoria	Child		5
Mari del Carmel	Child		2
Maria Josefa Borsoley	Widow		59
Her son Juan Jose' Sanches	Single	Farmer	36
Aggregated Juan Bustamante	Youth		14
Maria Cafe			28
Enrrique Estocoman	Married	Carpenter	36
His wife Maria Dorcas			35
His children Enrrique Samuel	Youth		9
Javiel Estocoman	Youth		7
Anriete	Child		3
Juan Bautista Puaria	Married	Farmer	33
His wife Maria Juliana Noris			37
His children Jose' de los Reyes Cuerca	Single	Farmer	18
Enrrique Cuerca	Single	Farmer	15
Maria Lusaya			13
Moses Rovenson	Married	Farmer	29
His wife Maria Barbara Federique			39
His children Maria Elena			9
Jose' Santiago			7
Ygnacio Santos Coy	Married	Farmer	51
His wife Maria Getrudes Chirino			40
His son Jose' Andres	Youth		10
Aggregated Jose' Eugenio Peres	Single	Farmer	18
Maria Anta Losoya			11
Encarnacion Chirino	Married	Farmer	44
His wife Maria Candida Delgado			39
His children Jose' Maria Chirino	Youth		6
Maria Tomasa	Child		1
Aggregated Luis Pena	Youth		10
Nate Niel Noris	Married	Farmer	41
His wife Juana Puarie			34
His children María Presela Recia			11
Maria Clara			8
Jose' Agustin			7
Nateniel Feliciano	Child		2

1830 Census of Nacogdoches 119

Tomas Amador	Single	Farmer	30
Aggregated Maria Manuela Fuentes			25
Jose' Elauterio Lopes	Single	Farmer	30
Aggregated Maria Concpcion Ariola			25
Her child Mari Bernardina	Child		5
Elena Kimble	Widow		60
Slaves Sam	Male		76
Ysabel	Female		67
Nanse	Female		25
Maria Benancia Santa Cruz	Widow		50
Aggregated Juan Santa Cruz	Single	Farmer	28
Guillermo Santa Cruz	Single	Farmer	20
Migl Saco	Married	Merchant	50
His wife Favasina Puaso			26
His children Maria Rosa			7
Anamaria Rosa			5
Maria Teresa			4
Juano Bautista	Child		3
Slave Costansa	Female		50
Jose' Maria Musquiz	Married	Farmer	33
Mari Juana Lionor			24
Damian Arocha	Widower	Farmer	77
His children Jose' Maria Arocha	Single	Farmer	22
Maria Bernardina Arocha			19
Jose' Lazarin	Married	Farmer	63
His wife Maria Juana Rivas			58
His children Marselino	Single		29
Maria Cassida Lazarina	Widow		20
Her daughter Maria Luiza Barsenas	Child		2
Julio Lazarin	Single	Farmer	17
Jose'Guadalupe Lazarin	Married	Farmer	36
His children Maria de la Luz Epitafia			11
Maria Estafana			9
Gordiano Badillo	Single	Farmer	46
Candido Sanches	Single	Farmer	26
Aggregated Maria Encarnacion Flores			36
Her children Maria Marselina de Jesus			15
Maria Bitoria			9
Pedro Jose'	Youth		12
Jose' Luis de los Reyes			8
Jose' Candelario	Child		1
Juan Carmana	Married	Farmer	45
Maria de Jesus Benites			36
Maria Lina	Child		6
Masedoni Carmona	Married	Farmer	25
His wife Maria de los Angeles Tovar			18

Name	Status	Occupation	Age
His children Mari Biviana	Child		6
Maria Dolores	Child		1
Maria Casimira	Child		-
Maria Benites	Widow		40
Her child Maria Savina Dias			28
Her child Jose'	Child		3
Jose' Ignacio Estrada	Single	Shoemaker	34
Aggregated Maria de la Mersed	Child		1
Juan Lorenzo Boden	Married	Farmer	61
His wife Maria Modesta			52
Juan Cortes	Married	Farmer	45
His wife Maria de la Cruz Rodrigz			25
His children Jose' Felipe	Youth		9
Maria Dorotea			8
Maria Guadalupe			6
Maria Casimira de Jesus	Child		4
Jose' Anto Rodriguez	Married	Farmer	56
His wife Maria Tomaza a la millo			54
His grandchild Juan Fermen Tovar	Single	Farmer	16
Maria Ocasia Tovar			11
Aggregated Franco Javier de Peña	Widower	Farmer	60
Marian Mora	Married	Farmer	57
His wife Maria Trenidad Prosela			49
His grandchild Mariano	Youth		13
Trenidad Manzolo	Widower	Farmer	52
His daughter Maria Josefa	Single		24
Her son Jose' Maria	Youth		14
Maria Salome Cortes	Widow		40
Juan Jose' Acosta	Married	Farmer	30
His wife Mari Jasinta de Castro			30
Her children Jose' Guadalupe Donato	Youth		7
Jose' Romaldo			5
Maria Josefa	Child		3
Maria Relusinda	Child		—
Miguel Herrera	Married	Farmer	31
His wife Maria Josefa de Soto			17
His cousin Jose' de Jesus Rodrigz	Single	Farmer	20
Maria Telesforo Ybarvo			35
Her son Balentin Ybarvo			23
Juan Bautista Cosanava	Single	Farmer	50
His son Eduardo	Single	Farmer	29
Aggregated Teresa Linche	Widow		30
Her sons Pedro	Youth		8
Tomas	Youth		5
Juan Bautista	Child		2
Maria Soledad de los Santo Coy	Widow		59
Silvestre Poaso	Married	Farmer	48

1830 Census of Nacogdoches

His wife Maria Josefa Eser			21
His son Juan Barnardino	Child		3
Jose' Olivie Poaso	Single	Farmer	23
Aggregated His mother Maria Manuela Soto	Widow		73
Slaves Anto	Male		50
Juan	Male		70
Jose'	Male		8
Adolfo Estern	Married	Trader	29
His wife Maria Rosina			20
His daughter Eugenia	Child		1
His brother Santiago	Youth		8
Aggregated Xaime Hartz		Trader	22
Juan Esrrovte	Married		33
His wife Garieta			30
His children Licurges P. Rovet	Child		-
Juan T. Kalier	Youth		7
Jose' L. Gustes	Single	Trader	27
Elial Meltin	Single	Trader	32
Pedro Morfit	Single	Farmer	44
Emos Denebil	Widower	Carpenter	56
His son Guilian	Single	Carpenter	21
Vicenta Michel	Married	Farmer	37
His wife Maria Telesforo Prosela			18
His children Mari Matilde	Child		7
Blas Ramon	Child		6
Pedro Ybarbo	Married	Farmer	50
His wife Juana de la Garza			41
His children Remigio	Single	Farmer	20
Maria Josefa			18
Maria Canuta			16
Manuel Onoje	Single	Farmer	14
Luciano	Single		12
Juan Bautista			8
Mari Feliciana			5
Juan de Jesus	Child		3
Jose' Chirino	Married	Farmer	28
His wife Maria Rafaela Ybarvo			22
His children Maria Vencelada Chirino			5
Maria Remigia	Child		3
Jose' Encarnacion	Child		-
Alen C. Yone	Married	Carpenter	45
Heni Hone			24
His children Dilete			13
Quiton Hone	Youth		12
Santiago	Youth		11
Mimes	Youth		9
Charles	Youth		7

Mateo	Youth		6
Terice	Child		4
Clarese	Child		2
Juan Franco de Ariola	Single	Farmer	28
Aggregated Ma Guadalupe Ramon			35
Her children Estevan Rechur	Youth		8
Maria Franca	Child		3
Guadalupe	Child		1
Juan Tovar	Married	Farmer	57
His wife Maria Teresa			30
Melchor Manzolo	Single	Farmer	31
Aggregated Maria Madalena Boden			24
Her son Jose' Justo Lorenzo	Child		1
Maria Dorotea Churnaca	Widow		48
Her son Juan Bautista Manzolo	Single	Farmer	17
Davi Sanches	Married	Farmer	28
His wife Maria Dorotea Piñeda			16
His son Manuel Bictorio	Child		1
His nephew Juan Jose' Bustamante	Youth		5
Martin Prado	Married	Farmer	68
His wife Maria Getrudes de Soto			42
His children Jose' Anselmo	Single	Farmer	22
Juan Nepomuceno	Single		21
Maria Antoa			16
Maria Faustina			9
Santiago Erie	Married	Farmer	24
Maria Bibiana Toar			16
His son Gregorio Erie	Child		3
Manuel de Herrera	Married	Farmer	27
His wife Maria Masedonia Mora			20
Ramon Chavana	Married	Farmer	54
His wife Maria Josefa Sanches			46
His children Jose' Santiago	Single	Farmer	24
Jose' Faustino	Single	Farmer	16
Jose' Guillermo	Single	Farmer	14
Jose' Fermin de Jesus			6
Maria de los Remedios			9
Maria Anta			7
Maria Ursula	Child		-
Andres Gonzales	Married	Farmer	36
His wife Ma Getrudes Amador			28
His children Masimo			5
Jose' de Jesus			4
Jose' de Manuel Gonzales			3
Sinforiano			1
Meliton	Child		-
Aggregated Jose' Maria Gonzales	Married	Farmer	58

1830 Census of Nacogdoches 123

His wife Maria Getrudes Dias			55
Patricio de Torres	Married	Farmer	46
His wife Catarina Amador			26
Aggregated Ma Josefa de la Garza	Widow		60
Maria Josefa de Torres	Widow		44
Her niece Maria Carmel			9
Franco Rosales	Single	Farmer	34
Guillermo Roberto	Single	Merchant	30
Tomas Gestin	Single	Merchant	25
Jose' Pineda	Married	Farmer	53
His son David Pineda	Youth		12
Juan Jose' Medina	Married	Farmer	68
Francisca Delila	Single	Baker	38
Her son Guillermo	Child		6
Guiare Tomas	Married	Trader	32
His wife Emele Margarita			27
His daughter Maria Luayes	Child		1
His slaves Sedra	Female		17
Feliz	Female		37
Llulie	Female		5
Fane	Female		4
Meltin Eslocom	Single	Printer	27
Jesus de los Santos Coy	Married	Farmer	30
His wife Maria Luiza			20
His niece Mari Clara			11
Juan Musquiz	Single	Farmer	26
His mother Trenidad Ybarvo	Married		43
Luis Prosela	Married	Tailor	38
His wife Dolores Soto			39
His slave Barnarda	Child		7
Pedro Roblo	Married	Farmer	61
His wife Madalena Pridonso			47
His children Jose' Nepomuceno	Single	Farmer	15
Maria Tranquilo			14
Maria Teresa			9
Maria			7
His slaves Franco	Male		15
Maria Rosa	Female		14
Aggregated Eustaquio Baldes	Single	Blacksmith	50
Jese Alifonzo Dominguez	Married	Farmer	28
His wife María Catarina Soliñe			20
His children Maria Barbara	Child		2
Maria Salome	Child		-
Franco Antonio Flores	Married	Farmer	36
His wife Maria Seleste Burasa			35
His children Mari Luisa			19
Madalena			17

124   1830 Citizens of Texas

Adelfin			15
Maria Antonia			11
Jose' Anto	Youth		10
Lusen	Youth		9
Selesten	Child		6
Anto Grillete	Widow	Farmer	50
His children C. Grillete	Single	Farmer	21
Maria Adel			8
Maria Constancia	Child		3
His slave Jacovo	Male		16
Remi Totan	Married	Farmer	51
His wife Mari Teresa Bascoqui			39
His daughter Mari Modesta			12
His slaves Samuel	Male		46
David	Male		30
Margarita	Female		25
Maria	Female		19
Her children Manuel	Male		9
Juan Pedro	Male		7
Marcelita	Female		5
Jose' Andres Torres	Married	Farmer	36
His wife Maria Jesus de Lion			30
His children Anamaria			10
Jose' Nasario	Child		6
Jose' Julian	Child		3
Aggregated Maria Isabel Flores	Married		47
Juan Doste	Married	Trader	29
His wife Marie Matilde			22
His children Luiza Doste	Child		2
Maria Benigna Doste	Child		-
Aggregated Maria Falen	Widow		52
His slaves Hiris		Blacksmith	30
Felipe			23
Samuel			31
Ysaque			20
Yesi			26
Neli			29
Arrtura			19
Leyda			5
Jacovo			13
Andres			3
Maria			-
Jesus Gomes	Married	Farmer	30
His wife Ma Gregoria Sanches			29
His children Pedro	Child		6
Maria Eudonia	Child		5
Jose' Bernardo	Child		3
Maria Andrea	Child		1

1830 Census of Nacogdoches 125

Manl Santos Coy	Married	Farmer	45
His wife Maria Guadalupe Chirino			35
His children Juan Pablo	Single	Trader	17
Benigno de los Santos	Single	Farmer	15
Maria Antonia			11
Maria Camela			9
Jose' Andres de Acosta	Widower	Farmer	86
His son Juan Manuel	Single	Carpenter	48
Jose' Morin	Single	Farmer	35
Tomas Fenequine	Married	Trader	28
His wife Ma Nanse			32
His slave Maria	Female		22
Maria Josefa Peres	Widow		51
Her children Maria Trinidad	Widow		27
Jose' Falcon	Single	Farmer	22
Juan Falcon	Single	Farmer	20
Her grandson Franco	Single	Farmer	16
Bentura Sanches	Single	Farmer	21
Ma Berulda Arriola	Widow		57
Jose' Anto Saliz	Married	Farmer	36
His wife Ma del Pilar Sehaznaca			28
His children Maria Anta			13
Jose' Dolores	Youth		11
Jose' Fernando	Youth		7
Bentura			5
Maria Pioquinta	Child		-
Franco Perez	Married	Farmer	27
His wife Ma del Carmen Treviño			29
His children Ma Juliana	Child		3
Jose' Ma Perez	Child		2
Juan Perez	Child		-
Pedro Medina	Married	Farmer	25
His wife Maria Anta Lione			19
His children Ma Guadalupe	Child		2
Maria Teresa	Child		-
Jose' Ma Soto	Single	Farmer	32
Aggregated Maria Castañeda	Widow		49
Franco Soto	Single	Farmer	19
Juan Jose' Martines	Youth		12
Ma Josefa Castañeda			35
Her children Juan Longoria	Single	Farmer	15
Maria Getrudes			10
Maria Carmen			5
Batis Tecie	Single	Farmer	60
Aggregated Juana Oliber	Widow		50
Jose' Leonicio Lopes	Married	Farmer	56
His wife Ma Guadalupe Cordova			50

His children Juan	Single	Farmer	23
Gregorio	Youth		13
Pedro Lopes	Single	Farmer	15
Jose' Anto Chirino	Married	Farmer	78
His wife Maria Anta de los Santos			50
His granddaughter Maria Tomasa			15
Aggregated Blaz Lozolla	Youth		12
Andres Mermea	Married	Farmer	33
His wife Juana Cadena			29
His granddaughter Anta Bermea	Child		5
Pedro Sanches	Single	Farmer	46
Jose' Felis Lopes	Single	Farmer	36
Aggregated Ma Luiza Benites			30
Juan Blea	Single	Blacksmith	30
Carlos H. Simen	Single	Trader	29
Car Estela	Single	Trader	23
Bernardo Pantalion	Married	Farmer	33
His wife Ma Ulali			24
His children Olibie	Child		4
Moriel	Child		2
His slave Ma Yini	Female		38
Juan Maquedagnel	Single	Trader	27
Jose' Justo Comb	Married	Doctor	43
His wife Ma Ana			43
His daughter Aneta			17
Samuel B. Machel	Single	Trader	26
Guillermo Goyn	Single	Blacksmith	34
Aggregated Ma Petra			32
Her son Genere	Youth		11
Her slave Sale	Female		30
Her children Luiza	Female		6
Juliana	Female		3
Gorge Polito	Single	Tanner	35
Fros Ton	Married	Trader	35
His wife Ma Susana			22
Aggregated Jose' Eduardo	Single	Trader	15
Atanacio Lopes	Single	Farmer	34
Aggregated Ma Cosiana Poleto			20
Her son Jose' Benigno	Child		-
Tomas de la Garza free mulatto	Single	Farmer	21
His mother Ma Guadalupe Nieves			60
[The foregoing two names were lined out]			
Simon Sanches	Married	Farmer	23
His wife Ma Apolian Suares			22
Mariano Sanches	Married	Farmer	59
His wife Ma Paubla Ruiz			65

1830 Census of Nacogdoches   127

His children Jose' Maria	Single	Farmer	24
Jose' Anto	Single	Farmer	18
Jose' Ignacio	Single	Farmer	16
His niece Ma Rosalia Toscano			12
Aggregated Ma Josefa Morvan	Widow		31
Her son Jose' Romaldo	Child		4
Jose' Damacio Sanches	Married	Farmer	47
His wife Manuela Morvan			29
His child Ma Antonia			9
Julio Saballes	Married	Farmer	23
His wife Mari Jordana Sanches			23
Julian Sanches	Single	Farmer	37
Aggregated Ma Concpcion Santa Cruz	Widow		59
Luis Sanches	Married	Farmer	26
His wife Ma del Pilar Caro			19
His child Ma Concpcion	Child		-
Daniel Claque	Widower	Farmer	51
His slaves Else	Female		35
Sale	Female		20
Boyne	Female		18
Live	Female		15
Sayras	Male		22
Estivin	Male		18
Aysam	Male		17
Sibne	Male		12
Toble	Female		4
Ysta	Female		-
Guiliam Hesmite	Single	Trader	24
Jose' Doste	Married	Farmer	39
His wife Ma Olaya Dil			34
His son Jose' Santiago	Youth		10
His slaves Mosle	Female		25
Matilde	Female		9
Scharles	Male		7
Maraya	Female		5
Aggregated Dolores Cortina	Single	Farmer	15
Sebastian Mancha	Youth		10
Estevan Mora	Married	Farmer	43
His wife Ma Getrudes de la Serda			30
His children Juan	Youth		13
Jose' de los Santos	Youth		8
Eulogio	Youth		6
Mauricio	Child		3
Maria Luiza	Child		-
Maria Getrudes Cordova	Widow		27
Her children Juan Jose' de Luna	Youth		12
Maria Barbara			10

1830 Citizens of Texas

Jose' Gregorio			8
Jose' Matias	Child		2
Juan Martines	Widower		50
His children Domingo Servantes	Single	Farmer	32
Jose' Agapito	Single	Farmer	30
Jose' Andres	Single	Farmer	20
Jose' Maria	Single	Farmer	18
Jose' Lorenzo	Youth		10
Tomas Noris	Married	Farmer	34
His wife Maria Puarie			21
His children Jose' Guillermo	Child		2
Franco Sarapio	Child		.
Juan Noris	Married	Farmer	30
His wife Selestina Estocoman			19
His children Maria Juliana	Child		2
Jose' Santiago	Child		—
Aggregated Maria Selestina Tega	Widow		70
Julian Fonteno	Single	Farmer	49
Aggregated Mari Petra Dias	Married		30
Jose' Maria Martines	Single	Farmer	35
Juan Robas	Single	Farmer	36
Aggregated Ma Yne Gomes			21
Her son Jose' Lionardo	Child		2
Catarino Mendes	Single	Farmer	33
Dolores Martines	Married	Farmer	46
His children Mari Candelaria	Married		18
Faustina Ayala			7
Aggregated Ma Trinidad Garcia			40
Jose' Cordova	Married	Farmer	59
His wife Ma Tiburcia Ybarbo			43
Genere Guev	Single	Farmer	26
Manuel de la Garza	Married	Farmer	47
Domingo Ybarbo	Married	Farmer	51
His wife Maria Elena Sanches			44
His children Maria Estefania			23
Maria Alegandra			23
Maria Barbara			21
Juan Jose'	Youth		14
Juan Antonio	Youth		12
Juan Bautista	Youth		10
Maria Dorotea			8
Jose' Lauriano	Child		6
Maria de la Luz	Child		1
Maria Ybarvo			27
Her child Juana Tovar	Child		2
Guilian Eliete	Married	Farmer	34
His wife Ma Pole			24

His children Juan Santiago	Child		2
Tomas	Child		-
Jose' Maria Prosela	Married	Farmer	53
His wife Maria Manuela de la Serda			49
His children Jose' de Jesus	Single	Farmer	21
Jose' Policarpio	Single	Farmer	15
Maria Vicenta			13
Maria del Pilar			11
Jose' Antonio Lionires	Child		4
Telesforo Cordova	Single	Farmer	23
Aggregated Manuela Cruz	Married		23
Her children Crisanto	Youth		11
Estevan	Youth		9
Jose' Alifonzo	Youth		7
Maria Juliana	Child		2
Maria Andrea	Child		-
Jose' de los Santos Coy	Married	Farmer	58
His wife Ma Concpcion Topa			46
His slave Fane			30
Her child Merden			7
Jose' Antonio de los Santos Coy	Married	Farmer	21
His wife Mari Anta Menchaca			16
Juan Jose' Ybarbo	Married	Farmer	40
His wife Ma Garcia			30
Gregorio	Single	Farmer	18
Juan	Single		14
Manuel Chirino	Married	Farmer	40
His wife Martina Ybarbo			36
His children Apolonio	Single	Farmer	18
Jose' Antonio	Single	Farmer	16
Maria Faustina			14
Anestacio Ysidoro	Youth		12
Maria Gorgonia			10
Franco Mora	Single	Farmer	65
Aggregated Juana Ballanova	Widow		53
Manual Ybarbo	Married	Farmer	39
His wife Getrudes Calderon			31
His children Jose' Maria	Youth		10
Jose' de Jesus	Youth		8
Maria Brijida			5
Jose' Arcario	Child		-
Juan Escolton	Married	Farmer	40
His wife Ma Llino			24
His slave Maria Boto			34
Her son Ma Polo			4
Marcos de la Garza	Married	Farmer	38
His wife Dolores Manzolo			22

His son Jose'	Youth		9
Jose' Maria Mora	Married	Farmer	48
His wife Mari Anta Prosela			24
His children Jose' Anestacio	Youth		11
Jose' Maria	Child		2
Maria Eduvijen			10
Maria Elena			5
Juan Bautista Michem	Married	Trader	49
His wife Maria Calorina			27
His children Jose'	Youth		7
Antonia	Youth		6
Maria	Youth		4
Manuel	Child		2
His slave Eme			39
Franco Cordova	Married	Farmer	34
His wife Ma Ricarda Caro			28
His children Ma Severiana			8
Maria Asencion			7
Jose' Manuel	Child		4
Antonio Chavana	Married	Farmer	31
Pablo Leone	Single	Farmer	29
Moses Flom	Single	Farmer	28
Donato Leone	Single	Farmer	14
Andres Morales	Married	Farmer	32
His wife Ma Encarnacion			30
His son Jose' Miguel	Child		2
Roberto Quese	Single	Carpenter	32
Jose' Menchaca	Married	Farmer	43
His wife Dolores Gonzales			31
His child Martin	Child		3
Maria Adeli	Married		25
His son Jose'	Child		2
Jose' Maria Gomes	Married	Farmer	34
His wife Josefa Esparza			23
Eduardo Ariola	Married	Carpenter	44
His wife Candelaria Simes			38
His mother Anamaria Exis	Widow		63
His children Mari Olaya			19
Jose' Franco	Single	Farmer	17
Jose' Mariano	Youth		11
Juan	Youth		13
Jose' Teodoro	Youth		10
Jose' Ylario	Child		6
Gregorio	Child		3
Aggregated Prudencio Alami	Single	Farmer	22
Dolores Arriola	Married	Farmer	21
His wife Ma Jaime			15

Juan Bautista Gañe	Widower	Farmer	40
Aggregated Bautista Bandal	Single	Farmer	59
Jose' Ma Villareal	Single	Farmer	22
Vicenta Dias	Widow		32
Her children Maria			9
Maria Juana			6
Maria Getrudes			4
Juan Jose' Alvarado	Married	Farmer	47
His wife Ygnacia			32
His children Jose' Santos	Single	Farmer	18
Jose Gil	Child		5
Damacio Ybarbo	Married	Farmer	42
Juan Palbado	Married	Farmer	55
His wife Leonor Tecie			60

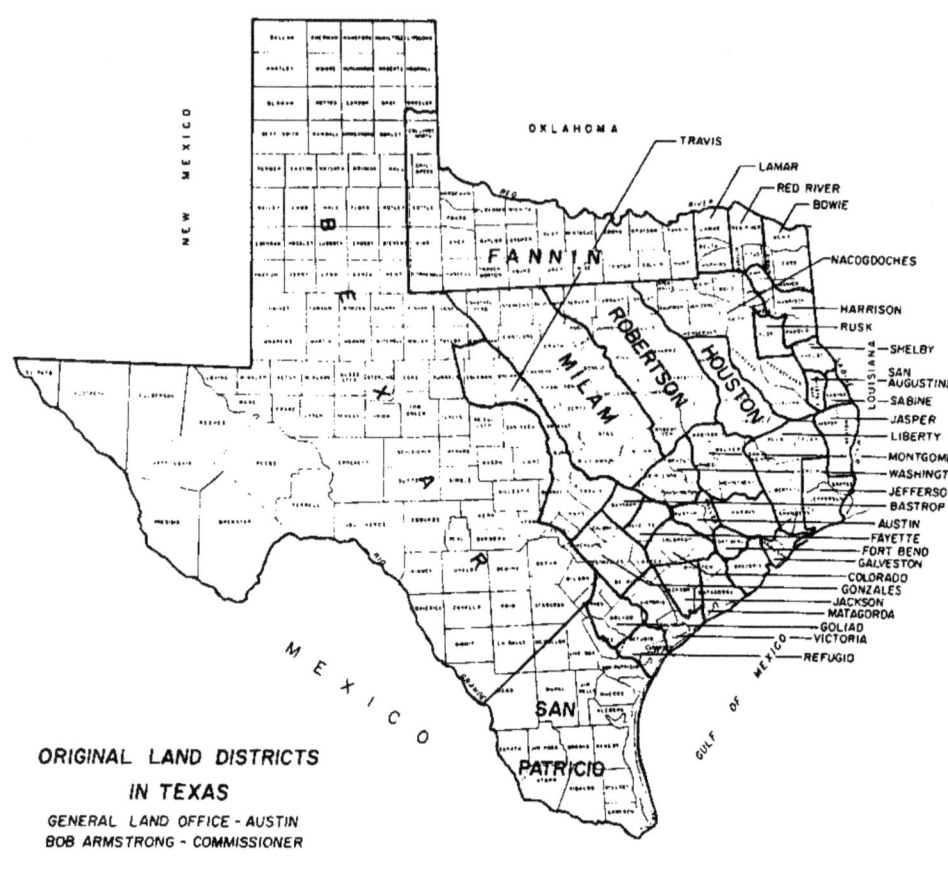

GENERAL LAND OFFICE RECORDS

Anglo-American immigration into Texas began in earnest in 1823 with the opening of Austin's first colony. New arrivals continued to accept Mexican citizenship and cheap land for more than ten years more, up to the Texian declaration of independence from Mexico on March 2, 1836. The constitution and laws of the new Republic of Texas then gained control of the land and the people until Texas joined the Union in late 1845. Even after statehood, Texas still administered the granting or sale of its public lands so that the land records of Texas are unique among the states as a history of its citizens.

Immigrants to Texas before 1836 did not always receive a title to their land from the Mexican government because the mechanism for making land grants was not evenly administered. In the Austin Colony, petitions were usually processed with speed but this clearly did not apply to the eastern part of Texas. Many settlers waited more than 10 years to receive grants in 1835, and many more were still waiting when the Texian Revolution closed the land offices in 1835.

Several publications which list the names of those receiving Mexican grants before 1835 may be consulted for the names of early settlers in Texas, although it will not usually be clear what year the person might have arrived.

Under colonial law, a head of a family (a married man or a widowed person with dependents) was entitled to a league of land. A single man over the age of 17 years could receive ¼ of a league. If he married later, he was entitled to apply for an "augmentation" to a full league.

Under the land laws spelled out in the new Texian constitution of 1837 and the laws of the new Congress, immigrants arriving before March 2, 1836 were settlers of the First Class and entitled to a league and a labor of land, or to 1/3 league as single men. In the Appendix will be found an excerpt from the land law that lists the requirements to be met.

In brief, a person desiring land in Texas after the Revolution of 1836 was required to appear before a Board of Land Commissioners in his county of residence where he would recite the answers to questions listed in the law. He had to bring two witnesses who could swear to the information he would give. The local Board of Land Commissioners would issue a certificate to each successful applicant, stating the amount of land to which he might be entitled.

The settler had to find vacant land to his liking, on his own initiative. It might not be in the county of his residence or original application. He then paid for a survey and for filing in the General Land Office. Eventually a patent would be issued (or denied) as perfected proof of ownership.

It should be noted that the Texian law was more liberal than the Mexican immigration law because it allowed a labor (177 acres) more to heads of families, and 1/3 rather than ¼ league to single men. This last augmentation accounts for the entires of 369 (or 370) acres granted to some applicants in 1838. The increased entitlements brought many of the old settlers or their heirs and assignees into the 1838 records when they applied for and proved their right to the increase.

There were a surprising number of immigrants in Texas before 1836 who had not received land under Mexican grants. Their petitions appear in the 1838 and 1839 records.

The General Land Office indexes and reports have been read and the names of applicants who arrived 1830 or earlier have been abstracted. By still being here in 1838, and swearing to continuous residence, any date of 1830 or earlier is proof of residence in Texas in 1830.

Some special hints will be helpful in using these lists.

Application had to be made in the county of residence. The Index in the General Land Office gives the county where the land was finally located. The grantee may never have lived in the county where he found the vacant land and had it surveyed. Perhaps he even sold the right to the land and never saw it. The right to land could be sold at any point in the chain, so that many settlers appear by 'Assignee.'' The record still had to be initiated in the name of the original claimant, and the date of his arrival is the one stated in the record. Any remarks on marital status, etc. will refer to him. The name of the assignee is not usually of any genealogical significance. He was often a speculator.

Deceased persons entitled to land during their lifetimes were represented by their heirs or assignss. An application in 1838 that proved arrival before 1830 does not prove that the person was living in 1830. Entries of this kind have been included, even though the ambiguity makes other research necessary to establish the date of death.

March 2, 1836 was the date of the Declaration of Independence and a "cut-off" date in the land law. In the record will be found statements like "Married at the D of I." This means that the claimant was married on or before that date; that is, such a statement reflects status on March 2, 1836. Likewise, "seventeen years old on the D of I" only proves a minimum age, although it usually applies to a young man about whom the question of age might be raised.

An "Augmentation" is an increase in the amount of land due a settler because of a change in status. Usually this was through marriage, or because of the change in the law after the Republic was established. Some apparently odd amounts of land were granted in this way.

INDEX A

Among the records of the General Land Office is a book with the title "An Alphabetical List of Returns from the Different Boards of Land Commissioners, Book A." It contains an alphabetical list of the First Class Grantees (those arriving before March 2, 1836), as they applied for original grants or newly allowed increases under the new Texas Constitution in 1838. No more than the first two reports, nominally made in January and February of 1838, are tabulated. Not all counties are represented. It appears there should be a Book B and so on but none is now known. The present Book A is almost surely a copy of an earlier work because it is written in a uniform hand and does not appear as old as known records of 1838.

The General Land Office has a complete modern alphabetic list of names, but "Index A" has the advantage of (1) giving the year of immigration and (2) giving the county in which the applicant lived where he applied by law. Current lists and records stress the county in which the vacant land was finally located, which proves nothing about the grantee.

In using this list, reference should be made to the map showing the different land districts, which were more or less the same as the counties then in existence. Only a resident of the district could appear before their board with a claim for land.

The immigration date is that of the original settler, and not of any assignee or heirs. The word "Native" should mean born in Texas, although it may sometimes mean born in Mexico.

An Alphabetical List of Returns from Different Boards of Land Commissioners
Book A

No.	Name	Leagues	Lab	Emigrated	County	Report No.
5	Allen Benjamin	1/3		Aug 1826	Jefferson	1
8	Allen Moses	1	1	1826	Jefferson	1
15	Allen Elijah	1/3		1827	Jefferson	1
16	Allen Hannah	1	1	1827	Jefferson	1
17	Allen Elisha	1/3		1827	Jefferson	1
68	Andrus William	1/3		April 1829	Fort Bend	1
33	Allen James W.	1/3		1827	Liberty	1
	Thos W. Key Attorney					
2	Allen George		1	1826	Jefferson	2
21	Arnold Holly	1	1	March 1826	Montgomery	1
25	Arnold Daniel	—	1	March 1826	Montgomery	1
36	Atkins William	—	1	Dec 1829	Montgomery	1
35	Allsberry W<u>m</u> W.	1/3		1828	Gonzales	1
123	Alexander George decd	1/3		1825	Matagorda	1
	To heirs & representatives					
144	Albright Jacob	1/3		1830	Matagorda	1
29	Andrews John Jr.	—	1	Jan 1826	Jackson	1
30	Alley William	1/3		1825	Jackson	1
17	Arocha Jose' Ramon	1	1	Native	Bexar	1
	Wm H. Steel & Ludovick Colquhoun assignees					
21	Arreola Gabriel	1	1	Native	Bexar	1
37	Alcorte Marcelo	1	1	Native	Bexar	1
	Jose' Ant<u>o</u> de la Garza assignee					
82	Arocha Juan Jose'	1/3		Native	Bexar	1
	Steel & Colquhoun assignees					
87	Alcantura Rafael	1	1	Native	Bexar	1
	John McMullen assignee					
94	Arreola Simon	1	1	Native	Bexar	1
	Rafael de la Garza assignee					
110	Alaniz Maria Gertrudis de	1	1	Native	Bexar	1
	John W. Smith assignee					
117	Almansar Ignacia	1	1	Native	Bexar	1
	Hezekiah Bissell assignee					
127	Arocha Antonio	1	1	Native	Bexar	1
	do	do				
152	Almaguei Eusebio	1	1	Native	Bexar	1
	Steel & Colquhoun assignees					
158	Arocha Jose' Maria	1/3		Native	Bexar	1
	do	do				
182	Arocha Antonio the Elder	1	1	Native	Bexar	1
	Wm H. Steele assignee					
191	Alderete Dolores	1	1	Native	Bexar	1
	John Sutherland assignee					

General Land Office Records 137

207	Ampara Maria	1	1	Native	Bexar	1
	Jas A. Haynie assignee					
234	Aperlado Jose'	1/3		Native	Bexar	1
	Wm H. Steel assignee					
266	Arocha Maria Josefa	1	1	Native	Bexar	1
	Ignacio Castro assignee					
42	Aken Collin M	1	1	Nov 1827	Red River	1
59	Aken James	1/3		Nov 1827	Red River	1
262	Akens William	1	1	Nov 1827	Red River	1
111	Andracia Jose' Maria	1	1	Native	Nacogdoches	1
	Seth Sheldon assignee					
76	Aguelaria Jose' Fecundo	1/3		Native	Nacogdoches	1
	Ambrose Crane assignee					
48	Anderson Vincent decd	1	1	1825	S. Augustine	1
244	Anderson Bailey	1	1	1822	S. Augustine	1
278	Allen George	—	1	1830	Montgomery	2
440	Allcorn John H	1/12		1825	Washington	2
21	Anderson Wm H	1/3		Aug 1830	Fannin	1
	Allan John M decd	1/12		1829 or '30	Austin	3
	J. B. Johnson Admr					
347	Alameda Francisco	1/3		Native	Bexar	2
	John Sutherland assignee					
351	Arocha Jose' Ma the Elder	1	1	Native	Bexar	2
389	Arocha Lino	1/3		Native	Bexar	2
	J. P. Henderson assignee					
423	Alderete Rafael	1/3		Native	Bexar	2
	Wm Richardson assignee					
76	Bell Thomas	—	1	1826	Austin	1
92	Birtrong Thomas	1	1	1830	Austin	1
96	Best Stephen	1	1	1825	Austin	1
86	Battle Mills M	—	1	March 1825	Fort Bend	1
89	Bradley Daniel	1/3		July 1825	Fort Bend	1
140	Borden Pascal P	3/4	1	May 1830	Fort Bend	1
48	Baker Caleb	1/3		1830	Liberty	1
	A. B. Hardin assignee					
63	Buxten Alexander	1	1	1827	Liberty	1
136	Barrow Benjamin	1	1	1827	Liberty	1
138	Barrow Solomon 3,320,000	sq varas		1824	Liberty	1
139	Barrow Levi	1	1	1830	Liberty	1
142	Barrow Reuben Senr	1	1	1824	Liberty	1
145	Barrow Vincent	1	1	1830	Liberty	1
	Benj Barrow Admr					
105	Burrell Robert	1	1	1828	Liberty	1
3	Bowen Michl	1	1	Dec 1828	Milam	1
52	Barrow Jno M	1/4		1830	Milam	1
103	Boring Nancy	—	1	1828	Milam	1
119	Busby William	—	1	May 10, 1830	Montgomery	1
45	Burnham Wm O	1	1	Dec 1821	Fayette	1
46	Burnham John H	1/3		Dec 1821	Fayette	1

138   1830 Citizens of Texas

10	Berry Francis	—	1	1830	Gonzales	1
11	Berry James	1/3		1830	Gonzales	1
20	Bridger Henry	1/3		1830	Gonzales	1
9	Burns Arthur	—	1	July 1826	Victoria	1
82	Brigham Saml B	1/3		1830	Matagorda	1
161	Bowman Jo.	1	1	1822	Matagorda	1
	To heirs & Representatives					
203	Burknap L	1/3		1830	Matagorda	1
	To heirs & representatives					
213	Bostwick C. R.	1/2	1	1822	Matagorda	1
	To heirs & representatives					
253	Bayse Henry L	1	1	1826	Matagorda	1
293	Betts Jacob	1/2	1	1825	Matagorda	1
	To heirs & representatives					
333	Bright George	1/3		1826	Matagorda	1
	To heirs & representatives					
25	Batey Edward	—	1	1828	Jackson	1
26	Brown Daniel D	1/3		1829	Jackson	1
45	Brackin William	1/3		Aug 1826	Jackson	1
87	Burns Squire	1/12		1826	Jackson	1
134	Bradberry James	1	1	1829	Washington	1
178	Berry Jackson	1/3		1828	Washington	1
209	Boren Matthew	1	1	1828	Washington	1
238	Belcher Isham G	3/4	1	1825	Washington	1
288	Berry John	1	1	1828	Washington	1
289	Berry Joseph	1/3		1828	Washington	1
326	Becam Mary & heir	1	1	1830	Washington	1
20	Barclay Anderson	—	1	1829	Jasper	1
39	Bevil Jehu	3/4	1	1829	Jasper	1
49	Blount Penelope	—	1	1830	Jasper	1
11	Becerra Jose' Maria	1	1	Native	Bexar	1
	Jones & Smith assignees					
25	Botello Francisco	1	1	Native	Bexar	1
	John McMullen assignee					
60	Benites Antonio	1/3		Native	Bexar	1
	Steel & Colquhoun assignee					
74	Bustillos Clemente	1	1	Native	Bexar	1
	Alex F. Gayle assignee					
77	Bustillo Jose' Maria	1	1	Native	Bexar	1
	Anderson M. Berry assignee					
129	Bustillos Alexos	1	1	Native	Bexar	1
	Steel & Colquhoun assignees					
143	Barrera Jose' Antonio	1	1	Native	Bexar	1
	Steele & Colquhoun assignees					
150	Bustillo Casimero	1	1	Native	Bexar	1
	do	do				
208	Bustillos Josefa	1	1	Native	Bexar	1
	James A. Haynie assignee					
	Black Albert	1/3		1827	Bastrop	1

General Land Office Records 139

	Name			Date	Place	
	Black Joseph	1	1	1823	Bastrop	1
	Bennett D. W.	1/3		1830	Bastrop	1
	S. C. Bennett Admr					
	Barton Wayne	1/3		1829	Bastrop	1
	Barton William	—	1	1828	Bastrop	1
	Barton Jefferson	1/3		1830	Bastrop	1
86	Boren Elisha decd	1	1	1828	Robertson	1
	M. Boren Admr					
166	Barksdale Lewis	3/4	1	June 1830	Fort Bend	2
169	Bell Joseph T	1	1	Aug 1830	Fort Bend	2
139	Borden Gail Jr.	—	1	1830	Harrisburg	1
	Thomas H. Borden Atty					
360	Brenson Enoch	—	1	1828	Harrisburg	1
245	Barrow Benj Jr.	1/3		1830	Liberty	2
80	Brinlee George	1	1	Feb 1824	Red River	1
107	Burkham Chas	1	1	March 1820	Red River	1
140	Bird John	1/3		June 1830	Red River	1
279	Byers Westly	1	1	Nov 1824	Red River	1
288	Barkham James	1	1	1820	Red River	1
	Boren Jos	1	1	1828	Milam	2
56	Barbo Ramigeo Y	1/3		Native	Nacogdoches	1
	By Chas Chevallier & Bernard Pantaleon					
67	Barbo Gregorio Y	1/3		Native	Nacogdoches	1
	do	do				
81	Barbo Maximilian Y	1/3		Native	Nacogdoches	1
	Bernard Pantaleon assignee					
86	Barilla Jose' Antonio	—	1	Native	Nacogdoches	1
	Moses L. Pattent assignee					
87	Barbo Miguel Y	—	1	Native	Nacogdoches	1
	M. L. Pattent & Wm M. Keeling assignee					
142	Barbo Candraiks Y	1/3		Native	Nacogdoches	1
	Jesse Burdett assignee					
143	Barbo Jesus Y	1/3		Native	Nacogdoches	1
	do	do				
186	Barbo Manuel M. Y	1/3		Native	Nacogdoches	1
	Saml Maas assignee					
190	Barbo Luciana Y	1/3		Native	Nacogdoches	1
	Jas Walling assignee					
224	Barbo Jose' Antonio Y	1/3		Native	Nacogdoches	1
	Jesse Burdett assignee					
240	Bordan Juan Lorenzo	—	1	Native	Nacogdoches	1
	David Rusk assignee					
245	Barbo Juan Benigno Y	1/3		Native	Nacogdoches	1
	Stephen Collins assignee					
249	Barbo Antonio Y	1	1	Native	Nacogdoches	1
	Jesse Burdett assignee					
250	Barbo Martin Y	—	1	Native	Nacogdoches	1
	Robt F. Millard assignee					
278	Bordon Juan Lorenzo	1	—	Native	Nacogdoches	1

1830 Citizens of Texas

P. A. Sublett & S. Houston assignees
[Notation]: Previously obtained land

#	Name			Date	Location	
279	Barbo Jose' Antonio Y	1	1	Native	Nacogdoches	1
	Jesse Burdett assignee					
154	Barbo Manuel M Y	1/3		Native	Nacogdoches	1
	Saml Maas assignee					
115	Bordine John	1	1	1825	S. Augustine	1
242	Bridges James	1	1	1821	S. Augustine	1
249	Brownrigg Geo. B.	—	1	1830	S. Augustine	1
256	Bullock James W.	—	1	1824	S. Augustine	1
294	Bullock Julius W	1/3		1827	S. Augustine	2
377	Blackwell Henry B	1	1	1828	S. Augustine	2
282	Burney William	—	1	1822	Montgomery	2
308	Black Marcus S. decd	1/12		1830	Montgomery	2
448	Bidy Abednigo	1	1	1826	Washington	2
15	Black Jacob	1	1	May 1825	Fannin	1
81	Buckman Oliver	1	—	1825	Fayette	2
	Geo W. Spear assignee					
195	Brown Joseph	1	1	1817	Sabine	1
	Martin D. White Admr					
	Bell James H	—	1	1830	Austin	3
	Bird Thomas	—	1	1830	Austin	3
	Bird John	—	1	1830	Austin	3
	Bailey Alexander	1/12		1827	Austin	3
	Best E. W.	1/3		1826	Austin	3
320	Borgas Frutosa	1	1	Native	Bexar	2
	Steel & Colquhoun assignees					
321	Braba Guadalupe	1	1	Native	Bexar	2
	John McMullen assignee					
363	Bargas Estevan	1/3		Native	Bexar	2
371	Buena Juana Francisca	1	1	Native	Bexar	2
	John N. Seguin assignee					
375	Baron Ginio	1	1	Native	Bexar	2
	Wm H. Daingerfield assignee					
380	Bueno Manuel	1/3		Native	Bexar	2
381	Botello Concepcion	1	1	Native	Bexar	2
409	Bustillo Francisco	1/3		Native	Bexar	2
413	Bustillos Teresa	1	1	Native	Bexar	2
	Hezekiah Bissell assignee					
435	Benites Trinidad	1	1	Native	Bexar	2
	Wm Richardson assignee					
437	Bustillos Juana Francisca	1	1	Native	Bexar	2
	Hez Bissell assignee					
452	Bustillos Domingo	1	1	Native	Bexar	2
467	Benites Beronica	1	1	Native	Bexar	2
	Vicente Garza assignee					
469	Berban Juan Jose'	1	1	Native	Bexar	2
	John Sutherland assignee					
470	Barrera Augustin	1	1	Native	Bexar	2

General Land Office Records 141

232	W. W. Ballard	1/3		1821	Montgomery	2
	[written over]: Battle					
45	Clap Elisha	—	1	1822	Houston	1
9	Cottle Eliza	1	1	1829	Jefferson	1
13	Cole Solomon	1/3		1830	Jefferson	1
14	Cole David	1/3		1830	Jefferson	1
53	Cooper Enos	1	1	1823	Austin	1
102	Cochrane James	3/4	1	1830	Austin	1
83	Cartwright Robert M	1/3	1	July 1826	Fort Bend	1
	Jesse H. Cartwright Admr					
53	Clark George	1/3		1830	Liberty	1
95	Coronado Jose'	—	1	1825	Liberty	1
107	Cherry William	1/3		1825	Liberty	1
156	Cherry John	—	1	1825	Liberty	1
157	Cope Thomas	1/3		1828	Liberty	1
161	Cherry Aaron	1/3		1827	Liberty	1
162	Choate David Senr	—	1	1825	Liberty	1
164	Choate John	1/3		1825	Liberty	1
192	Carroll M. A.	—	1	1828	Liberty	1
	E. A. Carroll Admr					
43	Chance Saml	2/3		1822	Milam	1
85	Corryall James	1/12		1828	Milam	1
	Massillon Farley Admr					
88	Castelman Mich.	1/3		1826	Milam	1
32	Cobby William	1/12		March 1830	Montgomery	1
97	Corner Evan	1	1	Nov 17, 1829	Montgomery	1
	C. B. Stewart assignee					
98	Corner James	1/3		Nov 17, 1829	Montgomery	1
99	Corner John	—	1	Nov 28, 1829	Montgomery	1
114	Corner Thomas	1/12		Nov 17, 1829	Montgomery	1
144	Clark Wm C	—	1	Dec 1821	Montgomery	1
216	Crothers Mary	1/4		1829	Montgomery	1
	Hugh McGuffin assignee					
4	Criswell William	1/3		Feb 1830	Fayette	1
5	Criswell LeRoy	1/3		Feb 1830	Fayette	1
31	Cummings Willie	1/3		1822	Fayette	1
44	Clift Jesse	1/3		Feb 1830	Fayette	1
54	Cottle Lee F.T.	1	1	Dec 1826	Fayette	1
66	Criswell John Y	—	1	Dec 1830	Fayette	1
68	Cocke Anne	—	1	Dec 1825	Fayette	1
74	Clift Jesse	2/3	1	Feb 1830	Fayette	1
1	Cook James decd	1/2	1	1824	Matagorda	1
	To heirs & representatives					
21	Curtis Hinton	—	1	1826	Matagorda	1
98	Cayce Henry	1/3		1830	Matagorda	1
142	Campbell Elizabeth	—	1	1828	Matagorda	1
300	Cook Maria	—	1	1825	Matagorda	1
335	Cavenah Charles	1	1	1828	Matagorda	1
44	Clare A. M.	—	1	1826	Jackson	1

142   1830 Citizens of Texas

#	Name			Year	Place	
89	Coleman Youngs	—	1	1828	Jackson	1
51	Chadoin Thomas	1	1	1829	Washington	1
226	Clements Austin	1/3		1830	Washington	1
244	Clark James	—	1	1828	Washington	1
260	Clark Haner decd	1/3		1828	Washington	1
	Jas Clark Admr					
341	Castleman Jacob	1/3		1826	Washington	1
357	Clark Abraham K.	1/3		1830	Washington	1
50	Conn James	—	1	1830	Jasper	1
2	Carillo Fernando	1	1	Native	Bexar	1
	John W. Smith assignee					
14	Casillas Juan Jose'	1/3		Native	Bexar	1
	Geo Sutherland assignee					
15	Casanova Juan	1/3		Native	Bexar	1
	Henry R. Allen assignee					
33	Casanova Anacleto	1	1	Native	Bexar	1
	Steel & Colquhoun assignee					
38	Casillas Mateo	1	1	Native	Bexar	1
	do	do				
51	Cherino Jose' Maria	1/3		Native	Bexar	1
	Geo Sutherland assignee					
58	Casillas Francisco	1/3		Native	Bexar	1
	Jno W. Smith assignee					
69	Carranza Maria Luisa	1	1	Native	Bexar	1
	Juan Andres Zambrano assignee					
75	Cortinas Gertrudis	1		Native	Bexar	1
	Nath Lewis Assignee					
76	Carrera Jose' Antonio	1	1	Native	Bexar	1
	A. M. Berry assignee					
80	Curbelo Juana	1	1	Native	Bexar	1
	Steel & Colquhoun assignees					
81	Carillo Pedro	1/3		Native	Bexar	1
109	Cuellar Jinio	1	1	Native	Bexar	1
	Rafael Garza assignee					
121	Casillas Manuel	1/3		Native	Bexar	1
	Jno W. Smith assignee					
122	Casillas Yrrineo	1/3		Native	Bexar	1
	do	do				
123	Calderon Jose'	1	1	Native	Bexar	1
	do	do				
151	Cardono Juan	1	1	Native	Bexar	1
	Steele & Colquhoun assignee					
171	Carillo Concepcion	1	1	Native	Bexar	1
	do	do				
178	Contreras Jose' Simon	1/3		Native	Bexar	1
	do	do				
196	Casillas Gabriel	1/3		Native	Bexar	1
	John Sutherland assignee					
201	Contes Julian	1/3		Native	Bexar	1

	Alex. Tims assignee					
202	Casillas Pablo	1/3		Native	Bexar	1
	do	do				
203	Cherino Gertrudis	1	1	Native	Bexar	1
	Rufus McClellan assignee					
206	Casanova Francisco	1/3		Native	Bexar	1
	Jas A. Haynie assignee					
218	Castanera Ramon	1/3		Native	Bexar	1
256	Curvier Antonio	1/3		Native	Bexar	1
	Jas L. Wood & Wm K. Steele assignee					
134	Coy Maria Luisa de los Santos	1	1	Native	Bexar	1
	Thos J. Green assignee					
	Chambers Talbot	1/3		1830	Bastrop	1
	Greenleaf Fisk assignee					
	Cottle Joseph	1/3		1827	Bastrop	1
	Thos Anderson assignee					
	Crawford James	—	1	1830	Bastrop	1
	Caldwell John	—	1	1830	Bastrop	1
	Curtis Elijah	1/3		1825	Bastrop	1
	Curtis James	—	1	1825	Bastrop	1
	Curtis James Sen heirs of	—	1	1825	Bastrop	1
100	Campbell Ruthy decd	1	—	1829	Robertson	1
	Thos Morrow admr					
102	Campbell Walter	1/12		1829	Robertson	1
107	Campbell Ruthy decd	—	1	1829	Robertson	1
	T. Morrow Admr					
67	Clopper Andrew M	1/3		Jan 1828	Harrisburg	1
75	Cheevers John	1/3		1829	Harrisburg	1
	Jas M. Manning Atty					
208	Chavenoe M.	1/3		1829	Liberty	2
235	Cherry Aaron Sen	—	1	1825	Liberty	2
22	Clark James	1	1	1830	Red River	1
50	Collum Charles	1	1	Feb 1822	Red River	1
51	Collum Jonathan	1	1	Oct 1827	Red River	1
82	Collum George	1	1	Feb 1822	Red River	1
259	Clapp William	1/3		May 1820	Red River	1
355	Collum Collin M decd	1	1	1824	Red River	1
	Levi M. Rice Admr					
20	Cherino Anastacio	1/3		Native	Nacogdoches	1
	F. J. Anthony assignee					
80	Cortez Philip	1/3		Native	Nacogdoches	1
	K. H. Douglass assignee					
153	Cortinas Dolores	1	1	Native	Nacogdoches	1
	H. H. Edwards assignee					
165	Cherino Jose'	1		Native	Nacogdoches	1
	Elisha Roberts assignee					
184	Caro Thomas	1	1	Native	Nacogdoches	1
	Albert Emanuel assignee					
189	Casanova Crisantus	1/3		Native	Nacogdoches	1

JAMES BOWIE
History of Texas, John Henry Brown, St. Louis 1892

		Jesse Walling & E. Roberts assignee					
238		Casanova Alfonzo	1/3		Native	Nacogdoches	1
		do	do				
239		Casanova Christa	1/3		Native	Nacogdoches	1
		do	do				
246		Chavana Antonio	—	1	Native	Nacogdoches	1
		J. S. Roberts & Geo Allen assignee					
27		Channley Thomas	1/3		1828	S. Augustine	1
41		Chunnley John	1	1	1826	S. Augustine	1
218		Cartwright W. G.	1	1	1825	S. Augustine	1
351		Cartwright Matthew	3/4	1	1825	S. Augustine	2
224		Castleman John R	—	1	Feb 1821	Montgomery	2
249		Crabbe H. M.	—	1	1830	Montgomery	2
269		Castleman Patience decd	1	1	1825	Montgomery	2
		John R. Castleman Admr					
276		Castleman Andrew decd	1/3		1829	Montgomery	2
		do	do				
277		Castleman Patience	—	1	1825	Montgomery	2
		do	do				
311		Corner Mary	—	1	Nov 1829	Montgomery	2
401		Cummins Susanna	—	1	1826	Washington	2
3		Carodine Robert	1	1	1829	Sabine	1
53		Clark James	1/12		1823	Sabine	1
59		Clark Henry	1	1	1823	Sabine	1
62		Clark Elijah (balance)			1823	Sabine	1
74		Chapple Corene	1	1	1822	Sabine	1
127		Carodine Isaac	1	1	1829	Sabine	1
171		Clark John	1	1	1823	Sabine	1
175		Clark William Sen	1	1	1824	Sabine	1
		Conrad Peter	1/12		1828	Austin	3
		Campbell Hul O.	1	1	1828	Austin	3
		Cooper James	—	1	1826	Austin	3
335		Castro Maria Josefa	1	1	Native	Bexar	2
		Wm N. Steele assignee					
338		Contes Siriaco	1	1	Native	Bexar	2
		L. B. Franks assignee					
358		Cuvier Fernando	1/3		Native	Bexar	2
		Andrew W. White assignee					
360		Cruz Antonio	1	1	Native	Bexar	2
366		Cervantes Dolores	1	1	Native	Bexar	2
		Wm E. Howth assignee					
367		Chaves Pedro Ramon	1/3		Native	Bexar	2
		John Sutherland assignee					
369		Carvajal Francisco	1	1	Native	Bexar	2
		John N. Seguin assignee					
404		Casanova Dolores	1	1	Native	Bexar	2
412		Cherina Maria Ignacia	1	1	Native	Bexar	2
		Hez Bissel assignee					
415		Casanova Estevan	1/3		Native	Bexar	2
		Wm Richardson assignee					

146   1830 Citizens of Texas

441	Cruz Juan de la	1/3		Native	Bexar	2
	Hez Bissell assignee					
442	Casillas Maria Guadalupe	1	1	Native	Bexar	2
	W<u>m</u> H. Steele assignee					
456	Colchado Jose' Maria	1/3		Native	Bexar	2
	John McMullen assignee					
457	Camona Cesario	1/3		Native	Bexar	2
	Jas S. Martin assignee					
464	Carriona Manuela	1	1	Native	Bexar	2
	Nath Lewis assignee					
476	Castañeda Dolores	1	1	Native	Bexar	2
275	Coy Emanuela de los Santos	1	1	Native	Bexar	2
	Howth & Boyd assignee					
278	Chaves Francisco	1	1	Native	Bexar	2
284	Castro Jose' Manuel del	1	1	Native	Bexar	2
	L. Colquhoun assignee					
287	Curvier Matias	1	1	Native	Bexar	2
	Joseph L. Hood assignee					
299	Castañon Maria Andrea	1	1	Native	Bexar	2
	A. M. Berry assignee					
302	Castro Mariquita	1	1	Native	Bexar	2
	Jas A. Haynie assignee					
326	Castro Maria Petra	1	1	Native	Bexar	2
	L. C. Harrison assignee					
55	Darst Patrick C	1/3		July 1829	Fort Bend	1
71	Darst John G	1/3		July 1829	Fort Bend	1
152	Darst Emery H	1/3		Sep 1829	Fort Bend	1
153	Darst Edmond C decd	1/3		Sep 1829	Fort Bend	1
	Samuel Damon Adm<u>r</u>					
79	Dunman Henry	1/3		1828	Liberty	1
80	Dunman Jas T	1	1	1828	Liberty	1
91	Dever Thomas	3/4	1	1825	Liberty	1
110	Dever P. P.	—	1	1825	Liberty	1
	A. B. Hardin Adm<u>r</u>					
113	Devers John C	1/3		1825	Liberty	1
152	Duncan William	—	1	1825	Liberty	1
	by heirs					
153	Duncan Meredith	—	1	1825	Liberty	1
183	Dorsett Charles	1/3		1829	Liberty	1
193	Dunman Martin	1		1829	Liberty	1
4	Demoss Lewis	1	1	1825	Matagorda	1
69	Dukes Thomas M	—	1	1822	Matagorda	1
271	Demoss William	1	1	1825	Matagorda	1
	To heirs & representatives					
309	Davis George W	—	1	1821	Washington	1
313	Dare George	1	1	1830	Washington	1
44	Daily Michael	1	1	1830	Jasper	1
22	Delgado Juana	1	1	Native	Bexar	1
	Juan Andres Zambrano assignee					

62	Diaz Jose' Maria	1	1	Native	Bexar	1
	A. M. Berry assignee					
66	Diaz Julian	1	1	Native	Bexar	1
	Hezekiah Bissell assignee					
93	Diaz Domingo	1	1	Native	Bexar	1
	Erasmo Seguin assignee					
95	Diaz Ma Escolastica	1	1	Native	Bexar	1
	Enoch Jones & Jno W. Smith assignee					
148	Delgado Josefa	—	1	Native	Bexar	1
	John W. Smith assignee					
155	Delgado Jose' Antonio	1	1	Native	Bexar	1
	do	do				
186	Diaz Polonio	1/3		Native	Bexar	1
	do	do				
	Duty Richard	1	1	1830	Bastrop	1
	Edwd Blakey Admr					
105	Dawson David	1/3		1828	Robertson	1
176	Dewitt Christopher C	1/3		1829	Harrisburg	1
258	Dunman Robert	1/3		1830	Harrisburg	1
259	Dunman John	1	1	1827	Harrisburg	1
361	Dodson Obediah decd	1	1	1828	Harrisburg	1
	A. Dodson Admr					
35	Donlan Patrick	3/4	—	1827	Victoria	2
10	David Lewis	—	1	Native	Nacogdoches	1
	K. H. Douglass assignee					
140	Durst James H	1/3		Fall of 1826	Nacogdoches	1
4	Davis Anna	1	1	1821	S. Augustine	1
240	Davis Edward B	3/4	1	1828	S. Augustine	1
324	Duncan Jas H	1/3		1830	Montgomery	2
398	Dunn Matthew	1/12		1830	Washington	2
	Davis William	—	1	1829	Houston	2
	Dennet Geo A	1	1	1830	Austin	3
	Durbin Basil	1/12		1827	Austin	3
306	Diaz Josefa	1	1	Native	Bexar	2
	Wm H. Steele assignee					
332	Delgado Encarnacion	1	1	Native	Bexar	2
	do	do				
340	Diaz Canuto	1	1	Native	Bexar	2
	John McMullen assignee					
354	Diaz Juan	1	1	Native	Bexar	2
	Rufus McLellan assignee					
417	Delgado Maria Ignacia	1	1	Native	Bexar	2
	Wm Richardson assignee					
468	Duran Pablo	1/3		Native	Bexar	2
	John Sutherland assignee					
477	Diaz Antonio	1	1	Native	Bexar	2
99	DeLeon Francisco	[blank]		Native		
	Erasmo Seguin [assignee?]					
7	Edwards John T	3/4	1	1822	Austin	1

148 1830 Citizens of Texas

#	Name			Date	Place	
72	Ellender Joseph	1/3		1825	Liberty	1
3	Earnest Felix B	1/12		1827	Jackson	1
108	Early Thomas	1/3		1825	Washington	1
9	Enriques Lucio	1/3		Native	Bexar	1
	John McCreary assignee					
45	Estrada Antonio	1/3		Native	Bexar	1
	Geo Sutherland assignee					
130	Estrada Asencio	1/3		Native	Bexar	1
	Cornelius Van Ness assignee					
131	Espinosa Jose' Ignacio	1/3		Native	Bexar	1
	Wm R. Daingerfield assignee					
138	Escalera Jose' Maria Sen	1	1	Native	Bexar	1
	Steele & Colquhoun assignee					
243	Escalera Manuel	1	1	Native	Bexar	1
	do	do				
244	Escalera Jose' Maria Jr	1	1	Native	Bexar	1
	do	do				
201	Everett Wm	—	1	1827	Liberty	2
	B. M. Green legal representative					
70	Erio Santiago	—	1	Spring 1828	Nacogdoches	1
180	Esparcia Jose'	1	1	Native	Nacogdoches	1
	J. Walling & Elisha Roberts assignee					
187	Escallon Anastacio Heirs of	1	1	Native	Nacogdoches	1
	[Office note]: Should be Juana Escalon see letter 14 Aug/39					
65	Earl Matthew	1	1	1824	Sabine	1
123	Earl William	1/3		1824	Sabine	1
198	Eastep Joseph	1	1	1821	Sabine	1
	Daniel Eastep Admr					
129	Easly James	1/3		1828	Sabine	1
	William Walker assignee					
376	Eddy Peleg	1/3		1827	Matagorda	2
327	Espinosa Jose' Maria	1	1	Native	Bexar	2
	Wood & Steele assignee					
372	Esqueda Justo	1/3		Native	Bexar	2
411	Escobar Francisco	1	1	Native	Bexar	2
	John W. Smith assignee					
36	Foster John Ray	1/12		1827	Austin	1
103	Fisher Reubin	1		1824	Austin	1
	James Cochrane assignee					
33	Fitzgerald John	1	1	Mar 1822	Fort Bend	1
132	Foster Moses A	1	1	Aug 30	Fort Bend	1
155	Foster Randolph	—	1	Dec 1829	Fort Bend	1
126	Fields Isiah S	—	1	1830	Liberty	1
79	Frazier William	1/3		1824	Milam	1
86	Frazier Stephen	1/3		1828	Milam	1
75	Fisher William	1/12		1823	Montgomery	1
137	Ford James	—	1	Jan 1830	Montgomery	1
152	Fulton Saml decd	—	1	Nov 17, 1829	Montgomery	1
	Hugh McGuffin Admr					

156	Flowers Elisha	1/2		1827	Matagorda	1
175	Fulcher James	1/3		1830	Washington	1
203	Fulcher John	—	1	1818	Washington	1
206	Furenash Robt Heirs of	1/3		1822	Washington	1
	Littleberry B. Franks asse					
263	Farmer James	1	1	1830	Washington	1
29	Fernandez Antonio	1	1	Native	Bexar	1
	John McMullen assignee					
111	Figeroa Juan	1	1	Native	Bexar	1
	Vincente Garza assignee					
153	Flores Bartolo	1	1	Native	Bexar	1
	Anderson M. Berry assignee					
192	Farias Eusebio	1	1	Native	Bexar	1
	John Sutherland assignee					
228	Flores Manuel	1	1	Native	Bexar	1
233	Flores Manuel Maria	1/3		Native	Bexar	1
	Wm H. Steele assignee					
250	Flores Guadalupe	1	1	Native	Bexar	1
	Jas A. Haynie assignee					
262	Flores Juan Garcia	1/3		Native	Bexar	1
	A. M. Berry assignee					
240	Fairchild Philo	—	1	Aug 1827	Fort Bend	2
15	Ford Wm W	1	1	1828	Sabine	1
242	Franks Burrell	1	1	1826	Liberty	2
168	Fishback Isaac H	1	1	Aug 1828	Red River	1
171	Fowler Bradford C	1	1	Aug 1830	Red River	1
299	Fizer John decd	1/3		Feb 1830	Red River	1
245	Foote Robert H	1/12		1830	S. Augustine	1
302	Fuqua Ephraim	—	1	1828	Montgomery	2
304	Fuqua Ephraim	1	—	1828	Montgomery	2
375	Furenash Charles	—	1	1820	Washington	2
378	Furenash Charles Jr	1/3		1822	Washington	2
379	Furenash Conrad	1/3		1820	Washington	2
382	Furenash John	1/12		1822	Washington	2
	L. B. Franks assignee					
	Falshear Churchill	—	1	1823	Austin	3
276	Flores Gaspar decd	1	1	Native	Bexar	2
	Saml A. Maverick assignee					
277	Fragoso Micaela	1	1	Native	Bexar	2
296	Fuentes Ana Maria	1	1	Native	Bexar	2
	Steele & Colquhoun assignee					
316	Franco Josefa	1	1	Native	Bexar	2
	Jno W. Smith assignee					
318	Flores Antonia	1	1	Native	Bexar	2
	Steele & Colquhoun assignee					
365	Flores Nicolas	1	1	Native	Bexar	2
370	Flores Jose' Sen	1	1	Native	Bexar	2
	John N. Seguin assignee					
448	Flores Francisco	1/3		Native	Bexar	2

	Jose' Antonio Navarro assignee					
461	Fuentes Juana	1	1	Native	Bexar	2
	John W. Smith assignee					
24	Garner David	1/3		1825	Jefferson	1
27	Garner Jacob H	1/3		1825	Jefferson	1
13	Green Richard	1	1	1830	Liberty	1
	By B. Green Curator					
15	Griffin W. R.	1/3		1830	Liberty	1
	Wm M. Logan legal representative					
44	Griger J. H.	1/3		1829	Liberty	1
	A. S. Roberts Curator					
61	Gill Presly	1	1	1824	Liberty	1
94	Gowen Nancy	1	1	1827	Liberty	
	By agent					
148	Green Amos	—	1	1828	Liberty	1
	James Knight Admr					
28	Galbraith George	7-1/3	lab	Oct 1830	Montgomery	1
31	Garrett Dickinson	—	1	June 1821	Montgomery	1
210	Greenwood Joel	—	1	1820	Montgomery	1
211	Greenwood Franklin J	1		1820	Montgomery	1
212	Greenwood H. B. decd	1	1	1820	Montgomery	1
	Joel Greenwood Admr					
84	Gove H. N.	1/12		1830	Matagorda	1
141	Graves Ransom O	1/3		1828	Matagorda	1
167	Gillilan Ellen	1	1	1829	Matagorda	1
178	George Nicholas	1	1	1829	Matagorda	1
243	George John	1/3		1830	Matagorda	1
244	George Holman	1/3		1829	Matagorda	1
247	George Jefferson	1/3		1829	Matagorda	1
250	George David	1/3		1829	Matagorda	1
266	George James	1/3		1829	Matagorda	1
	To heirs & representatives					
327	Griffith Noah	—	1	1829		
	Asa Yeamins purchaser					
328	Griffith Henry	—	1	1829	Matagorda	1
	Asa Yeamins purchaser					
31	Griffith Solomon	1	1	Jan 1826	Jackson	1
	To Clarissa Andrews & Abitha Ann Griffith heirs					
84	Gates William decd	—	1	1823	Washington	1
	Amos Gates Admr					
37	Gilchrist Anthonia J	1	1	1830	Jasper	1
4	Gaytan Margil	1	1	Native	Bexar	1
	John W. Smith assignee					
12	Guajardo Ignacio	1	1	Native	Bexar	1
	Geo Sutherland assignee					
39	Gaytan Agapito	1	1	Native	Bexar	1
	Ludovic Colquhoun assignee					
48	Gomez Antonio	1	1	Native	Bexar	1
	John W. Smith assignee					

59	Gaytan Felipe	1/3		Native	Bexar	1
	do	do				
68	Galvan Anselmo	1/3		Native	Bexar	1
	Nath Lewis assignee					
105	Gil Ignacio	1	1	Native	Bexar	1
	Wm K. Daingerfield & Wm E. Howth assignees					
114	Garcia Dolores	1	1	Native	Bexar	1
	Hezekiah Bissell assignee					
137	Garza Ignacio de la	1	1	Native	Bexar	1
	Juan N. Seguin assignee					
139	Galvan Jose' Maria	—	1	Native	Bexar	1
	John W. Smith assignee					
146	Gonzales Antonio	1/3		Native	Bexar	1
	Enoch Jones & Jno W. Smith assignees					
164	Gansava Luis	1/3		Native	Bexar	1
	Steele & Colquhoun assignees					
185	Gomez Francisco	1	1	Native	Bexar	1
197	Gomez Zaviana	1	1	Native	Bexar	1
	John Sutherland assignee					
199	Gonzales Antonio the older	1/3		Native	Bexar	1
	Nath Lewis assignee					
226	Garza Francisco de la	1	1	Native	Bexar	1
	Jose' Antonio Navarro assignee					
229	Garcia Maria de Jesus	1	1	Native	Bexar	1
	Wm H. Steele assignee					
230	Gimenez Maria Ignacia	1	1	Native	Bexar	1
	Jas A. Hynie assignee					
237	Guerra Maria de la Luz	1	1	Native	Bexar	1
	Enoch Jones & John W. Smith assignees					
240	Gomez Josefa	1	1	Native	Bexar	1
	Jas L. Hood & Wm H. Steele assignee					
242	Grande Lusgarda	1	1	Native	Bexar	1
	Steele & Colquhoun assignee					
248	Gaona Pedro	1/3		Native	Bexar	1
	Wm H. Steele assignee					
253	Guerra María Madelena	1	1	Native	Bexar	1
	Steele & Colquhoun assignees					
257	Guzman Juan Andres	1/3		Native	Bexar	1
	Wm H. Steele assignee					
259	Guerra Juan Jose'	1	1	Native	Bexar	1
	Wm Richardson assignee					
262	Garcia Juan alias Flores	1/3		Native	Bexar	1
	Andersen M. Berry assignee					
	Garretson Thomas	1/3		1829	Bastrop	
	Jas Smith Admr					
	Gilliland James	—	1	1828	Bastrop	1
	Garcier Francisco	1/3		1829	Bastrop	1
6	Grafton G.M.G.	1	—	Sep 1829	Robertson	1
7	Grafton G.M.G.	—	1	Sep 1829	Robertson	1

152   1830 Citizens of Texas

	T. Dillard assignee					
200	Green Benj M	—	1	1827	Liberty	2
52	Greenwood John	1	1	1818	Red River	1
75	Gragg Jacob	1/3		Dec 1820	Red River	1
99	Gragg Samuel	1/3		Dec 1820	Red River	1
106	Gragg John	1	1	Dec 1820	Red River	1
257	Gragg William	1	1	Dec 1820	Red River	1
300	Gragg Milton	1/3		Dec 1820	Red River	1
66	Garcia Jose' Maria	1	1	Native	Nacogdoches	1
	Albert Emanuel assignee					
115	Garcia Marcus Jr	1/3		Native	Nacogdoches	1
	Adolphus Sterne assignee					
171	Gallan Miguel	1	1	Native	Nacogdoches	1
	Wm Dankworth & Geo Bondes assignees					
173	Gertrudis Manuel	1	1	Native	Nacogdoches	1
	John Walling Jr assignee					
171	Gates Charles	1	1	1824	Nacogdoches	1
257	Groce Christian	1	1	1830	S. Augustine	1
293	Garrett William	1	1	1830	S. Augustine	1
296	Garrett Claiborne decd	3/4	1	1827	S. Augustine	1
327	Garrett Dickinson	2/3	1	June 1821	Montgomery	1
	Guthrie Robt decd	—	1	1825	Jackson	2
	per Admr					
71	Gaines E. P.	1	1	1822	Sabine	1
149	Gross Larkin	1	1	1828	Sabine	1
155	Gains John B	1/3		1824	Sabine	1
280	Gimenez Josefa	1	1	Native	Bexar	2
	Jas McGloin assignee					
282	Gonzales Ma Concepcion	1	1	Native	Bexar	2
285	Garcia Jose' de Jesus	1	1	Native	Bexar	2
	Steele & Colquhoun assignees					
292	Gil Leonardo	1	1	Native	Bexar	2
	Jose' Antonio Navarro assignee					
294	Gortaris Miguel	1	1	Native	Bexar	2
	Edward Dwyer assignee					
298	Garza Ma Josefa de la	1	1	Native	Bexar	2
	Anderson M. Berry assignee					
305	Gonsava Ascencion	1	1	Native	Bexar	2
	Wm K. Steele assignee					
322	Guerrera Guadalupe	1	1	Native	Bexar	2
	John McMullen assignee					
341	Gimenez Fermina	1	1	Native	Bexar	2
	do	do				
348	Garza Juana	1	1	Native	Bexar	2
	A. M. Berry assignee					
396	Garza Marcelino de la	1/3		Native	Bexar	2
	J. P. Henderson assignee					
401	Garza Rafael	1/3		Native	Bexar	2
416	Gamboa Ma Matilda	1	1	Native	Bexar	2
	Wm Richardson assignee					

451	Granada Francisco	1	1	Native	Bexar	2
466	Garza Vicente	1/3		Native	Bexar	2
18	Harmon David	1	1	1829	Jefferson	1
14	Hensley William	1/3		1830	Austin	1
112	Hunter Robert H	1/3		May 1829	Fort Bend	1
122	Hodge William	1/3		Dec 1825	Fort Bend	1
134	Hodge Alexander E	1/3		Aug 1830	Fort Bend	1
135	Hodge Alexander decd Alex E. Hodge Executor	—	1	Nov 1827	Fort Bend	1
136	Hodge Wm decd Heirs of Alex E. Hodge Guardian	—	1	April 1828	Fort Bend	1
147	Harris Abner	1/2	1	April 1826	Fort Bend	1
4	Hardin Franklin	1/12		1825	Liberty	1
23	Hardin William	—	1	1827	Liberty	1
34	Harper Clayton Wm Hardin Admr	1	1	1826	Liberty	1
46	Hardin B. W.	—	1	1827	Liberty	1
59	Hardin A. B.	1/2	1	1825	Liberty	1
127	Hubert Matthew	—	1	1828	Liberty	1
135	Janey James	1	1	1826	Liberty	1
155	Hardin Jerusha	1	1	1828	Liberty	1
2	Hibbens John decd Claibourn Stinett Admr	—	1	1829	Gonzales	1
6	Hall J. C.	1	1	1829	Matagorda	1
46	Hanson Thomas	1/3		1830	Matagorda	1
83	Hall Joseph decd	1	1	1829	Matagorda	1
143	Hall Elisha To heirs & representatives	—	1	1830	Matagorda	1
191	Hearst Lewis To heirs & representatives	1	1	1826	Matagorda	1
233	Hadden William	1/3		1825	Matagorda	1
234	Hadden Henry	1/3		1825	Matagorda	1
245	Hadden Jackson To heirs & representatives	1/3		1826	Matagorda	1
270	Huff John	1/2	1	1825	Matagorda	1
273	Haden John To heirs & representatives	1/4	1	1826	Matagorda	1
331	Hunter Ely To heirs & representatives	—	1	1826	Matagorda	1
341	Henderson C To heirs & representatives	1	1	1825	Matagorda	1
49	Hatch Sylvanus	—	1	1829	Jackson	1
103	Hall James Jr	—	1	1830	Washington	1
104	Hall John	3/4	1	June 3, 1830	Washington	1
163	Harbour George W	1/3		1830	Washington	1
186	House John P	1	1	1830	Washington	1
252	Hope Richard	1/3		1825	Washington	1
349	Hope Adolphus	3/4	1	1827	Washington	1
358	Hope Prosper	3/4	1	1825	Washington	1

ROBERT M. WILLIAMSON
History of Texas, John Henry Brown, St. Louis 1892

General Land Office Records 155

36	Howard Mordecai	1/3		1830	Jasper	1
7	Huizar Seferino	1	1	Native	Bexar	1
	John W. Smith assignee					
10	Herrera Toribio	1	1	Native	Bexar	1
	E. Jones & J. W. Smith assignees					
52	Herrera Francisco	1	1	Native	Bexar	1
	John W. Smith assignee					
86	Herrera Rafael	1	1	Native	Bexar	1
	Nathaniel Lewis assignee					
147	Huizar Jose' Francisco	1/3		Native	Bexar	1
	Jas McGloin assignee					
194	Hernandez Manuel	1	1	Native	Bexar	1
	John Sutherland assignee					
214	Hernandez Vicente	1/3		Native	Bexar	1
	Archibald Bass assignee					
239	Hernandez Candido	1	1	Native	Bexar	1
	Steele & Colquhoun assignees					
249	Herrera Pedro	1	1	Native	Bexar	1
	Jas L. Hood & Wm L. Steele assignees					
260	Huizar Carlos	1	1	Native	Bexar	1
	Wm Richardson assignee					
263	Hernandez Timoteo	1	1	Native	Bexar	1
	Edward Dwyer assignee					
	Harris Wiley	1/3		1822	Bastrop	1
	Thos Anderson assignee					
64	Harris Enoch	1	1	1823	Bastrop	1
	B. Sims assignee					
	Harris Isaac	—	1	1823	Bastrop	1
	Hornsby W. W.	1/3		1830	Bastrop	1
112	Hendrez Pedro	1/3		Native	Nacogdoches	1
269	Hendricks Thos D	1/3		1825	S. Augustine	2
311	Horton Alexander	2/3	1	1824	S. Augustine	2
314	Horton H. P.	1	1	1825	S. Augustine	2
378	Hanks Isabella	1	1	1829	S. Augustine	2
382	Hanks Wyatt	1	1	1828	S. Augustine	2
399	Hendricks Edwin	1	1	1824	S. Augustine	2
231	Holland Tapley decd	1/3		1823	Montgomery	2
	Francis Holland Admr					
409	Harbour James M	1/3		1824	Washington	2
34	Hall Burges	1/3		1828	Sabine	1
97	Hill Moses	1	1	1822	Sabine	1
	Hedy S. E. decd	1	1	1829	Austin	3
	Elizabeth Hedy Admrx					
	Hedy W. decd	1/3		1829	Austin	3
	Holley Arnold Admr					
295	Hernandez Jose' Maria	1	1	Native	Bexar	2
	John McMullen assignee					
319	Herrera Guadalupe	1	1	Native	Bexar	2
	Steele & Colquhoun assignees					

1830 Citizens of Texas

323	Herrera Victor	1/3		Native	Bexar	2
	John McMullen assignee					
339	Hernandez Ma Francisco	1	1	Native	Bexar	2
	do	do				
359	Herrera Hilario	1/3		Native	Bexar	2
	Wm E. Howth assignees					
384	Hernandez Geraldo	1	1	Native	Bexar	2
	Ambrosia Rodrigues assignee					
385	Hernandez Ma Juliana	1	1	Native	Bexar	2
393	Herrera Antonio	1/3		Native	Bexar	2
	J. P. Henderson assignee					
454	Hernandez Jose' Antonio	1	1	Native	Bexar	2
	Rhodes & Lewis assignees					
455	Herrera Blas	1	1	Native	Bexar	2
	Elisha A. Rhodes assignee					
473	Hernandez Juan Antonio	1	1	Native	Bexar	2
	Jose' Anto de la Garza assignee					
91	Henson David	1/3		1828	Harrisburg	1
115	Hudson John	1	1	Oct 1829	Robertson	2
	Delila McCullough assignee					
108	Hopkins Richard M	1	1	Dec 1824	Red River	1
109	Hopkins Jas E	1	1	Nov 1824	Red River	1
118	Hughart Edward	1	1	June 1830	Red River	1
177	Hampton Adam	1	1	Sep 1824	Red River	1
212	Humphres John decd	1	1	July 1818	Red River	1
216	Humphres John	1/3		1818	Red River	1
246	Hickman Asa	1/3		Sep 1825	Red River	1
305	Hansoame Aaron	1/3		1825	Red River	1
329	Hampton Andrew	1	1	March 1826	Red River	1
112	Hendrez Pedro	1/3		Native	Red River	1
6	Johnson John	1	1	1829	Jefferson	1
86	Jackson Isaac decd	—	1	1830	Austin	1
	Tillah Jackson Admr					
113	Jones Henry	—	1	Dec 1825	Fort Bend	1
114	Jones John decd	1/12		May 1826	Fort Bend	1
	Henry Jones Admr					
9	Johnston Hugh B	—	1	1825	Liberty	1
124	Jackson Hugh	1/3		1823	Liberty	1
134	Johns William	—	1	1830	Liberty	1
8	Jett James	1	1	1824	Jefferson	2
17	Isaacs William	1/3		1821	Milam	1
66	Jones Allen C	1	1	July 1, 1826	Montgomery	1
87	Jones Kelton	1/3		July 1, 1826	Montgomery	1
63	Ingram John	3/4		Dec 1823	Fayette	1
64	Ingram John	—	1	Dec 1823	Fayette	1
108	Ingram Seth	3/4	1	1823	Matagorda	1
211	Jameson Thomas	—	1	1824	Matagorda	1
13	Jones William	1/3		1829	Washington	1
84	Jordan William	1	1	1830	Jasper	1

120	Jaime Antonio	1	1	Native	Bexar	1
	Cornelius Van Ness assignee					
200	Ilaniz Prudencio	1	1	Native	Bexar	1
	John Sutherland assignee					
225	Juares Juan Nepomuceno	1/3		Native	Bexar	1
	John W. Smith assignee					
103	Ingram Elijah	1	1	1829	Bastrop	1
197	Jesus Colesto decd	1/3		Native	Fort Bend	2
	Randal Jones assignee					
199	Jones Emily	—	1	May 1830	Fort Bend	2
256	Jones Jno Brown	1/3		1830	Harrisburg	1
232	Jermain Saml	1/3		1830	Liberty	2
	E. T. Branch Admr					
337	James Joseph decd Heirs of	1	1	Nov 1824	Red River	1
17	Jones Geo W	1	1	1829	S. Augustine	1
114	Johnson William	1/12		1822	S. Augustine	1
192	Irvine W. D.	1/3		1830	S. Augustine	1
197	Irvine Josephus S	1/3		1830	S. Augustine	1
309	James Thomas	—	1	1830	Montgomery	2
394	Jones John H	—	1	1830	Washington	2
444	Jackson Isaac decd	—	1	1827 or 28	Washington	2
	To heirs					
	Isaacs George	1/3		1821	Houston	2
156	Isaacs William	1	1	1824	Sabine	1
353	Jaime Maria Josefa	1	1	Native	Bexar	
	Rufus McLellan assignee					
50	Kuykendall Adam	1/3		1822	Austin	1
51	Kuykendall Thornton P	1/3		1825	Austin	1
58	Kelly William	1	1	1828	Austin	1
101	Kuykendall William	3/4	1	1830	Austin	1
117	Kuykendall John	1/3		1827	Austin	1
82	Kuykendall Robt H	1	1	July 1825	Fort Bend	1
148	Kuykendall Joseph	—	1	Aug 1823	Fort Bend	1
78	Kirkham S	—	1	1830	Liberty	1
141	Knight James	—	1	1828	Liberty	1
101	Kinnard William	1/3		May 1830	Montgomery	1
107	Kinnard Michael	1/3		May 14, 1830	Montgomery	1
126	Kinnard A. D. Sen	—	1	May 14, 1830	Montgomery	1
127	Kinnard A. D. Jr	1/3		May 14, 1830	Montgomery	1
7	Kornegay David S	1/3		April 1830	Fayette	1
157	Kinchelow Lewis	1/12		1824	Matagorda	1
180	Kemp Caleb	1	1	1829	Matagorda	1
	To heirs & representatives					
205	Kemp Jonathan	1	1	1830	Matagorda	1
239	Kincheloe Augustus	1/3		1830	Matagorda	1
18	Kerr James	—	1	1824	Jackson	1
315	Kennetly Everton	1	1	1830	Washington	1
202	Kinne Louisiana	—	1	May 1828	Fort Bend	2
224	Kigans John	1/3		May 1828	Fort Bend	2

158   1830 Citizens of Texas

#	Name			Date	Place	
225	Kigans Washington	1/3		May 1828	Fort Bend	2
439	Kiggins James decd	—	1	1825	Washington	2
	To Nancy Kiggins & Heirs					
	Kuykendall Barzillai	3/4	1	1821	Austin	3
	Kuykendall Gibson	—	1	1821	Austin	3
141	Lightfoot John W decd	1/12		Aug 1830	Fort Bend	1
	Wilson T. Lightfoot Admr					
46	Lightfoot Wilson T	1/12		April 1830	Fort Bend	1
31	Lanier Benjamin	—	1	1829	Liberty	1
60	Lani Alfred	1	1	1830	Liberty	1
75	Louis Frederick	1/3		1830	Liberty	1
	A. S. Roberts Curator					
88	Labadie N. D.	1	1	1830	Liberty	1
17	Landrum William	—	1	Jan 1830	Montgomery	1
18	Landrum Letitia	—	1	Jan 20, 1830	Montgomery	1
50	Lindley Joseph	—	1	April 1827	Montgomery	1
88	Lindley James N	1/3		April 4, 1827	Montgomery	1
95	Landrum John	—	1	Dec 30, 1829	Montgomery	1
44	Lockhart Charles	—	1	1830	Gonzales	1
23	Linn John J	1	1	1830	Victoria	1
44	Lawrence Adam	3/4	1	1822	Washington	1
100	Lynch James	—	1	1825	Washington	1
192	Lawrence Samuel	—	1	Feb 1830	Washington	1
215	Lewis William Sen	1	1	1828	Jasper	1
71	Lewis James	1/3		1828	Jasper	1
56	Landin Cruz	1	1	Native	Bexar	1
	Luciano Navarro assignee					
63	Lazo Xavier	1/3		Native	Bexar	1
	John W. Smith assignee					
99	Leon Francisco de	1	1	Native	Bexar	1
	Erasmo Seguin assignee					
103	Leal Manuel	1	1	Native	Bexar	1
	Wm P. Delmour assignee					
135	Leal Jose' Maria	1	1	Native	Bexar	1
	R. T. Higginbotham assignee					
159	Losoya Toribio decd	1	1	Native	Bexar	1
	John W. Smith Admr					
217	Leal Melchor	1		Native	Bexar	1
251	Leal Maria Ignacia	1	1	Native	Bexar	1
	Steele & Colquhoun assignees					
258	Leal Juana Isidora	1	1	Native	Bexar	1
	Wm Richardson assignee					
264	Leal Jeronomo	1	1	Native	Bexar	1
270	Lazo Chapita	1	1	Native	Bexar	1
	Jas R. Cooke assignee					
	Litton John	1	1	1827	Bastrop	1
181	Lewis Franklin	1/3		1829	Bastrop	1
351	Lynch N. Heirs of	—	1	1828	Harrisburg	1
	F. Lynch Admr					

352	Lynch Benj F	1/3		1828	Harrisburg	1
	G. M. Patrick Guardian					
210	Levins Joseph	1	1	1818	Red River	1
217	Levins James decd	1/3		1818	Red River	1
273	Levins Nicholas	1/3		1820	Red River	1
280	Lawson Josiah D	1	1	Feb 1823	Red River	1
330	Lankford Benjamin	1	1	Sep 1825	Red River	1
338	Landford Eleanor	1	1	1826	Red River	1
341	Levins Jas decd Heirs of	1	1	1819	Red River	1
351	Levins Jas Jr decd	1/3		1818	Red River	1
46	Linn Charles	1/3		1830	Victoria	2
	J. J. Linn Admr					
48	Linn Edward	1/12		May 2d 1830	Victoria	2
28	Lazarine Julian	1/3		Native	Nacogdoches	1
	Jas Riley assignee					
108	Lavigena Jose' Palmora	1/3		Native	Nacogdoches	1
	A. Sterne assignee					
128	Love John G	1	1	June 1826	S. Augustine	1
273	Lewis Geo W	1/3		1826	S. Augustine	2
397	Loyd Wm M	1/3		1828	S. Augustine	2
318	Larrison Thomas	1/3		1829	Montgomery	2
410	Lockhart Saml decd	—	1	1830	Washington	2
	To heirs					
429	Lee Hiram decd	1/12		1830	Washington	2
	Landford Woodman Admr					
164	Lowe Joel	1/3		1828	Sabine	1
175	Lowe Isaac	1	1	1828	Sabine	1
206	Lowe Jesse	1	1	1828	Sabine	1
350	Linville Aaron	1/3		1823	Matagorda	2
	To heirs & representatives					
355	Lidstrand Ludowick	1/3		1828	Matagorda	2
290	Leal Francisco	1	1	Native	Bexar	2
	Jose' Luis Carrajal assignee					
297	Leiba Ma Gertrudis Gil de	1	1	Native	Bexar	2
	Ignacio Castro assignee					
307	Losoya Isabel	1	1	Native	Bexar	2
	Steele & Colquhoun assignee					
317	Losoya Concepcion	1	1	Native	Bexar	2
	A. M. Berry assignee					
349	Leal Maria de Jesus	1	1	Native	Bexar	2
	Wm E. Howth assignee					
355	Leal Josefa	1	1	Native	Bexar	2
	Edward Dwyer attorney					
383	Lombraño Antonio	1/3		Native	Bexar	2
407	Longaville Francois	1/3		Native	Bexar	2
463	Lazo Antonio	1	1	Native	Bexar	2
	Nath Lewis assignee					
465	Leal Jose' Antonio	1		Native	Bexar	2
11	Masters Henry	—	1	Jan 1829	Houston	1

24	Murchison Martin	—	1	1829	Houston	1
56	Masters Jacob Sen	—	1	1829	Houston	1
57	Masters Jacob Jun	—	1	1829	Houston	1
19	McDonald William	—	1	1828	Jefferson	1
23	McFaden Jr Wm	—	1	1830	Jefferson	1
39	Marshall Hugh L.	1/3		1829	Austin	1
40	Marshall John Senr	1	1	1828	Austin	1
41	Marshall John Jr	1	1	1830	Austin	1
42	Marshall Samuel	1	1	1829	Austin	1
43	Marshall Joseph	1/3		1830	Austin	1
55	Martin John decd	3/4		1826	Austin	1
	McHenry Winburn assignee of one third					
32	Morton John S	1	1	April 1822	Fort Bend	1
65	McCoy Alexander	1/12		July 1823	Fort Bend	1
	James Perry Admr					
80	McGary Isaac	—	1	1830	Fort Bend	1
14	Martin Josiah C	1/3		1825	Liberty	1
17	McCoy James	1	1	1827	Liberty	1
103	Martin James	—	1	1825	Liberty	1
	J. C. Martin Admr					
178	Moore William	1		1829	Liberty	1
1	McFadin James	—	1	1825	Jefferson	2
5	Morrow Thos	1	1	1827	Milam	1
	John Teal Admr					
13	Monroe Daniel	—	1	1830	Milam	1
36	Milton Eliel	1/3		1829	Milam	1
	J. L. Hood Admr					
44	Maiden Isaac	1/12		1824	Milam	1
1	McIntire William	3/4	1	Aug 1825	Montgomery	1
8	McIntire Robert	1/3		1825	Montgomery	1
27	McGuffin John F	1/12		Jan 24, 1829	Montgomery	1
53	McDonald William	—	1	June 1830	Montgomery	1
69	Montgomery Edley	1/12		Oct 1829	Montgomery	1
76	McIntire Margaret	—	1	Aug 1825	Montgomery	1
213	Miller Ruth	—	1	1821	Montgomery	1
60	Miles Sarah	—	1	June 1820	Fayette	1
61	McDaniel Benj	1/3		June 1830	Fayette	1
3	McHenry John	—	1	June 1830	Victoria	1
11	McCoy Thomas	1/2	1	1823	Matagorda	1
163	Mason Robert	1	1	1822	Matagorda	1
	To heirs & representatives					
177	Morrisson William	1	1	1829	Matagorda	1
209	McFarlane Dugald	—	1	1830	Matagorda	1
226	Moore James	—	1	1829	Matagorda	1
329	McCroskey John	1/3		1826	Matagorda	1
	To heirs & representatives					
5	Menefee George	1/3		Nov 1830	Jackson	1
12	McNutt Nicholas	1	1	1826	Jackson	1
38	Menefee Thomas	—	1	1830	Jackson	1

39	Menefee Heirs of	—	1	1830	Jackson	1
40	Menefee John S	1/3		1830	Jackson	1
71	McNutt Elizabeth heirs of	1	lab	1824	Jackson	1
80	Milican William	—	1	1830	Jackson	1
82	Middleton Saml P	3/4	1	1829	Jackson	1
235	McCoy Prospect	1/3		1828	Washington	1
232	Menchaca Jose' Maria	1/3		Native	Bexar	1
	Wm H. Steele assignee					
265	Menchaca Antonio	1	1	Native	Bexar	1
	Edwin Alexander assignee					
	Miller John R	1	1	1822	Bastrop	1
	McDevitt John	1/3		1830	Bastrop	1
153	McLaughlin Wm	1	1	1822	Bastrop	1
	Miller Samuel	—	1	1822	Bastrop	1
	C. B. Stewart assignee					
8	Morrow Thomas	—	1	Dec 1829	Robertson	1
65	Millican A. A.	1	1	June 1822	Robertson	1
81	Morrow Thomas	1		Dec 1829	Robertson	1
89	Mumford David	—	1	1828	Robertson	1
106	McCullough Jas A	1/3		1830	Robertson	1
168	Murray Bartlett	1/3		1828	Harrisburg	1
280	McCormick Michael	1/3		1830	Harrisburg	1
282	McCormick A. decd	—	1	1830	Harrisburg	1
	To widow & heirs					
359	McGahea James	—	1	1830	Harrisburg	1
	[Note]: Cert. to McGaley					
250	Munson M. B.	—	1	1825	Liberty	1
	Eli Whiting Admr					
15	McKinney Blackly	1/3		1824	Red River	1
36	McKinney Hiram C	1	1	Nov 1826	Red River	1
40	Morris Lee	1/3		Oct 1824	Red River	1
41	McKinney Daniel	1/3		Nov 1824	Red River	1
58	Morris Robert	1/3		Feb 1824	Red River	1
60	McKinney G. Y.	1/3		Nov 1824	Red River	1
70	Milam Jefferson	1	1	Nov 1826	Red River	1
89	McKinney Ashley	1	1	Nov 1824	Red River	1
98	McKinney Collin	1	1	Dec 1824	Red River	1
100	McKinney Younger S	1/3		Dec 1824	Red River	1
149	Mitchell Reuben	1/3		Dec 1824	Red River	1
170	McDaniel James	1/3		Dec 1820	Red River	1
204	Morton John	1	1	Dec 1826	Red River	1
283	McKinney Wm	1	1	Nov 1824	Red River	1
306	Martin Gabriel decd	1	1	1828	Red River	1
333	Mays Squire	1	1	Sep 1826	Red River	1
339	McKinney Jas decd Heirs of	1	1	Nov 1824	Red River	1
248	Millican John H	1/3		Previous to 1830	Washington	1
250	McCoy Green	1/3		1828	Washington	1
304	Miller Saml S	—	1	1823	Washington	1
36	Martinez Bruno	1/3		Native	Bexar	1

162   1830 Citizens of Texas

John W. Smith assignee						
43 Martinez Manuel	1	1	Native	Bexar	1
Anderson W. Berry assignee						
44 Morales Francisco Flores	1	1	Native	Bexar	1
Nathaniel Lewis assignee						
47 Montoya Nepomuceno	1	1	Native	Bexar	1
Geo Sutherland assignee						
64 Mancho Pablo	1	1	Native	Bexar	1
Steele & Colquhoun assignees						
97 Martinez Ferman	1/3		Native	Bexar	1
Joseph Baker assignee						
102 Menchaca Ramon	1/3		Native	Bexar	1
Wm H. Daingerfield assignee						
124 Mata Miguel	1/3		Native	Bexar	1
A. M. Berry assignee						
132 Menchaca Leonor	1	1	Native	Bexar	1
Hezekiah Bissell assignee						
156 Montalvo Simon	1/3		Native	Bexar	1
John S. Simpson assignee						
165 Montalvo Juan Manuel	1	1	Native	Bexar	1
Steele & Colquhoun assignees						
166 Martinez Jose' Maria Sen	1	1	Native	Bexar	1
do	do				
167 Martinez Jose' Maria Jr	1/3		Native	Bexar	1
do	do				
174 Menchaca Gertrudis	1	1	Native	Bexar	1
do	do				
179 Moraido Jose' Maria	1/3		Native canclld	Bexar	1
190 Montes Jose'	1/3		Native	Bexar	1
Wm H. Steele assignee						
193 Mancha Tomas	1/3		Native	Bexar	1
John Sutherland assignee						
205 Mendez Nicolas	1	1	Native	Bexar	1
Jas A. Haynie assignee						
219 Molino Jose' Maria	1/3		Native	Bexar	1
Archibald W. Bass assignee						
221 Menchaca Manuel	1	1	Native	Bexar	1
Alex Dunlap assignee						
227 Martinez Nicolas	1/3		Native	Bexar	1
John Sutherland assignee						
231 Maldonado Juan	1	1	Native	Bexar	1
11 Milhome Francis	—	1	June 1830	Nacogdoches	1
58 Medro Batiste	1/3		Native	Nacogdoches	1
R. H. Douglass assignee						
90 Martinez Guadalupe	1	1	Native	Nacogdoches	1
R. H. Douglass assignee						
151 Morales Jose' R	1/3		Native	Nacogdoches	1
R. H. Douglass assignee						
201 Mora Jose' Sefrana	1	1	Native	Nacogdoches	1

General Land Office Records 163

	Horatio Griffith assignee					
221	Mendez Vicente	1	1	Native	Nacogdoches	1
	J. Walling & Elisha Roberts assignees					
222	Martinez Juan Jose'	1/3		Native	Nacogdoches	1
	do	do				
297	Moore Daniel T. D.	—	1	1826	S. Augustine	2
365	McGinness John	1	1	1830	S. Augustine	2
387	McDonald Donald	—	1	1830	S. Augustine	2
323	Montgomery Wm decd	—	1	1822	S. Augustine	2
	John Montgomery Admr					
402	Mencha Jose' Francisco	1	—	1824	Washington	2
425	Mancha Antonio		11	1823	Washington	2
	Thos Gay assignee					
426	Mancha Antonio	—	1	1823	Washington	2
	do	do				
	Moore John	—	1		Houston	2
	Mitchell Thos S	1	1	March 1830	Houston	2
	McLean Hannah	—	1	1825	Houston	2
2	McKean John	1	1	1829	Sabine	1
25	Martin Henry	1	1	1822	Sabine	1
35	Maxamillian John Sen	1	1	1822	Sabine	1
42	Mason James	1	1	1830	Sabine	1
56	Murphy Willis	—	1	1825	Sabine	1
115	McKim James	1	1	1825	Sabine	1
117	McKim William	1/3		1825	Sabine	1
121	McKim Charles	1/3		1827	Sabine	1
130	Mason William	1	1	1830	Sabine	1
172	Melton Elizabeth	1	1	1822	Sabine	1
67	Maxamillian John Jr	1	1	1825	Sabine	1
	D. A. Cunningham assignee					
279	Martinez Pedro	1	1	Native	Bexar	2
	Saml A. Maverick assignee					
281	Montes Jose'	2/3	1	Native	Bexar	2
	Jos L. Hood assignee					
301	Martinez Gregoria	1	1	Native	Bexar	2
	Jno W. Smith assignee					
309	Martinez Juana	1	1	Native	Bexar	2
	Wm Richardson assignee					
313	Moraido Jose' Maria	1	1	Native	Bexar	2
	Steele & Colquhoun assignees					
328	Martinez Josefa	1	1	Native	Bexar	2
329	Martinez Juana	1	1	Native	Bexar	2
	John McMullen assignee					
345	Martinez Refugia	1	1	Native	Bexar	2
	Wm E. Howth assignee					
352	Martinez Josefa	1	1	Native	Bexar	2
	Clapten & Mosely assignees					
361	Martinez Cesario	1/3		Native	Bexar	2
	Andrew W. White assignee					

164   1830 Citizens of Texas

373	Moral Martina del	1	1	Native	Bexar	2
	George Sutherland assignee					
379	Martinez Lugarda	1	1	Native	Bexar	2
388	Martinez Anavato	1	1	Native	Bexar	2
402	Martinez Manuel the Elder	1	1	Native	Bexar	2
	Ambrosio Rodrigues assignee					
405	Mancha Benino	1/3		Native	Bexar	2
410	Mancha Agapo	1/3		Native	Bexar	2
	[Note]: Annulled by previous sale					
421	Muñoz Eugenio	1/3		Native	Bexar	2
	Wm Richardson assignee					
428	Mesa Maria Ignacia	1	1	Native	Bexar	2
	do	do				
429	Menchaca Serafina	1	1	Native	Bexar	2
	do	do				
433	Martinez Juan	1/3		Native	Bexar	2
	J. P. Henderson assignee					
434	Menchaca Rafael	1/3		Native	Bexar	2
	Wm Richardson assignee					
438	Martinez Maria Dolores	1	1	Native	Bexar	2
	Jas A. Haynie assignee					
444	Menchaca Carmel	1	1	Native	Bexar	2
447	Menchaca Ma de los Santos	1	1	Native	Bexar	2
453	Monjaras Manuel	1	1	Native	Bexar	2
187	Newman Felix	1	1	1828	Liberty	1
28	Norton James	1/3		1826	Matagorda	1
6	Navarro Nepomuceno	1/3		Native	Bexar	1
	John W. Smith assignee					
54	Navarro Nicolas	1	1	Native	Bexar	1
	Steele & Colquhoun assignees					
98	Niesta Jose' Bernardino	1/3		Native	Bexar	1
	John W. Smith assignee					
116	Navarro Desedoro	1/3		Native	Bexar	1
	Antonio de la Garza assignee					
141	Nuñez Nepomuceno	1/3		Native	Bexar	1
	Jose' Antonio de la Garza assignee					
175	Nuñez Maria Josefa	1	1	Native	Bexar	1
	Steele & Colquhoun assignees					
	Neill George J	1/3		1830	Bastrop	1
232	Neil John A	—	1	1830	Harrisburg	1
266	Nicholson Stephen	—	1	1830	Harrisburg	1
358	Nash Hannah	—	1	1828	Harrisburg	1
261	Nall Martin G	1	1	Jan 1820	Red River	1
278	Nall John	1	1	Jan 1820	Red River	1
327	Nugent John	1	1	Nov 1826	Red River	1
168	Neato Jose'	1/3		Native	Nacogdoches	1
	W. W. Wingfield assignee					
172	Nevaro Lorenzia	1/3		Native	Nacogdoches	1
	J. S. & L. M. Thorne assignee					

397	Newman Jonathan	—	1	1830	Washington	2
	New William	1/12		1830	Jackson	2
354	Noble Benjamin	1/3		1829	Matagorda	2
	Joseph O'Neil assignee					
375	Ness David	1/3		1827	Matagorda	2
	Heirs & representatives					
362	Nieto Andres	1/3		Native	Bexar	2
443	Navarro Nepomuceno	2/3	1	Native	Bexar	2
20	Orr Thomas	1/3		1824	Liberty	1
225	Osburn John L	1	1	1826	Matagorda	1
230	Osburn Charles	1/3		1826	Matagorda	1
240	Osburn Thomas	1/3		1826	Matagorda	1
106	Ortega Facundo	1/3		Native	Bexar	1
	Daingerfield & Howth assignees					
128	Ortiz Jose'	1/3		Native	Bexar	1
	Hezekiah Bissell assignee					
136	Ortiz Juan	1	1	Native	Bexar	1
	Steele & Colquhoun assignees					
163	Ortiz Pablo	1	1	Native	Bexar	1
	Hezekiah Bissell assignee					
176	Otelo Matias	1/3		Native	Bexar	1
	Steele & Colquhoun assignees					
180	Olivar Casimero	1/3		Native	Bexar	1
	do	do				
268	Olivarri Placido	1/3		Native	Bexar	1
	Colvin Emmons assignee					
270	Owin Mary decd	1	1	1828	Harrisburg	1
	J. Owins & P. Reels Curators					
174	Oment Washington	1/3		1824	Sabine	1
395	Ortiz Jesus	1/3		Native	Bexar	2
	Wm Richardson assignee					
436	Ortega Desidora	1	1	Native	Bexar	2
	Jas H. Haynie assignee					
11	Pattillo George A	—	1	1830	Jefferson	1
104	Perry Polly	1	—	1830	Austin	1
	James Cochrane assignee					
61	Perry James	—	1	Dec 1830	Fort Bend	1
81	Pentecost Jr Geo W	1/3		Jan 1828	Fort Bend	1
107	Pentecost Geo S	—	1	May 1830	Fort Bend	1
6	Pruett Martin	1/3		1823	Houston	2
	Daniel Parker assignee					
20	Pruett Levi	1	1	1823	Houston	2
49	Pruett Jesse	1	—	1824	Liberty	1
	A. S. Roberts Curator					
60	Pool John C	1/3		Native of Tex.	Milam	1
148	Parker Jesse	—	1	Mar 12, 1822	Montgomery	1
39	Ponton Andrew	1/12		1830	Gonzales	1
40	Ponton Isabella	—	1	1830	Gonzales	1
	Widow of Wm Ponton. Andrew Ponton assignee					

12	Page J. W.	3/4	1	1824	Matagorda	1
275	Payton J. C.	—	1	1826	Matagorda	1
276	Payton Alex G	1/3		1829	Matagorda	1
293	Pankey Mary Ann	—	1	1828	Washington	1
93	Pry Peter B	—	1	1829	Jasper	1
32	Perez Gregorio	1	1	Native	Bexar	1
	Ignacio Castro assignee					
46	Perieda Maria del Pilar	1	1	Native	Bexar	1
	John W. Smith assignee					
55	Padilla Rafael	1	1	Native	Bexar	1
	R. T. Higginbotham assignee					
67	Pacheco Jose'	1	1	Native	Bexar	1
	Hezekiah Bissell assignee					
78	Peña Jacinto	1/3		Native	Bexar	1
	Steele & Colquhoun assignees					
79	Padilla Gabriel	1/3		Native	Bexar	1
	Steele & Colquhoun assignees					
96	Perez Antonio	1	1	Native	Bexar	1
	Wm H. Steele assignee					
100	Pacheco Antonio	1/3		Native	Bexar	1
	Steele & Colquhoun assignees					
170	Pacheco Weneslado	1/3		Native	Bexar	1
	do	do				
172	Perez Francisco	1/3		Native	Bexar	1
	do	do				
188	Perez Manuel	1/3		Native	Bexar	1
245	Perez Valentine	1	1	Native	Bexar	1
	Steele & Colquhoun assignees					
254	Pulido Maria Encarnacion	1	1	Native	Bexar	1
	do	do				
255	Perez Maria Jeusita de	1	1	Native	Bexar	1
	Ludovic Colquhoun assignee					
269	Perez Francisco the elder	1/3		Native	Bexar	1
	Wm H. Steele assignee					
	Pace Dempsey	1/3		1828	Bastrop	1
	L. C. Cunningham assignee					
	Pruett Elisha	1/3		1820	Bastrop	1
	Pace James R	1/3		1828	Bastrop	1
	Pace Gideon Heirs of	1	1	1828	Bastrop	1
229	Pruett Beasly	1	1	1825	Liberty	2
248	Pruett Jesse	—	1	1824	Liberty	2
	A. S. Roberts Curator					
310	Pendergrass Sarah	1	1	1825	Red River	1
	Wm M. Williams Admr					
	Pearson J. H.	1/12		1829	Milam	2
102	Peneda Jose' Maria	1/3		Native	Nacogdoches	1
	A. Sterne assignee					
150	Piertecha	1	1	Native	Nacogdoches	1
	Isaac Lee assignee					

General Land Office Records 167

221	Prather Freeman	1	1	1821	S. Augustine	1
279	Peterson John	—	1	1822	Montgomery	2
53	Peck Ancil C	1/3		1830	Fannin	1
	Pruett Jacob	—	1	1822	Houston	2
39	Parker Matthew	1	1	1822	Sabine	1
159	Pace John	1/3		1826	Sabine	1
163	Pace Isaac F	1/3		1826	Sabine	1
370	Philips Isham B	—	1	1827	Matagorda	2
	Pettus Saml O decd	—	1	1830	Austin	3
	John York Admr					
	Pettus John F	1	1	1830	Austin	3
308	Porras Ma Caledonia de	1	1	Native	Bexar	2
	Wm H. Steele assignee					
334	Perez Rosalia	1	1	Native	Bexar	2
	Jas R. Cooke assignee					
336	Padilla Jose'	1/3		Native	Bexar	2
	Wm E. Howth assignee					
350	Pacheco Policarpia	1	1	Native	Bexar	2
	A. M. Berry assignee					
368	Perez Malena	1	1	Native	Bexar	2
	Jas H. Morris assignee					
376	Perez Domingo	1	1	Native	Bexar	2
382	Planes Juana Maria	1	1	Native	Bexar	2
422	Pacheco Luciano	1/3		Native	Bexar	2
	Wm Richardson assignee					
440	Perez Jose' Antonio	1/3		Native	Bexar	2
	John W. Smith assignee					
145	Quevedo Guillermo	1	1	Native	Bexar	1
	Anderson M. Berry assignee					
3	Rice Clinton A	1	1	1828	Houston	1
6	Rice Lemuel	1	1	1828	Houston	1
49	Russell Reuben R	—	1	1829	Houston	1
72	Roberts William	1	1	1826	Austin	1
21	Rector Claiborne	1	1	Jan 1830	Fort Bend	1
98	Roark Leo	1/3		Jan 1825	Fort Bend	1
11	Rogers James	1/3		1823	Liberty	1
98	Rogers Robert	1	—	1823	Liberty	1
	Jas Rogers admr					
20	Ritchie Uel	1/12		1826	Jefferson	2
	Hannah Simmons admrx					
21	Ritchie William	1	1	1826	Jefferson	2
	Hannah Simmons admrx					
68	Rivers Antonio	—	1	Native	Montgomery	1
	Benaniah Jones assignee					
26	Rogers Raleigh	—	1	Dec 1830	Montgomery	1
37	Rigby Benjamin	—	1	Dec 1829	Montgomery	1
48	Robinson Geo W	1/3		Dec 24, 1829	Montgomery	1
56	Robbins Cintha	—	1	May 1, 1829	Montgomery	1
58	Robert William	1/3		1826	Montgomery	1

1830 Citizens of Texas

74	Raper Daniel	1/3		Feb 1830	Montgomery	1
131	Rankin Wm M	—	1	Dec 1829	Montgomery	1
177	Rankin Thos B	1/3		Dec 29, 1829	Montgomery	1
201	Robbins Joshua	1		1818	Montgomery	1
202	Robbins Joshua James Mitchell assignee	—	1	1818	Montgomery	1
203	Robbins Rebecca In trust for her heirs	1	—	June 1818	Montgomery	1
204	Robbins Rebecca In trust for her heirs	—	1	June 1818	Montgomery	1
205	Robinson William	—	1	Dec 24, 1829	Montgomery	1
62	Robinson James	—	1	Dec 1830	Fayette	1
26	Reeder Mary Ann	1	1	1825	Matagorda	1
71	Robinson George	1/2	1	1822	Matagorda	1
94	Robinson Oscar	1/3		1830	Matagorda	1
217	Reed Ely To heirs & representatives	1	1	1829	Matagorda	1
223	Ryon William To heirs & representatives	1	1	1830	Matagorda	1
241	Rawles George To heirs & representatives	1/3		1826	Matagorda	1
274	Roberts Redding	1/3		1830	Washington	1
279	Robinson Andrew Jr.	1	1	1821	Washington	1
191	Robinson S. W. decd Mary Fulcher Admrx	1	1	1824	Washington	1
3	Rivas Jose' Geo Sutherland assignee	1/3		Native	Bexar	1
8	Rodrigues Ambrosio	1	1	Native	Bexar	1
13	Rolen Francisco Enoch Jones & John W. Smith assignee	1	1	Native	Bexar	1
19	Rubio Cristobal Jas F. Johnson assignee	1/3		Native	Bexar	1
24	Rivas Juan Manuel John McMullen assignee	1/3		Native	Bexar	1
27	Ramirez Edourdo do	1 do	1	Native	Bexar	1
42	Ruiz Francisco Antonio	1	1	Native	Bexar	1
49	Reyes Damasio de los Wm E. Howth assignee	1/3		Native	Bexar	1
70	Rodriguez Rufino Saml McCullouch assignee	1	1	Native	Bexar	1
73	Ramos Vicente Geo Sutherland assignee	1/3		Native	Bexar	1
107	Rosas Jose' Maria Anto de la Garza assignee	1/3		Native	Bexar	1
144	Ruiz Esmerigildo decd John W. Smith Admr	2/3		Native	Bexar	1
157	Ruiz Esmerigildo Joseph Baker assignee	1/3		Native	Bexar	1

General Land Office Records 169

160	Rodriguez Antonio	1	1	Native	Bexar	1
	Steele & Colquhoun assignees					
181	Rodriguez Justo	1	1	Native	Bexar	1
	Steele & Colquhoun assignees					
187	Rubio Ramon	1	1	Native	Bexar	1
195	Rendon Joaquin	1	1	Native	Bexar	1
	John Sutherland assignee					
271	Ramon Rosario	1	1	Native	Bexar	1
	Saml A. Maverick assignee					
	Rosseau Mosea	—	1	1829	Bastrop	1
82	Robertson Geo W	—	1	Nov 1829	Robertson	1
215	Randen John Heirs of		1	May 1828	Fort Bend	2
	G. W. Parker Guardian					
	Rowark Jackson	1/3		1830	Austin	2
	Wm Jones assignee					
271	Roberts Geo H	1	1	1828	Harrisburg	1
342	Richardson Geo F	1/12		1830	Harrisburg	1
214	Robinson James	—	1	1825	Liberty	2
240	Rankin James M	—	1	1827	Liberty	2
208	Robbins John	1	1	1818	Red River	1
302	Ragsdale Wm decd	1	1	1825	Red River	1
40	Rios Raphael	1	—	1829	Victoria	2
	J. J. Linn assignee					
255	Ruddle Archibald decd	1	1	1824	St. Augustine	1
300	Ray Robert	3/4	1	Dec 1822	Montgomery	2
319	Robbins John	1	—	1819	Montgomery	2
320	Robbins John	—	1	1819	Montgomery	2
321	Robbins Thomas decd	1/3		1819	Montgomery	2
	John Robbins Admr					
322	Robbins Nat. decd	—	1	1819	Montgomery	2
	John & Lucy Robbins Admrs					
451	Robinson Wm decd	—	1	1830	Washington	2
	Robt Stevenson Admr					
	Rice Joseph	1	1	1828	Houston	2
	Roberts Charles	1/12		1830	Houston	2
20	Renfro Isaac	1	1	1825	Sabine	1
23	Rians James	1/3		1829	Sabine	1
152	Richards Francis	1/3		1830	Sabine	1
	David Renfro assignee					
180	Robert Wm	1/3		1822	Sabine	1
	Saml Stivers assignee					
	Robbins Early decd	1/12		1823	Austin	3
	Mary Robbins Admx					
	Robert Josias	1/3		1830	Austin	3
273	Ruiz Fernando decd	1	1	Native	Bexar	2
	Juan Andres Zambrano Admr					
300	Rodrigues Jose'	1	1	Native	Bexar	2
	Hez Bissell assignee					
311	Ramos Vicente	2/3	1	Native	Bexar	2
	Geo Sutherland assignee					

1830 Citizens of Texas

342	Roble Maria Ignacia	1		1	Native	Bexar	2
343	Ruiz Bernardino	1		1	Native	Bexar	2
374	Reyes Jose' de los	1/3			Native	Bexar	2
	Wm H. Daingerfield assignee						
390	Ramon Ma Canuta	1		1	Native	Bexar	2
	Wm S. Richardson assignee						
394	Rivera Matilde	1		1	Native	Bexar	2
	Wm S. Richardson assignee						
397	Ramirez Locario	1/3			Native	Bexar	2
	do	do					
406	Rodrigues Ma Antonio	1		1	Native	Bexar	2
414	Rodrigues Gil	1/3			Native	Bexar	2
	Wm Richardson assignee						
427	Ramos Maria Luisa	1		1	Native	Bexar	2
	do	do					
679	Ross John Heirs of	1		1	1820	Red River	6
7	Stephenson William	—		1	1828	Jefferson	1
28	Scott Noah	1		1	1829	Austin	1
77	Stephenson Thomas B	1/3			1826	Austin	1
34	Shipman John M	1/3			April 1826	Fort Bend	1
59	Shipman Edward decd	3/4			July 1825	Fort Bend	1
	John M. Shipman Admr						
90	Scott Simpson	1/3			May 1830	Fort Bend	1
93	Scott David	1/3			May 1829	Fort Bend	1
115	Stiles William decd	—		1	May 1826	Fort Bend	1
	Henry Jones Admr						
10	Spencer Nancy	—		1	May 1824	Fort Bend	1
23	Smith Luther	1		1	1829	Houston	2
29	Smith William	1/3			1830	Liberty	1
62	Swail Amy	—		1	1824	Liberty	1
65	Smith Silas	1		1	1830	Liberty	1
85	Stephenson Elisha	1			1829	Liberty	1
109	Strang Samuel	—		1	1825	Liberty	1
175	Self Taylor B	1/3			1823	Liberty	1
	Wm M. Logan Admr						
176	Self Jacob E	—		1	1823	Liberty	1
	Wm M. Logan Admr						
143	Stubblefield Thos	1		1	1830	Liberty	1
29	Smith James B	1/3			1830	Jefferson	2
90	Scott James W	—		1	1826	Milam	1
3	Shannon Jacob	—		1	1821	Montgomery	1
221	Stewart C. B.	3/4			1830	Montgomery	1
80	Smith Willie	3/4			April 9, 1828	Montgomery	1
81	Smith Willie	—		1	April 9, 1828	Montgomery	1
146	Shannon Margaret	—		1	Dec 1821	Montgomery	1
3	Stinett Claibourn	1/12			1830	Gonzales	1
19	Smothers Archibald	1/3			1829	Gonzales	1
20	Smally Andrew decd	1		1	1826	Matagorda	1
	To heirs & representatives						

General Land Office Records 171

151	Scott Levy P	1/3		1830	Matagorda	1
267	Scott John	1/3		1829	Matagorda	1
278	Shropshier H	1/3		1829	Matagorda	1
	To heirs & representatives					
279	Shropshier Harrison	1	1	1829	Matagorda	1
	To heirs & representatives					
343	Selkerk William	—	1	1825	Matagorda	1
	To heirs & representatives					
2	Stapp Darwin M	3/4	1	Dec 1830	Jackson	1
4	Scott Andrew	1/3		1827	Jackson	1
7	Scarbrough Paul	1/3		1830	Jackson	1
17	Scott Jonathan	3/4	1	1829	Jackson	1
24	Stapp Elijah	—	1	1830	Jackson	1
64	Scott Patrick heirs of	—	1	1829	Jackson	1
94	Stapp William P	1/12		1830	Jackson	1
100	Sutherland George	—	1	1830	Jackson	1
114	Stevens John M Jr	1	1	1829	Washington	1
218	Stevens Thomas	—	1	1830	Washington	1
272	Stephens Jas R	1/3		1830	Washington	1
283	Sessum Michael	—	1	Previous 1830	Washington	1
59	Slaydon John	1/3		1825	Jasper	1
83	Slaydon Arthur	1	1	1825	Jasper	1
26	Selinas Pablo	1	1	Native	Bexar	
	John McMullen assignee					
61	Sosa Manuel	1/3		Native	Bexar	1
	Steele & Colquhoun assignees					
115	Silba Matias	1	1	Native	Bexar	1
	Anto de la Garza assignee					
126	Sanchez Antonia Gomez	1	1	Native	Bexar	1
	Cornelius van Ness assignee					
161	Saes Jose' Maria	1/3		Native	Bexar	1
	Steele & Colquhoun assignees					
162	Suniga Maraquita	1	1	Native	Bexar	1
	do	do				
189	Sanchez Trinidad	1	1	Native	Bexar	1
	John Sutherland assignee					
198	Sanchez Jose' Maria	1/3		Native	Bexar	1
	John Sutherland assignee					
220	Santos Guadalupe de los	1/3		Native	Bexar	1
252	Sosa Maria Francisca	1	1	Native	Bexar	1
	Steele & Colquhoun assignees					
267	Selva Maria Josefa	1	1	Native	Bexar	1
	Cornelius van Ness assignee					
	Smithwick N[oah]	1	—	1827	Bastrop	1
	L. C. Cunningham assignee					
	Sims Bartlett	—	1	1822	Bastrop	1
	Standiferd Jacob	1/3		1829	Bastrop	1
	Standiferd Elizabeth	—	1	1829	Bastrop	1
42	Smith John D	3/4	1	March 1828	Robertson	1

172 1830 Citizens of Texas

171	Shipman Jas R	1/3		Aug 1829	Fort Bend	2
227	Shipman Moses G	1/3		May 1828	Fort Bend	2
232	Stafford Adam	1/3		Nov 1825	Fort Bend	2
85	Spilman Jas H	1	1	1830	Harrisburg	1
167	Sawyer Jane	1	1	1830	Harrisburg	1
286	Somers W. W.	3/4	1	Jan 1830	Harrisburg	1
330	Strange James	1/3		1828	Harrisburg	1
234	Smith Stephen	—	1	1830	Liberty	2
239	Smith Wm M	1	1	1827	Liberty	2
241	Scott Rozelia	1	1	1830	Liberty	2
246	Shaw Jones	1	1	1829	Liberty	2
110	Saul Chas	1/3		1825	Robertson	2
153	Slingland William	1	1	Aug 1820	Red River	1
	Simons John	1/3		1830	Milam	2
	Selinas Pedro	—	1	Native	Milam	2
	John Teal Admr					
109	Sana Silvestus	1/3		Native	Nacogdoches	1
	K. H. Douglas assignee					
229	Stiddum Samuel	1	1	1828	S. Augustine	1
334	Sythe Francis	1	—	1828	S. Augustine	2
384	Simms James	1	1	1830	S. Augustine	2
233	Sandifer M.D.	—	1	1823	Montgomery	2
305	Sidic Antonio	1/3		1828	Montgomery	2
306	Sidic John B	—	1	1824	Montgomery	2
330	Scriers James	—	1	1824	Montgomery	2
332	Sidic Peter decd	—	1	1825	Montgomery	2
	Antonio Sidic Admr					
442	Stevens Jacob	—	1	1826	Washington	2
443	Stewart John W decd	1	1	1830	Washington	2
	Jas D. Allcorn Admr					
	Sheriden John decd	—	1	1829	Houston	2
	Lucinda Sheridan Admx					
	Shupe Samuel	1/12		1827	Jackson	2
	Scott John Heirs of	1/12		1828	Jackson	2
89	Smith Major	—	1	1828	Sabine	1
212	Smith Philip	1/3		1830	Sabine	1
345	Savage Emilius	—	1	1830	Matagorda	2
	Smith William decd	1/3		1824	Austin	3
	Wm Hunter Admr					
288	Santos Guadalupe de los	2/3	1	Native	Bexar	2
	Jas L. Hood assignee					
310	Sanches Juana Francisca	1	1	Native	Bexar	2
	Geo Sutherland assignee					
344	Sanches Barbara	1	1	Native	Bexar	2
	Thos W. Mather assignee					
378	Sandoval Beriana	1	1	Native	Bexar	2
408	Sitala Margarita	1	1	Native	Bexar	2
	Juan Andres Zambrano assignee					
420	Sanches Antonio	1/3		Native	Bexar	2

	Wm Richardson assignee					
424	Sierra Noverto	1/3		Native	Bexar	2
	do	do				
446	Sotela Baltasar	1/3		Native	Bexar	2
	Saml A. Maverick assignee					
460	Segura Ma Antonia	1	1	Native	Bexar	2
	Wm. H. Steele assignee					
120	Tyler Daniel	1/12		1826	Austin	1
10	Thompson Hiram M	1/3		May 1824	Fort Bend	1
11	Thompson Jesse decd	—	1	May 1824	Fort Bend	1
	Hiram M. Thompson Admr					
19	Thompson Jas M	1/3		Jan 1824	Fort Bend	1
20	Thompson Jesse	1/3		Jan 1824	Fort Bend	1
55	Tanner Edward	1	—	1827	Liberty	1
56	Tanner Edward	—	1	1827	Liberty	1
66	Targenton Burton	1	1	1827	Liberty	1
73	Tanner James R	1/3		1829	Liberty	1
108	Taylor Jane	—	1	1830	Liberty	1
154	Tier Polly	1	1	1828	Liberty	1
	E. T. Branch agent					
17	Tevis Andrew J	1/3		1827	Jefferson	2
22	Tevis George W	1/4		1824	Jefferson	2
25	Tevis Nancy	1/2	1	1825	Jefferson	2
18	Teal Richard S	1/3		1827	Milam	1
19	Teal John	1	1	1827	Milam	1
16	Tong John B	3/4	1	March 1827	Montgomery	1
218	Tumlinson Peter	1	—	1830	Montgomery	1
222	Tumlinson Peter	—	1	1830	Montgomery	1
49	Tanehill Jesse C	—	1	April 1828	Fayette	1
56	Thompson John decd	1	1	Dec 1825	Fayette	1
	J. S. Lester atty for heirs					
17	Trudo Margaret	—	1	Fall of 1826	Victoria	1
29	Tone Thomas J	1/2	1	1826	Matagorda	1
135	Thompson Thomas	1/3		1829	Matagorda	1
	To heirs & representatives					
136	Thompson Isham	1	1	1829	Matagorda	1
140	Thompson Charles	1/3		1829	Matagorda	1
	To heirs & representatives					
49	Turner Elizabeth	—	1	1826	Jackson	1
40	Tarrin Manuel	1	1	Native	Bexar	1
	L. Colquhoun assignee					
71	Tarrin Vicente	1/3		Native	Bexar	1
	Steele & Colquhoun assignees					
104	Torres Maria Lucia	1	1	Native	Bexar	1
	Wm E. Howth assignee					
112	Texada Clemente	1	1	Native	Bexar	1
	Hezekiah Bissell assignee					
125	Texada Jose'	1/3		Native	Bexar	1
	John W. Smith assignee					

174   1830 Citizens of Texas

140	Toro Guadalupe del	1/3		Native	Bexar	1
	Steele & Colquhoun assignees					
168	Texada Sebastian	1/3		Native	Bexar	1
	Steele & Colquhoun assignees					
	Turner Winslow	3/4	1	1827	Bastrop	1
	Trammel James	1/3		1828	Bastrop	1
	Trammel Burke	1/3		1829	Bastrop	1
	Jas Trammell Admr					
215	Taylor Anson	1	1	1828	Liberty	2
	Chas Wilcox Admr					
236	Thompson Wm	1	1	1830	Liberty	2
132	Tinnin Caleb	1/3		Nov 1829	Robertson	2
	J. Tinnin Admr					
25	Taylor Josiah	1/3	1	1829	Victoria	2
26	Taylor Creed	1/3		1829	Victoria	2
	Jas Tumblinson Atty					
29	Taylor William	—	1	1830	Victoria	2
37	Taylor Joshua	—	1	1830	Victoria	2
	To Hepsibeth Taylor and heirs					
9	Texada Ventura	—	1	Native	Nacogdoches	1
	K. H. Douglass assignee					
147	Tuscano Santiago	1/3		Native	Nacogdoches	1
	James Smith assignee					
129	Thomas Shadrac D	1	1	1826	S. Augustine	1
130	Teal Edward J.	1	1	1826	S. Augustine	1
	By assignee					
246	Teal Henry decd	1/3		1828	S. Augustine	1
247	Thomas Jackson	1/3		1823	S. Augustine	1
371	Thomas Theophilus	1	1	1825	S. Augustine	2
307	Taylor Levi decd	—	1	1830	Montgomery	2
	Henry Fanthorpe Admr					
	Tyler Edward	1	1	1823	Houston	2
79	Thompson Thomas	—	1	Dec 1824	Fayette	2
173	Toban Joan Ferrian	1	1	1822	Sabine	1
	Thos Garner assignee					
315	Torres Guadalupe	1	1	Native	Bexar	2
	Wood & Steele assignees					
386	Treviño Ramon	1	1	Native	Bexar	2
387	Treviño Maria de Jesus	1	1	Native	Bexar	2
	Van Ness & Daingerfield assignees					
391	Trevino Jose'	1/3		Native	Bexar	2
	Richardson & Henderson assignees					
418	Tarrin Juan Maria	1/3		Native	Bexar	2
	Wm Richardson assignee					
425	Toro Margarita del	1	1	Native	Bexar	2
	John W. Smith assignee					
426	Toro Mateo del	1/3		Native	Bexar	2
	Wm Richardson assignee					
430	Toro Cipriano del	1	1	Native	Bexar	2

	John W. Smith assignee					
445	Tigerina Jose' Manuel	1/3		Native	Bexar	2
	Saml A. Maverick assignee					
20	Urriegas Juan Manuel	1	1	Native	Bexar	1
	Jose' Anto de la Garza assignee					
50	Urrutia Vicente	1/3		Native	Bexar	1
	John W. Smith assignee					
119	Urrutia Maria Rosa	1	1	Native	Bexar	1
	Howth & Daingerfield assignees					
142	Urrutia Jose' Maria	1/3		Native	Bexar	1
	Steele & Colquhoun assignees					
173	Urriegas Ramona	1	1	Native	Bexar	1
	do	do				
304	Urrutia Encarnacion	1	1	Native	Bexar	2
	Jas A. Haynie assignee					
471	Urrutia Juan Anto	1	1	Native	Bexar	2
	John W. Smith assignee					
159	Vince Richard	1/2	1	Aug 1824	Fort Bend	1
221	Vandom Isaac	1/2	1	1826	Matagorda	1
290	Vandivier C. H.	—	1	1830	Matagorda	1
77	Vess Jonathan	—	1	1829	Jackson	1
85	Veremendi Marco Anthony	1/3		Native	Bexar	1
108	Varcinas Andres	1/3		Native	Bexar	1
	Joseph Baker assignee					
113	Villegas Jesusa Perez de	1	1	Native	Bexar	1
	R. T. Higginbotham assignee					
118	Velasco Juan Jose'	1/3		Native	Bexar	1
	Hezekiah Bissell assignee					
169	Valverde Luciano	1/3		Native	Bexar	1
	Steele & Colquhoun assignees					
184	Villagran Gabriel	1/3		Native	Bexar	1
	Daingerfield & Howth assignees					
235	Valverde Anselmo	1/3		Native	Bexar	1
	Wm H. Steel assignee					
238	Villanueva Candelario	1/3		Native	Bexar	1
	Steele & Colquhoun assignees					
162	Vince John T decd	1/12		May 1828	Fort Bend	2
	Richard Vince Admr					
257	Vince Wm	1/3		1830	Harrisburg	1
	by his father Allen Vince					
314	Villagran Gabriel	2/3	1	Native	Bexar	2
	Daingerfield & Howth					
324	Valdez Geronimo	1	1	Native	Bexar	2
	Joel McMullen assignee					
346	Vasquez Juan	1	1	Native	Bexar	2
	Steele & Colquhoun assignees					
356	Valdez Jose' Antonio	1/3		Native	Bexar	2
377	Villapando Pablo decd	1	—	Native	Bexar	2
	Ma Anta Mancha Admrx					
458	Varcinas Trinidad	1/3		Native	Bexar	2

176   1830 Citizens of Texas

	John W. Smith assignee					
462	Vela Sebastiana	1	1	Native	Bexar	2
	Nath Lewis assignee					
29	Ware Mary	1	1	1830	Houston	1
40	Wilson George W	—	1	1830	Houston	1
99	Wright Felix decd	1/3		1830	Houston	1
	James Cochrane Admr					
8	Wickson Asa	3/4	1	July 1826	Fort Bend	1
15	Wickson Dyrun	1/3		July 1826	Fort Bend	1
16	Wickson Eli	1/3		July 1826	Fort Bend	1
100	Wickson Cyrus	1/3		Jan 1830	Fort Bend	1
35	Whitlock Robert	1/3		1827	Liberty	1
37	Whitlock Mary	—	1	1827	Liberty	1
70	Wallis E.H.R.	1	1	1824	Liberty	1
76	Whitcher N	1/3		1829	Liberty	1
	By Atty Saml Rogers pr Curator A. S. Roberts					
77	White James T	1	1	1828	Liberty	1
83	Winfrie A.B.J.	1	1	1827	Liberty	1
86	Williams William	1/3		1828	Liberty	1
92	Winfrie J. F.	1	1	1827	Liberty	1
120	Wilcox Charles	1/3		1830	Liberty	1
129	Walless William	1	1	1825	Liberty	1
172	Williams Hezekiah	1/3		1828	Liberty	1
	By agent					
181	Welch C. P.	—	1	1829	Liberty	1
194	Williams T. J.	1	1	1827	Liberty	1
	A. B. Hardin Admr					
14	Williams Absalom			1828	Jefferson	2
51	Webb Charles	1	1	1822	Milam	1
51	Webb Isham G	1	1	Mar 1830	Montgomery	1
67	Wallace Caleb	—	1	Feb 1825	Montgomery	1
138	Whittaker Peter decd	1	1	1821	Montgomery	1
	Joseph Barnett Admr					
166	Whiteside John J	—	1	Dec 1824	Montgomery	1
168	Walker Tandy H	1	1	Mar 11, 1828	Montgomery	1
169	Walker Danl heirs of	1	1	Mar 11, 1828	Montgomery	1
170	Walker John C	1	1	Mar 11, 1828	Montgomery	1
175	Wingfield Jane, Matilda	1	1	Feb 1825	Montgomery	1
	& Henry. Caleb Wallace Guardian					
176	Wingfield H (insane)	1/3		Feb 1825	Montgomery	1
	Caleb Wallace Guardian					
199	Winn James	—	1	May 1825	Montgomery	1
67	Woods Zadock	—	1	Sep 1823	Fayette	1
70	Woods Norman	—	1	Dec 1825	Fayette	1
5	Williams Thos J	1	1	1825	Matagorda	1
27	Wightman Elias R	3/4	1	1825	Matagorda	1
55	Williams Thomas Sen	—	1	1823	Matagorda	1
80	Wilkins Jane	—	1	1824	Matagorda	1
124	Williams John decd	1	1	1824	Matagorda	1
	To heirs & representatives					

General Land Office Records 177

126	Williams R. H.	—	1	1825	Matagorda	1
186	Wallace J. W. E.	—	1	1830	Matagorda	1
197	Williams Henry	—	1	1829	Matagorda	1
201	Williams George W	1/3		1828	Matagorda	1
207	Williams N. B.	1	1	1828	Matagorda	1
	To heirs & representatives					
312	Woodward Alvin	1/3		1829	Matagorda	1
313	Wightman B	—	1	1829	Matagorda	1
	To heirs & representatives					
334	Wightman John	1/3		1824	Matagorda	1
	To heirs & representatives					
1	White James G	1/3		1830	Jackson	1
20	Whitson Benjamin	1	1	1830	Jackson	1
21	Williams Malkijah	3/4	1	1827	Jackson	1
32	White John M	1	1	1830	Jackson	1
37	White Samuel A	1/3		1830	Jackson	1
44	White Peter	—	1	1826	Jackson	1
74	Ward Russel	3/4	1	1830	Jackson	1
113	Walker John M	1	1	1829	Washington	1
133	Williamson J. W.	1/4		1829	Washington	1
138	Wood William R	1/3		1830	Washington	1
145	Williams Jno decd	1	1	1829	Washington	1.
	W. Y. McFarland Admr					
86	Wilson William	1	1	1830	Jasper	1
	Williams John	1/3		1825	Bastrop	1
	Wm Cannen assignee					
	Wilbarger Josiah	—	1	1827	Bastrop	1
	Webber John F	1/2	1	1824	Bastrop	1
	Walters John B	—	1	1825	Bastrop	1
	Williamson R. M.	3/4	1	1826	Bastrop	1
	Wells Weyman F	1/3		1829	Bastrop	1
	Wells Martin J	1/3		1829	Bastrop	1
192	Wickson Barna	—	1	June 1830	Fort Bend	2
87	Wilcox James	1/3		1830	Harrisburg	1
	Thos J. Gazley assignee					
339	Whitehead Edward P	1/12		1830	Harrisburg	1
213	Wilcox Charles	2/3	1	1830	Liberty	2
218	White Wm M	1/3		1825	Liberty	2
249	Whiting Saml	—	1	1827	Liberty	2
92	Ward James	1	1	April 1820	Red River	1
121	Ward Wm B decd	1/3		April 1820	Red River	1
127	Wright Geo W	1	1	Jan 1830	Red River	1
142	Ward Wm C	1	1	Dec 1830	Red River	1
151	Wilson William	1/3		Feb 1830	Red River	1
169	Ward Jos J	1	1	Dec 1830	Red River	1
194	Ward James J Senr	1	1	April 1820	Red River	1
271	Wright Francis G	1/3		Jan 1828	Red River	1
303	Wright Wm F decd	1/3		1828	Red River	1
307	Witmore Geo C decd	1	1	1820	Red River	1

1830 Citizens of Texas

340	Willett Andrew decd Heirs of	1	1	Dec 1819	Red River	1
348	Wood Joseph decd heirs of	1/3		1820	Red River	1
42	Wiley John	1	1	1828	Victoria	2
42	Wiley William To John Wiley heir	1/3		1828	Victoria	2
262	Warren Daniel Jacob Shannon Admr	1/3		1830	Montgomery	2
263	Wallace James	—	1	1826	Montgomery	2
295	Whittaker Alex	1/12		1822	Montgomery	2
393	Wootton Thos J	—	1	1830	Washington	2
395	Wootton Greenville T.	1/3		1830	Washington	2
	Ware Hardy	1	1	1825	Houston	2
	White Archibald S	—	1	1830	Jackson	2
1	Walker Jacob decd Absalom F--- Admr	1	1	1829	Sabine	1
126	White Elizabeth	1	1	1828	Sabine	1
193	Warren Lewis L. C. Randolph Admr	1	1	1825	Sabine	1
199	White Martin D D. A. Cunningham assignee	1	1	1822	Sabine	1
211	White Benjamin	1	1	1823	Sabine	1
356	Wright Buford	1	1	1826	Matagorda	2
	Whitehead N	1/12		1826	Austin	3
	Westner Christian	1/3		Feb 1830	Fayette	
392	Ximenes Casiano Richardson & Henderson assignees	1/3		Native	Bexar	2
419	Ximenes Ponceano Wm Richardson assignee	1/3		Native	Bexar	2
459	Ximenes Jose' Joseph L. Hood assignee	1/3		Native	Bexar	2
280	Ximenes Josefa	1	1	Native	Bexar	2
29	York James A	1/3		1829	Austin	1
30	York Thomas decd Jas A. York & Noah Scott Admr	1	1	1829	Austin	1
321	Yeamins Elias To heirs & representatives	1/3		1829	Matagorda	1
322	Yeamans Erastus To heirs & representatives			1829	Matagorda	1
325	Yeamans Joseph	1	1	1829	Matagorda	1
326	Yeamans Asa	—	1	1829	Matagorda	1
53	Ynojosa Benturo R. T. Higginbotham assignee	1	1	Native	Bexar	1
247	Ybarbo Jesus Steele & Colquhoun assignees	1/3		Native	Bexar	1
56	Ybarbo Ramigeo By Chas Chevalier & Bernard Pantaleon	1/3		Native	Nacogdoches	1
67	Ybarbo Gregorio do	1/3 do		Native	Nacogdoches	1
81	Ybarbo Maximilian	1/3		Native	Nacogdoches	1

General Land Office Records 179

	Barnard Panteleon assignee					
87	Ybarbo Miguel	—	1	Native	Nacogdoches	1
	Msrs. L. Pattent & Wm M. Keeling assignees					
142	Ybarbo Candraises	1/3		Native	Nacogdoches	1
	Jesse Burdett assignee					
143	Ybarbo Jesus	1/3		Native	Nacogdoches	1
	do	do				
186	Ybarbo Manuel M	1/3		Native	Nacogdoches	1
	Saml Maas assignee					
190	Ybarbo Luciana	1/3		Native	Nacogdoches	1
	Jas Walling assignee					
224	Ybarbo Jose' Antonio	1/3		Native	Nacogdoches	1
	Jesse Burdett assignee					
245	Ybarbo Juan Benigno	1/3		Native	Nacogdoches	1
	Stephen Collins assignee					
249	Ybarbo Antonio	1	1	Native	Nacogdoches	1
	Jesse Burdett assignee					
250	Ybarbo Martin	—	1	Native	Nacogdoches	1
	Robt F. Maillard assignee					
279	Ybarbo Jose' Antonio	1/3		Native	Nacogdoches	1
	Jesse Burdett assignee					
154	Ybarbo Manual M	1/3		Native	Nacogdoches	1
	Saml Maas assignee					
286	Yglesias Dionisio	1	1	Native	Nacogdoches	2
400	Yndo Miguel	1/3		Native	Nacogdoches	2
	York John	1	1	1825 or '26	Austin	3
64	Zuber Wm P	1/3		June 18, 1830	Montgomery	1
30	Zambrano Juan Andres	1	1	Native	Bexar	1
154	Zerda Nemecio de la	1	1	Native	Bexar	1
237	Zuber Abraham	—	1	June 1830	Montgomery	2
312	Zerda Pedro de la	1	1	Native	Bexar	2
	Hez Bissel assignee					
325	Zota Maria Pabla	1	1	Native	Bexar	2
	John W. Smith assignee					
337	Zepeda Catarina	1	1	Native	Bexar	2
	Philip Dimmitt assignee					
357	Zunega Jose'	1	1	Native	Bexar	2
	John McCrary assignee					
472	Zepeda Vicente	—	1	Native	Bexar	2
18	Casillas Juan	1/3		Native	Bexar	1
	Henry R. Allen assignee					
439	Leon Ma Josefa de	1	1	Native	Bexar	2
	Wm Richardson assignee					

DAVID G. BURNET
President ad-interim 1836

— *History of Texas,* **John Henry Brown,** St. Louis 1892

CLERK'S RETURNS AND REPORTS

The Boards of Land Commissioners were appointed in 1838 in each land district (generally coinciding with an original county) to receive petitions from the residents of their district for the right to land. The Clerk of the Board was required by law to make prompt returns of the lists of the persons who had been given certificates entitling them to vacant land. The General Land Office referred to these reports when a survey based on a certificate might be filed for a patent. A few reports are in the form of complete minutes bound in manuscript books but most are in vertical files. They are not complete and are not part of the file which is separately kept on each grant.

All these secondary files were read and information on all settlers arriving by 1830 or earlier was abstracted. The date of arrival appears in the petitions because the law required it among the questions asked of the claimants. It was critical in determining the size of the land entitlement. All the names and information not contained in "Index A" are tabulated here. Most of the personal facts were given in reply to the specific questions of the land law; occasionally extra bits of information will appear.

Many of the oldest settlers applied for land for the first time in 1838 because sections of Texas were not served by the Mexican land system in an orderly fashion, or they delayed because fees had to be paid. Others appeared to obtain the additional labor (177 acres) or whatever augmentation the new law allowed. Whatever the cause, most of the land owners of Texas appear in these records in some way in clearing up their affairs or taking advantage of liberalized regulations.

The reasons for grants of odd size are several and one of the accounts of the complex history of Texas land may need to be consulted to extract maximum information from each record.

CLERK'S RETURNS
Information not contained in
"Index A"

No.	Grantee	Leagues	Labors	Date of Emigr.	Remarks
		AUSTIN CO.			
January 1838 Return No. 1					
81	Micajah Bird decd	—	1	1826	Oliver Jones Admr
95	James Small estate of	1	1	1827	
	For the use of Nathaniel Townsend				
99	Felix Wright decd	1/3		1830	James Cochrane Admr
February 1838 Return No. 2					
	Jackson Howard	1/3		1830	William Jones assignee
	Charles Breen	—	1	1830	
May 1838 Return No. 4					
	Job Fisher	1/3 less 1/4		1830	
	Rich M. Swift	1	1	1829	
June 1838 Return No. 5					
Elizabeth Kuykendall representative of the heirs of					
	Jos [Jas] Kuykendall decd	1 labor		1825	
	Baker Larkin estate	1/3		1828	J.W.Burton Admr
July 1838 Return No. 6					
	Isaac Weldon	369 ac		1830	
August 1838 Return No. 7					
	John Campbell	1/3		1828	
October 1838 Return No. 8					
250	Gared E. Groce Jr.	1	1	1822	
	By George A. Denett representative				
January 1839 Return No. 9					
259	Robert Lewis estate	1/3		1825	Franklin Lewis Admr
		BASTROP CO.			
Return No. 2, March 1838					
	Elias Marshall	1/3		1829	
	Saml Wooddy	—	1	1830	To heirs
	Malcom M. Hornsby	1/3		1830	
	Jno B. Berry	1/3		1827	
	Edward Jinkins	—	1	1830	To heirs
	Elisha Barton	—	1	1830	
	Matthew Moss	2/3	1	1830	
	Stephen Cottle	—	1	1827	To heirs
	Sylvanus Cottle	370 ac		1827	
	Washt Curtis	370 ac		1825	To heirs

James Stewart	1/3		1823	
Charles Tapp	1/3		1825	
Lenard Cottle	1/3		1827	
William Harris	1/3		1824	
Samuel Hazlatt	—	1	1827	
Solimon Duty	—	1	1822	
James Standiferd	—	1	1829	
Joseph Duty	—	1	1822	
Reuben Hornsby	—	1	1820	
Samuel Highsmith	—	1	1827	
Martin Wells	—	1	1829	
Joseph Hornsby	1/3		1830	

Return No. 3, April 1838

William Duty	1/3		1822
Cassia Stewart	—	1	1823

Return No. 4, July 1838

J. D. Morris	370 ac	1827

Return for July 1839 through January 1840

John A. Haynie	1/3	Novr 1829
John B. McNautt	1/3	1826

BEXAR CO.

March 1838 Return No. 2

472	Vicente Tejada	1	1	Native	Widower at D of Ind
473	Juan Antonio Hernandez	1	1	Native	Widower at D of I
	Jose' Antonio de la Garza atty & assignee				
477	Antonio Diaz	1	1	Native	Married at D of Ind
478	Manuel Arocha	1/3		Native	By assignee
479	Luz Navarrete	1	1	Native	Widow at D of Ind
	By assignee				
480	Joaquin del Toro Alias Chiver. Known by his mothers				
	name of Chiver	1	1	Native	By assignee
481	Jose' Olivarri	1	1	Native	Married at D of Ind
	By assignee				
482	Ignacio Castillo	1	1	Native	Married at D of Ind
	By assignee				
483	Louis Romero	1	1	Native	Married at D of Ind
	By assignee				
484	Antonia Torres	1	1	Native	Widow at D of Ind
485	Marcelo Garcia	1/3		Native	By assignee
	In Texian service at the siege of Bexar, prisoner in Matamoros, escaped.				
486	Iginio Tejada	1	1	Native	Married at D of Ind
	By assignee				
487	Julio Contis	1	1	Native	Single. By assignee
488	Concepcion Losoya	1	1	Native	Widow at D of Ind
	By assignee				
489	Pedro Flores	1	1	Native	Single at D of Ind
	But has since married				
490	Gertrudis Diaz, widow of	1	1	Native	By assignee

Crescensio Fuentes. Was a widow at the Dec of Independence

April 1838

491	Maria Jesus Ximenes	1	1	Native	Mother of children By assignee
492	Cornelio Gonzales	1/3		Native	Single
493	Alejandro Gortar	1	1	Native	By assignee

Widower at Dec of Independence. After D of Ind went to Laredo to daughter, now lives at Bexar

494	Gregorio Hernandez	1/3		Native	By assignee
495	John N. Seguin	2/3	1	Native	Married at D of I
496	Ana Petra dela Peña	1	1	Native	Widow. By assignee
497	Maria Teresa Bernal	1	1	Native	Mother of children By assignee
498	Manuel Lopez	1/2		Native	By assignee

Report No. 3 May 1838

501	Nasario Manchaca	1	1	Native	Married at D of Ind
506	Manuel Arciniega	1	1	Native	
507	Manuel Zepeda	1	1	Native	
	By Maria Antonia Padilla Admx				
508	Benito Rocha	1	1	Native	
509	Manuel Hernandez	1/3		Native	By assignee
510	Crenscensio Rodriguez	1	1	Native	
	Married at D of Ind. By assignee				
512	Juana Carillo	1	1	Native	Widow at D of Ind. By assignee
513	Manuel Tejada	1	1	Native	Married at D of Ind. By assignee
514	Manuel Estrada	1/3		Native	By assignee
516	Follaria Dolores Diaz	1	1	Native	Widow at D of I By assignee
517	Estevan Villareal	1/3		Native	By assignee
519	Juan Ignacio Diaz	1	1	Native	Married at D of Ind By assignee
523	Maria Trinidad Guerra	1	1	Native	Widow at D of I By assignee
524	Andres Fileno	1/3		Native	By assignee
525	Crescencio Montes	1	1	Native	Married at D of I By assignee
526	Cayetano Leruia	1	1	Native	Married at D of I By assignee
527	Clemente Diaz	1/3		Native	By assignee
528	Jose' Maria Contis	1/3		Native	By assignee
529	Maria Malena Miranda	1	1	Native	Mother of children By assignee
530	Rafael Vasquez	1	1	Native	Married at D of Ind By assignee
531	Maria Francisca dela Garza	1	1	Native	
	By assignee. Mother of children				
532	Ignacio Flores	1	1	Native	Widow

533 Juan Jose' Cervantes	1	1	Native	Married at D of I

11 May 1838

535 Nepomuceno Flores	1	1	Native	Was single at D of
Independence has since married				
536 Manuel Chaves	1	1	Native	Was widower at D of I
537 Juan Jose' Berban	1/3		Native	
538 Miguel Franco	1/3		Native	By assignee
Was a soldier in Col. Seguin's Company				
539 Thomas Pereida	1	1	Native	Married at D of Ind
541 Miguel Pechea	1	1	Native	Married at D of Ind

28 May 1838

542 Jose' Antonio dela Garza	1	1	Native	By assignee
543 Eugenio Navarro decd	1/3		Native	John W. Smith Admr
544 Gertrudis Rodriguez	1	1	Native	by assignee
Widow at Declaration of Independence				
546 Vicente dela Garza	1	1	Native	by assignee
Married at the Declaration of Independence				
547 Juan Manuel Rivas	1	1	Native	by assignee
Married at the Declaration of Independence				
548 Trinidad Garcia	1	1	Native	by assignee
Widow at the Declaration of Independence				
549 Auselmo Pre	1	1	Native	by assignee
Married at the Declaration of Independence				
550 Miguel Benites	1/3		Native	by assignee

30 June 1838

551 Andres Soto	1	1	Native	by assignee
Married at the Declaration of Independence				
552 Juana de Leon	1/3		Native	
553 Juan Jose' Sanches	1	1	Native	by assignee
554 Maria Dorotea Jesus	1	1	Native	
de Treviño	Widow at Dec of Ind. By assignee			
555 Felipe Jaime	1	1	Native	by assignee
556 Jose' Maria Gil de Leilea	1/3		Native	by assignee
557 Antonia Curvier	1	1	Native	Widow
558 Maria Rodriguez	1	1	Native	by assignee
559 Guadalupe Najar	1/3		Native	by assignee

6 July 1838

562 Juana Francisca Gonzales	1	1	Native	Widow. By asee
563 Justa Flores	1	1	Native	Widow. By assignee
564 Guadalupe Flores	1	1	Native	Married
565 Margarita Ximenes	1	1	Native	by assignee
Mother of children				
567 Simon Garcia	1/3		Native	Single. By assignee
568 Margricio Rodriguez	1	1	Native	Married. By asee
569 Mariano Romano	1	1	Native	Married. By assignee
572 Maria Josefa Guerra	1	1	Native	Widow. By assignee
573 Jacinto de la Garza	1	1	Native	Married. By assignee
574 Leandro Escamillo	1	1	Native	Married. By assignee

575	Maria Candida Zuniga	1	1	Native	Widow. By assignee
576	Santos Rodriguez	1	1	Native	Married at D. of Ind.
577	Francisco Carillo	1	1	Native	By assignee
	Married at Declaration of Independence				
578	Mariano Tejeda	1/3		Native	Single
579	Jose' Maria Garcia	1/3		Native	Single. By assignee
580	Leandro Chaves	1	1	Native	Married at Dec of Ind
	By assignee				

7 July 1838

581	Gabriel Martinez	1	1	Native	Married at Dec of Ind
582	Maria Juanita Treviño	1	1	Native	By assignee
	Mother of children				
583	Juan Rodriguez	1	1	Native	Married. By assignee
584	Roberta Estrada	1	1	Native	By assignee
	Mother of children				
587	Maria Catalina Selines	1	1	Native	Widow. By assignee
589	Juana Rodriguez	1	1	Native	By assignee
	Was married at the Dec of Ind., mother of children, husband abandoned her more than 6 years ago, out of the country at Natchitoches.				
590	Juana de Dios Nieto	1	1	Native	Widow. By assignee
591	Trinidad Martinez	1/3		Native	Single. By assignee
593	Eduardo Rivas	1/3		Native	Single
594	Estevan Serrano	1/3		Native	Single. By assignee
595	Juana Francisco Flores	1	1	Native	By assignee
	Was widow at the Dec of Ind				
597	Pablo Ortiz	1/3		Native	Single. By assignee
598	Julio Romero	1	1	Native	Was single at D of I
599	Concepcion Martinez	1	1	Native	By assignee
	Married, separated since 1834, husband left country in Nov 1836, his name Felipe dela Garza, children still under age.				
601	Francisco Ruiz	1/3		Native	
	Brother-in-law of Deaf Smith				
602	Cayetano Rivas	1	1	Native	Married at Dec of Ind
603	Antonia Losoya	1	1	Native	Widow at Dec of Ind
604	Francisco Lopez	1/3		Native	Single

12 July 1838

605	Isidro Ramos	1	1	Native	Married at Dec of Ind
600	Ana Maria dela Garza	[blank]		Native	Widow at Dec of Ind
608	Jesus Hernandez	1	1	Native	Single. By assignee
609	Ignacio Herrera	1/3		Native	Single. By assignee

16 July 1838

611	Salvador Flores	1/3		Native	Single
612	Carlos Flores	1/3		Native	Single

10 October 1838

613	Estifana dela Garza	1	1	Native	Widow at Dec of Ind
614	Jose' Casima	1	1	Native	Married at Dec of Ind
	Emigrated to Texas in 1824				
615	Carmel Ramon decd	1	1	Native	To heirs by assignee
	Was a resident at Dec of Ind, was a widow at death				

616 Jesus Ortiz heir of Jose' Maria Ortiz decd.	1	1	Native	By assignee
618 Maria Gertrudis Sanches	1	1	Native	Widow at D of Ind
619 Gabriel Martines y Nuñes	1	1	Native	Married at D of I
620 Francisco Gonzales	1	1	Native	Married at Dec of Ind
621 Francisco Cardines	1	1	Native	Married at Dec of Ind
622 Santos Blanco By assignee	1/3		Native	Single. 21 years old
623 Pedro dela Garza	1	1	Native	Then married. By asee
625 Jose' Maria Martinez y Perez Single at Dec of Ind, since married	1/3		Native	By assignee
626 Pablo Farias	1/3		Native	Single
627 Isabel Gotari	1	1	Native	Widow at Dec of Ind
628 Jose' Albino Carrasco	1/3		Native	Single. By assignee
629 Maria Paula Tejada	1	1	Native	Head fam at Dec of Ind
630 Hipolito Sotelo	1	1	Native	Widower. By asee

25 October 1838

631 Ana Maria Baca	1	1	Native	Widow at Dec of Ind
632 Jose' Antonio dela Garza (Zanzabino) Was married at Dec of Ind	1	1	Native	
633 Victor Pedrasa By assignee	1	1	Native	Married at D of Ind
634 Antonio Rodrigues (Valdes)	1	1	Native	Married at DI

June 1839, Clerk's Return

644 Gertrudis Flores	1	1	Native	Widow
645 Maria Polonia Garza	1	1	Native	Widow. By assignee
646 Juan Carollas	1/3		Native	By assignee
647 Juana Granado	1	1	Native	

She was married to Jose' Maria Jaime who died about 1818 or 19. She has lived with Santos Flores who is now on the west side of the Rio Grande, went in 1836. She has two or three small children.

Sept., Oct. & Nov. 1839, Clerks Return

652 Blas Duran	1/3			Emigrated to Texas 1829
653 Maria Ramona Vela	1	1	Native	Widow, head of family
655 Ana Maria Vaea	1	1	Native	Widow, head of family
657 Concepcion Manchaca	1	1	Native	Widow
659 Manuel Martines	1	1	Native	
660 Antonio Zalazar	1	1	Native	
662 Jose' Atocha	1	1	Native	
663 Rafael Garza	2/3	1	Native	

Nov. & Dec. 1839, Clerk's Return

664 Jose' Rivas	1/3		Native	By assignee
665 Jose' Antonio Salinas	—	1	Native	By assignee
666 Francisca Carbier	1	1	Native	By assignee

COLORADO CO.

No. 1 January through 27 April 1838

11 Jesse Robinson	3/4	1	1822
34 Joseph Highland	1/3		1829

59 Abraham Alley	1	1	1822
68 William Neuman	1	1	1830
70 William Waters	1/3		1830
89 Jasper Gilbert	1	1	1822
90 Thomas Rabb	—	1	1822
99 Nathaniel Osburn	1/2	1	1823
116 John Cryer [Crice]	—	1	1830

No. 2 to Sept 1838

129 James Nelson	—	1	1823

Nov 1838

140 Levi Mercer	2/3	1	1830

In addition to 1/3 league granted when a single man

141 Preston Gilbert	—	1	1824

FANNIN CO.

April 1838

David C. Strickland	1/3		1825

FAYETTE CO.

May 1838

87 Leander Woods decd	1/3 less 1/4	1823

Zadock Woods legal rep [resentative]

93 William Kuykendall	1/3	1830

March 1839 to Jan 1840

163 Ingram John	299-9/10 ac Aug [mentation]	1822
104 Taylor Felix	1 —	1825

Donation for permanent wound in Service of Country

FORT BEND CO.

June 1838

Leo Roark	2/3	1	1825	

July 1838

George Carpenter decd	1	1	1825	M.M. Battle Admr

Oct 1839

370 Elizabeth E. Parrott formerly Eliz E. Lippincott. M.M. Battle knew her as early as 1826. Had received 1 lg, now wants one labor.

GOLIAD CO.

Clerk's Return No. 1 1838

7 Incarnacion Vasques	1	1	Native
8 Antonio Vasques	1	1	Native
9 Gregorio Flores	1	1	Before 1830. Married
By assignee			
10 Jose Olivares	1/3		Before 1830
18 Martin Toole	1/3		15 Aug 1830
19 Felicia Mancha	1	1	Native

No. 2 Aug-Sept 1838

Anastatio Varon	1/3		Native
Juan Igenin Henon	1/3		Native

Clerk's Returns and Reports 189

Manuel Munguio	1/3		Native	
Manuel Dias	1/3		Native	
Jose Cunia	1/3		Native	
Benigno Gomay	1/3		Native	
Rafael Alderete	1/3		Native	
Jose Angel Leal	1	1	Native	
Gustavus Flores	1	1	Native	By assignee
Mareano Vidal	1/3		Native	

Sept-Oct 1838

Atago de Gregoria Gonzales	1	1	Native	To assignee
Miguel Bouttar	1	1	Native	
Jose Ignacio Varmor	1	1	Native	
Miguel Villigas	1	1	Native	
Louis Mandosa	1	1	Native	
Miguel Zoto	1	1	Native	
Carlos Molino	1	1	Native	
Juan Ruta	1	1	Native	
Pedro Gonzales de Flores	1/3		Native	
Leonardo Gonzales	1/3		Native	
Martias Varias	1	1	Native	To assignee
Antonio Ramon	1	1	Native	
Francesco Carrara	1/3		Native	
Francisca Salinas	1/3		Native	

Nov 1838

Francisco Mandiola	1	1	Native	
Auginio Varron	1	1	Native	
Jacobo Barrea	1	1	Native	
Juan Lazaro Ramirez	1	1	Native	
Manuel Cameros	1	1	Native	
Manuel Delgado	1	1	Native	
Naravio Seraes	1	1	Native	
Jose Vantura Parra	1/3		Native	
Miguel Alderete Admr Jesus Alderete	1	1	Native	
Pablo Garcia	1	1	Native	

GONZALES CO.

May 1838 Return No. 2

Andrew Lockhart	—		1	Feb 5, 1829. Married
George Blair	—		1	In year 1829. Married
Andrew Kent decd	—		1	1830 H. H. Baldriege Admr
Adam Zumalt	—		1	1829
Isaac Hall decd	—		1	1825. Arthur Floyd Admr
Chs. Lockhart decd	1/3			1829 Andrew Lockart Admst
John Lockhart decd	1/3	less 1/4		1829 Andrew Lockhart Admr
Byrd B. Lockhart	1/3	less 1/4		1830
Eben Haven	—		1	1830 Married
Geo Blair Admr of James Fulton	1/3			1829
Almond Dickerson decd	—		1	1830 Wm A. Mathews Admr

Eliza Hardiman one labor to which she is entitled under the name of
Eliza DeWitt — 1 1830

August 1838   Return No. 4

Jas May Guardian of the heirs of P. Say	1	1	1828	
John McCoy	—	1	1830	Married
Estate of Benj Fulcher	369 ac		1829	Single
Silas Fuqua	—	1	1830	Single
James Hinds	1	1	1830	Married
George Tumlinson	1/3		1830	Single. By Admr

HARRIS CO.

January 1838. Minutes of the Board of Land Commissioners

William F. Neal	3/4	1	1826	Head of family
James H. Spilman	1	1	1830	Married about 4 years
Mrs. Hanna Nash	—	1	About 10 years ago	
Widow of Coleman Nash				
Richard Faulk	1/3		1824	Single, in Army
Michale McCormick	1/3		1829	Single, in Army
About 19 years old now				
Jesse White	3/4	1	1830	Married, in Army
Mary Owns decd	1	1	1828 or '29	
John Owns & Patrick Reels, Curators				
Mrs. Delila Morris alias	1	1	1829	
Mrs. Armstrong				
About 1830 she married Hugh Kilgore, decd. her last marriage				
John Owen	1	1	1828	
Henry Tierwester	1/3		1829	Single, in Army
John Iiames	1/3		1829	Single, in Army
Edward P. Whitehead	1/12		1830	Single
James Earl	1/3		1824	Single, in Army

February 1838

Henry K. Lewis decd	1/3		1828	Died about 1834
Jane Sawyer	1	1	1830	
Widow of Samuel Sawyer who died about 1832				
Hugh Kilgore decd	1	1	1830	Married 1831
By Edwd Wray, Guardian of heirs				
Mrs. Arthur McCormick	—	1	1830	Head of a family
Widow of Arthur McCormick				
John Kerlew decd	1/3		1830	Single. Died 1835
Daniel Shipman	1/2	1	1825	Head of family, Army
Obadiah Dodsons	1	1	1828	Died 1833
Archeloes Dodson, Admr. Family has one son				

March 1838

William Lynch	1/3		1828-30	Single
William Barker	1/3		1829	Single
Luke Moore	—	1	1830	Died 12 months ago
Thos Earl Jr Guardian of heirs				
Nicholas Clopper	—	1	1829-30	

Age about 65, brought 3 sons				
Joseph House Junr	—	1	1830	Head of family
Jethrow R. Bancroft	1/3		1830	Single, in Army
Page Bellow decd	1/2	1	1825	By Admr Enoch Brinson
Green DeWitt decd	1	1	1829	
By widow and heirs, died 1835				
George White	—	1	1825	Married 8 years
John R. Faulk	—	1	1824	Head of family
Henry White	2/3	1	1824	Married a widow
George Fisher	1/3		1830	Head of a family
Spyars Singleton	1	1	1830	Head of family
Reuben White	—	1	1824	Head of family

May 1838

James W. Singleton	2/3	1	1828	Marr. one week ago
Mrs. Maria Josepha Fernandez	1	1	13 years ago	
Widow of Francisco Fernandez				

June 1838

Joseph Richie	1/12		1828	Single, in Army
Samuel McKerley	—	1	1824	

July 1838

John R. Harris decd	—	1	1828	Widow and family
Died in the U.S. on a visit				
Abraham Roberts	999,800 vs		8 or 9 years ago. Family	
Crawford Burnett decd	—	1	1828	
By Matthew Burnett, Guardian for heirs				
Wm Rankin Junr	—	1	1830	Family

JACKSON CO.

July 1838

Heirs of Wm Alley decd	—	1	1826
Thomas Alley	1/3 less 1/4		1826
Samuel Shupe	2/3 lg & labor less 1280 ac		1827

August 1838

Francis G. Keller	—	1	1830

JASPER CO.

March 1838

John Dickenson	1	1	1830	Thomas B. Huling Assee
Jacob Becker	1/3		1830	
James Chessher Senr	1	1	1829	
Thomas Williams	1	1	1830	
Harman Lewis	1/3		1830	Thomas Williams Assee
Mrs. Polly Ryan	—	1	1830 or 1831	
Eliza Isaacs	—	1	1830	
Benjamin Burke	—	1	1830	
Hiram Watts	1/3		1827	
Benjamin Richardson	1	1	1830	
Joseph E. Thompson	1	1	1829	

	Stephen Williams Junr	1/3		1830	
	William McFarland	—	1	1830	
	George W. Smyth	—	1	1830	Mitchael Martin Ase
	James B. Willson	1/3		1829	Joseph Crisswell Ae
	William Lewis Junr	1/3		1828	Geo W. Glasscock Ae
	Andrew Richardson	1/3		1830	
	William Richardson	1/3		1830	

June 1838

	Rachel Sawl	1	1	1827	Joseph M Glasscock Ae
	Gadi West	1	1	1828	Thos B. Huling Ase
	Seaborn Berry	1	1	1830	Glasscock & Huling A
	Samuel Isaacs	1	1	1825	
	Elizabeth Bridges	1	1	1830	
	Mrs. Matilda Cherry	1	1	1830	Thos H Espy Ase
	John B. Robinson	1	1	1830	Wm H Stark Assee
	Thos Watts	—	1	1825	

July 1838

	Mrs. Margaret Swift	1	1	1830

August 1838

493	John R. Sawlsbury decd	1	—	1813	James Hoggatt heir
432	John Slaydon	2/3	1	1825	
223	Mrs. Sarah Winfrey	1	1	1829	
444	Alexander Wright	—	1	1823	
298	Joel Robinson	2,089,333 sq varas		1829	

December 1838

499	Daniel McNeal decd	1	1	1826	Martin Parmer Admr
454	John Wright decd	1	1	1823	
	Sherrod Wright, Alexander Wright, Susan Harvey heirs				
507	Charles Gilchrist	—	1	1830	
371	Rebecca Beley	1	1	1830	John Droddy Assee
436	A. E. Winfrey	1/3		1830	John Droddy Assee

January 1839

	Stephen Williams Senr	2/3	1	1830
	Joseph McGee	1/3		Native
	Spicy Taylor	1	1	July 1829
	John W. Taylor	1	—	1826

August 1839   New Board

349	Alexander Lamb	1	1	1830
353	Lawrence Humphrey	1	1	1830
364	Emily Brown	1	1	1830
366	Allen Goodridge	1	1	1830
369	Franklin Baton	1	1	1830
371	Jane Moore	1	1	1830

January 1840

	J. Becker	2/3	1	August 1830

JEFFERSON CO.

1838 Minutes of the Board of Land Commissioners

Mrs. Eliza Cottle	1	1	1829	Head of family
Mrs. Nancy Tevis	1/2	1	1825	Head of family
Wm McFadden Jr	1	1	1825	Marr. August 1837
Mrs. Hannah Allen	—	1	1827	Head of family
Thomas Lewis	1	1	July 1830	
Wm McFadden	—	1	1830	Head of family
Absalom Jett	1	1	1824	Head of family
Claiborn West	—	1	1825	Head of family
Clark Beach	1	—	1830	Married
Wm Ritchie died 1832			1826	Mrs. Hannah Simmons Admx
Gilbert Stephenson	1	1	1828	Married
John Cole			1828	Married
James Cole			1829	Head of family
John Jett	1	1	1826	
Duncan St. Clair			1828	Married
George Stephenson			1829	Single
John Stephenson			1830	Married
Isaac Garner			1828	
M. J. Brake decd			1830	Wm H. Irion Admr
Died after 2 March 1836				
Henry Griffith			1830	Head of family
Bradley Garner			1828	Head of family
Wilson W. Gill			1828	Single
Hiram Ritchey			1826	Head of family
Jacob Townsend			1829	Single
Silas Palmer			1830	Head of family
Jacob Grigsby			1828	Head of family
Nathaniel Grigsby			1828	Single
Enoch Grigsby			1829	Single
Hiram Bunch			1830	Married
John Stephenson Sr deceased			1828	Married
Lydia Stephenson Admx				
Thomas D. Yocum			1830	Head of family
Mary Ann Cottle			1829	Widow on 2 March 1836
John McGuffie			1828	Marr. before 2 Mar 1836
Thomas Court			1829	Marr. before 2 Mar 1836
Lorenzo D. Cottle	1/3		1829	Single. Age 20 now

March 1838   Return No. 3

James Drake	1	1	1825	
James Stephenson	1	1	1829	
William Carr	1	1	1827	
David Burrill	1	1	1828	
Wilson W. Sills	1/3		1828	
William D. Smith	—	1	1830	
Bradley Garner Sr	1	1	1828	
Bradley Garner Sr administrator of the estate of				
John Stewart Dd	—	1	1828	

1830 Citizens of Texas

    Claiborne West by Power of Attorney from Sarah Jett Admx of the
Estate of Stephen Jett Decd — 1 1830

April 1838
    John Jett — 1 1826
        Hannah Simmons admtr of the estate of Archibald Ritchie, entitled to one league and labor, certificate issued for
                1 — 1826
      William H. Irion Administrator of the Estate of
    Michael J. Brake   1/3   1830
    John Harmon   5,922,250 sq varas   1830

1839
    Jacob M. Garner   2/3   1   1825   Marr. 19 Nov 1838
    James H. Pattillo   320 ac   1830   Now arrived at 18 years
44 William Grigsby   320 ac   1828   Now arrived at 18 yrs
56 Hiram Peace decd   1   1   1830   Thomas D. Yocum Admr
57 Westley Garner   320 ac   1830   Now arrived at 17 years in July 1839
159 Mary Ann Cottle   —   1   1829
165 Wm H. Smith   1   1   1829
    G. W. Tevis   1   1   1824
        Previously appeared, proved emigration in 1824 and the head of a family since 6th July 1837

LIBERTY CO.

January 1838. Minutes of the Board of Land Commissioners
13 Richd Green by Benj Green, Admr. Was married by bond, died before 2 March 1836 in Liberty   1   1   1830
15 W. R. Griffin by Wm M. Logan, representative. Died about 1832, no kin in Texas
              1/3   1830
32 Clayton Harper decd. William Hardin, Guardian to one minor heir in Texas. Harper died at Liberty   1   1   1826
37 Mary Whitlock   —   1   1827   Widow with family
44 Jacob H. Geiger   1/3   1829   Single
    Alexr S. Roberts, Curator
49 Jesse Pruett by Alexr S. Roberts, Curator ad litem. Head of family, died 1832, children in Texas   1   —   1824
61 Presley Gill   1   1   1824   Marr bef 2 Mar 1836
62 Amy Swail   —   1   1824   Head of family
69 E.H.R. Wallis   1   1   1824   Came with family
75 Frederic Lewis decd   1/3   1830
    Died single in the fall of 1835
76 Nathaniel Whitaker   1/3   1829   Single
77 James T. White   1   1   1828   Came with family
80 James T. Dunman   1   1   1828
    Came single, now heads a family
83 A.B.J. Winfree   1   1   1827   Came with family
85 Elisha Stephenson   1   1   1829   Is 21 years of age
    Married since 3 March 1836
88 N. D. Labadie   1   1   1830   Head of family 1832

Clerk's Returns and Reports   195

89	James Humphreys	1	1	1827	Head of family 1832
91	Thomas Devers	3/4	—	1825	Was in service
	Married since 2 March 1836				
92	Jacob F. Winfrie	1	1	1827	Came with family
94	Nancy Gowen	1	1	1827	By Edwd T. Branch, Atty
	Came with her family, children now in Texas; died 1832.				
95	Jose Coronado	—	1		Came with family
103	Jas Martin	—	1	1825	By J. C. Martin, Admr
	Died 1836, heirs in the country				
105	Robert Burrill	1	1	1828	Came with family
108	Jane Taylor	—	1	1830	Came with family
110	P. P. Dever decd	—	1	1825	A. B. Hardin Admr
	Died 1836. Was married. Children here now				
119	Wm Heron decd	1/3		1829	H. W. Farley Admr
	Single. Died fall of 1835				

February 1838

120	Chs Willcox	1/3		1830	
124	Hugh Jackson	1/3		1823	Now about 21
127	Matthew Hubert	—	1	Winter 1828.	Brought family.
134	Wm Johns	—	1	1830	Came with family
129	Wm Walless	1	1	1825	Married in 1828
135	James Haney	1	1	1826	Family here 1829
136	Benjamin Barrow	1	1	1827	Marr. on 4 Jun 1835
137	John White	1/3		1829	Single
	Was over 17 on 2 March 1836				
138	Soln Barrow	5,320,000 sq varas			Came with family in 1824
139	Levi Barrow	1	1	1830	Married in 1827
141	Jas Knight	—	1	1825	Married in 1828
142	Reuben Barrow Senr	1	1	1824	Marr. 7 Jan 1832
143	Thos Stubblefield	1	1	1830	
	Married since 2 March 1836				
145	Vincent Barrow decd	1	1	1830	Benjn Barrow Admr.
	Came with family. Died 1835				
148	Amos Green decd	—	1	1825	Jas Knight Admr
	Came with family. Died 1834				
152	Wm Duncan heirs	—	1	1825	Came with family
	Died in 1836				
152	M. Duncan	—	1	1825	Marr. Feb 1832
152	Polly Tier decd	1	1	1828	E. T. Branch Atty
	Brought child Mary, here now. Died 1830				
155	Jerusha Hardin	1	1	1828	Head of family
	Husband died 1829				
156	John Cherry	—	1	1825	
	Had a wife and 2 or 3 children in 1825				
162	David Choate Senr	—	1	1825	Came with family
163	Edmund Choate	1/3		1825	Single
	Son of David Choate Senr; over 17 on 2 Mar 1836				
175	Taylor B. Self	1/3		1823	Wm M. Logan Admr
	Died 1837. Over 17 on 2 Mar 1836				

1830 Citizens of Texas

176 Jacob E. Self — 1 1822 or '23 Died 1831
    Wm M. Logan Admr. Came with wife and children
181 C. P. Welch — 1 1829 Married in 1830
187 Felix Newman 1 1 1828 Marr. fall of 1835
192 Moses H. Carroll decd — 1 1828 Mary C. Carroll Admx
    Married in 1833, heirs in this country
194 T. J. Williams 1 1 1827 Died 1830
    Came with family, here now

March 1838
197 Charles Tilton 1 1 1829 Married in 1831
200 Benjn M. Green — 1 1827 Married in 1832
201 Wm Everett — 1 1827 Died in Liberty 1831
    Married in 1828, heirs here now
214 James Robinson — 1 1825 Came with family
215 Ansen Taylor 1 1 1828 Head of family
    Died in Liberty in 1831
228 Edward Dorr 1/3 1825 Single
229 Beasley Pruett 1 1 1825 Marr. 2 July 1837
    Served in the Army
232 Jas San Germain 1/3 1830 Edward T. Branch
    Admr. Single, heirs in Texas. Died in Liberty 1835
235 Aaron Cherry Senr — 1 1825 Came with family
236 Wm Thompson 1 1 1830
    Married Jan 1837. Served in the Army
239 Wm M. Smith 1 1 1827 Marr. fall 1835
240 James M. Rankin — 1 1827 Marr. some yrs ago
241 Rozelia Scott 1 1 1830 Came with family
    By F. W. Johnson Agent
242 Burrell Franks 1 1 1826 Came with family

March to November 1838
244 Amos Barber 1/3 1829 Single, 23 yrs
245 Benj Barrow Jr. 1/3 1830 Over 17 on D I
246 Jones Shaw 1 1 1829 Came with family
250 Elizabeth Whiting widow of M. B. Munson died 1827
    — 1 1825
257 Esther Clark 1 1 1829 Clark died 1836
    Youngest son born 4 July 1809
260 Rebecca Coleman decd, A. B. Hardin Admr. Died 1836
    1 1 1825 Came with fam
262 James B. Woods — 1 1829 Marr in 1830
267 Jno. Barber 1/3 1829 Single
    Born 27 July 1818
274 Wm Dobie decd. Sterling N. Dobie Admr. Died 1835 on a visit to U.S. Has heirs in Texas 3/4 1 1830
275 B. M. Spinks — 1 1825 Came with family
285 Jos Laurence 1 1 1824 Marr in 1830
295 Jno. Saul — 1 1825 Came with fam
296 John Watts — 1 1825 Marr about 1827
300 Robt Wiseman 1/2 1 1827 Came with fam

Clerk's Returns and Reports 197

301 Theo. Dorsett   —   1   1825   Came with fam
307 George Orr died 1834 or 35. Reason Green Admr.
            —   1   1824   Came with fam
313 James Roberts died in Liberty about 1832. N. D. Labadie Admr. No heirs in
    Texas   1/3   1830
315 Matthew G. White died in Liberty about 1830 to 32. Lucy & Wm White Admrs.
    Came with his family   —   1   1825
325 Stephen Jones died in Liberty in 1834. D. Choate Senr Admr. Came with
    his family   1   1   1830
335 Edwd Miles died in Liberty in 1832. Ewd Miles, Admr. Came with family, son
    now living was minor in 1832.
            1   1   1830
   Wm Johns   —   1   1830   Came with fam

MATAGORDA CO.
Report of Thos Morewood. [See note at the end]

January 1838
  26 Mary Ann Reeder   1   —   1827
    If her husband has not got before
  80 James Hughson   —   1   1824
    As a purchase from Mrs. Jane Wilkins
  83 The heirs & representatives of Joseph Hall Decd
    Thos M. Drake Admr   1   1   1829
  94 Oscar Robinson   1/3   1830
    Under age at the Declaration of Independence
126 Robert H. Williams   —   1   1825
125 Andrew Vanslyke as a purchase from R. M. Greene
          1/3   Previous to the Dec of Ind
    Has got an honorable discharge from the Army
141 Heirs & representatives of   1/3   1828
    Ransom O. Graves   Killed with Fannin. Isham Thompson took the oath
    as Admr
143 Heirs & Repres of Elisha   —   1   1830
    Hall Decd   Isham Thompson took the oath before a J.P. as Admr & Curator
144 Jacob Allbriecht   1/3   1830
156 Elisha Flowers   1/2   —   1827
    Doubtful is no Citizen being 13 years away left an orphan here not been
    here except on a visit
161 Heirs & Repres of Joseph   1   1   1822
    Bowman Decd. His son John Bowman claims the land as admr
163 Mrs Jane Wilkins   1   1   1822
    J. Wilkins claimed the land as widow of Robert Matson [Mason] who
    came to the Country in 1822 and died in the same year.
167 Ellen Gillilan   1   1   1829
    Claims the land by her atty R. R. Royall as a widow
177 Wm Morrison   1   1   1829
    Doubt in this country
180 Heirs & Repres of Caleb   1   1   1829
    Kemp Decd. Nicholas George took the oath before a J.P. as admr.

1830 Citizens of Texas

203 Heirs & Representatives of Leonard Balknapp Decd
    R. H. Wynne is now admr.   1/3   1830
207 Heirs & Repres of N. B.   1   1   1829
    Williams   George W. Williams admr. Killed with Fannin
213 Heirs & Repres of Caleb   1/2   1   1822
    R. Bostwick
217 Heirs & Repres of Elsy   1   1   1829
    Reed Decd   Woman of family
221 Isaac Vandorn   1/2   1   1826

February 1838

239 Augustus Kinchelow   1/3   1830
    Ent[itled] if was 17 at the passing of the law
240 Thos Osburn   1/3   1826
    Ent[itled] if was 17 at the passing of the law
241 Heirs & Repres of George   1/3   1826
    Rawls Decd. Fought at St Jacinto   Benj Rawls admr
243 John George   1/3   1830 Ent[itled] if old enough
250 David George   1/3   1829
    Gave a power of attorney to Jefferson George, not known whether old enough
267 Heirs & Repres of John   1/3   1829
    Scott decd
275 Heirs & Repres of Jonathan —   1   1826
    C. Payton decd
276 Alexander G. Payton   1/3   1829 If old enough, ent[itled]
278 Heirs & Repres of Hicks   1/3   1829
    Shropshire.   Jefferson George Adm
279 Heirs & Repres of   1   1   1829
    Harrison Shropshire   Jefferson George Adm
293 Heirs & Repres of Jacob   1/2   1   1825
    Betts   Mary Kincheloe admr, if not having his land before
300 Heirs & Repres of Maria   1 labor   1825
    Cook   H. L. Cook Adm
312 Alvin Woodward   1/3   1829
    Received 1/4 league in 1836
334 Heirs & c of George   1/3   1826
    Bright decd.   W. D. Lacy Adm
341 Heirs & c of Chs   1   1   1825
    Henderson decd
356 Ralph Wright   1   1   1826

March 1838

376 Heirs & Representatives   1/3   1827 Died in 1828
    of Eeley Eddy decd

April 1838

383 Heirs & Representatives   1/3   1828 Died in '32 or '33
    of James Johnston Eweart decd
390 Silas Dinsmore &   —   1   1824
    A. J. Dalton by purchase from Peter Demoss
391 Heirs & Representatives of 1/3   1822
    Peter L. White

394 Heirs & Representatives   —   1   1828
       of Elisha Moore decd
May 1838
404 Heirs & Representatives of 1/3   1828
       Wm Scott decd
405 Heirs & Representatives   1   1   1828
       of Jonathan Scott decd
June 1838
414 Chas Johnston   1   1   1830
415 Heirs & Representatives of 1   1   1830
       Wm M. Rivers
January 1839
432 John Huff   1/2   1825

[Special Note: Because of widespread reports of land fraud, the President of the Republic authorised the Commissioner of the General Land Office on 15 April 1839 to appoint several agents to audit the local boards. The list that appears above is part of the report of Thos Morewood for Matagorda County. The remarks after many of the names are the informal information obtained by Morewood. Although they are probably true, they were not part of the sworn record, which he reported to have been badly kept. Morewood's report is now with the Clerk's Report under Matagorda Co. in the General Land Office files.]

July 1839 Clerk's Return [New numbers]
  64 Lopez Jose' Maria   1/3   Native of the Country
  81 William Spence heirs &   1/3   1827
        representatives
  82 David Butler heirs &   1/3   1829
        representatives

MILAM CO.

January 1838
  Margaret Taylor late Margaret Frazier widow
                              —   1   1824   Received 1 lg
  Nancy Boring widow   —   1   1828   Received 1 lg
January 1840, New Board
  42 Monroe Sampier   640 ac   March 1824
  43 Joseph Sampier   640 ac   March 1824

MONTGOMERY CO.

February 1838
  3 Jacob S annon   —   1   1821
     John Jones decd   Previous to 1827
     Charles B. Stewart assige of Nancy Jones, now Nancy Tullus, obtained a certificate of heirship in the Estate of John Jones, decd.
174 A. C. Grimes decd   1/3   1825
       A minor, by his father Jesse Grimes
March 1838
323 John Montgomery   —   1   1822
       Admr of Wm Montgomery decd

336	John Caruthers	—	1	Feb 1830
340	Mary Crothers	3/4	1	1829
341	Elizabeth Ray	—	1	1825
343	Cyrus Dykeman assignee of Matthew Morse	1/3		1830
346	Jesse Young	—	1	1823
349	Martin Varner assignee of Francis Holland	1/3		1823
350	William Burney Admr of Francis Holland decd	—	1	1822
351	Wm Burney Admr of Tapley Holland decd	1/3		1822
359	H. H. Goff	1/3		1823

July 1838

399	Wiatt Anderson	1/3		1824
402	Mill McDowell	—	1	1824
404	James Bennett	1/3		1827
406	Nancy Norman	—	1	1820
407	Alexander Thompson	1	1	1820
409	Danl L. Richardson assee of Massine Arriola	1/3		1824
412	Margaret Hampton Admx of the Est of William Hampton decd	1	1	1830
414	John F. McGuffin	2/3	1	24 Jany 1829

August to November 1838

424	James Cox	—	1	1830	
439	William Brooks	1/4	1	1826	Augmentation
440	A. G. Perry and James W. Smith assignee of Wm Brooks	1/2		1826	Augmentation
442	John Potter	1/3		1823	
445	Philip Martin	—	1	1828	
446	John H. Pierson	2/3	1	1830	

NACOGDOCHES CO.

August to December 1839

699	Heirs of John Eberhard Roof	1	1	1827
700	Lewis Velard	1/3		1827
723	Heirs of Michael Sacco by Manuel Guterres Admr	1 labor & 119 ac		1829

RED RIVER CO.

No. 6 up to Novr 2, 1838

57	Levi M. Rice	1	1	1824
69	Joseph J. Ward	1	1	28 Oct 1830
212	John Hampton Decd	1	1	July 1818
297	Frances Hopkins decd	1	1	Nov 1824
305	Aaron Hansome	1/3		1825
345	Heirs of Joseph Wood decd	1/3		1820
373	Henry S. Janes	1/3		1826

384	Jacob Barkman	1/3		1824
385	Heirs of Barkley Nall decd John Nall Admr	1/3		1819
390	Hugh B. Shaw	1	1	March 1823
391	Henry Stout	1	1	1823
393	James Stout	1/3		1823
395	Jarrel James	1	1	1822
397	Bryant Homes	1	1	May 1822
398	Robert Hall	1	1	December 1822
400	Heirs of Daniel Cornelius decd Samuel B. Young Admr	1	1	December 1820
401	Benage Loyd	1/3		June 1, 1821
402	Hirom Loyd	1/3		June 1, 1821
403	David Clapp	1	1	March 1820 [or 1826]
409	John H. Nall	1	1	October 1830
413	Heirs of John Lick Sen decd William B. Stout Admr	1	1	1820
414	Jonathan Cochran decd	1	1	1824
415	Heirs of Isaac Murfy decd James Rodes Admr	1	1	1824
416	James Rodes	1	1	1826
417	Heirs Jasper Woods decd John H. Hall Admr	1	1	1820
427	Isaac Clover	1/3		1822
430	Heirs William Shaw Jur decd William B. Steel Admr	1/3		1823
443	William H. H. Hopkins	1	1	December 1824
444	Hugh B. Shaw Admr of Wm Shaw Jur decd	1/3		1824
448	Charles Y. Douglass Admr of the heirs of Richard M. Hopkins decd	1/3		1824
451	Heirs of John Hanks	1	1	1824 James Clark Admr
453	John Walker	1	1	September 30, 1829
459	Heirs of Eldridge Hopkins decd	1	1	April 1824
462	John Walker	1	1	1822 John Martin assignee
465	John E. Janes	1/3		Native born citizen
467	James Osgood	1	1	1826
468	William Burnside	1/3		September 9, 1824
471	The heirs of Samuel Burnsides	1	1	1828
472	The heirs of John Daniel	1	1	1820
477	Richard H. Finn	1	1	February 1822
480	Jacob Blair	1	1	1824 Robert Hamilton Admr
491	Heirs of Daniel McKinney	1	1	Novemr 5, 1824
506	Isaac Taylor	1	1	1824
507	Abijah Burkham	1/3		A native born citizen
509	William McFarland	1	1	2 January 1825
511	Massack H. Janes	1	1	29 Nov 1825

515	The Heirs of Sherrod Dunman	1	1	2 January 1825
518	Heirs of William Collum Decd	1	1	1824
519	Heirs of John Barkam	1/3		1824
526	Heirs of Abner Azkey Decd	1	1	1822
533	Heirs of Samuel Barnam	1	1	1830
539	Heirs of Preston Kitchens	1/3		1827
541	Heirs of Joseph Stricklen	1	1	1825
546	John Davis	1	1	1824
557	Jacob Buzzard	1	1	March 1826
569	Richard Rhodes	1	1	1827
570	Heirs of Henry Vincent Decd, Henry Stout Admr	1	1	1822
572	James R. Nyro, W. B. Stout Admr	1	1	1824
603	Lewis Dayton	1/3		1824
604	John Edmonson	1	1	April 1825
606	David Stricklen Decd John Stricklen Admr	1	1	1824
612	Francisco Longordia	1/3		Native Born
614	Lewis Richardson	1/3		June 1830
616	James Holland Decd John Robbins Admr	1/3		1822
619	Alexander W. Wright	1/3		Native Born
620	James Wimbley	1/3		Native
639	Johnson Bowers	1	1	Apr 1820
645	Heirs James Barker decd	1	1	1830
650	Heirs Adam Wright decd George W. Wright Admr	1/3		1828

Novr 1838 to March 1839

714	Samuel Bush	1/3		1830
716	Heirs Hugh McCelay decd	1	1	1824
721	Heirs Abraham Ogden decd	1	1	1825
723	Travis G. Wright	2/3	1	1828
729	John Askins	1/3		1818
737	Heirs Alexander O. Witmore decd	1	1	1825
739	Heirs Luke Roberts decd	1	1	1820
743	John Levins	1/3		Native Born

October-December 1839

George Bason Admr of Emanuel Grubbs	1/3		1829
Joseph J. Ward	1/3		1830
Heirs of Joseph Ferguson decd	1/3		1825
Heirs of Daniel Thompson deceased	1/3		June 1830

Clerk's Returns and Reports

Jany 1840

James Rhodes Junr	320 ac			Native of the country
Thomas Thombison Heirs of Thomas Thombison Senr	1	1	1825	
Francis Rosseau	1	1	1830	
Nelson Roubdoux	1/3		1830	

ROBERTSON CO.

February to April 1838

	John Latham	1	1	1821
	Mary Rohus	1	1	1828
	Philip Graves	1	1	1825
	James Bowling	1	1	1827
	Marreah Assovose, H. L. Wiggins assignee			1826
	Henry G. Strickland	1/3		1823
	Ahira Butler	1	1	1829
	John Buckley	1	1	1823
	William McFaddin	1	1	1822
	Jonathan Bittick	3229 ac		1830
	King Latham	1	1	1821
139	Saml W. White	—	1	1829
	Est Saml C. Smith decd	369 ac		1828
169	John Marlin	—	1	1830

January 1840, New Board, Report No. 1

1	Henry Dawson	320 ac		1828
20	John Stokes	320 ac		1828

SABINE CO.

January 1838

67	John Maximillion Junr By assignee	1	1	1825	Married 1831
74	Corene Chapple D. A. Cunningham assignee	1	1	1822	Married 1834
173	Joan Ferdan Johan	1	1	1822	By Thos H Garner

March 1838

233	Neely John M	1	1	1830	Head of family
234	Harden Thomas	1	1	1830	Benj Fuller Assee
235	Charles McKay	1/4	1	1825	Nancy McKey Admx
247	Wood Prissa	1	1	1830	Jas T White Admr
248	Daverson Saml	1	1	1830	
308	William Pace	1	1	1826	Isaac F Pace Admr
314	Marshack Tebosha	1	1	1826	Fredk Fay Assee
321	McKim James		2	1828	Head of family
486	Smith John		1	1830	Head of family
252	Crowder John	1/3		1828	Wm Isaacs Admr
273	Delass Charles	1	1	1829	C Thompson Assee
374	Johnson Abraham	1	1	1829	S. H. Smith Assee
383	French Edmond	1	1	1829	S. H. Smith Assee

325	White William F	1	1	1829	S. F. Clark Assee
327	Lake John W	1	1	1828	Saml Clark Assee
332	Day Aron L	1	1	1830	Saml Clark Assee
337	Burke George T	1	1	1829	S. F. Clark Assee
339	Young Horatio	1	1	1829	S. F. Clark Assee
349	Summers Henry	1	1	1830	S. F. Clark Assee
351	Roberds Richard	1	1	1829	S. F. Clark Assee
357	Forbes B. T.	1	1	1830	S. F. Clark Assee
407	Hall R. G.	1	1	1830	E. W. Cullen Assee
408	Flint H	1	1	1830	E. W. Cullen Assee
409	Pool G	1	1	1830	E. W. Cullen Assee
410	Scott T. W.	1	1	1830	E. W. Cullen Assee
411	Powe A	1	1	1830	E. W. Cullen Assee
430	Gray L. P.	1	1	1830	Thos H. Garner assee
431	Lee Wm L.	1	1	1828	Thos H. Garner assee
432	Gray S. P.	1	1	1828	Thos H. Garner assee
433	Saul James B.	1	1	1827	Thos H. Garner assee
434	Little John	1	1	1830	Thos H. Garner assee
437	Penn Eli	1	1	1828	Thos H. Garner assee
438	Duncan S.	1	1	1828	Thos H. Garner assee
439	Richey, J. S.	1	1	1828	Thos H. Garner assee
440	Kean Jas E.	1	1	1828	Thos H. Garner assee
461	Rowson K.	1	1	1827	Jas T. White assee
462	Goodley J.	1	1	1827	Jas T. White assee
473	White G. L.	1	1	1830	Thos H. Garner assee
476	Allen Davis	1	1	1820	Thos H. Garner assee
482	Tanner Daniel	1	1	1826	Had family
484	Gains James	1	1	1812	
491	Jones Frederick	1	1	1829	Wm S. Lewis assee
497	Jones Ira D.	1	1	1828	Wm S. Lewis assee
505	Trew Demion	1	1	1829	Wm S. Lewis assee
511	Williams Johnson	1	1	1830	Thos H. Preston assee
512	Gray Samuel	1	1	1829	Thos H. Preston assee
513	Jones Everett	1	1	1830	Thos H. Preston assee

April 1838

541	Cieders Lisabel	1	1	1828	B. J. Thompson Assee
550	Jackson Emory	1/3		1830	
566	Reeve James R	1/3		1829	
576	Porter James G	1/3		1830	
582	Lacy M. K.	1	1	1830	
583	Nobles E. M.	1	1	1830	
584	Rariden Thomas M	1	1	1830	
585	Flinn Simpson F	1	1	1830	

June 1838

618	Lowe Eliz	—	1	1828	
619	do	1	—	do	
620	Evans Joseph	2/3	1	Saml D. McMahan Admr	
621	Irion Jas H	—	1	1830	
622	Hines Elbort	1	1	1823	

Clerk's Returns and Reports 205

623 Hines Davis	1/3		1823	
626 Nicholas Robert	1/3		1828	
627 Mcadams John D	2/3	1		
628 Easly Daniel	—	1	1830	
629 Holt Thomas C	1/3		A. G. Kellogg assignee	
630 Mitchal A. J.	1	1	1836	

July 1838

638 Renfro David	1	1	1828
644 Pace J. F.	2/3	1	1828
Married & rendered service			
645 Taylor John	—	1	1823
646 McKim Charles	2/3	1	Native
Married. Rendered service.			
655 Hines Ransom	1	1	1829
659 Taylor Truman	1	1	1829
673 Coulter Abram	1	1	1829

[1838 list]

748 Gescom [?] Nathan	1	1	1830
708 Story Benjamin	1	1	1830
717 Yates Phillip	1	1	1830
718 Stibbens Benj	1	1	1830
819 Foote Wilson	1	1	1829
785 Davis Nathan Jr	—	—	1830
668 Hoffman Andrew	1	1	1829
738 Atherton Benj	1	1	1829
741 Harper Isaac D	1	1	1830
686 Newell Samuel W	1	1	1829
687 Singleton Ira	1	1	1830
754 Graves Reubin	1	1	1830
769 Richmond Truman	1	1	1830
770 Richmond John R	1	1	1830
773 Potter Steven	1	1	1830
775 Warren Jesse	1	1	1830
776 Warren Nehemiah	1	1	1830
790 Robinson Thomas	1	1	1830
796 Love David W	1	1	1830
808 Stewart Jackson P	1	1	1830
839 Walthington Andrew	1	1	1829
840 Denton Jesse	1	1	1830
842 Sargent Frederick	1	1	1830
843 Sargent Thomas	1	1	1830
844 Sargent Ralph	1	1	1830
847 Phillips Jarvis	1	1	1830
848 Phillips Nathaniel	1	1	1830
851 Sewell John C	1	1	1830
852 Irving W$\underline{m}$ D	1	1	1830
859 Prentiss George P	1	1	1830
864 Graves Franses	1	1	1830
871 Hartwell Steven	1	1	1830

206   1830 Citizens of Texas

891	Mourhouse Seymour	1	1	1830
894	Ellison Jared P	1	1	1830
901	Thomas J. Francis	1	1	1830
904	Doone Grason	1	1	1830
922	Laurance Preston T	1	1	1830
947	Truworthy Thos T	1	1	1830
950	Northrop Orvill	1	1	1829
917	Prese Jose Anto	1	1	1830
919	Joseph Irion	1	1	1830
688	Stearn John W	1	1	1830
689	Stockton Epps G	1	1	1830
690	Manson Reubin	1	1	1828
691	Richards Jacob	1	1	1829
720	Richardson Lemuel	1	1	1830
725	Stone Wm J	1	1	1830
731	Dennis Gerry	1	1	1830

[written later]: Denniston

Traveling Auditor Reports written May-June 1839

2 Isaac H. Low, emigrated 1828. Issued June 7, 1839, 1/3 lea. (A young man 17 years of age at the declaration).

3 Isaac Low with family, emigrated on or before September 1828. 15 labors. Said Low received a title from the Mexican Govt.

7 Matthew Parker Adm of Willis Parker, deceased, W. P. emigrated 1824, died September 1828. 1/3 league.

SAN AUGUSTINE CO.

1838 Returns

418	Samuel Moss decd	1	1	1826	
420	John Holloway	1/3		1821	
421	Thos S. McFarland	3/4	1	1830	
426	John Cartwright	—	1	1825	
435	Martin V. Lout	2/3	1	1830	
437	Charity Sanders	1	1	1830	
445	David Earl decd	1	1	1824	
451	Wm Quirk decd	1	1	1824	
460	Andrew Spears	—	1	1826	
461	David Harris	1	1	1827	
465	A. A. Lewis	1/3		1828	
467	Martha Renfro	1	1	1824	
503	Williams W. M.	1	1	1830	Issued to self
511	Andrews George	1	1	1830	Issued to self
512	Linn Isaac W.	1	1	1830	Issued to self
516	Vaughan Theo	1	1	1827	Issued to self
517	Thaya Michl	1	1	1830	Issued to self
519	Mooney James	1	1	1829	Issued to self
520	Tipps Thos	1	1	1829	Issued to self
524	Roberts Elisha	1	1	1830	Issued to self
529	Matthews S. S.	1	1	1829	Issued to self
533	Carney P. L.	1	1	1829	Issued to self
547	Davis Warren decd	1	1	1824	Edwd Davis Admr

Clerk's Returns and Reports 207

584	McHenry Andrew	1		1	1827	To Self
586	Stratton David	1		1	1837	To Self
587	Morse Willie	1		1	1828	To Self
592	Cole Philo K.	1		1	1827	Morris May Assee
593	King Jno S.	1		1	1829	Morris May Assee
602	Peterson Elijah	1		1	1826	To Self
603	Bass Ambrose	1		1	1828	To Self
590	Littleton White	1		1	1830	To Self
605	Simpson Gains	1		1	1829	Issued to self
611	Moore Nathl B.	1		1	1829	Issued to self
612	Patterson Lewis Y.	1		1	1827	Issued to self
615	Allen Jno M.	1		1	1828	Issued to self
622	Jones James	1		1	1830	Issued to self
623	Dumas Saml	1		1	1829	Issued to self
627	Jowers John	1		1	1829	Issued to self
633	Tinsley Nathl	1		1	1826	Issued to self
634	Baker John W.	1		1	1830	Issued to self
635	Williams Cary W.	1		1	1829	Issued to self
645	Moss Silas	1		1	1830	To Saml E. Powers
668	Holloway Simpson	1		1	1826	To Self
670	Garrett Jacob			6	1824	To Self
673	Lindsey Benj	1/3			1824	To Self
746	Walker Leonard	1		1	1830	To Saml E. Powers
747	Reed Martin T.	1		1	1830	To Saml E. Powers
750	Stephen Elias	1		1	1830	To Saml E. Powers
751	Sparks Aaron	1		1	1830	To Saml E. Powers
752	Dewees Ellis	1		1	1830	To Saml E. Powers
753	Smith Felix	1		1	1830	To Saml E. Powers
754	Pearce Rufus	1		1	1830	To Saml E. Powers
755	Carter Andw	1		1	1830	To Saml E. Powers
756	Tyres James	1		1	1830	To Saml E. Powers
763	Starks Moses	1		1	1830	To Saml E. Powers
611	Moore Nathl B	1		1	1829	To Self

Return for July 1838

775	Moring Charles	1		1	1829	To Self
777	Collins Sewall	1		1	1829	To Self
781	Dunham Cary W.	1		1	1829	To Self
784	Jones Norris H.	1		1	1829	To Self
785	Beckett Dayton	1		1	1829	To Self
788	Harrell Ezekiel	1		1	1829	To Self
794	Sutton Phillip	1		1	1830	S. E. Powers Assee
795	Sutton James	1		1	1830	S. E. Powers Assee
796	Fury Elias	1		1	1830	S. E. Powers Assee
799	Worrell Wm	1		1	1829	To self
801	Knap Asa	1		1	1829	To self
804	Rice Claiborn	1		1	1830	Saml E Powers Ae
810	Smith Reuben H	1		1	1830	Saml E Powers Ae
813	Browning Lucas	369 ac			1830	To self
816	Lang Jackson D	1		1	1830	To self

208   1830 Citizens of Texas

817	Lang Wm E	1	1	1829	To self
818	Manning Noel	1	1	1830	To self
819	Whetstone Silas	1	1	1829	To self
824	Allen Jackson C	1	1	1830	Saml E Powers Ae
827	Passing James	1	1	1830	Saml E Powers Ae
828	Masters Lawrence	1	1	1830	Saml E Powers Ae
829	Graves Minos	1	1	1830	Saml E Powers Ae
833	Pope Caesar	1	1	1829	To self
834	Purnell Chas S	1	1	1830	To self
835	Purnell Wm S	1	1	1830	To self
840	Carroll Levi H	1	1	1829	To self
845	Whetstone Edwd	1	1	1829	To self
847	Battell Wm T	1	1	1829	To self
850	Pickens Charles	1	1	1828	To self
851	Carroll Peter N	1	1	1829	To self
852	Carroll Dennis C	1	1	1829	To self
894	Holloway Lewis	—	1	1821	To self
897	Davis Elias K	—	1	1825	To self
924	Brightman Jos W decd	1/4		1830	Richd Haley Admr
1009	Snyder John	1	1	1830	To self
958	Irvine R. Boyd	369 ac		1830	To self

October 1838

1109	Willson Robert H	1	1	1828	To self
1110	Lakey William	1	1	1829	To self
1111	Thompson Danl	1	1	1829	To self
1112	Parron Wm E	1	1	1829	To self
1114	McDonough Wm	1	1	1827	To self
1115	Graves Hezekiah	1	1	1829	To self
1116	Turner Edmond	1	1	1826	To self
1121	Lagow David	1	1	1829	To self
1125	Manna Robert	1	1	1828	To self
1126	Malvin Johnson	1	1	1827	To self
1127	Moore David L	1	1	1830	To self
1128	Mason John S	1	1	1828	To self
1129	Newton Jacob	1	1	1828	To self
1130	Lumpkin Richd C	1	1	1827	To self
1131	Moore Saml T	1	1	1829	To self
1133	Newton John	1	1	1829	To self
1134	McElroy Wm	1	1	1828	To self
1137	Graham Thos R	1	1	1827	To self
1138	Monroe Peter	1	1	1826	To self
1139	McLain James	1	1	1830	To self
1143	Malvin Richd	1	1	1830	To self
1144	Monroe John	1	1	1826	To self
1145	McRe John	1	1	1829	To self
1146	Monroe Wm T	1	1	1828	To self
1166	Allbright Edmond	1	1	1828	To self
1167	Calvertson Jas T	1	1	1828	To self
1168	Caloway Phillip	1	1	1826	To self

Clerk's Returns and Reports

1169 Calvertson Henry	1	1	1828	To self
1171 Newell David	1	1	1829	To self
1176 Larkin Peter	1	1	1829	To self
1179 McBride Edward	1	1	1829	To self
1180 Eldridge Elisha	1	1	1827	To self
1185 Allsup Elisha	1	1	1830	To self
1187 Duvaul Thos	1	1	1828	To self
1188 Hundley Jas C	1	1	1826	To self
1203 Woodruff Zachy	1	1	1828	To self
1205 McMullen Joseph	1	1	1826	To self
1207 McMullen Chas	1	1	1828	To self
1208 Sowell M	1	1	1826	To self
1211 Walkins Alfred	1	1	1825	To self
1212 Ashton Jno T	1	1	1830	To self
1214 Sowell Jno T	1	1	1830	To self
1219 Cravens Edwin R	1	1	1829	To self
1220 Ballard Archd	1	1	1827	To self
1221 Ray Allen S	1	1	1826	To self
1222 Burgess Dickson	1	1	1828	To self
1223 Bridgeman Jas T	1	1	1826	To self
1224 Fuller Seth W	1	1	1826	To self
1225 Parker Richd V	1	1	1826	To self
1226 Brown Selwin L	1	1	1828	To self
1227 Rogers James	1	1	1829	To self
1228 Bacon Richard	1	1	1830	To self
1229 Lee Thomas	1	1	1828	To self
1230 Williams Tilmon	1	1	1829	To self
1231 Estes Henry W	1	1	1829	To self
1232 Burney Abel	1	1	1826	To self
1233 Gorman Abner	1	1	1830	To self
1234 Childs Geo W	1	1	1826	To self
1235 Nobles John	1	1	1826	To self
1236 McDavid John	1	1	1830	To self
1237 Leroy Wm	1	1	1828	To self
1238 Morton James	1	1	1827	To self
1239 Morton Peter	1	1	1827	To self
1240 Tomlinson Wm S	1	1	1826	To self
1241 Mask Jno	1	1	1827	To self
1242 Tomlinson Thos S	1	1	1825	To self
1243 Purdue James	1	1	1828	To self
1244 Collins Lemuel	1	1	1827	To self
1245 Hambleton Frances	1	1	1828	To self
1247 Ziegler Edmund	1	1	1826	To self
1248 Comb Saml	1	1	1830	To self
1250 Goodall Adam	1	1	1826	To self
1252 Andrews Jas S	1	1	1828	To self
1253 Mask Jas V	1	1	1830	To self

November 1838

1270 Horton Susanna	—	1	1825	To self

1830 Citizens of Texas

April 1839
1389 Irvine Josephus S   2/3   1   1820   To self

SHELBY COUNTY   Clerk's Returns

No. 1 February 1838

John English	1	1	1825
Stephen English	1	1	1825
Dortrick McDavid	1/3		1829
Henry Assabranner	1	1	1830
Nathan Davis	1	1	1822
John Forsythe	1	1	1821
Silby Forsythe	1	1	1822
George Butler	—	1	1830
Elizabeth Lewis	1	1	1822
Harrison Davis	1	1	1822
Samuel McFaddin	1	1	1821
Jonathan McFaddin	1/3		1825
William T. English	1/3		1827
Moses Wooten	1	1	1823
Sarah English	1	1	1825
Monair Smyth	1	1	1824
Bailey Anderson	1	1	1825
Jesse McCelvey	1/3		1824
William English	1	1	1825
Squire Humphres	1/3		1825
James McCelvey	1	1	1824
Joseph English	1	1	1829
George English	370-1/3 ac		1829
Lewis Latham	1	1	1824
Alva R. Johnson	—	1	1830
Jonathan Anderson	1	1	1819
Rachael Story	1	1	1827
John C. Payne	1	1	1825
James Forsythe	1	1	1821
E. Rains	—	1	1822
David Strickland	1	1	1826
Richard Haley	1	1	1825
James Bowling	1	1	1827
Edward A. Merchant	1	1	1825
Mason M. Van	1	1	1825
Jose Santos	1	1	1830
Domingo Gonzales	1	1	1830
David Wilkason	1	1	1823
Elizabeth Choate	1	1	1821
Mary Strickland	1	1	1821
Amos Strickland	1	1	1822
Peter Stockman	1	1	1830
Elizabeth Rogers	1	1	1823
Elizabeth Graves	1	1	1825
Pierre Murvoir	1	1	1816

Clerk's Returns and Reports 211

Anteoine Douboiae	1	1	1818	
Susan Brewno	1	1	1823	
Antioine Duboiae Jr	1	1	1818	
Anastasha Carr	1	1	1830	D. A. Cunningham A<u>e</u>
Joseph S. Polvadore	1	1	1825	
Anderson Whetstone	1/3		1830	
Peter Whetstone	1	1	1830	
Hiram Thompson Adm<u>r</u>	1	1	1825	
of the Estate of Chas Thompson dec<u>d</u>				
Samuel Strickland Adm<u>r</u>	1	1	1826	
of the Estate of William Humphries dec<u>d</u>				
Thomas Haley	1	1	1821	
Susannah McCelvey	1	1	1826	
Nancy Smyth Adm<u>x</u> of	1	1	1830	
the Estate of William Smith dec<u>d</u>				
William Humphreys	---	1	1828	
James English Adm<u>r</u>	1	1	1822	
of the Estate of Even Lowery				
Matthew Dayne	1/3		1825	
Wiet Anderson	1/3		1822	
Elenor Harrison	1	1	1825	
Mary Haley	1	1	1825	
Asa Lankford	1/3		1830	Ahiea Butler Ass<u>ee</u>
Mary Arocha	1	1	1827	
Elizabeth Nail Adm<u>x</u> of	1/3		1824	
the Estate of George Humphres				
Nancy Mays [Mayo?]	1	1	1828	
Baley McFaddin	1/3		1821	
Hannah Dayne	1	1	1825	
John Little	---	1	1827	
Richard Haley Sen	1	1	1824	
Richard Haley Sen Adm<u>r</u>	1	1	1825	
of the estate of Richard Haley Sen dec<u>d</u>				
Archibald Smyth	1	1	1826	Mark Haley Ass<u>ee</u>
John R. Haley	1/3		182-	
Lucy Maragte	1	1	1830	F. Fay Ass<u>ee</u>

No. 2 March 1838

Andrew McFaddin	1	1	1830	Albert S. Kellog A<u>e</u>
Antonio Carr	---	1	1826	
Marsele Carr	1/3		1826	
Beniete Alderata	1	1	1828	
Stephen Holmes	1/3		1826	
John Applegate	1	1	1826	
Hampton Anderson	1	1	1825	
Gemedey Anderson	1/3		1821	
Bailey Anderson Sen	1/3		1821	
assignee of Bailey Anderson Jr				
Wiet Anderson dec<u>d</u>	1	1	1822	
John Latham Jr. Adm<u>r</u>	1	1	1821	

of John Latham Sen decd
Anteoin Barb Admr of   1   1 1826
    Estate of Ocela Bard decd

No. 3   April 1838
Clement Tutt   1   1 1824
John McGrew   1   1 1824   Chas Q. Haley Assee
Marela Algese   1   1 1830
Samuel Strickland   1   1 1824
Alfred Lout   1   1 1823
Richard Haley Jr Admr   1   1 1824
    of the Estate of Felician Gonzales decd

May 1838
Daniel Farmer Admr of   1   1 1824
    Estate of John Taner decd
Mary Alexander   1   1 1824   John Stout Assee
James Forsythe   1   1 1819
Amos Strickland Admr of 1/3   1826
    the Estate of Benj Strickland
Samuel Norris   1   1 1806   [1826?]
Edward Irons   1/3   1823   James Forsythe Ase
Catharine Stockman   1   1 1824   Seth Sheldon Assee
Joseph S. Good Admr of 1   1 1824
    the Estate of Henry Quirk decd
Humphrey C. Hag··   1   1 1821   R. O. Lusk Assee

Burton's Reports   May 24, 1838
328 Jose Ben Aldsevata 1   1 1828
 78 Hampton Anderson   —   1 1825
215 Wm King   1   1 1828
359 Jno M. Boadly assee 1   1 1825
    of E. Story
341 Hayward Anderson   1   1 1829
 74 Alfred Lout   1   1 1823
 50 Clement Tutt   1   1 1824
453 Jas H. King   1/3   1827   Wm King Assee
455 Jas Forsythe Admr of 1/3   1830
    Jno Man
A. D. Martinas   1   1 1827   Richard Haley Assee

Clerk's Return   June 1838
George T. Assabranner   1/3   1830
William Van   1/3   1829
George Glass Estate   1/3   1827   William Clark Admr

August 1838
Henry T. Stockman   1/3   1827
Wm F. Allen Estate   1   1 1830   Jas Forsythe Admr
Joseph Butler   —   1 1830   Moses F. Roberts Ae
Antonio Barbose   1/3   1815
Joseph Valentine   1   1 1823
John Haley   1/3   1825   Allen Haley Assee

Clerk's Returns and Reports   213

No. 1 July 1839 New Board
638 Susan Latham   1   1 1820 A. Sterne Assee

VICTORIA CO.

January-February 1838
  41 Rios Raphael by assignee   1   1 1829 Married
     John J. Linn
  42 John Wiley   1   1 1828 Married
  43 John Wiley only heir   1/3   1828 Single
     of Wm Wiley
  47 Charles Linn by Admr   1/3   1830 Single
     John J. Linn
  49 Edward Linn   369 ac   2 May 1830 Single
March through July 1838
  68 Richard Morgan by his   1/3   Fall of 1826 [1836?]
     Admr John P. Henry. Single.
  69 Patrick Dalton by his   1/3   1830 Single
     Admr John McHenry
  71 Patrick Quinn   369 ac   1824 Single
  73 Robert Burns by his   1/3   1830 Single
     Admr Arthur Burns
  75 Edward Perry   —   1 1828 Married
August to Novr 1838
  103 Margaret Trudo   1   — 1827 Widow
  115 William Hill Adminis-   1   1 1829
      trator of the Estate of Patrick McGloin. Married
  122 Bridget Hart Administra- —   1 1829 Married
      trix of the Estate of John Hart

WASHINGTON CO.

January 1838
   31 Andrew Miller   —   1 1824
  313 George Dare   1   1 1830
February 1838
  382 Furenash Jehu   1/12   1822
  402 Menchaca Jose' Francisco 1   — 1824
      by John Allcorn assignee
April 1838
  456 William T. Millican   1/3 less 1/4 Previous to 1825
  457 Aaron & Margaret Calvin 1   1 1823
      administrators of the Estate of Saml Shields decd
  464 John L. Sleight   1/3   1830
  481 William P. Tumlinson   1/3   1822
  482 Ellis Sessum   1/3   before 1830
      John T. Eubanks and Chas T. White assignees
May 1838 Report No. 5
  483 John Williams   1/3   1822
  486 John Furenash   1   1 1822

490 Elizth Hensley for the   —   1   before 1830
      Heirs of Harman Hensley decd
500 Saml Gates decd   —   1   1822
      Amos & Catherine Gates Executors of the estate
504 Charles Hensley   1/3   May 1829   James Hughes assignee

June 1838   Report No. 6
506 Prudence Kimble formerly   1 labor   1829
      Prudence Nash for the heirs of Nash
517 David Frost   1/3 less 1/4   1830   Augmentation
527 Elisha Whiteside   1/3   1825
529 Christopher C. Williams   1/3 less 1/4   1830

July 1838   Report No. 7
535 Abner Lee   —   1   1828
536 John Millican   1/3 less 1/4   1822   Augmentation
539 James R. Stevens   1/3 less 1/4   1829   Augmentation
542 Jackson Hensley   1/3 less 1/4   1829   Augmentation

August 1838   Report No. 8
563 James Stevens   —   1   1829
564 John Shaw   —   1   1828
565 William H. Smith   1/3   1830
566 Nancy Walker heir at   3/4   1   year 1825 or '26
      law of Wm Walker decd

October 1838   Report No. 10
572 Alfred Kinyon decd   1   —   1825
      James & Jemima Jones, administrators of the estate

December 1838
581 George W. Whiteside   —   1   1824
578 Moses Cumins   —   1   1829

REGISTERED VOTERS OF 1867

After the end of the Civil War, Texas and Louisiana formed one of the military districts set up by the Federal Government under the Reconstruction Acts. *Texas in Turmoil* by Ernest Wallace, Steck-Vaughn, Austin 1965, for example, explains the control over the registration of voters in that period.

". . . the Second Reconstruction Act . . . provided that the qualified citizens of each county should be registered before September 1, 1867, and that each registrant should take an oath that he had never held any legislative, executive, or judicial office in any state, or taken an oath as an officer to support the Constitution of the United States, and afterwards engaged in insurrection against the United States or given aid or comfort to its enemies . . . A board of three registrars for each subdistrict, usually a county, proceeded slowly with registration from May until August 31, and again from September 23 to 28. Many whites who were eligible did not register . . . Sheridan disqualified many who were eligible. In some instances, one radical wrote, "secessionists have been excluded almost without exception." The final count was 59,633 whites and 49,497 Negroes."

Each voter signed a special printed loyalty oath form in which he gave personal information, and his name was enrolled in a voter register. Registrations from each county were compiled into a set of very large books, now in the Archives of the Texas State Library. More than half of the entries give the number of years the voter had lived in the State, County, and precinct, as well as his local address and where he was born. The other half merely give the legal minimums of residence as required by law.

From this information, a voter who had lived in Texas for at least thirty-seven years (or 38 or 39 years depending on the registration date) could be assumed to have been living in Texas in 1830. Names of such voters have been abstracted for this compilation.

Although most Confederate veterans were disfranchised, this register is important because it gives personal data on blacks and those of Mexican origin. Years of residence have sometimes been given in round figures like 40 or 50 years, but since the statement was sworn, it must in the main have been correct.

THOMAS JEFFERSON CHAMBERS
— *Courtesy: San Jacinto Museum of History Association*

Various estimates of the percentage of Confederate disfranchised have been made. It seems to have varied from almost all in some counties to almost none in others.

Notations appear in the Register to denote a black voter. Since ethnic origin did not appear as a blank to be filled out in the printed oath taken by the voter, it is not apparent how this information was obtained. It appears in the Voters Registration now in the Archives in the form of red ink notations. The words vary from Colored through Col., C., F.M.C. and others whose meaning should be clear although they vary from one county to the next.

The 1867 Voters Register is in books too large to copy in a copy machine. They are available in the Archives Division of the Texas State Library, Austin, for research work.

1867 REGISTER OF VOTERS

No.	Date	Name	St.	How long in Co.	Pct.	Where Born
		ANDERSON CO.				
475	Aug 1867	Wm Y. Lacy	37	8	8	KY
1961	Nov 1867	John Murchison	39	28		SC
		ANDERSON CO.				
210	Aug 1867	Lysurgus S. Roberts	37	13	13	TX
406	Aug 1867	Samuel Burris	38	38		TX
		ATASCOSA CO.				
20	Jul 1867	Antonio Paddillo	60	10	10	TX
62	Jul 1867	Robert E. Neill	37	12	12	KY
84	Jul 1867	Ignacio Sotello	40	7	7	TX
121	Jul 1867	Absalom T. Tumlinson	40	11	11	Indian Terr.
149	Jul 1867	Henriques Esparza	39	12	12	TX
177	Jul 1867	Jose M. Cardenas	71	9	9	TX
178	Jul 1867	Crecencio Rodriguez	50	8	8	TX
189	Jul 1867	Ventura Gonzales	54	2	2	TX
214	Jul 1867	Fernando Cuviel	47	10	10	TX
229	Jul 1867	John Taylor	40	5	5	TX
243	Jul 1867	Angel Lial	62	1	1	TX
249	Jul 1867	Manuel Flores	67	15	15	TX
255	Jul 1867	Jesus Garza	42	3	3	Mexico
260	Jul 1867	William W. Adkins	37	4	4	SC
278	Jul 1867	Jose J. Hernandez	41	13	13	TX
281	Jul 1867	Miguel Pechi	56	55	55	TX
284	Sep 1867	Pablo Oliveravi	39	3 mo		TX
313	Sep 1867	Hendrick Thompson	38	4		TX
326	Sep 1867	Juan de Leon	54	3		TX
327	Sep 1867	Pasqual Cadena	41	6 mo		TX

218   1830 Citizens of Texas

334	Jan 1868	William B. Morris	37	12	12	AL	
335	Jan 1868	Antonio de los Santos Coy	47	8	8	Mexico	
		Emigrated to Texas in the year 1819					
348	Nov 1869	Tomas Perez	40	15	15	TX	
406	Nov 1869	Augustine Bernal	42	1	1	Mexico	
409	Nov 1869	James C. McDonald	40	13	5	LA	
467	Nov 1869	John Perkins	40	2	2	TX	

AUSTIN CO.

401	Jul 67	John Campbell	39	30		AR	
513	Jul 67	Ado Spade	40	1		NC	
534	Jul 67	Harold Lewis	37	21		TX	Col
616	Aug 67	David Shelby	45	30		PA	
1013	Aug 67	Alexander Spriggs	42	42		TX	Col
1023	Aug 67	George Carter	38	38		VA	Col
1049	Aug 67	Wm Logins	46	46		SC	Col
1067	Aug 67	Pickins Livingston	46	46		SC	Col
1081	Aug 67	Frederick J. Calvit	43	6 mo		MS	
1107	Aug 67	Stephen Webb	43	6 mo		VA	Col
1121	Aug 67	Franklin Johnson	46	46		TX	Col
1124	Aug 67	Spencer Livingston	47	47		TN	Col
1125	Aug 67	Thomas Hawkins	45	20		Guinea, Africa	Col
1143	Aug 67	Wm Lucas	38	38		VA	Col
1150	Aug 67	Abraham Lilly	46	46		SC	Col
1155	Aug 67	Johnson Hensley	49	30		TN	
1156	Aug 67	Abraham Cleggett	47	47		TX	Col
1184	Aug 67	Robert Boyd	46	46		AL	Col
1188	Aug 67	Thomas Banfield	45	9		KY	Col
1201	Aug 67	Leven Childs	38	38		——	Col
1224	Aug 67	James Bennet	40	6		PA	
1244	Aug 67	Jacob Hillyard	46	46		VA	Col
1451	Aug 67	Archilles R. Brookshire	37	37		MS	Col
1452	Aug 67	Benjamin Cooper	39	39		TX	
1461	Aug 67	James S. Brookshire	37	20		MS	
1474	Aug 67	John Jackson	44	44		SC	Col
1629	Sep 67	Stepney Jackson	40	40		TX	Col
1742	Sep 67	Alfred Roberts	46	2		MS	Col
1755	Sep 67	Robert Rice	37	37		TX	Col
1756	Sep 67	Peter Rice	40	40		KY	Col
1776	Jan 68	Moses Boyd	46	46		GA	Col
1782	Jan 68	Lewis Goodin	47	47		AL	Col
1974	Jan 68	Samuel McMillen	40	2		TX	Col
2040	Jan 68	John Hutchins	45	20		TX	
2062	Jan 68	James Boren	40	10		TX	
2100	Nov 69	Washington Collins	48	48		AL	Col
2173	Nov 69	Henry Johnson	50	50		GA	Col
2203	Nov 69	Henry Byers	42	42		TX	Col
2419	Nov 69	Nelson Livingston	46	46		TX	Col
2421	Nov 69	G. W. Grimes	40	38		KY	
2445	Nov 69	Steven Vaughn	39	39		SC	Col

Registered Voters of 1867

2559	Nov 69	Noel Smith	39	6 mo		LA	

BANDERA CO.

102	Jan 69	Joseph Miller	40	10		U.S.	

BASTROP CO.

520	Jul 67	Ruben Coleman	30			VA	Col
709	Jul 67	Freeman Blalock	38			TX	Col
717	Jul 67	Claiborne Osborn	41			TX	
722	Jul 67	James W. Standefer	37			AL	
762	Jul 67	Jonathan P. Scott	38			AL	
763	Jul 67	Timothy Scott	38			AL	
824	Jul 67	Oliver H. P. Cole	42			TX	
876	Jul 67	David Scott	39			AL	
1056	Jul 67	William Highsmith	38			MO	
1134	Jul 67	Anderson Qualls	44			TN	
1149	Aug 67	Joshua W. Collom	39			TX	
1214	Aug 67	James S. Gaines	40			TX	
1315	Aug 67	John H. Jenkins	40			AL	
1425	Aug 67	Zebulon P. Cottle	40			MO	
1429	Aug 67	Wade Jacob	40			AL	Col
1615	Jan 68	H. B. Wells	39			AL	

BEE CO.

42	Jul 67	Martin Pool	38	32	32	Ireland	
		Naturalized by coming into U.S. under age					
54	Aug 67	Charles S. Lockhart	37	9	9	TX	
69	Aug 67	Abner Yancey	50	7	7	VA	Col
70	Aug 67	Robert Carlisle	45	12	12	KY	
95	Jan 68	Roswell Gillett	50	6 mo		KY	

BELL CO.

1037	Nov 69	John Kegans	44	14	14	Native born	

BEXAR CO.

5	Jul 1, '67	Nat Lewis	40	31	15	MA
212	Jul 5, '67	M. A. Veramende	48	48	1	TX
277	Jul 6, '67	Jose' Antonio Navaro	70	70	70	TX
283	Jul 6, '67	F. de los Santos Gortari	50	50	50	TX
285	Jul 6, '67	Antonio Manchaca	67	67	67	TX
310	Jul 6, '67	H. L. Thompson	45	15	15	MO
345	Jul 8, '67	Antonio Sierra	37	37	37	TX
351	Jul 8, '67	Francisco R. Morales	57	57	57	TX
364	Jul 8, '67	Adrien Cardenas	38	38	38	TX
412	Jul 8, '67	E. Rivas	53	53	53	TX
413	Jul 8, '67	Damasco de los Reyes	54	54	21	TX
416	Jul 8, '67	Miguel Benitas	49	49	49	TX
471	Jul 8, '67	Leandro Chaves	58	58	58	TX
483	Jul 10, '67	Matias Cortizo	59	59	2	TX
487	Jul 10, '67	Augustine Barrera	63	63	63	TX
499	Jul 10, '67	Juan Rodriguez	40	40	10	TX

220   1830 Citizens of Texas

506	Jul 10, '67	Refugio Salasar [by mistake]	45	45	12	Mexico
507	Jul 10, '67	Jose' A. Cardena	39	39	7	TX
554	Jul 10, '67	Juan Jimenes	57	57	11	TX
563	Jul 10, '67	Rosario Perez	38	38	21	TX
571	Jul 10, '67	Benj Thomas	44	20	2	NC
606	Jul 10, '67	Antonio Hernandez	57	57	57	TX
618	Jul 10, '67	Jesus Perez	53	53		TX
579	Jul 13, '67	Francisco Flores	60	60		TX
711	Jul 13, '67	A. Sepeda	38	38	38	TX
712	Jul 13, '67	J. T. Cassiano	38	38	1	TX
713	Jul 13, '67	Manuel Martinez	40	40		TX
750	Jul 13, '67	Y. P. Alsbury	42	17		KY
756	Jul 15, '67	John Anto Montes de Oca	47	47	10	TX
758	Jul 15, '67	Jose Rivas	49	49		TX
762	Jul 15, '67	Jose M. Valdez	55	55	2	TX
784	Jul 15, '67	Ferman Martinez	46	46	46	TX
789	Jul 15, '67	Juan Garcia	39	39	39	Mexico
828	Jul 15, '67	Aniseto Martinez	51	51	37	TX
850	Jul 15, '67	Jose A. Gutierres	65	65	65	TX
903	Jul 15, '67	Monico Ortis	37	37	37	TX
927	Jul 16, '67	Calletano Rivas	52	52		TX
959	Jul 17, '67	Jose' Chavez	45	45	45	TX
996	Jul 17, '67	Juan J. Flores	63	63	63	TX
1011	Jul 17, '67	Ignacio Espenasa	53	53		TX
1013	Jul 17, '67	Gabriel Villareal	41	26		TX
1033	Jul 17, '67	Jose Delgado	43	43		LA
1049	Jul 19, '67	Renijio Mojaras	39	39		TX
1055	Jul 20, '67	Salomon Delgado	37	37		LA
1059	Jul 20, '67	Juan Valdes	50	50		TX
1062	Jul 20, '67	Jose de la Baume	63	40		TX
1074	Jul 20, '67	Jesus Gomes	48	48	3	TX
1083	Jul 22, '67	Juan Lasoya	46	46		TX
1084	Jul 22, '67	Lusiana Cabrera	54	54		TX
1085	Jul 22, '67	Lino Arocha	49	49		TX
1089	Jul 22, '67	Agapito Servantes	50	50		Tx
1093	Jul 22, '67	Dorateo Muñis	45	45		TX
1094	Jul 22, '67	Macario Tarin	43	43	43	TX
1095	Jul 22, '67	Simon Casanova	47	47	47	TX
1096	Jul 22, '67	Juan de Leon	47	47		TX
1100	Jul 22, '67	Ylario Martines	54	9	9	TX
1102	Jul 22, '67	Mariano Treviño	39	39		TX
1103	Jul 22, '67	Antonio Rodriquez	40	40	22	TX
1107	Jul 22, '67	Pablo Farias	45	45	37	TX
1120	Jul 22, '67	Remijio Casanova	53	53		TX
1125	Jul 22, '67	Lino Garcia	46	46		Mexico
1126	Jul 22, '67	Joaquin Tarin	47	47		TX
1127	Jul 22, '67	Jose Jaimes	50	50		TX
1128	Jul 22, '67	C. F. Beitel	39	18	18	PA
1132	Jul 22, '67	Francisco Herrera	39	39	20	TX

Registered Voters of 1867 221

1133	Jul 22, '67	Jose Miguel de la Garza	47	47	15	TX
1134	Jul 22, '67	Blas Herrera	65	65	22	TX
1135	Jul 22, '67	Benito Herrera	37	37	22	TX
1136	Jul 22, '67	Jose Antonio de la Garza	43	43	15	TX
1138	Jul 22, '67	Jesus Basques	45	45		TX
1140	Jul 22, '67	Antonio Lombrano	58	58	19	TX
1147	Jul 22, '67	Francisco Ruis	54	54	54	TX
1148	Jul 22, '67	Jesus Hernandez	55	55	22	TX
1150	Jul 22, '67	Manuel Estrada	59	59	59	TX
1186	Jul 27, '67	Nicolas Delgado	49	49		TX
1191	Jul 27, '67	Mariano Serna	37	37	6	TX
1192	Jul 27, '67	Blas Serna	40	40	6	TX
1215	Aug 2, '67	Roque Flores	60	60		TX
1230	Aug 6, '67	Plasido Olibarri	52	52	52	TX
1249	Aug 6, '67	Vivian Huron	38	38	20	TX
1261	Aug 7, '67	Anavato Martines	51	51	51	TX
1274	Aug 7, '67	Esteban Uron	41	41	20	TX
1292	Aug 8, '67	J. F. de la Garza	62	62	16	TX
1296	Aug 8, '67	Pedro Espinosa	58	40	16	TX
1342	Aug 10, '67	Carlos Sandoval	40	40	40	TX
1395	Sep 24, '67	Domingo Losoya	83	83		TX
1413	Sep 25, '67	Seferino Vizar	60	60		TX
1419	Sep 26, '67	Jesus Bustillo	41	41	6	TX
1420	Sep 26, '67	Lucas Sanches	42	42	42	TX
1448	Sep 28, '67	Alejo Montes de Oca	42	42	42	TX
1477	Jan 28, '68	J. A. Chavez	40	40		TX
1543	Jan 30, '68	Claudio Guerrero	41	41	41	TX
1551	Jan 30, '68	Antonio Huisar	40	40	40	TX
1552	Jan 30, '68	Nicholas Sanches	38	38	38	TX
1554	Jan 30, '68	Benino Arocha	40	40	40	TX
1582	Jan 31, '68	Jeremiah Claunch	38	2		AL
1682	Nov 16, '69	Lorenso Sausedo	40	40	40	TX
1637	Nov 16, '69	Clements Bustillo	54	54	54	TX
1657	Nov 16, '69	Jose Apelado	56	56	56	TX
1743	Nov 18, '69	Jose Alemeda	50	50	50	TX
1775	Nov 18, '69	Santiago Gutierres	39	39	39	TX
1812	Nov 19, '69	Canute Dias	60	60	60	TX
1813	Nov 19, '69	Maximo Bernal	40	40	40	Mexico
1814	Nov 19, '69	Mateo Casias	62	62	62	TX
1815	Nov 19, '69	Gabriel Martines	62	62	62	TX
1853	Nov 20, '69	Macedonia Arocha	40	40	40	TX
1869	Nov 20, '69	Juan Dias	42	42	42	TX
1912	Nov 23, '69	Ramon Menchaca	55	55	55	TX
1913	Nov 23, '69	Juan Ramon Augilar	50	50	50	TX
1915	Nov 22, '69	Acencio Baca	65	6	6	Mexico
1924	Nov 22, '69	Rufius Rodriguez	58	57	57	TX
1928	Nov 22, '69	Sebastian Degado	57	57	57	TX
1941	Nov 22, '69	Juan Sanches	61	61	61	TX
1942	Nov 22, '69	Ervin McRoss	39	4	4	TX	Colored

1830 Citizens of Texas

1944	Nov 22, '69	Antonio Leal	58	58	58	TX	
2016	Nov 24, '69	Juan Martines	44	44	44	TX	
2017	Nov 24, '69	Manuel Hernandes Sr	55	55	55	TX	
2038	Nov 24, '69	Louis Gomez	64	40	40	Mexico	
2042	Nov 24, '69	Gabriel Gonzales	43	30	30	Mexico	
2049	Nov 24, '69	Silverio Gomez	48	48	48	TX	
2054	Nov 24, '69	Antonio Seguin	43	43	43	TX	
2075	Nov 24, '69	Santos Blanco	45	20	20	TX	
2080	Nov 24, '69	Jesus Arranaga	58	58	58	TX	
2081	Nov 25, '69	Pedro Tejeda	51	51	51	TX	
2083	Nov 25, '69	Andreas Mata	39	39	39	TX	
2142	Nov 26, '69	Nepusera Navaro	56	10	10	TX	
2151	Nov 26, '69	Ygnacio Sandoval	42	42	42	TX	
2155	Nov 26, '69	Manuel Gil	41	41	41	TX	
2163	Nov 26, '69	Gil Silas	40	40	40	TX	
2166	Nov 26, '69	S. Rodrigues	46	46	46	TX	
2171	Nov 26, '69	Antonio Dariah	48	48	48	TX	
2172	Nov 26, '69	Herinomo Leal	64	64	64	TX	
2175	Nov 26, '69	Francisco Casas	40	40	40	TX	
2178	Nov 26, '69	Jose Maria Ocon	55	28	28	Mexico	
2205	Nov 26, '69	Jose M. Guerrero	29	30	30	Mexico	
2227	Nov 26, '69	Jesus Vasquez	47	47	47	Mexico	
		BLANCO CO.					
1	Jul 17, '67	John McCoy	45	4	4	KY	
132	Nov 16, '69	Augustus Pharr	43	11		MS	
		BRAZORIA CO.					
21	Jul 30, '67	George Nabner	37	37	37	NC	Col
38	Jul 30, '67	Thomas Hardeman	37	37	37	TN	Col
41	Jul 30, '67	Jefferson Bryant	43	43	43	VA	Col
52	Jul 30, '67	William Thomas	36	36	36	VA	Col
83	Jul 31, '67	Ennin Johnson	42	42	42	VA	Col
91	Jul 31, '67	Francis Churchill	42	42	42	VA	Col
93	Jul 31, '67	Ambrose Harrison	40	40		KY	Col
107	Jul 31, '67	Louis Lewis	40	40		AL	Col
109	Jul 31, '67	William Davis	37	37		TX	Col
131	Aug 1, '67	Isaac Franklin	50	50		LA	Col
136	Aug 1, '67	Jeremiah Miller	40	40		TX	Col
156	Aug 1, '67	Ralph Ramsey	39	39		KY	Col
164	Aug 1, '67	Thomas Hayes	41	4		GA	Col
172	Aug 1, '67	Matthew Channin	38	38		TN	Col
185	Aug 1, '67	Abraham Hampton	40	40		TX	Col
214	Aug 2, '67	Madison Crutcher	40	40		NC	Col
301	Aug 3, '67	Marshall Blake	40	40		VA	Col
316	Aug 3, '67	Jeremiah Freeman	42	42		VA	Col
318	Aug 3, '67	Willis Littleton	39	39		TN	Col
327	Aug 3, '67	Levi Lipkins	39	39		TN	Col
332	Aug 5, '67	Jacob Gonner	39	17		NC	Col
394	Aug 6, '67	London Watson	40	40		GA	Col

407	Aug 7, '67	Jackson Johnson	38	38		TX	Col
477	Aug 9, '67	Dennis Lucker	40	40		TX	Col
540	Aug 12, '67	William C. Tony	40	40		MS	Col
544	Aug 12, '67	James Davis	39	39		MD	Col
584	Aug 12, '67	Jack Story	45	45		GA	Col
657	Aug 14, '67	Thomas Bowler	45	45		LA	Col
780	Aug 14, '67	Henry Thomson	40	40		TN	Col
841	Aug 15, '67	Anthony McNeal	40	40		KY	Col
876	Aug 15, '67	Alfred Brown	44	44		TN	Col
916	Aug 16, '67	Burt Willey	40	40		MD	Col
934	Aug 21, '67	Samuel McCullough	39	39		GA	Col
957	Aug 21, '67	Joshua G. Lipkins	40	40		TN	Col
974	Aug 21, '67	Charles Brown	43	43		GA	Col
1000	Aug 22, '67	Abraham George	40	40		GA	Col
1003	Aug 22, '67	Solomon Williams	45	45		KY	Col
1025	Aug 22, '67	Charles George	38	38		AL	Col
1107	Aug 23, '67	Isiah Porter	40	40		TN	Col
1119	Aug 24, '67	Milburn James	37	37		AL	Col
1120	Aug 24, '67	Henry Hilyard	44	44		GA	Col
1169	Aug 24, '67	Gabriel Lewis	40	40		GA	Col
1180	Sep 3, '67	Peter Bell	38	38		GA	Col
1209	Sep 5, '67	Norris Wiggins	37	37		TX	Col
1269	Sep 7, '67	Francis Umstead	38	38		NC	Col
1302	Sep 10, '67	William Williams	44	44		AL	Col
1333	Sep 24, '67	Edward Porter	40	40		VA	Col
1381	Sep 28, '67	Pleasant D. McNeil	45	45		KY	
1382	Sep 28, '67	John Smelzer	40	40		TN	
1498	Nov 20, '69	Milburn James	39	39		AL	Col
1559	Nov 24, '69	James C. Louis	39	39		TN	
1560	Nov 24, '69	John M. Louis	39	39		TN	
1561	Nov 24, '69	W. F. Louis	39	39		AL	
1604	Nov 26, '69	J. T. Tinsley	39	39		TN	

BRAZOS CO.

51	Jun 21, '67	A. C. Neill	38	6	6	Native	
511	Jun 28, '67	Harry Williams	50	50	50	——	Colored
729	Jul 2, '67	A. J. Hall	37	1	1	——	
733	Jul 2, '67	Barry Millican	40	40	40	——	Colored
761	Jul 3, '67	McCoy Brown	45	36	36	——	Colored
1441	Nov 19, '69	Aaron Bailey	40	2		——	Colored
1461	Nov 19, '69	J. Walter White	41	8		——	
1467	Nov 19, '69	Tom Newsom	40	10		——	Colored
1428	Nov 19, '69	Tom Lewis	40	1		——	Colored
1539	Nov 20, '69	Joseph Greer	40	1		——	Colored
1657	Nov 22, '69	Wm Burton	40	1		——	Colored
1723	Nov 23, '69	James Harris	40	1		——	Colored
1745	Nov 23, '69	Chesterfield Polk	40	1		——	Colored
1879	Nov 25, '69	J. R. Stewart	40	12		——	

1830 Citizens of Texas

BURLESON CO.

31	Jul 2, '67	A. M. Williams	37	1		Native
191	Jul 5, '67	Jos Chrisman	40	20	20	Native Col
415	Jul 9, '67	Isaac Jackson	40	10	10	Native
418	Jul 9, '67	Wm Jackson	42	14	14	Native
660	Jul 15, '67	S. Lorance	40	20	20	Native
1107	Jan 27, '68	Horatio Chrisman	46	24	24	Native

CAMERON CO.

77	Jul 15, '67	Juan Miguel Longoria Carvazas	40	2	2	Mexico
128	Aug 2, '67	Melchor Salinas	46	46		Mexico
130	Aug 2, '67	Clementas Larvana	48	43		Mexico
132	Aug 2, '67	Francisco Garcia	45	45	45	TX
133	Aug 2, '67	Luis Puabla	45	45	21	Mexico
140	Aug 3, '67	Pedro Garcia	38	38	38	Mexico
146	Aug 5, '67	Francisco Salinas	38	38	38	Mexico
167	Aug 9, '67	Jose M. Trevino	38	38	38	TX
162	Aug 9, '67	Jose Antonio de la Garza Urest	60	60	60	TX
165	Aug 9, '67	Apuricio Cantuu	64	64	64	TX
166	Aug 9, '67	Valentine Sallas	41	2	2	TX
167	Aug 9, '67	Jose Ignacio E. Trabieso	67	2	2	TX
171	Aug 9, '67	Carlas Esparez	40	40	40	TX
182	Aug 10, '67	Manuel Mantolvo	48	48	48	Mexico
254	Aug 28, '67	Antonio Ramon	47	47	47	TX
270	Aug 30, '67	Juan Antonio Vargues	42	42	42	Mexico
272	Aug 30, '67	Jose Enjenio	39	2	2	TX
274	Aug 31, '67	Jose Marien Bocanegro	50	37		TX
278	Aug 31, '67	Agapito Guerro	42	42		Mexico
309	Jan 27, '68	Jose Aguerro	41	2		TX
410	Nov 18, '68	Margil Salinas	47	2	2	TX
445	Nov 18, '68	Ygnacio Trevino	50	50	50	TX
446	Nov 18, '68	Jose Maria Espaza	54	54	54	Mexico
458	Nov 19, '68	Slin Barcena	41	41	41	Mexico
465	Nov 19, '68	Levcadio Salinas	59	59	59	TX
467	Nov 19, '68	Pablo Cano	38	38	38	Mexico
507	Nov 20, '69	Salustiana Cantu	50	2	2	Mexico
519	Nov 20, '69	Amciti Ramirez	48	25		TX
530	Nov 22, '69	Pedro Gonzales	39	39	39	Mexico
532	Nov 22, '69	Isidro Hernandez	40	40	40	Mexico
541	Nov 22, '69	Eugenio Guzman	44	7	7	TX
545	Nov 22, '69	Casme Torres	45	45	45	TX
547	Nov 22, '69	Jesus Becarra	65	27	27	TX
567	Nov 69	Pedro Garza	50	11	11	TX
585	Nov 69	Js Defond Flores	46	46	46	Mexico
586	Nov 69	Comdio Bazguez	45	45	45	TX
590	Nov 69	Antonio Carascas	43	43	43	Mexico
591	Nov 69	Manuel Carascas	43	18	18	Mexico
596	Nov 69	Felipe Mirales	44	3	3	TX
619	Nov 69	Matias Garcia	43	43	43	Mexico

Registered Voters of 1867 225

659	Nov 69	Raphael Vela	49	1	1	Mexico	
661	Nov 69	Ramon Garcia	55	55	55	Mexico	

CHAMBERS CO.

11	Aug 67	Henry Jackson	49	16	16	VA	Col
39	Aug 67	Jerry Toran	39	39	39	VA	Col
97	Aug 67	Henry Griffith Sr	40	40	40	PA	b 1797
109	Aug 67	Charles Wilcox	37	36	36	R.I.	b 1785
124	Aug 67	Nathaniel Brown	40	40	40	SC	Col
126	Aug 67	Jacob Blue	40	40	40	LA	Col
127	Aug 67	J. T. White	38	38	38	TX	b 1829
135	Aug 67	Benjamin Barrow	40	40	40	LA	b 1808
136	Aug 67	Reuben Barrow	38			LA	b 1815
165	Aug 67	Benj Barrow	38	38	38	LA	b 1817
190	Aug 67	Elisha Stephenson	39	29	29	LA	b 1817
191	Aug 67	Alexander Edgar	37	6	6	Scotland	
192	Aug 67	John Jackson	44	21	21	LA	b 1820
193	Aug 67	James Jackson	44	21	21	LA	b 1822
216	Sep 67	J. C. Fisher	39	25	25	LA	b 1819
219	Jan 68	W. S. McManus	40	40	40	TX	Col

COLORADO CO.

269	Jul 67	William Alley	42	42	42	MO	
333	Jul 67	George W. Smith	38	18	18	TX	Col
335	Jul 67	Frank Jenkins	40	16	16	TX	Col
406	Jul 67	S. R. Bostick	38	36	36	AL	
645	Jul 67	Frank Ansland	45	45	45	VA	Col
655	Jul 67	Major Jerrell	37	½	½	NC	Col
1100	Aug 67	W. B. Scates	38	20	20	VA	
1178	Aug 8, '67	T. W. Hunter	40	4	4	TX	
1894	Nov 16, '69	John W. Keith	46	1	1	FL	
1935	Nov 17, '69	W. Thompson	40	7	7	AL	Col
1995	Nov 18, '69	Shadrach Cayce	39	2	2	TN	

COMAL CO.

4	22 Aug 67	Joseph Rumsey	48	7 mo		KY	Freedman
198	25 Jul 67	Sandford Graves	48	13		KY	Freedman
846	Nov 26, '69	George T. Neill	39	14		TN	b 1830

COMANCHE CO.

59	Aug 22, '67	R. B. Smith	38	8 mo		MS	

COOKE CO.

86	Jul 24, '67	Hugh Gray [struck]: Gone	40	1	1	AR	

DALLAS CO.

1302	Jan 31, '69	Geo W. Guess	41	14	14	NC	

DE WITT CO.

84	Jul 17, '67	Gabriel Jones	37	14	14	U.S.A.	Color.
287	Jul 22, '67	Joseph Tumlinson	42	20	20	U.S.A.	
290	Jul 22, '67	Walter Anderson	44	16	16	U.S.A.	

341	Jul 23, '67	William Ratliffe	43	15	15	U.S.A.
348	Jul 23, '67	Joseph A. Newman	39	3 mo		U.S.A.
375	Jul 23, '67	Alfred Friar	37	26	26	U.S.A.
571	Jul 31, '67	Robert Peebles	38	21	21	U.S.A.
643	Jul 31, '67	Pero Torres	47	over 1		U.S.A.
786	Aug 7, '67	George C. Tennelle	41	20	20	U.S.A.
839	Sep 27, '67	P. B. Taylor	38	20	20	U.S.
840	Sep 27, '67	Jonathan York	40	20	20	U.S.
888	Nov 16, '69	Wyatt Anderson	45	18	18	LA

ELLIS CO.

219	Jul 27, '67	Wm M. Boren	37	15		TX
799	Aug 31, '67	Joseph Boren	48	19	19	KY
56	Jul 28, '67	N. B. Rankin	38	16	16	TX

EL PASO CO.

7	Aug 19, '67	Luciano Guerre	46	46	46	Texas
8	Aug 19, '67	Benito Marujo	58	58	58	Texas
9	Aug 19, '67	Jose Tellos	38	38	38	Texas
13	Aug 19, '67	Jose Ma Telles	55	55	55	Texas
15	Aug 20, '67	Gregorio Paiz	37	37	37	Texas
16	Aug 20, '67	Higinio Duran	39	39	39	Texas
17	Aug 20, '67	Faustin Duran	59	59	59	Texas
21	Aug 20, '67	Santiago Duran	40	40	40	Texas
22	Aug 20, '67	Tomas Duran	48	48	48	Texas
24	Aug 20, '67	Benito Rodila	40	40	40	Texas
26	Aug 20, '67	Martin Duran	50	50	50	Texas
28	Aug 20, '67	Tomas Granillo	52	52	52	Texas
36	Aug 20, '67	Martin Lopez	45	45	45	Texas
40	Aug 20, '67	Encarnacion Granillo	50	50	50	Texas
42	Aug 20, '67	Rafel Diaz	40	40	40	Texas
43	Aug 20, '67	Tinisted Trujillo	58	58	58	Texas
45	Aug 20, '67	Feliz Duran	80	80	80	Texas
47	Aug 20, '67	Nicolas Padilla	43	43	43	Texas
48	Aug 20, '67	Siriaca Marguez	72	72	72	Texas
49	Aug 20, '67	Ricardo Telles	44	44	44	Texas
53	Aug 20, '67	Marcial Telles	41	41	41	Texas
55	Aug 20, '67	Jose Apodaco	50	50	50	Texas
56	Aug 20, '67	Isidro Colmenero	38	38	38	Texas
57	Aug 20, '67	Rafel Padillo	50	50	50	Texas
59	Aug 20, '67	Benito Apodaco	38	38	38	Texas
61	Aug 20, '67	Fabian Granillo	43	43	43	Texas
62	Aug 20, '67	Jesus Guerre	40	40	40	Texas
64	Aug 20, '67	Francisco Gonzales	50	50	50	Texas
65	Aug 20, '67	Juan Alderete	43	43	43	Texas
67	Aug 20, '67	Victoriano Piarote	41	41	41	Texas
76	Aug 21, '67	Madalino Marquez	40	40	40	Texas
78	Aug 21, '67	Manuel Telles	38	38	38	Texas
84	Aug 21, '67	Francisco Tapia	60	60	60	Texas

Registered Voters of 1867

87	Aug 21, '67	Claro Garcia		37	37	37	Texas
95	Aug 21, '67	Pablo Telles		37	37	37	Texas
97	Aug 23, '67	Rafel Telles		39	39	39	Texas
98	Aug 23, '67	Crisoto Carrascas		45	45	45	Texas
99	Aug 23, '67	Inez Frescas		46	46	46	Texas
100	Aug 23, '67	Marcos Telles		68	68	68	Texas
101	Aug 23, '67	Jesus Estrada		44	44	44	Texas
102	Aug 23, '67	Gregorio Ortiz		50	50	50	Texas
106	Aug 23, '67	Felix Palanco		66	66	66	Texas
107	Aug 23, '67	Vicente Cadena		60	60	60	Texas
109	Aug 23, '67	Marcelo Prudencio		46	46	46	Texas
111	Aug 23, '67	Juan Ligon		62	62	62	Texas
116	Aug 23, '67	Jose D. Sepulvera		38	38	38	Texas
117	Aug 23, '67	Rosalio Astrada		42	42	42	Texas
120	Aug 23, '67	Francisco Garcia		45	45	45	Texas
124	Aug 23, '67	Ignacio Guerre		53	53	53	Texas
125	Aug 23, '67	Antonio Paiz		59	59	59	Texas
129	Aug 23, '67	Jose Ligon		72	72	72	Texas
134	Aug 23, '67	Anastasio Apodeca		39	39	39	Texas
135	Aug 23, '67	Demacio Cortez		50	50	50	Texas
140	Aug 23, '67	Higinio Frescas		47	47	47	Texas
141	Aug 23, '67	Tomas Lopez		46	46	46	Texas
144	Aug 23, '67	Jose Gomez		40	40	40	Texas
146	Aug 23, '67	Andreas Provencio		44	44	44	Texas
147	Aug 23, '67	Juan J. Montoyo		52	52	52	Texas
154	Aug 23, '67	Altegracia Chavas		62	62	62	Texas
156	Aug 23, '67	Filipe Olguin		56	56	56	Texas
159	Aug 23, '67	Luciana Giron		50	50	50	Texas
161	Aug 23, '67	Juan R. Jurada		80	80	80	Texas
162	Aug 23, '67	Antonio Perez		70	70	70	Texas
163	Aug 23, '67	Alexandro Urtiaga		54	54	54	Texas
166	Aug 23, '67	Manuel Pruvencio		38	38	38	Texas
170	Aug 23, '67	Calistro Olguin		60	60	60	Texas
172	Aug 23, '67	Ramon Sisnera		65	65	65	Texas
175	Aug 23, '67	Florentino Padilla		56	56	56	Texas
179	Aug 23, '67	Blas Provencio		62	62	62	Texas
183	Aug 23, '67	Apolonio Olguin		67	67	67	Texas
187	Aug 23, '67	Pedro Carasca		54	54	54	Texas
192	Aug 23, '67	Polito Marquez		40	40	40	Texas
196	Aug 23, '67	Juan R. Gomez		60	60	60	Texas
200	Aug 24, '67	Santos Telles		40	40	40	Texas
209	Aug 24, '67	Martias Pedrazo		38	38	38	Texas
210	Aug 24, '67	Juan Jose Gomez		50	50	50	Texas
212	Aug 24, '67	Jose de la Gandara		62	62	62	Texas
215	Aug 24, '67	Pedro Gandara		48	48	48	Texas
219	Aug 24, '67	Guadalupe Lopez		41	41	41	Texas
220	Aug 24, '67	Tomas Sanches		53	53	53	Texas
221	Aug 26, '67	Jose Chaves		50	50	50	Texas
224	Aug 26, '67	Juan de Aro		50	50	50	Texas

227	Aug 26, '67	Julian Chaves	50	50	50	Texas
230	Aug 26, '67	Militon Apodaca	39	39	39	Texas
233	Aug 27, '67	Nicolas Juarez	50	50	50	Texas
234	Aug 27, '67	Andres Astrada	48	48	48	Texas
237	Aug 27, '67	Panfilo Lucero	39	39	39	Texas
239	Aug 27, '67	Pedro Lopez	43	43	43	Texas
241	Aug 27, '67	Jesus Medina	50	50	50	Texas
244	Aug 27, '67	Tomas Maise	49	49	49	Texas
245	Aug 27, '67	Ambrosia Olguin	40	40	40	Texas
253	Aug 27, '67	Telesforo Montez	47	47	47	Texas
258	Aug 27, '67	Perfecto Ortega	42	42	42	Texas
259	Aug 27, '67	Dolores Apodaca	50	50	50	Texas
260	Aug 27, '67	Jose Peris 1st	50	50	50	Texas
261	Aug 27, '67	Sostenes Beltran	60	60	60	Texas
270	Aug 27, '67	Perfecto Ortiz	49	49	49	Texas
278	Aug 27, '67	Jose Guerre	60	60	60	Texas
284	Aug 27, '67	Juan Jose Nunez	53	53	53	Texas
286	Aug 27, '67	Pedro Arroyes	40	40	40	Texas
288	Aug 27, '67	Placido Herrera	40	40	40	Texas
293	Aug 27, '67	Victoriana Oporto	48	48	48	Texas
299	Aug 27, '67	Higinio Duran	40	40	40	Texas
301	Aug 27, '67	Albino Olivarez	46	46	46	Texas
302	Aug 27, '67	Tumin Caballero	60	60	60	Texas
305	Aug 27, '67	Icundo Alberado	50	50	50	Texas
315	Aug 27, '67	Jesus Duran	43	43	43	Texas
318	Aug 27, '67	Ricardo Valencia	42	42	42	Texas
320	Aug 27, '67	Anecleto Escajada	38	38	38	Texas
323	Aug 27, '67	Matias Benavidas	43	43	43	Texas
325	Aug 27, '67	Santos Lucero	67	67	67	Texas
329	Aug 28, '67	Regina Olguin	45	45	45	Texas
330	Aug 28, '67	Jose Ma Chavez	53	53	53	Texas
331	Aug 28, '67	Vicento Lucero	40	40	40	Texas
336	Aug 28, '67	Andreas Olguin	50	50	50	Texas
337	Aug 28, '67	Nacario Gomez	48	48	48	Texas
338	Aug 28, '67	Berabas Jerez	58	58	58	Texas
340	Aug 28, '67	Eusibia Gomez	48	48	48	Texas
342	Aug 28, '67	Alcaria Loya	47	47	47	Texas
343	Aug 28, '67	Antiqui Olguin	40	40	40	Texas
345	Aug 28, '67	Jose Ma Almengor	39	39	39	Texas
347	Aug 28, '67	Loquario Loya	46	46	46	Texas
349	Aug 28, '67	Trinidad Parada	42	42	42	Texas
350	Aug 28, '67	Jose Dios Gandara	38	38	38	Texas
352	Aug 28, '67	Elatario Lucero	67	67	67	Texas
407	Aug 31, '67	Augustine Barilla	61	61	61	Texas
408	Aug 31, '67	Jose Ma Alderete	43	43	43	Texas
410	Aug 31, '67	Manuel Jimines	38	38	38	Texas
412	Aug 31, '67	Francisco Telles	66	66	66	Texas
416	Aug 31, '67	Martin Paiz	43	43	43	Texas
432	Aug 31, '67	Jose Ma Durand	48	48	48	Texas

434	Aug 31, '67	Esteban Pirote	40	40	40	Texas	
443	Jan 30, '68	Jose Ma Gonzales	42	42	42	Texas	
445	Jan 30, '68	Narcia Loya	38	38	38	Texas	
449	Jan 30, '68	Gregoria Garcia	49	49	49	Texas	
450	Jan 30, '68	Gorgonio Alrian	40	40	40	Texas	
451	Jan 30, '68	Martin Lujan	51	51	51	Texas	
452	Jan 30, '68	Martin Alderete	49	49	49	Texas	
454	Jan 30, '68	Marilo Barila	49	49	49	Texas	
459	Nov 17, '69	Juan de Dios Carrasco	65	65	65	Texas	
461	Nov 17, '69	Justo Heradio	60	60	60	Texas	
462	Nov 17, '69	Ygnosento Biscarra	40	40	40	Texas	
464	Nov 17, '69	Jose Ma Berrere	50	50	50	Texas	
466	Nov 17, '69	Nichelos Romaro	61	61	61	Texas	
470	Nov 17, '69	Amicacio Tarin	50	50	50	Texas	
483	Nov 18, '69	Jesus Lujan	55	55	55	Texas	
484	Nov 18, '69	Ylario Albilar	50	50	50	Texas	
493	Nov 19, '69	Leandro Padia	49	49	49	Texas	
496	Nov 19, '69	Victor Maruja	69	69	69	Texas	
497	Nov 19, '69	Andres Duran	45	45	45	Texas	
517	Nov 20, '69	Christobal Brisceno	42	42	42	Texas	
518	Nov 20, '69	Jose Ma Lopez	61	61	61	Texas	
525	Nov 20, '69	Juan Pablo Carasco	39	39	39	Texas	
550	Nov 22, '69	Jesus Medina	50	50	50	Texas	
553	Nov 22, '69	Ancleto Olgin	50	50	50	Texas	
556	Nov 22, '69	Gregorio Olguin	49	49	49	Texas	
558	Nov 22, '69	Julian Chaves	50	50	50	Texas	
561	Nov 22, '69	Concepcion Arras	40	40	40	Texas	
566	Nov 22, '69	Julian Arras	50	50	50	Texas	
582	Nov 22, '69	Luis Semboaner	46	46	46	Texas	
583	Nov 23, '69	Bernard Trujillo	42	42	42	Texas	
595	Nov 23, '69	Polonio Zorlosols	50	50	50	Texas	
598	Nov 23, '69	Torinio Lusere	40	40	40	Texas	
623	Nov 24, '69	Juan Jose Medina	42	42	42	Texas	
631	Nov 24, '69	Gregorio Albrado	42	42	42	Texas	
633	Nov 24, '69	Gregorio Carbajel	40	40	40	Texas	
634	Nov 24, '69	Hilario Padilla	42	42	42	Texas	
648	Nov 25, '69	Juan S. Gonzales	54	54	54	Texas	
649	Nov 25, '69	Jose Lujaro	74	74	74	Texas	
657	Nov 25, '69	Jose Gonzales	88	88	88	Texas	
658	Nov 25, '69	Bentina Lopez	50	50	50	Texas	
689	Nov 26, '69	Victor Balencia	40	40	40	Texas	
697	Nov 26, '69	Nipomeseno Sembranon	55	55	55	Texas	
700	Nov 26, '69	Lino Guerre	40	40	40	Texas	
		FAYETTE CO.					
12	Jul 8, '67	Quin M. Menifee	37	20		AL	
145	Jul 10, '67	Wm H. Matthews	44	19	12	AL	
273	Jul 12, '67	Jno H. Moore	46	30	30	TN	
384	Jul 13, '67	Moses Williams	46	17		LA	Colored
390	Jul 13, '67	Wm B. Moore	39	39	39	Texas	

397	Jul 13, '67	Ulysses Rabb	37	29	29	VA	
597	Jul 17, '67	Tom Rivers	39	1½	1½	NC	
735	Jul 22, '67	James T. Ross	47	23	23	AR	
1179	Jul 31, '67	W. F. Lyons	37	37	37	OH	
1181	Jul 31, '67	C. C. Ragsdale	46	24	16	AR	
1383	Aug 9, '67	Henry Hardeman	37	½	½	TN	Color.
2288	Jan 31, '68	William Hodge	41	13	13	TX	

FORT BEND CO.

583	Aug 10, '67	W. Thompson	40	8		Native	Color.
587	Aug 10, '67	Jefferson Gay	41	25		Native	Color.
627	Aug 12, '67	Tom Taylor	43	6 mo		Native	Color.
631	Aug 13, '67	Phil Franklin	38	15		Native	Color.
651	Aug 13, '67	Richard Prater	40	40		Native	Color.
654	Aug 13, '67	Egay Texas	40	39		Native	Color.
720	Aug 13, '67	Theodore Carter	41	5 mo		Native	Color.
793	Aug 15, '67	Alph Thompson	41	12		Native	Color.
801	Aug 15, '67	Kemp Plummer	40	20		Native	Color.
858	Aug 15, '67	Uleses Lambert	46	46		Native	Color.
936	Aug 17, '67	Anderson Randen	39	39 [struck]		Native	Color.
951	Aug 17, '67	Geo Martin	38	38		Native	Color.
989	Aug 19, '67	Carson King	40	4		Native	Color.
1067	Aug 20, '67	Levi Morris	40	2		Native	Color.
1083	Aug 21, '67	Geo Kelser	45	11		Native	Color.
1119	Aug 23, '67	Charles Addison	40	1		Native	Color.
1148	Aug 24, '67	Abner Eckols	37	37		Native	Color.
1178	Aug 26, '67	Jacob Stewart	40	13		Native	Color.
1200	Aug 26, '67	Fred Long	39	39		Native	Color.
1201	Aug 26, '67	Geo Staffen	37	3		Native	Color.
1258	Sep 4, '67	William P. Huff	43	20		Native	
1363	Jan 31, '68	Daniel Texas	50	2 mo		Native	Color.
1365	Jan 31, '68	Harry Texas	50	2		Native	Color.
1370	Jan 31, '68	Thomas J. Hunter	46	38		Native	
1367	Nov 17, '69	Pleasants, G. W.	39	32	32	NC	
1492	Nov 24, '69	Newell, J. D.	40	12	12	NC	
1503	Nov 24, '69	Gale, Adam	50	20	20	VA	Color.
1587	Nov 27, '69	Thompson, H. W.	45	35	25	AL	
1618	Nov 29, '69	Foster, Ran	48	48	48	MS	
1626	Nov 29, '69	Shipman, J. R.	45	44	44	SC	
1642	Nov 29, '69	Thompson, Jesse	40	35	35	AL	
1650	Nov 29, '69	Jackson, Cato	57	3	3	VA	Color.

FREESTONE CO.

1627	Nov 24, '69	William Anderson	45	18 mo		Texas	

GALVESTON CO.

116	Jun 5, '67	Edmond Hickman	40	40	4 mo	Native	Col
340	Jun 8, '67	Luke Hall	37	24		Native	Col
562	Jun 12, '67	Charles McGale	40	14 m		Native	Col
722	Jun 14, '67	Thomas Ellis	40	40	12	Native	Col
743	Jun 14, '67	Granville Penn	37	4 m		Native	Col

Registered Voters of 1867

770	Jun 15, '67	Thornton Burrell	45	2		Native	Col
815	Jun 18, '67	Michael Andrews	40	40	40	Native	Col
1376	Jul 3, '67	L. W. Groce	46	4 m		Native	
1395	Jul 6, '67	Roben Wills	37	18	13	Native	
1496	Jul 9, '67	George H. Treat	40	40	2	Native	
1661	Jul 13, '67	David G., Burnet	41	8	1	Native	[Struck]

GOLIAD CO.

91	Jul 17, '67	Leander, Raphael	40	16	16	U.S.A.	
119	Jul 19, '67	Alderett, Raphael	51	16	16	Texas	
126	Jul 19, '67	Lasso, Charles	75	16	16	Native	
130	Jul 19, '67	Salusar, Ehinis	41	41	41	Native	
131	Jul 19, '67	Leander, Antonio Sr.	62	62	62	Native	
133	Jul 19, '67	Mendez, Ignacio	49	49	49	Native	
166	Jul 19, '67	Cabrena, Mariano	55	55	55	Native	
167	Jul 19, '67	Flores, Dionicio	45	45	45	Native	
168	Jul 19, '67	Losano, Antonio	42	22	22	Native	
210	Jul 22, '67	Carvjal, Juan	44	44	44	Native	
217	Jul 22, '67	Cavrara, Juan	40	16	16	Native	
249	Jul 25, '67	Amador, Antonio	58	58	58	Native	
258	Jul 25, '67	Harmandes, Dolores	50	50	50	Native	
370	Jul 30, '67	Flowers, R.	37	13	13	U.S.A.	
404	Aug 2, '67	Gado del Juan	47	47	47	Mexico	
405	Aug 2, '67	Gado del Antonio	37	37	37	Mexico	
527	Nov 24, '69	Goins, Robert	40	4	4	USA	Color
519	Nov 24, '69	Kuykendall, James W.	40	15	1	USA	
558	Nov 24, '69	Seeligson, Edward	40	1	1	USA	

GONZALES CO.

206	Jul 13, '67	Eli Mitchell	42	36	36	USA	
230	Jul 13, '67	John R. Smith	40	14	14	USA	
334	Jul 16, '67	Ebin Haven	37	37	37	USA	
	[Struck, probably as of 1869]: Dead						
660	Jul 20, '67	James Haley	37	5 m		USA	
	[Struck]: Removed						
809	Jul 25, '67	John Stewart	43	12	12	USA	
906	Jul 29, '67	G. C. Wiseman	42	12	12	USA	
1137	Aug 7, '67	R. C. McCoy	40	30		USA	
1148	Aug 7, '67	Joseph McCoy	38	38		USA	
1288	Aug 9, '67	G. W. Bailey	37	1		USA	
1328	Aug 16, '67	Jacob Jackson	39	20		USA	Color.
1443	Sep 24, '67	Jesse K. Davis	38	38	38	USA	
1462	Sep 26, '67	Larkin N. West	43	20		USA	

GRIMES CO   All "12 mos" through 2050

2222	Nov 18, '69	Henry Johnson	52	52		USA	
2355	Nov 19, '69	Edmund Williams	40	40	40	USA	

HARDIN CO.

39	Jul 24, '67	David Choate	37	8	7	LA	
133	Aug 13, '67	Seaborne Berry	43	2	2	LA	

226	Nov 23, '69	James Chessher	46	10	10		GA	
		HARRIS CO.						
153	Jun 13, '67	Charles Pryor	40	7 mo			Native	Color
391	Jun 17, '67	Lewis Watkins	38	13			Native	Color
403	Jun 17, '67	Tenola Edwards	39	19			Native	Color
836	Jun 22, '67	Robert McFarland	39	14 mo			Native	White
859	Jun 22, '67	George Ewing	37	15			Native	White
993	Jun 24, '67	John Goodlow	55	2			Native	Color
1162	Jun 26, '67	Abram Wilson	38	18 mo			Native	Color
1169	Jun 26, '67	John Hardy	38	7			Native	Color
1388	Jun 29, '67	Isaac Yearly	40	40			Native	Color
1498	Jul 1, '67	William K. Wilson	40	40			Native	White
1675	Jul 3, '67	W. S. Bowles	40	25			Native	White
		[Struck]: Judge of Elec., J.P. Raised a Co. for Confed Ser						
1696	Jul 3, '67	Osborne Smith	39	39			Native	Color
1755	Jul 5, '67	John Iiams	45	45			Native	White
2265	Jul 30, '67	Solomon Watts	42	4			Native	White
2447	Aug 3, '67	T. C. Bell	44	9 mo			Native	White
2615	Jan 28, '68	Henry Lewis Senr	40	1 ¼			Native	Color
2977	Nov 17, '69	Dow, Loranzo	40	40			Native	Color
		HIDALGO CO.						
33	Jul 24, '67	John F. Webber	44	14	14		VT	White
34	Jul 30, '67	Pacifico Ochoa [Struck]	61	61	61		TX	White
35	Jul 30, '67	Mariano Mangilla	51	51	51		TX	White
40	Jul 30, '67	Ignacio de Ochoa	62	62	62		Mexico	White
42	Jul 30, '67	Peter Vela	40	40	40		Mexico	White
43	Jul 30, '67	John B. Munguia	63	63	63		TX	White
50	Aug 10, '67	Gregorio Villareal	40	40	40		TX	White
60	Aug 21, '67	Indalacio Dominguez	55	55	55		TX	White
61	Aug 21, '67	Antonio Bajene	54	54	54		TX	White
63	Aug 21, '67	Francisco Cavazos	52	52	52		TX	White
66	Aug 22, '67	Antonio Seguia	46	3	3		Mexico	White
67	Aug 22, '67	Cipriano Hinojosa	50	50	50		TX	White
80	Nov 19, '69	Sixto Dominguez	40	40	7		TX	White
		HILL CO.						
391	Aug 22, '67	O. K. Anderson	46	4	4		IN	White
493	Aug 28, '67	S. G. Hanks	51	1	1		IN	White
496	Aug 28, '67	John Miller	18	1 m	1 m		NC	White
590	Aug 31, '67	J. Y. Rogers	38	7	7		LA	White
		HOOD CO.						
467	Nov 12, '69	M. G. Noll	50	1	1		TN	White
		HOUSTON CO.						
183	Jul 25, '67	William Earl	43	14			LA	White
438	Aug 7, '67	James Benton	37	17 mo			TN	Color
975	Aug 23, '67	Robert Price	40	40			VA	Color
1299	Sep 23, '67	William N. Sheridan	39	39			LA	White

Registered Voters of 1867

1457	Jan 29, '68	Ned Masters	40	40		MS	Color
1474	Jan 30, '68	John English	40	13		NC	White
1501	Jan 31, '68	James McLean	45	45		TN	White

JACKSON CO.

25	Jul 1, '67	W<u>m</u> Rollins	52	52	52	U.S.	Color
30	Jul 1, '67	King Parson	38	38	38	U.S.	Color
274	Jul 15, '67	Neal Williams	40	40	40	U.S.	White
344	Jul 16, '67	Nelson Barnes	37	37	37	U.S.	Color

JEFFERSON CO.

38	Jul 23, '67	Blanchett, Jack	40	21	21	Amer.	Color
131	Jul 30, '67	Texas, A. J.	45	45	45	Amer.	White
	[Struck]: Sheriff before & during rebellion						
287	Nov 25, '69	George Burell	40	20	20	Amer.	White

KARNES CO.

114	Jul 22, '67	John R. Rice	38	12	12	TX	White
176	Aug 1, '67	John J. Ratliff	44	10	10	TX	White
212	Jan 30, '68	William R. Calloway	41	9	9	TX	White

KAUFMAN CO.

513	Aug 21, '67	N. D. Wootan	40			TX	
	[Struck]: Not taken amnesty oath						
628	Aug 28, '67	M. D. McCallister	48			TN	

LAVACA CO.

610	Jul 16, '67	Scath, Geo W.	44	4	4	U.S.	
969	Jul 27, '67	Bridger, Henry	38	20	20	U.S.	Color
979	Jul 30, '67	Crabb, H. M.	37	4	4	U.S.	
1018	Aug 20, '67	Bland, Simon	40	6	1	U.S.	Color
1074	Aug 5, '67	Sawey, James	39	20	20	U.S.	
1400	Nov 25, '69	S. M. Stevens	42	2	2	U.S.	
1417	Nov 25, '69	Jessie Robinson	48	20	2	U.S.	

LEON CO.

516	Aug 15, '67	Sutton, Polk	40	12		TN	Color
517	Aug 15, '67	Andrew Harris	39	2		TX	Color
560	Aug 17, '67	Jacob Washington	40	20		MS	Color
588	Aug 19, '67	D. A. Lindsey	43	15	15	TX	

LIBERTY CO.
[First 629 names without time data.]

672	Nov 19, '69	Frank Harden	40	40		TN	
682	Nov 20, '69	Michael Linney	47	27		KY	
692	Nov 20, '69	Robert Whitlock	45	43		LA	
758	Nov 25, '69	Bryan Smith	39	38		LA	
779	Nov 26, '69	C. Devore	40	40		LA	
783	Nov 26, '69	George Smith	45	45		TN	Col.

LIMESTONE CO.

318	Jul 22, '67	Grimes A. J.	40	11	11	TN	
428	Jul 30, '67	Polveda, Joseph	40	12	12	LA	

234 1830 Citizens of Texas

814	Sep 23, '67	Ware, Hardy	40	12	12	TX	

LLANO CO.
[This tabulation gives the year date, instead of years elapsed]

40	Aug 29, '67	Mathew Moss	1829	1857	1857	TN	
113	Sep 16, '67	J. W. Harrington	1825	1856	1856	AL	
122	Sep 16, '67	H. Dunman	1825	1856	1856	GA	

MADISON CO.

328	Aug 24, '67	Charlton Steward	45	10	10	TX	
584	Nov 24, '69	G. W. Robinson	39	18	18	AR	

MARION CO.

1775	Nov 16, '69	Peter Flemming	40	10 mo		KY	Color

MASON CO.

101	Sep 17, '67	Creed Taylor	40	3 mo		U.S.	
125	Sep 27, '67	Mathew A. Doyal	40	1		U.S.	

MATAGORDA CO.

20	Aug 5, '67	Peyton, Edmund	40	15	2	VA	Color
99	Aug 9, '67	Franten, Alfred	37	37	1	TX	Color
175	Aug 13, '67	Odon, Sam	40	1	1	Africa	Color
202	Aug 14, '67	Armstrong, Thomas	45	5	5	MD	Color
212	Aug 14, '67	Powell, Sam	40	26	17	OH	—
219	Aug 14, '67	Van, Odee	40	40	40	Africa	Col.
220	Aug 14, '67	Williams, David	38	2	2	TX	Col
258	Aug 20, '67	Henry Holmes	37	37	8 m	TX	?
292	Aug 20, '67	Thomas Jamison	46	46	46	TN	
375	Aug 21, '67	Henry Isaac	40	30		AL	
376	Aug 21, '67	John Jackson	42	42		TX	
446	Aug 21, '67	W. G. Warren	37	16	16	NC	
	[Struck]: Rejected on Revision						
471	Aug 22, '67	George Hearst	44	40	9	MO	
640	Sep 28, '67	William Taylor	42	42	42	TX	

MAVERICK CO.

20	Aug 22, '69	Bentara Solis	42	6	6	[blank]	
21	Aug 22, '69	Firmin Chavanna	45	4	4	[blank]	
55	Nov 22, '69	Nepomocena Longoria	53	17	17	[blank]	

MILAM CO.

892	Aug 9, '67	W. M. Pierson	39	6 m	6 m	TX	
994	Aug 12, '67	W. M. Pool	37	6 m	6 m	TX	
1002	Aug 11, '67	David Gilleland	45	20	20	VA	
1111	Aug 16, '67	Wm F. Gee	37	13	13	TN	
1162	Aug 20, '67	P. M. Lampier	40	12	12	TX	
1202	Sep 28, '67	A. Stephens	38	12	12	TX	
1243	Jan 31, '68	H. W. Stephens	43	14	14	TX	

MONTAGUE CO.

153	Sep 28, '67	Ruben Deck	40	12	12	TX	
170	Nov 16, '69	Richard Boren	44	10	3	AR	

MONTGOMERY CO.

10	Jul 29, '67	Billy Sapp	61	6 mo	6 mo	GA	Col.
147	Jul 30,. '67	Henry Clay	40	40	40	VA	Col
353	Aug 3, '67	M. W. Shannon	47	43	43	TX	
725	Aug 14, '67	J. F. McFadden	40	7	7	AR	
911	Aug 27, '67	Thornton Henry	40	40	40	TX	Col
928	Aug 22, '67	T. B. Rankin	37	38	38	AL	
1168	Nov 18, '69	J. M. Shannon	40	38		TX	

NACOGDOCHES CO.

20	Jul 15, '67	Isaac Lee	39	39	39	KY	Col
22	Jul 15, '67	Moses Walton	39	30	30	KY	Col
29	Jul 16, '67	Juan Prado	50	30	30	TX	
41	Jul 16, '67	John F. Roberts	40	14	14	AL	
116	Jul 18, '67	Gregorio Luna	45	45	45	TX	
192	Jul 20, '67	Ramon Cordova	46	40	40	TX	
674	Aug 7, '67	Lucien Ybarbo	50	50	50	LA	
683	Aug 8, '67	Jose M. Montes	44	44	44	TX	
714	Aug 9, '67	Jose M. Chirino	44	44	44	TX	
715	Aug 9. '67	Fernando Solis	45	45	45	LA	
739	Aug 10, '67	Bartlett Garrett	40	2	2	MO	Col
953	Aug 16, '67	Juan Ybarbo	40	40	40	TX	
970	Aug 17, '67	Jose D. Cordova	38	38	38	TX	
1115	Aug 21, '67	John Norris	61	61	61	LA	
1124	Aug 21, '67	Guadalupe Ariola	39	39	39	TX	
1151	Aug 22, '67	Emedia Mora	37	37	37	TX	
1200	Aug 23, '67	Luis Chirino	45	45	45	Mexico	
1236	Aug 24, '67	Juan P. Bustamente	44	44	44	LA	
1255	Aug 24, '67	James Chirino	55	55	55	TX	
1429	Nov 22, '69	Stephen Richards	46	45	45	LA	
1505	Nov 25, '69	James Hargis	40	40	20	TX	

NEWTON CO.

82	Sep 4, '67	John Wright	43	19	19	LA	
98	Sep 5, '67	Albert Nantz	40	2	1	LA	
253	Sep 27, '67	G. A. Gilchrist	37	37	15	TX	

ORANGE CO.

283	Nov 25, '69	John Harmon	41			LA	
241	Nov 25, '69	John Wilson	47			LA	
245	Nov 25, '69	Wm Richardson	42			TX	
258	Nov 25, '69	Leroy Patillo	43			LA	

NAVARRO CO.

145	Jul 20, '67	Charles Vaughn	48	6 mo		U.S.	Color.
149	Jul 20, '67	Britten Dawson	41	19	19	U.S.	
911	Aug 30, '67	Samuel Bowman	47	22	22	U.S.	

NUECES CO.

3	Jun 18, '67	Dolores Acosta	45	18	18	TX	
45	Jun 20, '67	John Rabb	42	9		TX	

90	Jun 25, '67	Troy Eggleston	40			MS	Color.
111	Jun 29, '67	Fermin Salas	40	27	10	Mexico	
184	Jul 18, '67	Locadio Salinas	45	15		TX	
212	Jul 26, '67	Alexandro Garcia	49	15		TX	
213	Jul 27, '67	Jose Ma Hinojosa	40			TX	
330	Nov 18, '69	Sam R. Miller	47	19	19	VA	
332	Nov 18, '69	Refugio Hinojosa	39	39	39	TX	
337	Nov 18, '69	Laurence Falcon	48	48	48	Mexico	
374	Nov 20, '69	Samuel Harrison Page	48	7	7	MS	
381	Nov 22, '69	Felipe de la Garza	55	5	5	TX	
449	Nov 22, '69	Basilio Aguirre	40	40	40	Mexico	
465	Nov 25, '69	Justo Salas	40			Mexico	
502	Nov 26, '69	Antonio Lazarin	40	6	6	TX	
511	Nov 26, '69	Pedro Perezda	40	20	20	Mexico	
		DUVAL CO.					
3	Jul 27, '67	Cecilio Balero	40	15		Mexico	
5	Jul 27, '67	Eugenio Alanis	45	15		Mexico	
		PALO PINTO CO.					
99	Nov 17, '69	J. J. Ward	45	12		TN	White
	[born] 1820 Davidson Co.						
127	Nov 22, '69	J. A. Hines	45	10		MS	White
	[born] 1814 Pike Co.						
		ROBERTSON CO.					
462	Aug 2, '67	Sharper Haley	37	1	1	GA	Color.
550	Aug 6, '67	Judson Brooks	37	½		MD	Color.
1252	Aug 17, '67	Lewis Ables	40	12	12	VA	Color.
1589	Nov 24, '69	Harry Bartin	40	40	40	SC	Color.
1828	Nov 26, '69	Bob Kerkindoli	40	2	2	KY	Color.
		RUSK CO.					
541	Jul 20, '67	Elias Vansickle	40	25	25	AR	
1058	Jul 29, '67	Dan R. Clark [Struck]	37	20	6 mo	TX	
		SABINE CO.					
4	Jul 18 [67]	R. H. Smith	39	39	20	NC	
29	Jul 20	George W. Cartwright	40	40	10	TN	
39	Jul 20	Richard Earle	40	40	6 mo	TX	
130	Jul 26	Edward Manuel	39	39	6 mo	SC	
360	Aug 7	William Hines Jr.	40	40	14	GA	
390	Aug 14	Franklin Clark	39	39	16	TX	
410	Aug 22	John Clark Jr.	44	44	4	MS	
432	Aug 28	J. C. Norris	37	6 m		TX	
603	Nov 26, '69	Henry Cartwright	40	20	20	MS	F.M.C.
		SAN PATRICIO CO.					
9	Jul 1, '67	John Choate	40	11	11	LA	
	[Struck, possibly 1870]: Dead						
37	Jul 17, '67	Patrick Hart	40	40	40	Ireland	

SHELBY CO.

503	Aug 21, '67	Tyre Buckley	44	42	6	MS	
570	Aug 21, '67	John Critchfield	40	8 mo		TX	
593	Aug 21, '67	John C. Payne	42	42	4	TN	
609	Aug 21, '67	Bailey Lout	47	27	27	IN	
657	Aug 27, '67	John Lout	40	40	12	TX	
895	Nov 20, '69	R. H. Latham	53	6 m	6 m	LA	

STARR CO.

65	Nov 17, '69	Teodoro Garcia	49			TX	

TARRANT CO.

509	Aug 16, '67	D. C. Harrison	38	12	12	TX	
725	Aug 29, '67	J. T. Gilliland	39	14	14	TN	

TRAVIS CO.

8	Jul 1 [67]	Thomas Merry	37	12 m		TN	C.
13	Jul 1 [67]	Washington Hemphill	47	12 m		KY	C.
1074	Jul 24 [67]	John Burditt	37			TN	C.
1393	Aug 13 [67]	Richard Armstrong	37			NC	C.

UPSHUR CO.

901	Aug 5, '67	Alfred Booker	37	6 m		VA	Col.

VAN ZANDT CO. None

VICTORIA CO.

774	Nov 17, '69	F. R. Daughtery	over 40	17	17	U.S.	
818	Nov 23, '69	Francis Gusman	40	40	40	Mexico	

WALKER CO.

816	Aug 27, '67	Simon Shannon	42	26	26	TX	
878	Aug 27, '67	Jerry Palmer	48	12	11	TN	Col.

WASHINGTON CO.

24	Jun 12, '67	T. J. Allcorn	45	45	45	Native	
42	Jul 12, '67	James M. Harbour	43	43	43	Native	
153	Jun 13, '67	John M. Walker	43	43	43	Native	
245	Jun 5, '67	Joe Green	40	40	40	Native	
624	Jun 19, '67	W. W. Buster	40	30	30	Native	
748	Jun 21, '67	Daniel Shipman	45	1	1	Native	
1077	Jun 24, '67	Wm Dever	43	43	43	Native	
1388	Jun 28, '67	Geora Bostick	37	22		Native	
1415	Jul 1, '67	G. W. Harbour	40	40		Native	
1431	Jul 1, '67	Henry Foster	40	40		Native	Col
2045	Jul 9, '67	Henry Taylor	44	1		Native	Col
2336	Jul 10, '67	Amos Gates	46	46		Native	
2241	Jul 10, '67	F. G. Roberts	42	8		Native	
2271	Jul 10, '67	Moses Harrington	50	1		Native	Col
2323	Jul 22, '67	Reuben Lockridge	37	37		Native	Col
2517	Jul 26, '67	E. D. Jackson	40	20		Native	
3463	Jan 30, '67	M. Austin Bryan	37	4		Native	

[Dates appear inconsistent, but are copied as given]

WEBB CO.

2	Aug 12, '67	Clemento Salinas	40	40	40	Native	
6	Aug 13, '67	Isidro Martines	46	46	46	Native	
7	Aug 13, '67	Doreteo Martines	48	48	48	Native	
46	Nov 16, '69	Miguel Doraliria	50	50	50	Native	

WILSON CO.

42	Jul 12, '67	James Nians Sr	45	7 mo		MD	Col
43	Jul 12, '67	Burrell Montgomery	45	6 mo		VA	Col
119	Jul 19, '67	Daniel Bird [Struck]	38	18	18	GA	
149	Jul 25, '67	Antonio Herrera	45	1	1	Mexico	
150	Jul 25, '67	Melchor Ximene	42	30	30	TX	
159	Jul 25, '67	Antonio Leal	41	20	20	Mexico	
160	Jul 25, '67	Jose M. Roxo	44	44	40	TX	
161	Jul 25, '67	Augustin Bernal	41	18	1	Mexico	
162	Jul 25, '67	Jose Antonio Perez	47	7	5	TX	
165	Jul 25, '67	Manuel Gallardo	54	1	1	Mexico	
172	Jul 29, '67	Francisco Ximenes	45	39	18	TX	
176	Jul 29, '67	Manuel Zepeda	67	21	21	TX	
177	Jul 29, '67	Miguel Yendo	40	16	16	Mexico	
183	Jul 29, '67	Crecencio Hernandez	37	17	17	TX	
186	Jul 29, '67	Antonio Ruiz	46	14	14	TX	
187	Jul 29, '67	Pedro Flores	61	61	61	TX	
188	Jul 29, '67	Gregorio Areciniega	37	1	1	TX	
193	Jul 29, '67	Lorenzo Trevinio	40	16	16	TX	
199	Jul 29, '67	Juan M. Rodriguez	39	19	19	TX	
203	Jul 29, '67	Lino Mata	40	40	40	TX	
204	Jul 29, '67	Susano Corralles	45	32	13	Mexico	
208	Jul 29, '67	Mariano Vidal	40	40	40	TX	
209	Jul 29, '67	Nepomuceno Flores	55	55	55	TX	
218	Jul 30, '67	Gil Zimenes	48	5	5	TX	
219	Jul 30, '67	Cosme Arredondo	67	20	20	TX	
235	Jul 30, '67	Jose Ruiz	47	47	47	TX	
236	Jul 30, '67	Helario Montoya	60	60	60	TX	
238	Jul 30, '67	Ignatio Gil	50	14	14	TX	
258	Aug 1, '67	Macedonia Miranda	40	12	12	TX	
271	Sep 27, '67	Matias Carbier	40	40	20	TX	
275	Sep 27, '67	Manuel Salinas	40	40	10	TX	
315	Nov 20, '69	Santiago Hernandes	50	30	30	Mexico	
319	Nov 22, '69	Jinio Tajada	50	10	10	TX	
338	Nov 22, '69	Jesus Peres	40	20	20	TX	
344	Nov 22, '69	Martin Montoya	44	6	6	TX	
366	Nov 24, '69	Julian Soza	49	5	5	TX	
369	Nov 24, '69	Remigio Garcia	44	1	1	TX	
416	Nov 26, '69	Ilario Martines	57	10	10	TX	

WOOD CO.

916	Jan 31, '68	Emory Raines	48	13	13	TN

ZAPATA CO.

65	Nov 25, '69	Marcos Bottella	43	43	43	Native
66	Nov 25, '69	Barnardo Nevarro	50	50	50	Native

APPENDIX A

POPULATION STATISTICS FOR TEXAS

[See p. ix for Population of Texas chart.]

Historians of Texas make varying estimates of the early population of Texas before statehood in 1845. Most of the estimates are based on early official reports and on the guesses of visitors. Hubert Howe Bancroft in his "Works" made a thorough review of these sources in Vol. XVI, "History of the North Mexican States and Texas," San Francisco 1889. Most estimates seem to have been for persons under government control, of whatever ethnic origin, and excluded "wild" Indians.

In 1806, Almonte reported the population of the three principal settlements to be 2,000 at San Antonio de Bejar, 1,400 at Goliad, and 500 at Nacogdoches, for a total of 3,900.

In 1807, Major Pike passed through and thought that the Spanish creoles, some French, some Americans, and a few civilized Indians and half-breeds amounted to fewer than 7,000.

Bancroft thought an estimate of 4,000 in the principal settlements in 1811 to be reasonable, but that the population later suffered some shrinkage and he thought it not over 3,500 in 1821.

Anglo-Americans began coming to Texas in 1821 in some numbers, and immigrants began arriving in 1822 who expected to meet Stephen F. Austin. This year must have been the turning point, and by 1827 the Mexican census gave a total of 10,800 souls. Bancroft repeated an estimate of nearly 20,000 for 1830.

In 1834, Almonte gave the civilized population at 21,000 apportioned as follows:

Department of Bejar	4,000
Department of the Brazos (includes the Austin Colony)	8,000
Department of Nacogdoches	9,000
Indians not counted above	15,300

Bancroft quoted Kennedy as thinking these estimates to be low, and placed the 1834 count of Anglo-Texans at 30,000 with 2000 blacks.

In 1836, President Andrew Jackson sent Henry W. Morfit to Texas to report on the situation there, and he numbered the Anglo-Americans at 30,000, Mexicans at 3,470, blacks at 5,000 and Indians at 20,000. Excluding Indians, this adds to about 38,500 souls for late 1836. His figures are consistent with the general trend. There were other estimates that appear exaggerated, perhaps to reinforce some personal interest or bias.

Using the 1840 ad valorem tax rolls, I have estimated the 1840 free population at 50,000 (including those of Mexican origin) and 17,000 blacks. The Indians were being pushed out by this time and were almost excluded from any part in settling Texas. After 1840, they were usually not numbered in the population estimates.

There was a state census in early 1847, not long after statehood. It was made by the county tax assessors and its accuracy cannot be checked. Beginning in 1850 the usual Federal decennial census was taken. The tabulations are as follows:

	1847	1850	1860
White	102,961	154,034	421,600
Black	38,753	58,161	182,566

These data show an almost constant population of about 4,000 civilized persons up to 1821. Beginning in 1822, the surge of Anglo-American immigration started. Although it surely must have flowed unevenly from year to year, yet it shows a geometrical growth when plotted versus time. It doubled about every 6 years from 1821 through 1850. It tapered off a bit by 1860, and then the Civil War became a discontinuity in the history of the nation and new forces began to control growth in Texas.

APPENDIX B
LAND LAWS

An Act ". . . relating to the establishment of a General Land Office"

Sec. 11. Be it further enacted, That there shall be elected by joint vote of both houses of congress, a commissioner, who shall be president of the board, and two associate commissioners, for each and every county.

Sec. 12. Be it further enacted. That every person who shall claim a title to land in this government by virtue of the colonization laws, or by residence in the country at the declaration of independence, shall be required to take and subscribe to the following oath: "I do solemnly swear, that I was a resident citizen of Texas at the date of the declaration of independence, that I did not leave the country during the campaign of the spring of 1836, to avoid a participation in the struggle, that I did not refuse to participate in the war, and that I did not aid or assist the enemy, that I have not previously received a title to my quantum of land, and that I conceive myself justly entitled, under the constitution and laws, to the quantity of land for which I now apply." They shall also be required to prove, by two or more good and creditable witnesses, as the commissioners may require, that they were actually citizens of Texas at the date of the declaration of independence and have continued so to the present time; and they shall also be required to prove, in a like manner, whether they were married or single at the time of the declaration of independence, and what amount of land they were entitled to under the law . . .

Sec. 14. Be it further enacted. That there shall also be elected for the several counties, a clerk, by joint vote of both houses of congress, who shall keep, in a well bound book to be kept by him for that purpose, a correct account of all the transactions of the board of land commissioners, the name of every person to whom a certificate shall be given, the amount of land granted to each person, the time of their emigration to the country, and the name or names of witnesses, by whom the claimants severally proved their claims . . .

Sec. 22. . . . That each and every individual under the age of seventeen, who shall have volunteered in the service of their country, and who have received honorable discharges, shall be entitled to the same quantity of land as a head right, that they would be though they were twenty-one years of age, and upon the same conditions.

Sec. 23. . . . That all single men who were in the republic at the date of the declaration of independence, and entitled under the constitution to one-third of a league of land, and who have since married, or may marry within the next twelve months, shall be entitled to the additional quantity of two-thirds of a league and labor of land. Provided, that the benefits of this section shall only extend to those who have contributed to the support and defence of their country; and provided, this additional quantity shall not be allowed to any whose wife has received a league of land of this government.

Sec. 29. . . . That every volunteer who arrived in this republic after the 2nd day of March, 1836, and before the 1st of August, 1836, and has received . . . an honorable discharge . . . or who may have died, shall receive the quantity of land by this act secured to original colonists . . .

Vetoed by the president, and passed the house . . . and senate. Dec. 14, 1837.

Laws of the Republic of Texas, H.P.N. Gammel, Austin 1898 I-1404.

An Act Amending an act . . . relating to the establishment of a General Land Office.

Sec. 1. Be it enacted . . . That the chief justices of counties, the associate justices, and the county clerks, of each and every county of this Republic, shall be and they are hereby constituted boards of Land Commissioners for their respective counties: the chief justice shall be president, and the county clerks shall be clerks, to said boards.

Sec. 2. Be it further enacted, That the boards of Land Commissioners shall be governed by the same laws . . .

Sec. 4. Be it further enacted, That this act shall take effect from and after the second Monday of January, eighteen hundred and thirty-nine, and shall continue in force to the second Monday in January, eighteen hundred and forty, and no longer.

Approved, January 26, 1839.   MIRABEAU B. LAMAR

Gammel II-112

BIBLIOGRAPHY

Colonial Period to 1835

Marion Day Mullins, *The First Census of Texas*, Special Pub. of the National Genealogical Soc., No. 22 (Washington D.C. 1959).

Mary McMillan Osburn, "The Atascosita Census of 1826," Texana *1*, 299 (1963).

Ethel Zively Rather, "DeWitt's Colony," Southwestern Historical Quart. *VIII*, 95. (1904).

Austin's Register of Families, Spanish Archives of the General Land Office, Austin. (Manuscript originals).

Nacogdoches Archives, Texas State Library, Austin.

Bexar Archives, University of Texas Library, Austin.

Mattie Austin Hatcher, *The Opening of Texas to Foreign Settlement 1801-1821*, Univ. of Texas Bulletin N. 2174: April 8, 1927.

Republican Period 1836-46.

Gifford White, *The 1840 Census of the Republic of Texas*, Austin 1966.

Marion Day Mullins, *Republic of Texas Poll Tax Lists for 1846*, Genealogical Pub. Co., Baltimore 1974.

Land Grant Records

Virginia H. Taylor, *The Spanish Archives of the General Land Office of Texas*, The Lone Star Press, Austin 1955.

Abstract of Land Titles of Texas in 2 volumes, Shaw & Blaylock, Galveston 1878.

An Abstract of the Original Titles of Record, Houston 1838. Reprinted by The Pemberton Press, Austin 1964.

Lester G. Bugbee, "The Old Three Hundred," Southwestern Histor. Quart. *I*, 108 (1897).

INDEX TO 1830 CITIZENS

This Index is for 1830 Citizens only and does not include assignees, administrators and others tied only to later dates. Different common spellings are often grouped together. All variations and common errors should be considered in a search.

Abbott, Elizabeth, 41
  Joshua, 41
Ables, Lewis, 236
Acosta, Dolores, 235
  Franco Deciderio, 117
  Jose' Andres de, 125
  Jose' Guadalupe, 120
  Jose' Maria del Pilar, 117
  Jose' Mariano, 117
  Jose' Nicolas, 117
  Jose' Romaldo, 120
  Juana Franca, 117
  Juan Jose', 120
  Juan Jose' de la C., 117
  Juan Manuel, 125
  Juan Ysidro, 117
  Maria Anta, 117
  Maria Concpion, 117
  Maria de los Angeles, 117
  Ma Dominga, 117
  Maria Getrudes, 117
  Maria Josefa, 120
  Maria Luiza, 117
  Maria Relusinda, 120
Adair, William J., 4
Adams, Francis, 25
Addison, Charles, 230
Adeli, Jose, 130
  Maria, 130
Adkins, William W., 217
Agilar, Consepion, 90
  Francisca, 88
Aguelaria, Jose' Fecundo, 137
Aguerro, Jose, 224
Aguirre, Am--, 90
  Basilio, 236
  Feliciana, 90
  Ygno, 90
Aken, Collin M., 137
  James, 137
Akens, William, 137
Alameda, Francisco, 137
Alami, Prudencio, 130
Alanis, Eugenio, 236
Alaniz, Maria Gerrudis, 136

Alberado, Icundo, 228
Albilar, Ylario, 229
Albrado, Gregorio, 229
Albright, Jacob, 136, 197
Alcantar, Ma Micaela, 93
  Perfecta, 81
  Rafael, 102
Alcantura, Rafael, 136
Alcorte, Marcelo, 136
Aldape, Franco, 96
Alderate, Beniete, 211
  Carmel, 90, 98
  Dolores, 84, 136
  Jesus, 189
  Jose' Ma, 228
  Juan, 226
  Martin, 229
  Miguel, 189
  Rafael, 137, 189, 231
Aldrich, Peter, 22
Aldsevata, Jose Ben, 212
Alemeda, Jose, 221
Alexander, Caleb P., 65
  George, 136
  Mary, 212
Algese, Marela, 212
Alkins, Phoebe, 20
  William, 20
Allbriecht, Jacob, 136, 197
Allbright, Edmond, 208
Allcorn, J. D., 43
  James D., 12
  John H., 16, 43, 137
  Sarah, 16
  T. J., 237
  Thomas Jeff., 16
  Wm E., 16
Allen, Benjamin, 136
  Davis, 204
  Elijah, 136
  Elisha, 136
  George, 67, 136, 137
  Hannah, 136, 193
  Jackson C., 208
  John M., 41, 137, 207
  James W., 136

  Lydia, 39
  Moses, 136
  Richard, 24
  Wm F., 212
Alley, 7
  Abraham, 188
  Thomas, 18, 191
  William, 136, 191, 225
  William M., 7
Allsberry, Wm W., 136
Allsup, Elisha, 209
Almaguei, Eusebio, 136
Almansa, Ygnacia, 112
Almansar, Ignacia, 136
Almengor, Jose Ma, 228
Almquis, Juana, 89
Alrian, Gorgonio, 229
Alsbury, Y. P., 220
Alvarado, Jose Gil, 131
  Jose' Santos, 131
  Juan Jose', 131
  Ygnacia, 131
Amador, Antonio, 231
  Catarina, 123
  Franca, 82
  Ma Getrudes, 122
  Tomas, 119
Ampara, Maria, 137
Anda, Anestacia de, 105
Anderson, Anne, 32
  Bailey, 137, 210
  Bailey Sen, 46, 211
  Bailey Jr., 46, 211
  Benjamin, 46
  C. H., 46
  Ephraim, 33
  Gemedey, 211
  Hampton, 211, 212
  Hayward, 212
  Hazzard, 46
  Holland, 46
  John, 32
  Jonathan, 46, 210
  Milton J., 33
  O.K., 232
  Vincent, 137

244   1830 Citizens of Texas

Walter, 225
William, 230
W<u>m</u> H., 137
Wyatt, 200, 211, 226
Andracia, Jose' Maria, 137
Andrews, Clarissa, 150
  Edmund, 35
  George, 206
  Isabella, 36
  Jas S., 209
  John Jr., 136
  Michael, 231
  Richard, 30
Andrus, William, 136
Ansland, Frank, 225
Anthony, Frederick, 46
Apelado, Jose', 221
Aperlado, Jose', 137
Apodeca, Anastacio, 227
  Benito, 226
  Dolores, 228
  Jose', 226
  Militon, 228
Applegate, John, 46, 211
Arañaga, Loreta, 97
Arauza, Josefa, 90
Arecealeado, Polinario, 96
Arciniega, Dolores, 81
  Gregorio, 81, 238
  Jose' Miguel, 81
  Juliana, 81
  Manuel, 81, 184
  Maria de Jesus, 81
  Petra, 81
Arebalo, Ma Anta, 97
  Clara, 97
  Pedro, 97
Arenales, Manuel, 87
Arenaser, Andres, 82
Argullo, Ramon, 105
Ariola, Eduardo, 130
  Gregorio, 130
  Guadalupe, 235
  Jose' Franco, 130
  Jose' Mariano, 130
  Jose' Teodoro, 130
  Jose' Ylario, 130
  Juan, 130
  Juan Franco de, 122
  Mari Bernardina, 119
  Maria Concpcion, 119
  Mari Olaya, 130
Armstrong, Delila, 16, 190
  Henry T., 18
  Richard, 237

Thomas, 234
Arnold, Daniel, 15, 136
  Holly, 136
  Rachel, 15
Aro, Juan de, 227
Arocha, Anta, 98, 100, 106
  Antonio, 89, 106, 136
  Antonio (Elder), 136
  Benigno, 106
  Benino, 221
  Bonifacia, 112
  Damian, 119
  Franca, 107
  Gertrudis, 106
  Jesusa, 106
  Jose', 187
  Jose' Anto, 108
  Jose' Ma (Elder), 137
  Jose' Maria, 84, 92, 119, 136
  Jose' Ramon, 136
  Juan Jose', 136
  Lino, 106, 137, 220
  Macedonio, 106
  Macedonia, 221
  Manuel, 92, 98, 183
  Manuela, 108
  Maria Bernardina, 119
  Maria Josefa, 98, 137
  Mary, 211
  Nepomuceno, 109
  Paula, 109
  Ramon, 92
  Refugio, 108
  Tomas de, 108
  Da Yga, 80
  Ygno, 108
Arranaga, Jesus, 222
Arras, Concepcion, 229
  Julian, 229
Arredondo, Cosme, 238
  Eugenia, 108
Arreola, Gabriel, 136
  Simon, 136
  Teresa, 97
Arrington, William W., 74
Arriola, Dolores, 130
  Graviel, 83
  Leandro, 83
  Ma Berulda, 125
  Ma Josefa, 116
  Massine, 200
  Simon, 83
  Teresa, 83
Arrista, Dolores, 44

Arroyes, Pedro, 228
Ashabranner, Henry, 46
Ashby, John M., 69
Ashton, Jno T., 209
Askins, John, 202
Assabranner, George T., 212
  Henry, 210
Assovose, Marreah, 203
Astrada, Andres, 228
  Rosalio, 227
Astrigo, Toribo, 88
Atherton, Benj, 205
Atkins, William, 136
Augilar, Juan Ramon, 221
Austin, H., 44
  Henry, 33
  Joanna, 41
  John, 6
  Stephen F., 6, 7, 9, 74
  William T., 6, 41
Azkey, Abner, 202

Baca, Acencio, 221
  Ana Maria, 82, 187
  Anto, 109
Bacon, Richard, 209
Bacoqui, Batis Andre, 117
  Marcemiliano, 117
  Maria Eme, 117
  Maria Madalena, 117
Bacchus, John E., 22
  Mary, 22
Badillo, Gordiano, 119
Badio, Jesusa, 91
Bailey, Aaron, 223
  Alexander, 24, 140
  G. W., 231
  Gaines, 31
Baire, Henry L., 13
Bajene, Antonio, 232
Baker, Anne, 36
  Caleb, 137
  Colbert, 36
  Isaac, 73
  John W., 207
  Moses, 67
Balberde, Anselmo, 101
Balderas, Franco, 108
  Jesus, 108
  Juan, 108
  Manuel, 108
  Maria Calmel, 95
  Trenidad, 108
Baldes, Eustaquio, 123
  Polonia, 108

Index   245

Teresa, 103
Balencia, Victor, 229
Balero, Cecilio, 236
Balknapp, Leonard, 198
Ballanova, Juana, 129
Ballard, Arch<u>d</u>, 209
    W. W., 141
Balle, Rosa del, 109
Balmaceda, Jose M<u>a</u>, 105
    Petra, 105
    Vicente, 105
Balverde, Luciano, 110
Bancroft, Jethrow R., 191
Bandal, Bautista, 131
Banfield, Thomas, 218
Barb, Anteoin, 212
Barber, Amos, 196
    Jno, 196
Barbo see Ybarbo
Barbo, Antonio Y, 139
    Candraiks Y, 139
    Gregoria Y, 139
    Jesus Y, 139
    Jose' Antonio Y, 139, 140
    Juan Benigno Y, 139
    Luciano Y, 139
    Manuel M Y, 139, 140
    Martin Y, 139
    Maximilian Y, 139
    Miguel Y, 139
    Ramigeo Y, 139
Barbose, Antonio, 212
Barcena, Slin, 224
Barclay, Anderson, 138
Bard, Ocela, 212
Bargas, Estevan, 140
    Margarita, 95
Barilla, Augustine, 228
    Jose' Antonio, 139
    Marilo, 229
Barkam, John, 202
Barker, James, 202
    Lemon, 19
    William, 190
Barkham, Jacob, 201
Barkham, James, 139
Barksdale, Lewis, 41, 139
Barlow, Rebecca J, 36
    Samuel H, 36
Barnam, Samuel, 202
Barnes, Nelson, 233
Barnet, Thomas F., 6
Barney, Anne Eliza, 34
    Jabez, 34

Baron, Ginio, 140
Barr, Alanson, 46
Barrera, Augustine, 87, 140, 219
    Dolores, 87
    Guadalupe de, 93, 99
    Jacobo, 189
    Jose' Antonio, 138
    Jose Domingo, 99
    Juan Man<u>l</u>, 99
    Man<u>l</u>, 99
    Mariquita, 83
    Mig<u>l</u>, 93
Barret, Elizabeth, 12
    William, 12
Barron, Thomas, 46
Barrow, Benjamin,, 137, 195, 225
    Benj Jr., 139, 196
    Jno M., 137
    Levi, 137, 195
    Reuben, 225
    Reuben Senr, 137, 195
    Solomom, 137, 195
    Vincent, 137, 195
Barsenas, Maria Luiza, 119
Barton, B., 21
    Elisha, 182
    Elisha W., 18
    Harry, 236
    Jefferson, 139
    Kimber W., 69
    Stacy, 17
    Susana, 18
    Wayne, 139
    William, 17, 139
Bascoqui, Maria Eme, 117
    Mari Teresa, 124
Basques, Antolino, 96
    Comdio, 224
    Cristoval, 96
    Encarnacion, 96
    Jesus, 96, 221
    Maria de Jesus, 96
    Rafael, 96
    Ydurige, 96
Bass, Ambrose, 207
Bateman, Simon, 64
Bates, Henry, 5
Batey, Edward, 138
Baton, Franklin, 192
Battell, W<u>m</u> T., 208
Battle, M. M., 188
    Mills M., 137
Baty, Edw<u>d</u>, 14

Baume see Labaume
Baume, Gertrudis de la, 47
    Joseph de la, 54, 75, 220
    Pedro Sancir de la, 46
Bayse, Henry L., 138
Beach, Clark, 193
Beardslee, Hester, 21
    James, 21
Becam, Mary, 138
Becarra, Jesus, 224
    Jose' Maria, 138
    D<u>a</u> Josefa, 89
Becker, J., 192
    Jacob, 191
Beckett, Dayton, 207
Bedford, Jose' Ramon, 73
Bega, Gregorio,. 108
    Maria de, 108
    M<u>a</u> Josefa de la, 115
Beitel, G. F., 220
Belcher, Isham G., 138
Beley, Rebecca, 192
Bell, 44
    Abigail, 10
    George A., 28
    J. H., 6
    James, 14, 32
    James H., 140
    Jane, 41
    Joseph T., 41, 139
    Peter, 223
    T. C., 232
    Thomas, 10, 137
    Winsey, 32
Bellow, Page, 191
Beltran, Sostenes, 228
Benavides, Matias, 228
Benites, Antonio, 107, 138
    Beronica, 140
    Felipe, 104
    Jose' Mig<u>l</u>, 107
    Maria, 120
    Maria de Jesus, 120
    M<u>a</u> Luiza, 126
    Miguel, 185, 219
    Rumalda, 107
    Trinida, 94
    Trinidad, 140
Bennet, Chs H., 34
    D. W., 139
    James, 16, 46, 200, 218
    S. C., 139
    Valentine, 72
Benton, James, 232

Beramendi see Veramendi
   Eufemia, 98
   Jose' Primo, 98
   Juan Martin, 98
   Juana Gertrudes, 98
   Marco Anto, 98
   Ma Anta, 98
   Ma Josefa, 98
   Teresa de los Ang., 98
   Ursula Frutosa, 98
Berban, Juan Jose', 140, 185
   Teresa, 101
Bergana, Dolores, 90
Bergara, Dolores, 94
   Enselmo, 94
   Franca, 91
   Franco, 94
   Maria del Carmel, 94
Bermea, Anta, 126
Bernal, Augustine, 218, 238
   Maria Teresa, 184
   Maximo, 221
   Teresa, 107
Berrere, Jose' Ma, 229
Berry, Esther, 65
   Francis, 65, 138
   Jackson, 138
   James, 138
   John, 138
   Jno B, 182
   John T., 19
   Joseph, 138
   Lucinda, 43
   Milly, 46
   Radford, 8
   Seaborne, 192, 231
   Thos O., 43
Bertrand, Anne W., 19
   Peter, 19
Bervan, Jose', 111
   Juan, 111
   Manuela, 111
   Pascual, 111
Best, E. W., 140
   Stephen, 137
Betts, Jacob, 138, 198
Bevil, Jehu, 138
Bidales, Mariano, 95
   Puceno, 95
Biddy, Abednigo, 7, 140
   Patsy, 7
Billa, Migl, 103
   Sabino, 103
Biña, Casimira la, 110
Birado, Francisco, 88

Manuel, 88
Birch, William, 31
Bird, Daniel, 238
   John, 37, 139, 140
   Micajah, 182
   Nancy, 32
   Sally, 37
   Thomas, 32, 140
Birtrong, Thomas, 137
Biscarra, Ygnosento, 229
Bittick, Jonathan, 46, 203
Black, Albert, 138
   Jacob, 140
   John S., 135
   Joseph, 139
   Marcus L., 39
   Marcus S., 140
   Mary, 35
Blackwell, Henry B., 140
Blair, E. Alexander Jr., 9
   George, 71, 189
   Jacob, 201
Blake, Marshall, 222
   Thomas M., 44
Blalock, Freeman, 219
Blanchett, Jack, 233
Blanco, Santos, 187, 222
Bland, Frances, 18
   Simon, 233
Blea, Juan, 126
Bloodgood, Wm., 46
Blossom, Hiram, 47
   Minor, 47
Blount, Penelope, 138
Blue, Jacob, 225
Bocanegro, Jose' Marien, 224
Boden, Juan Lorenzo, 120
   Maria Madalena, 122
Bolen, Franco, 111
Booker, Alfred, 237
Bordan, Juan Lorenzo, 139
Borden, Gail, 18
   Gail Jr., 19, 139
   Paschal P., 18, 137
   Penelope, 19
   Thomas H., 139
Bordine, John, 140
Boren, Elisha, 139
   James, 218
   Joseph, 139, 226
   M., 139
   Matthew, 39, 138
   Nancy, 39
   Richard, 233
   Wm M., 226

Borgas, Frutosa, 111, 140
Boring, Nancy, 137, 199
Borsoley, Maria Josefa, 118
Bosque, Juliana, 83, 87
Bostic, Benjamine, 47
   Geora, 237
   J. H., 28
   James H., 47
   Levi, 13
   Patsey, 13
   S. R., 225
Bostwick, C. R., 138
   Caleb R., 198
Bottella, Marcos, 238
   Concepcion, 140
   Francisco, 138
Boughan, James G., 5
Bouttar, Miguel, 189
Bowen, Almira, 16
   Michl, 137
   Sylvester, 16
Bowers, Johnson, 202
Bowie, James, 5
   Stephen, 47
Bowler, Thomas, 223
Bowles, Benjamin, 36
   Betsey, 36
   W. S., 232
Bowlin, James, 47
   Jeremiah, 47
   Mary Ann, 47
Bowling, James, 203, 210
Bowman, 44
   Abraham, 22
   John, 32
   Joseph, 138, 197
   Margaret, 32
   Samuel, 235
Boyd, Irvine R., 208
   Moses, 218
   Robert, 218
Boyden, Clarissa, 37
   Moses H., 36
Braba, Guadalupe, 140
Braberry, James, 23
Brackin, William, 138
Bracy, 44
Bradberry, James, 138
Bradley, Daniel, 137
Brake, M. J., 193
   Michael J., 194
Branch, Umphries, 72
Brand, David W., 71
Bray, Cynthia Anne, 38
   Thomas, 38

Index   247

Breen, Charles, 182
Brenson, Enoch, 139
Brewno, Susan, 211
Bridgeman, Jas T., 209
Bridger, Henry, 138, 233
Bridges, James, 140
    Elizabeth, 192
Brigham, A., 36
    Elizabeth S., 36
    Saml B., 138
Bright, George, 138, 198
Brightman, Jos W., 208
Brinlee, George, 139
Brisceno, Christobal, 229
Briseño, Jose Ma, 101
Brock, Caleb, 65
Brooks, Judson, 236
    William, 200
Brookshire, Archilles R., 218
    James S., 218
Brown, Alexr, 38
    Alfred, 223
    Charles, 223
    Daniel D., 138
    Emily, 192
    Jeremiah, 31
    John, 14, 39
    Joseph, 140
    McCoy, 223
    Nancy, 14
    Nathaniel, 225
    Robert, 15
    Sally, 38
    S. P., 10
    Saml P., 6, 28
    Selwin L., 209
    Susan, 28
Browning, Lucas, 207
Brownrigg, Geo B., 140
Bruff, Samuel, 22
Brush, John F., 34
Bryan, M. Austin, 237
Bryant, Jefferson, 222
Buchetti, Juan Francisco, 47
Buckley, John, 203
    Terry, 47
    Tyre, 237
Buckman, Oliver, 140
Buena, Juana Francisca, 140
    Juan Franco, 97
    Manuel, 140
    Ma Elena, 97
Bulloock, James W., 140
    Julius W., 140
    Robert, 20

Bunch, Hiram, 193
Bundick, S. C., 31
Burasa, Maria Seleste, 123
Burdgess, John, 34
    Margaret C., 34
Burditt, John, 237
Burgess, Dickson, 209
Burk, John C., 47
    Benjamin, 191
Burke, George T., 204
Burket, David, 72
Burkham, Abijah, 201
    Chas, 139
Burknap, L., 138
Burleson, Edwd, 30
    Sarah, 30
Burnett, Anne, 29
    Crawford, 29, 191
    David G., 231
    Matthew, 191
    Nancy, 26
    William, 26, 33, 47
Burney, Abel, 209
    Robert, 9
    Robert A., 4
    Susan, 17
    William, 17, 140
Burnham, John H., 137
    Stephen, 41
    Wm O., 137
Burns, Arthur, 69, 138, 213
    Robert, 213
    Squire, 68, 138
Burnside, Samuel, 201
    William, 201
Burrill, David, 193
    George, 233
    Robert, 137, 195
    Thornton, 231
Burris, Samuel, 217
Burrus, Thomas, 47
Burton, John M., 25
    Wm, 223
Bury, Charles, 10
Busby, William, 31, 137
Bush, Samuel, 202
Bustamante, Juan, 118
    Juan Jose', 122
    Juan P., 235
Buster, W. W., 237
Bustillo, Casimero, 138
    Clements, 221
    Francisco, 140
    Jesus, 221
    Jose' Maria, 138

Juana, 83
Bustillos, Alejos, 101
    Alexos, 138
    Bonifasio, 91
    Clemente, 101, 138
    Domingo, 87, 140
    Franco, 91
    Josefa, 101, 138
    Juana Francisca, 140
    Maria Calisma, 88
    Teresa, 140
Butieres, Anta, 94
    Anto, 94
Butler, Ahira, 47, 203
    David, 199
    George, 210
    Joseph, 212
Buxten, Alexander, 137
Buzzard, Jacob, 202
Byers, Henry, 218
    Westly, 139
Byrne, John, 38
    Pamelia, 38
Caballero, Tumin, 228
Cabasos, Polonia, 83
Cabrena, Mariano, 231
Cabrera, Fernando, 81
    Juan Jose', 81
    Luciano, 81
    Lusiana, 220
    Pedro, 83, 87
Cadena, Anta, 110
    Jesus, 110
    Juan Manl, 110
    Juana, 126
    Manl, 110
    Pasqual, 217
    Vicente, 227
Cafe, Maria, 118
Calbello, Juana, 111
Calderon, Antonio, 88
    Getrudes, 128
    Jesus, 88
    Jose', 142
    Jose' de Leon, 88
    Juan Francisco, 88
    Maria de Jesus, 88
Caldwell, John, 5, 143
    Matthew, 68
Calkins, Simon, 5
Calloway, William R., 233
Calmenero, Isidro, 226
Calorina, Maria, 130
Caloway, Philip, 208
Calrillo, Josefa, 107

Calvertson, Henry, 209
   Jas T., 208
Calvit, Frederick J., 10, 218
Calvo, Baltasar, 93
Camaguas, Silvestre, 101
Camaño, Jose Antonio, 94
Cameros, Manuel, 189
Camona, Cesario, 146
Campbell, Cyrus, 70
   Elizabeth, 18, 141
   Hill, 70
   Hul O, 145
   John, 70, 182, 218
   Joseph, 69, 70
   Rachael, 70
   Rufus, 70
   Ruthy, 143
   Walter, 143
Canado, Maria, 31
Cano, Pablo, 224
Cantu, Apuricio, 224
   Jesus, 75, 79
   Jesusa, 79
   Lucia, 79
   Maria de, 47
   Miguel, 70
   Salustiana, 224
Cantura, Ananazia, 92
Carabajal, Carmel, 106
Caradine, Isaac, 47
   Robert P., 47
Cararillo, Pedro, 108
Carascas, Antonio, 224
   Manuel, 224
Carasco, Juan Pablo, 229
   Pedro, 227
Carabajala, Juan, 92
Carbajal, Anto, 101
   Franco, 101
   Gregorio, 229
   Jose' Ma, 97
   Juan, 101
   Juan Franco, 101
   Luis, 101
   Manuel, 105
   Teodora, 105
Carbier, Francisca, 187
   Matias, 238
Cardena, Jose' A., 220
Cardenas, Adriano, 93
   Adrien, 219
   Francisco, 187
   Jesus, 93
   Jose', 93
   Jose' Ma, 93, 217

Ma Anta, 93
Cardona, Juan, 142
Carillo, Concepcion, 142
   Fernando, 142
   Francisco, 186
   Juana, 184
   Pedro, 142
   Ygna, 109
Carlisle, Robert, 219
Carmel, Ma del, 80
   Carmona, Juan, 119
   Mari Bibiana, 120
   Maria Casimira, 120
   Maria Dolores, 120
   Maria Gertrudes, 47
   Maria Lina, 119
   Masedoni, 119
Carmonales, Manuel, 47
Carney, P. L., 206
Carns, Noah, 43
Caro, Anto, 116
   Feliciano, 116
   Jose' Agaton, 116
   Jose' Alejandro, 116
   Jose' Anastacio, 116
   Jose' Anto Marselo, 116
   Jose' Encarnacion, 116
   Jose' Justo, 116
   Jose' Sebastian, 116
   Jose' Trivio, 116
   Juan, 116
   Ma Anta, 116
   Ma Bacilia, 116
   Maria Cleta, 116
   Maria de Jesus, 116
   Ma del Pilar, 127
   Maria Eulogia, 116
   Maria Gavina, 116
   Maria Leonicia, 116
   Maria Luciana, 116
   Maria Marcelina, 116
   Maria Olaya, 116
   Ma Ricarda, 130
   Maria Ysabel, 116
   Pedro Jose', 115
   Tomas, 116, 143
Carodine, Isaac, 145
   Robert, 145
Carollas, Juan, 187
Carpenter, George, 188
Carr, Agaton, 47
   Anastacea, 48, 211
   Antonio, 211
   Marsele, 211
   William, 193

Carranza, Maria Luisa, 142
Carrascas, Crisoto, 227
Carrasco, Jose' Albino, 187
   Juan de Dios, 229
Carera, Fabian, 104
   Franco, 104, 189
   Jose' Antonio, 142
Carillo, Isabel, 106
   Matias, 106
Carriona, Manuela, 146
Carroll, Dennis C., 208
   E. A., 141
   Edward S., 24
   Elizabeth, 48
   George, 4
   Levi H, 208
   M. A., 141
   Mary C., 196
   Moses H., 196
   Peter N., 208
Carter, Andw, 207
   George, 48, 218
   Theodore, 230
Cartwright, George W., 236
   Henry, 236
   Jesse H., 141
   John, 26, 48, 50, 206
   Mary, 26, 48
   Matthew, 145
   Robert G., 47
   Robert M., 141
   W. G., 145
Caruthers, John, 200
   Mary, 25
Carvajal, Francisco, 145
   Jose' Luis, 97
   Juan, 231
   Manl, 97
   Ma Luisa, 98
Carvazas, Juan Miguel L., 224
   Francisco, 232
Casanova, Alfonso, 145
   Anacleto, 142
   Anto, 81
   Anto 2d, 81
   Carl--, 87
   Christa, 145
   Crisantus, 143
   Dolores, 145
   Estevan, 81, 145
   Francisco, 143
   Juan, 81, 142
   Remigio, 81, 220
   Simon, 81, 220

Index   249

Casas, Estevan, 85
   Francisco, 85, 222
   Joaquin, 85
   Luis, 85
   Manl, 85
   Yga, 85
   Ygo, 85
Cash, George M., 23
Casias, Mateo, 221
Casillas, Francisco, 142
   Gabriel, 142
   Juan, 179
   Juan Jose', 142
   Juana, 89
   Manuel, 142
   Maria Guadalupe, 146
   Mateo, 142
   Pablo, 143
   Yrrineo, 142
Casima, Jose', 186
Cassiano, J. T., 220
   Jose', 90
   Jose' Ygnasio, 90
Castañeda, Dolores, 95, 146
   Francica, 95
   Francica de, 95
   Maria, 125
   Ma Josefa, 125
Castanera, Ramon, 143
Castañon, Dolores, 111
   Jesus, 111
   Jesusa, 111
   Luis, 111
   Maria Andrea, 146
   Pedro, 111
Castello, Lino, 111
   Simon, 111
Castillo, Ignacio, 183
   Jose' Antonio, 94
   Jose' Francisco, 95
   Jose' Ma, 111
   Jose' Nestor, 93
   Josefa, 80
   Manl Yturri, 103
   Maria del Rosario, 95
   Miguel, 94
   Ygno, 93
Castleman, Andrew, 145
   Andrew L., 19
   Jacob, 142
   John R., 145
   Mich., 141
   Patience, 145
Castro, Eugenia de, 111
   Feliciana de, 117

Franco de, 117
Jose' Manuel del, 146
Josefa, 106
Manl de, 96
Margarita, 94
Ma, 99
Maria Agapita de, 96
Mari Jasinta de, 120
Ma de Jesus, 103
Maria Josefa, 145
Maria Petra, 146
Mariquita, 146
Cavazos, Francisco, 232
Cavenah, Charles, 141
Cavrara, Juan, 231
Cayce, Hannah, 23
   Henry, 141
   Shadrach, 225
   Thomas, 22
Cedilla, Petra de P. 105
Cenoma, Maria, 89
Cervantes see Servantes
   Dolores, 145
   Jose', 48
   Juan Jose', 185
Chadoin, Mahely, 44
   Thomas, 44, 142
Chambers, Talbot, 29, 143
   Thomas J., 4
Chance, Joseph B., 22
   Nancy, 22
   Samuel, 7, 141
Chandler, Davis, 18
   Prissa, 18
Channin, Matthew, 222
Channley, Thomas, 145
Chapa, Anto, 104
   Gregoria, 104
Chappell, Sarah, 48
   Corene, 145, 203
Charle, Ma Alvina, 79
   Da Concepcion, 79
Chase, Eliza, 13
   William, 13, 48, 70
Chavana, Antonio, 130, 145
   Firmin, 234
   Jose Fermin de J., 122
   Jose' Faustino, 122
   Jose' Guillermo, 122
   Jose' Santiago, 122
   Maria Anta, 122
   Maria Guadalupe, 117
   Maria de los R., 122
   Maria Ursula, 122
   Ramon, 122

Chavenoe, M., 143
Chavas, Altegracia, 227
Chaves, Agustin, 96
   Francisco, 146
   Gertrudis, 102
   Ignacio, 96
   J. A., 221
   Jose', 220, 227
   Jose Ma, 96, 228
   Juan Anto, 96
   Juana Franca, 96
   Julian, 228, 229
   Leandro, 186, 219
   Manuel, 107, 185
   Margarita, 96
   Pedro Ramon, 145
   Pilar, 96
   Zomara, 96
Cherino, Anastacio, 143
   Gertrudis, 143
   Jose', 143
   Jose' Maria, 142
   Maria Ignacia, 145
Cherny, John, 44
Cherry, Aaron, 141
   Aaron Senr, 143, 196
   David, 44
   John, 141, 195
   Matilda, 192
   Smith R., 48
   William, 141
Chessher, Daniel, 48
   James, 48, 232
   James Senr., 191
Cheevers, John, 143
Chever, Henry, 9
   John, 43, 143
Childs, Geo W., 209
   Leven, 218
Chirino, Anestacio Y., 129
   Apolonio, 129
   Encarnacion, 118
   Gertrudis, 100
   James, 235
   Jose', 121
   Jose' Angel, 115
   Jose' Antonio, 126, 129
   Jose' Encarnacion, 121
   Jose M., 235
   Jose' Maria, 118
   Juan Bautista, 115
   Luis, 235
   Maria Faustina, 117, 129
   Maria Getrudes, 118
   Maria Gorgonia, 129

Maria Guadalupe, 125
Manuel, 129
Margila, 75, 106
Ma Maurisia, 115
Maria Remigia, 121
Maria Tomasa, 118, 126
Maria Vencelada, 121
Chisholm, Richard H., 70
Chiver, Joaquin, 183
Choate, David, 231
  David Sr., 141, 195
  Edmund, 195
  Elizabeth, 210
  Jane, 32
  John, 141, 236
  Thos, 32
Chriesman, H., 6
  Horatio, 224
  Jos, 224
Christie, Francis, 40
Chunnley, John, 145
Churchill, Francis, 222
Churnaca, Maria Dorotea, 122
Cieders, Lisabel, 204
Cierra, Anto, 112
  Jose' Maria, 112
  Juan, 112
  Julian, 111
  Noviesto, 112
Clampit, Catherine, 19
  Ezekiel, 19
  Susannah, 19
Clapp, David, 201
  Elisha, 141
  William, 34, 143
Claque, Daniel, 127
Clare, Abraham M., 39, 141
  Sarah, 39
Clarisa, Mary, 38
Clark, Abraham K., 142
  Alvin B., 18
  Anthony R., 13, 48
  Bershela, 40
  Dan R., 236
  David, 40
  Elijah, 48, 145
  Elizabeth, 18
  Esther, 196
  Franklin, 236
  George, 141
  Haner, 142
  Henry, 145
  James, 16, 142, 143, 145
  John, 21, 145

John Jr., 236
Rebecca, 32
Rhoda, 16
Silas, 21
William Senr, 145
Wm C., 32, 141
Claunch, Jeremiah, 221
Clay, Henry, 235
  Nancy, 10
  Nestor, 10
Cleggett, Abraham, 218
Clements, Austin, 142
  Joseph D., 71
Clift, Jesse, 26, 141
  Mary, 26
Clokey, Anne, 23
  Robert, 23
Clopper, Andrew M., 143
  Nicholas, 190
Clover, Isaac, 48, 201
Cobarubia, Santiago, 106
Cobby, William, 66, 141
Cochran, James, 31, 141
  Jonathan, 201
Cocke, Anne, 17, 141
  John, 17
Cockrill, Washington J., 5
Colchado, Jose' Maria, 146
Cole, David, 141
  James, 193
  John, 24, 193
  Oliver H. P., 219
  Philo K., 207
  Polly, 24
  Solomon, 141
Coleman, Lucy, 22
  Rebecca, 196
  Ruben, 219
  Youngs, 22
Colesto, Jesus, 157
Collantes, Cosme, 90
Collins, Lemuel, 209
  Sewall, 207
  Washington, 218
  William, 4
Collum, Charles, 143
  Collin M., 143
  George, 143
  Jonathan, 143
  Joshua W., 219
  William, 202
Colmenero, Isidro, 226
Colton, Daniel E., 32
Colvin, Aaron, 12
  Margaret, 12

Comb, Aneta, 126
  Jose' Justo, 126
  Ma Ana, 126
  Saml, 209
Conde, Anto, 92
  Felipe, 92
  Jose' Ano, 92
  Maria Anta, 92
  Pascual, 92
  Polonia, 92
  Ramona, 92
Cone, Albert, 24
Conklin, Elijah, 6
Conn, James, 142
Connell, John H., 33
  Matilda, 33
Connelly, E. M., 26
  Elijah M., 48
Conrad, Peter, 145
Contes, Jose' Maria, 184
  Julio, 183
  Julian, 142
  Siriaco, 145
Contreras, Jose' Simon, 142
Contrerra, Ma Anta, 107
Converse, Thos F., 9
Cook, H. L., 198
  James decd, 141
  Maria, 141, 198
Coonce, Philip, 33
Cooper, Benjamin, 218
  Enos, 141
  James, 145
  William, 46
Cope, Thomas, 29, 141
Copeland, James, 29
Cordero, Concision, 90
Cordova, Birenta, 91
  Damian, 116
  Evaristo, 97
  Franco, 130
  Jose', 128
  Jose' D., 235
  Jose Dario, 113
  Jose' Manuel, 130
  Jose' Severano, 115
  Julio, 109
  Manuela, 91
  Ma Anta, 113
  Maria Ascencion, 130
  Maria Dolores, 116
  Maria Getrudes, 127
  Ma Guadalupe, 125
  Ma Josefa, 115, 116
  Ma Severiana, 130

Index   251

Pedro Jose', 115
Ramon, 113, 235
Telesforo, 129
Vicente, 113
Ygno, 109
Cornaugh, Hannah, 38
Cornelius, Daniel, 201
Corner, Evan, 20, 141
    James, 141
    John, 20, 141
    Mary, 22, 145
    Prussia, 20
    Thomas, 21, 141
Cornwall, William, 48
Coronado, Felisiana, 90
    Jose', 141, 195
    Juan, 102
Corralles, Susano, 238
Corrizo, Matias, 219
Corryall, James, 141
Cortes, Catarina, 111
    Demacio, 227
    Dolores, 111
    Jose' Felipe, 120
    Juan, 120
    Maria Casimira de J., 120
    Maria Dorotea, 120
    Maria Guadalupe, 120
    Maria Salome, 120
    Melchora, 111
    Philip, 143
    Tomas, 111
Cortinas, Dolores, 127, 143
    Franco, 108
    Gertrudis, 142
    Jusefa, 95
    Maria Gertrudis, 112
Cosanova, Eduardo, 120
    Juan Bautista, 120
Cottle, Almond, 69
    Eliza, 141, 193
    George W., 74
    Harriet, 66
    Isaac, 74
    Jonathan, 63
    Joseph, 143
    Lee F. T., 141
    Lenard, 183
    Leonard W., 48
    Lorenzo D., 193
    Mary Ann, 193, 194
    Sally, 17
    Stephen, 17, 182
    Sylvanus, 182

Zebulon P., 219
Cotten, G. B., 9
Cotton, John, 48
Coulter, Abram, 205
Courseaux, Alfonse, 24
Court, Thomas, 193
Courteaux, Francis, 39
Couturier, Maria Louisa, 54
Cox, Christopher G., 22
    Cynthia, 10
    Harriet H., 22
    James, 38, 200
    Sarah, 38
    Thomas, 10
    Wm H., 7
Coy, Antonio de los S., 218
    Benigno de los Santos, 125
    Beralda de los S., 101
    Dolores de los S., 101
    Emanuela de los S., 146
    Jesus de los Santos, 123
    Jose' Andres, 118
    Jose' Antonio, 118, 129
    Jose' de los Santos, 129
    Juan Pablo, 125
    Manl Santos, 125
    Maria Antonia, 125
    Maria Camela, 125
    Maria Clara, 123
    Maria Luiza, 123
    Maris Luisa de los S, 143
    Maria Soledad de los, 120
    Martin de los Santos, 99
    Ygnacio Santos, 118
Crabb, H. M., 145, 233
Cravens, Ewin R., 209
Crawford, James, 8, 143
    Sarah, 8
Creagher, William, 48
Crice, John, 188
Crier, Kesiah, 40
Crisswell, John Y, 141
    LeRoy, 141
    William, 141
Critchfield, John, 237
Crosby, Clementine, 36
    Thos P., 36
Cross, James North, 30
Crothers, Mary, 141, 200
Crowder, John, 203
Crownover, Arter, 21
    Clarissa, 21
    Elizabeth, 40

John, 40, 43
Crozier, 4
    R. C., 6, 11
    Robert G., 5
    Sarah H., 11
Crutcher, Madison, 222
Cruz, Antonio, 145
    Crisanto, 129
    Estevan, 129
    Gualupe de la, 91
    Jose' Alifonzo, 129
    Juan de la, 146
    Juan Jose de la, 111
    Leonardo de la, 104
    Manuela, 129
    Maria Andrea, 129
    Ma Concpcion Santa, 127
    Maria Juliana, 129
    Ma Olaya, 115
    Mariana de la, 90
    Melchora de la, 111
    Paula de la, 111
    Petra de la, 111
Cryer, John, 188
Cuellar, Jinio, 142
    Jose' Luis, 103
    Maria de, 103
    Rafaela, 106
Cuerca, Enrrique, 118
    Jose' de los Reyes, 118
Cullum, Edwd N., 11
Cummings, Willie, 141
Cummins, M., 4
    Moses, 11, 214
    Susanna, 145
Cunia, Jose', 189
Curbela, Josepa, 88
    Juan Andres, 88
    Juana, 142
    Maria de Jesus, 88
    Maria Luisa, 88
    Miguela, 88
Curbier, Fernando, 84
    Matias, 84
    Vicenta, 82
Curtis, Elijah, 15, 143
    Hinto, 141
    James, 143
    James Sen, 143
    Washington, 15, 182
Curvier, Alexandra, 93
    Antonia, 93, 185
    Antonio, 143
    Josefa, 93

Ma Erlinda, 93
Matias, 146
Cuviel, Fernando, 217
Cuvier, Fernando, 145

Daily, Michael, 146
Dayly, Redmond, 49
Dalton, Patrick, 213
Daniel, John, 201
Danklin, Stephen F., 5
Dare, George, 146, 213
Dariah, Antonio, 222
Darst, Abraham, 14
  Edmond C., 146
  Emery H., 146
  Jacob C., 64
  Jemimah, 14
  John G., 146
  Patrick C., 146
Daughtery, F. R., 236
Daverson, Saml, 203
David, Batis, 117
  David, 117
  Lewis, 147
  Maria Selestina, 117
  Ma Ursina, 115
  Tiofilo, 117
Davis, 4, 6
  Alfred B., 49
  Allen, 204
  Anna, 147
  Daniel, 67
  Edward B., 147
  Elias K., 208
  Fanny, 41
  George W., 71, 146
  Harrison, 210
  James, 223
  James C., 67
  James D., 67
  Jesse K., 72, 231
  Jesse T., 45
  John, 71, 202
  Joseph, 5, 13
  Kinchen W., 41
  Nathan, 210
  Nathan Senr, 49
  Nathan Jr., 205
  Rachael, 13
  Timothy, 30
  Warren, 206
  William, 147, 222
  Zachariah, 68
Dawson, Britten, 235
  David, 147

Henry, 203
Day, Aaron L., 204
  James, 32
Dayne, Hannah, 211
  Matthew, 211
Dayton, Lewis, 202
Dearduff, William, 71
Deaver, William, 19
Deck, Reuben, 234
Defee, William, 49
Degado, Sebastian, 221
Delass, Charles, 203
DeLeon, Francisco, 147
Delgado, Andra, 109
  Antonio, 83, 90, 231
  Anta, 109
  Apolonia, 90
  Caledonia, 100
  D. Clemento, 90
  Encarnacion, 106, 147
  Jose', 90, 100, 109, 220
  Jose' Antonio, 147
  Josefa, 90, 147
  Juan, 100, 231
  Juana, 90, 107, 146
  Manuel, 189
  Manuela, 90
  Margarita, 100
  Maria, 90
  Maria Candida, 118
  Maria Ignacia, 147
  Maria Josefa, 117
  Ma de la Luz, 109
  Migl, 100
  Neo···, 109
  Nicolas, 221
  Pablo, 100
  Rita, 100
  Salomon, 220
  Silbestra, 90
  Vitor, 93
  Trenidad, 100
  Ygno, 100
Delila, Francisca, 123
  Guillermo, 123
Delores, Santiago, 89
del Rio see Rio
del Toro see Toro
DeMoss, Catherine, 9
  John, 58
  Lewis, 9, 58, 146
  Peter, 198
  William, 58, 146
Dempsey, Francis W., 36
  Maria, 36

Demsy, Peter, 58
Denebil, Emos, 121
  Guilian, 121
Dennett, George, 15
  Geo A., 147
  Sarah, 15
Dennis, Gerry, 206
Denniston, Getry, 206
Denton, Abraham, 72
  Jesse, 205
  John, 15
DeSoto, Juana, 95
Dever, P. P., 146, 195
  Thomas, 146
  Wm, 237
Devers, John C., 146
  Thomas, 195
Devore, C., 233
Dewees, Ellis, 207
Dewitt, Christopher C., 147
  Eliza, 64, 190
  Green, 63, 64, 75, 191
  James J., 8
Diaz, Antonio, 88, 147, 183
  Balentin, 103
  Canute, 221
  Canuto, 147
  Clemente, 184
  Dolores, 104
  Domingo, 89, 147
  Fiodora, 88
  Follaria Dolores, 184
  Franca, 90
  Franco, 91
  Gertrudis, 84, 183
  Gulupe, 88
  Jose', 103, 120
  Jose' Maria, 103, 147
  Josefa, 147
  Josefa de, 103
  Juan, 147, 221
  Juan Ignacio, 184
  Juan Jose', 88
  Juana, 90
  Julian, 147
  Manuel, 189
  Margarita, 88
  Maria, 131
  Ma Escolastica, 147
  Maria Juana, 131
  Maria Getrudes, 123, 131
  Mari Petra, 128
  Maria Savina, 120
  Paula, 104

Index   253

Perfecta, 99
Polonio, 88, 147
Rafael, 88, 226
Sapopa, 88
Vincenta, 131
Dibble, Henry, 36
Dickerson, Almond, 189
Dickinson, Almerion, 65
   Edward, 34, 72
   John, 191
   Lemuel, 7
Dikes, Miles G., 70
Dil, Ma Olaya, 127
Dillard, Abraham, 23
   John B., 49
   John T., 4
   Thomas, 49
Dimite, Felix, 85
   Josefa, 85
   Napolean, 85
   Santiago, 85
Dinning, Agnes, 13
Dinsmore, John, 31
Dobie, Wm., 196
   Sterling N., 196
Dodson, A., 147
   Archolaus, 40, 190
   Obediah, 147, 190
Dolan, Annie, 25
   Patrick, 25, 147
Domingues, Diego, 96
   Felipa, 96
   Indalacio, 232
   Jese Alifonzo, 123
   Maria, 96
   Maria Barbara, 123
   Maria del Rosario, 96
   Maria Salome, 123
   Sixto, 232
Donoho, Charles, 6, 44
   Isaac, 5
   Mortimer, 44
Doone, Grason, 206
Doralina, Miguel, 238
Dorr, Edward, 196
Dorsett, Charles, 146
   Theo, 197
Doste, Jose', 127
   Jose' Santiago, 127
   Juan, 124
   Luiza, 124
   Maria Benigna, 124
   Marie Matilde, 124
Dottery, Anne, 12
   Bryant, 12

Dow, Lorenzo, 232
Dowlearn, Patrick, 69
Doyal, Matthew A., 234
Drake, James, 193
Draughan, Abijah W., 20
Drogeides, Francisco, 87
   Jose' Antonio, 94
   Juana, 95
   Marie Josepa, 94
Dry, Daniel, 49
   John F., 49
   Paul, 49
Duboiae, Anteoine, 211
   Antione Jr., 211
Dudley, Pulaskey, 5
Dukes, Thomas M., 58, 146
Dumas, Saml, 207
Duncan, Benjamin, 67
   Jas H., 147
   M., 195
   Meredith, 146
   S., 204
   William, 146, 195
Dundass, Wm E., 24
Dunham, Cary W., 207
Dunlap, Dolly, 11
   Wm, 11
Dunman, H., 234
   Henry, 146
   Jas T., 146, 194
   John, 147
   Martin, 146
   Robert, 147
   Sherrod, 202
Dunn, Eliza, 25
   Matthew, 147
   Patrick, 32, 44
   R. L., 25
Dupuy, William, 36
Duran, Andres, 229
   Blas, 187
   Dolores, 95
   Faustin, 226
   Feliz, 226
   Higinio, 226, 228
   Jesus, 228
   Jose' Ma, 228
   Martin, 226
   Nicolos, 101
   Pablo, 147
   Santiago, 226
   Tomas, 226
   Vicente, 101
Durbin, Basil, 147
Durst, James H., 147

Duty, Joseph, 4, 183
   Matthew, 4, 12
   Richard, 147
   Solomon, 4, 183
   William, 58, 183
Duvaul, Thos, 209
Dwyer, Edward, 40
   Eliza, 33
   Jeremiah, 33
D'Ziekanshi, John, 20

Earl, David, 206
   James, 190
   Matthew, 49, 148
   Richard, 236
   William, 49, 148, 232
Early, M., 13
   Thomas, 148
Earnest, Felix P., 37
   Felix B., 148
Easly, Daniel, 205
   James, 148
Eastep, Daniel, 148
   Joseph, 148
Eaton, William, 8
Echavaria, Concepcion, 104
Eckle, William, 8
Eckols, Abner, 230
Eddings, Abram, 28
   Nancy, 27
   Theophalus, 27
Eddy, Eeley, 198
   Peleg, 148
Edgar, Alexander, 225
Edmonson, John, 202
Edwards, Amos, 16
   Charles, 26
   John F., 14
   John H., 15
   John T., 147
   Penelope, 16
   Polly Anne, 26
   Sarah Anne, 15
   Tenola, 232
Eggleston, Troy, 236
Elam, John, 6
Eldridge, Elisha, 209
Eliete, Gilian, 128
   Juan Santiago, 129
   Ma Pole, 128
   Tomas, 129
Ellender, Joseph, 148
Elliott, Nicholas, 49
Ellis, Richard, 6
   Thomas, 230

254   1830 Citizens of Texas

Ellison, Jared P., 206
Endt, Lewis, 29
    Mary, 29
Enett, Lewis, 49
    Mary, 49
English, George, 210
    James, 49
    John, 49, 210, 233
    Jonas, 49
    Joseph, 49, 210
    Joshua, 49
    Richard B., 49
    Sarah, 210
    Stephen, 49, 210
    Thomas, 49
    William, 210
    William T., 210
Enjenio, Jose', 224
Enriques, Fernando, 101
    Lucio, 102, 148
Erera, Maria Antonia, 95
    Ynacio, 95
Erie, Gregorio, 122
    Santiago, 122, 148
Ernandes, Jesus, 94
    Josepa, 85
Errera, Anto, 82
    Jose' Ma, 82
    Ma Anto, 82
    Victor de, 82
    Ylario, 104
Escajada, Anecleto, 228
Escalera, Concepcion, 105
    Dolores, 91
    Jose' Maria Sen, 148
    Jose' Maria Jr., 148
    Manuel, 148
Escallan, Anastacio, 148
Escalon, Juana, 148
Escamillo, Leandro, 185
Escandon, 97
Escobar, Francisco, 148
Escolton, Juan, 129
Escovedo, Bartolo, 117
Eser, Maria Josefa, 121
Eslocum, Meltin, 123
Esmite, Juan, 88
Esparez, Carlas, 224
Esparza, Ana, 103
    Enriques, 103
    Gregorio, 103
    Henriques, 217
    Jose', 148
    Josefa, 130
Esparea, Ma, 106

Espaza, Jose' Maria, 224
Espenasa, Ignacio, 220
Espinosa, Jose' Ignacio, 148
    Jose' Maria, 91, 148
    Margarita, 91
    Maria Jesus, 89
    Pedro, 221
    Vicente, 89
Esqueada, Justo, 148
Esrrovte, Garieta, 121
    Juan, 121
Estela, Car, 126
Estern, Adolfo, 121
    Eugenia, 121
    Maris Rosina, 121
    Santiago, 121
Estes, Henry W., 209
Estocoman, Anriete, 118
    Enrrique, 118
    Enrriques Samuel, 118
    Javiel, 118
    Maria Dorcas, 118
    Selestina, 128
Estrada, Antonio, 148
    Asencio, 148
    Jesus, 227
    Jose' Ignacio, 120
    Loreta, 93
    Manuel, 93, 184, 221
    Da Maria, 79
    Roberta, 186
    Trinida, 93
Etherton, Dan, 11, 43
Evans, Charlotte, 38
    Holden, 38, 50
    Jesse J., 50
    Jesse M., 7
    John S., 11
    Joseph, 204
    Sarah, 11
Everett, Wm., 148, 196
Eweart, James Johnston, 198
Ewing, Abbie B., 19
    Charles W., 19
    George, 4, 6, 11, 232
    Ex., Maria Miguela, 115
Exis, Ana Maria, 130

Fairchild, Mahaley, 21
    Philo, 21, 149
Falcon, Jose, 125
    Juan, 125
    Laurance, 236
Falen, Maria, 124
Farias, Anta, 91

Franco, 84
Eusebio, 149
Jose' Anto, 84
Josefa, 83
Ma de Jesus, 84
Ma Josefa, 84
Micaela, 84
Pablo, 84, 187, 220
Trinidad, 84
Farin, Josquin, 80
    Juan Maria, 80
    Macario, 80
    Vicente, 80
Farmer, Alext, 23
    Huott, 50
    James, 149
Faulk, John R., 191
    Richard, 190
Federique, Maria Barbara, 118
Fenequine, Ma Nanse, 125
    Tomas, 125
Fennell, John, 74
Ferguson, Joseph, 202
Fernandez, Antonio, 149
    Francisco, 191
    Maria Josepha, 191
Fields, Isiah S., 148
Figeroa, Juan, 149
Filano, Andres, 103, 184
Finley, Lydia V., 11
    William D., 11
Finn, Richard H., 201
Finney, Ambrose, 73
Fish, Joseph, 50
Fishback, Isaac H., 50, 149
Fisher, Anne, 23
    Elizabeth, 28
    George, 191
    J. C., 225
    Job, 182
    Jorge, 28
    Reuben, 148
    S. R., 43
    S. Rhoads, 123
    William, 148
Fite, Uabetia, 42
Fitzgerald, John, 148
    Nancy, 50
    William, 50
Fitzgibbons, Nancy, 26
    William, 26
Fizer, John, 149
Flack, Elisha, 29
Flanders, John, 6, 35

Index   255

Flasolla, Bisente, 95
Fleming, Peter, 234
Fletcher, Joshua, 10, 56
Flinn, Simpson F., 204
Flint, H., 204
Flom, Moses, 130
Flores, Adelfin, 124
   Antonia, 94, 149
   Antonio, 89
   Bartolo, 149
   Carlos, 93, 186
   Catarina, 84
   Clarita, 89
   Concepcion, 104
   Concion, 89
   Crisanta, 98
   Dionicio, 231
   Dolores, 93
   Eguardo, 89
   Faustino, 104
   Franca, 91, 98
   Francisco, 88, 89, 91, 102, 149, 220
   Franco Antonio, 123
   Gaspar, 103, 149
   George, 104
   Gertrudis, 87, 92, 187
   Gregorio, 188
   Guadalupe, 149, 185
   Gustavus, 189
   Hermengilda, 106
   Ignacio, 184
   Jesus, 98
   Js Defond, 224
   Jose', 89, 93
   Jose' Sen, 149
   Jose' Anto, 124
   Jose' Candelario, 119
   Jose' de Jesus, 105
   Jose' Luis, 119
   Jose' Maria, 93
   Juan, 116
   Juan Anto, 99, 124
   Juan Bautista, 103
   Juan Garcia, 149
   Juan J, 220
   Juan Jose', 85
   Juana, 89
   Juana Francisca, 186
   Juana Ma, 99
   Juaquin, 100
   Justa, 185
   Luisa, 102
   Lusen, 124
   Madalena, 123
   Mansioia, 108
   Manuel, 88, 90, 94, 98, 149, 217
   Manuel Maria, 149
   Manla, 84, 103
   Maria Antonio, 124
   Maria Bitoria, 119
   Ma Bitoriana, 116
   Ma de Jesus, 97
   Maria Encarnacion, 119
   Ma Gertrudis, 98
   Maria Isabel, 124
   Ma Josefa, 80, 88, 103
   Ma Luisa, 110, 123
   Maria Marselina de J, 119
   Monica de, 98
   Nepomuceno, 185, 238
   Nicolas, 103, 149
   Pedro, 88, 91, 92, 183, 238
   Pedro Gonz. de, 189
   Pedro Jose', 119
   Ponusena, 93
   Rita, 103
   Roque, 221
   Salvador, 93, 186
   Santos, 187
   Selesten, 124
   Tonides, 89
   Xabiera, 105
   Ygnacio, 93
Flowers, Elisha, 149, 197
   R., 231
Foche, Candido, 98
Foley, George, 68
Fonteno, Julian, 128
Foot, Robert F., 50
Foote, Robert H., 149
   Wilson, 205
Forbes, B. T., 204
Ford, D. S., 30
   Drury S., 50
   James, 148
   Wm W., 38, 149
Forsythe, James, 50, 210, 212
   John, 50, 210
   Silby, 210
Foster, Henry, 237
   James, 29
   John, 50
   John Ray, 148
   Moses A., 23, 148
   Randolph, 148, 230
Fowler, Bradford C., 149
Fragoso, Micaela, 149
Frailey, Nancy, 25
Francis, Sebastian, 50
   Thomas J., 206
Franco, Josefa, 112, 149
   Miguel, 185
Franklin, Isaac, 222
   Phil, 230
Franks, Burrell, 149, 196
Franten, Alfred, 234
Frayle, Patricia, 90
Frazier, Margaret, 199
   Stephen, 148
   William, 148
Freeland, Choyl, 50
   Isaac, 50
Freeman, Jeremiah, 222
French, Edmond, 203
Frescas, Higinio, 227
   Inez, 227
Friar, Alfred, 226
Frias, Jose', 95
Frost, David, 214
Fuentes, Ana Maria, 149
   Anamand, 88
   Carmel, 84
   Crescencio, 184
   Juana, 150
   Juliana, 91
   Loreta, 84
   Luisa, 108
   Maria Manuela, 119
   Martina, 84
   Polonia, 83
   Trenidad, 112
Fulcher see Fullshear
Fulcher, Benj, 190
   James, 149
   John, 149
   Mary, 168
Fuller, Daniel, 50
   Hannah, 41
   Samuel, 41
   Seth W., 209
Fulshear, Benjamin, 63, 64, 67, 75
   Churchill, 63, 75, 149
   Graves, 64, 75
Fulton, Elisabeth, 22
   James, 189
   Saml, 21, 148
Fuqua, Benjamin, 38, 73
   Ephraim, 32, 149
   Martha, 32
   Silas, 74, 190
Furenash, Charles, 149

Charles Jr., 149
Conrad, 149
Jehu, 213
John, 149, 213
Robt, 149
Fury, Elias, 207
Gado see del Gado
Gage, 44
Gailbreth, George, 37
Gaime, Felipe, 100
Gaines, E. P., 152
  James, 204
  James S., 219
  John B., 152
Galban, Ancelmo, 97
  Ma del Carmen, 109
Galbraith, George, 150
Gale, Adam, 230
Gallan, Miguel, 152
Gallardo, Franco, 105
  Jesusa, 82
  Luis, 82
  Manl, 82, 238
  Pedro, 82
Galona, Teresa, 88
Galvan, Anselmo, 151
  Jose' Maria, 151
Galvana, Coleta, 92
Gamboa, Ma Matilda, 152
  Matilde, 79
Gandara, Jose' de la, 227
  Jose' Dios, 228
  Pedro, 227
Gandy, Daniel R., 50
Gañe, Juan Bautista, 131
Gaona, Pedro, 151
Garcia, Alexandro, 236
  Anto, 112
  Claro, 227
  Dolores, 151
  Francisco, 151, 224, 227
  Gregoria, 229
  Jose' de Jesus, 104, 152
  Jose' Maria, 152, 186
  Juan, 151, 220
  Juana, 108
  Lino, 220
  Marcelo, 183
  Marcus Jr., 152
  Ma, 129
  Maria de Jesus, 151
  Ma Josefa, 81
  Ma Trinidad, 128
  Matias, 224
  Nieves, 104

Pablo, 189
Pedro, 224
Pilar, 111
Ramon, 225
Remigio, 238
Simon, 185
Teodoro, 237
Trinidad, 185
Garner, Bradley, 193
  Bradley, Sr., 193
  David, 150
  Isaac, 193
  Jacob, 150
  Jacob M., 194
  Westley, 194
Garrett, Bartlett, 235
  Claiborne, 152
  Dickinson, 150, 152
  Jacob, 50, 207
  William, 152
Garretson, Thomas, 17, 151
Garsilla, Francica, 95
  Maria Josepa, 88
Garvin, John E., 66
Gary Thomas, 51
Garza, Anto, 102, 107
  Anto de la, 102, 104
  Ana Maria de la, 186
  Carmel, 102
  Concepcion, 107
  Desiderio de la, 94
  Estafana de la, 104, 186
  Felipe de la, 104, 186, 236
  Franco de la, 89, 107, 151
  Gertrudis de la, 79
  Guadalupe, 107
  Guadalupe de la, 108
  Ignacio de la, 151
  J. F. de la, 221
  Jacinto de la, 185
  Jesus, 89, 102, 217
  Jose', 130
  D. Jose' de la, 80
  Jose' Anto, 107
  Jose' Anto de la, 79, 94, 185, 187, 221
  Jose' Manl de la, 108
  Jose' Miguel, 107
  Jose' Miguel de la, 221
  Josefa de la, 101
  Juaquin de la, 106
  Juan Anto, 109
  Juana, 152

Juana de la, 88, 105, 121
Juliana de la, 104
Manl, 110
Manuela de la, 105, 128
Marcelino, 152
Marcos de la, 129
Margarita, 102
Margarita de la, 105, 107
Ma Franca, 107
Maria Francisca de la, 184
Ma Josefa de, 84, 123, 152
Ma Luisa de la, 106
Maria Polonia, 187
Melchor de la, 107
Pedro, 224
Pedro de la, 109, 187
Cura Refugio, 104
Rafael, 102, 152, 187
Reducinda, 102
Soledad, 107
Tomas de la, 126
Ucebio de la, 89
Vicente, 102, 153
Vicente de la, 185
Garzia, Anestacia, 102
  Dionicio, 99
  Jose' Dolores, 103
  Jose' Maria, 90, 104
  Jusefa, 91
  Lorenzo, 98
  Ma de Jesus, 99
  Masimo, 103
  Migl, 99
  Trenidad, 103
  Ynacia, 98
Gasley, Eliza, 9
  Thomas J., 9
Gates, Amos, 28, 150, 214, 237
  Catharine, 214
  Charles, 23, 50, 152
  John, 30
  Lydia, 28
  Minerva, 23
  Saml, 214
  William, 150
Gay, Jefferson, 230
  Thomas, 29, 51
Gaytan, Agapito, 150
  Felipe, 151
  Margil, 150
Gee, Wm F., 234

Geffray, Irene, 17
    Louis, 17
Geiger, Jacob H., 194
George, Abraham, 223
    Charles, 223
    David, 150, 198
    Holman, 150
    J., 44
    James, 67, 150
    Jefferson, 10, 150, 198
    John, 150, 198
    Nancy, 15
    Nicholas, 15, 150
Gerra, Casilda, 99
    Juana, 107
    Magdalena, 93
Gerrero, Trenidad, 108
Gertrudis, Manuel, 152
Gescom, Nathan, 205
Gestin, Thomas, 123
Gibson, James, 73
Gil, Concepcion, 82
    Cornelio, 84
    Dolores, 101
    Gertrudis, 101
    Ignacio, 151, 238
    Jose' Ma, 82
    Justo, 101
    Leonardo, 152
    Manuel, 82, 222
    Maria Ugenia, 91
    Petinario, 91
    Silas, 222
Gilbert, Jasper, 188
    Preston, 188
Gilchrist, Anthonia J., 150
    Charles, 192
    G. A., 235
Gill, Mary, 34
    Michael, 34
    Presly, 150, 194
    Wilson W., 193
Gillen, Michael, 68
Gillet heirs, 34
    Roswell, 219
Gilleland, Daniel, 32
    David, 234
    Dianah, 15
    Ellen, 150, 197
    James, 15, 151
    J. T., 237
    Priscilla, 32
Gimenes see Ximenes
Gimenez, Fermina, 152
    Francica, 87

Getrudis, 87
    Josefa, 152
    Juliana, 87
    Maria Ignacia, 151
    Maria Josefa, 94
    Ynacia, 95
Gintero, Manl, 92
Giral, Margarita, 100
Giron, Luciana, 227
Glass, George, 212
Gleason, Cynthia, 21
    Phinneas, 21
Goff, H. H., 200
Goins, Robert, 231
Gomay, Benigno, 189
Gomes, Antonio, 89
    Encarnacion, 89
    Jesus, 124, 220
    Jose' Bernardo, 124
    Jose' Lionardo, 128
    Jose' Maria, 130
    Josefa, 91
    Juan, 89
    Juana Getrudes, 87
    Maria Andrea, 124
    Maria Eudonia, 124
    Ma Ynes, 128
    Panteolona, 85
    Pedro, 124
Gomez, Antonio, 150
    Eusibia, 228
    Francisco, 151
    Jose', 105, 227
    Josefa, 151
    Juan Jose', 106, 227
    Juan R., 227
    Juana, 106
    Louis, 222
    Maria de los Angeles, 89
    Nacario, 228
    Silverio, 222
    Zaviana, 151
Gonner, Jacob, 222
Gonsales, Alvino, 91
    Andres, 95
    Antonio, 95
    Concepn, 85
    Esteban, 95
    Jesus, 109
    Juana, 95
    Manl, 104
    Ma Josefa, 82
    Migel, 95
    Trenidad, 109
Gonsava, Ascension, 152

Loreta, 97
Luis, 151
Gonzales, Alexandra, 98
    Ana Ma, 98
    Andres, 122
    Antonio, 151
    Antonio elder, 151
    Anta, 97
    Arago de Gregoria, 189
    Cornelio, 184
    Dolores, 130
    Domingo, 210
    Felician, 212
    Franco, 89, 187, 226
    Gabriel, 222
    Jose', 229
    Jose' de Jesus, 122
    Jose' de Manuel, 122
    Jose' Maria, 122, 229
    Juana Francisca, 185
    Juan S., 229
    Leonardo, 102, 189
    Ma Concepcion, 152
    Masimo, 122
    Meliton, 122
    Pedro, 224
    Sinforiano, 122
    Ventura, 217
    Ysabel, 108
Goodall, Adam, 209
Goodin, Lewis, 218
Goodley, J., 204
Goodlow, John, 232
Goodridge, Allen, 192
Goodwin, Andrew W., 50
Gordon, Elizabeth, 25
    Horace, 23
    Samuel, 29, 50
Gores, Humphrey N., 32
Gorman, Abner, 209
Gortari, Alexandro, 79, 184
    Elijio, 75, 93
    F. de los Santos, 219
    Isabel, 187
    Ma de los Angeles, 93
    Miguel, 152
    Santa, 79
    D. Vincente, 79
Gove, H. N., 150
Gowen, Nancy, 150, 195
Goyn, Guillermo, 126
Grafton, G.M.G., 151
Gragg, Jacob, 152
    John, 50, 152
    Milton, 152

Samuel, 152
William, 152
Graham, Thos R., 208
Grammer, David, 6, 34
Granada, Francisco, 153
Granado, Juana, 187
Granados, Carlota, 84
  Fernando, 84
  Juana, 104
  Laureano, 84
  Ma de la Luz, 84
Grande, Lusgarda, 151
Granillo, Encarnacion, 226
  Fabian, 226
  Tomas, 226
Grason, P. W., 6
Graves, Elizabeth, 210
  Franses, 205
  Hezekiah, 208
  Minos, 208
  Ransom O., 150, 197
  Philip, 203
  Reubin, 205
  Sandford, 225
Gray, Hugh, 225
  L. P., 204
  S. P., 204
  Samuel, 204
Green, Amos, 150, 195
  B., 150
  Benj, 194
  Benj M., 152, 194, 196
  Elizabeth, 14
  Joe, 237
  Patrick, 14
  R. M., 197
  Richard, 150, 194
Greenwood, Anne, 37
  Franklin J., 33, 150
  H. B., 150
  Joel, 37, 150
  John, 152
  Mary Jane, 33
Greer, Joseph, 223
Gregg, Darius, 16
Grey, James D., 33
  Levina, 33
Griffin, W. R., 150, 194
Griffith, Abitha Ann, 150
  Ester, 24
  Henry, 34, 150, 193
  Henry Sr., 225
  Noah, 24, 150
  Solomon, 150
Griger, J. H., 150

Grigsby, Enoch, 193
  Jacob, 193
  Nathaniel, 193
  William, 194
Grillette, Anto, 124
  C., 124
  Clery, 51
  Maria Adel, 124
  Maria Constancia, 124
Grimes, A. C., 199
  A. J., 233
  Disey, 16
  Fredk, 16
  G. W., 218
  George, 16
  Jesse, 25, 199
  Rosanna, 25
Gro, Luz, 88
Groce, Christian, 152
  Jared E. Jr., 44, 182
  L. W., 231
  Leonard W., 16
Gross, Christian, 51
  Larkin, 152
Grounds, George, 51
Groves, Phillip, 51
Grubbs, Emanuel, 202
Guajardo, Ynacio, 89, 150
Guedes, Juana, 83
Guerre, Ignacio, 227
  Jesus, 226
  Jose', 228
  Lino, 259
  Luciano, 226
Guerro, Agapito, 224
  Juan Jose', 151
  Maria de la Luz, 151
  Maria Josefa, 185
  Maria Madelena, 151
  Maria Trinidad, 184
Guerrero, Claudio, 221
  Franco, 113
  Guadalupe, 152
  Jose' M., 222
  Teodora, 112
  Tomas, 115
Guess, Geo. W., 225
Guev, Genere, 128
Gusman, Francis, 237
Gustes, Jose' L., 121
Guthrie, Robt., 152
Gutierres, Catarina, 104
  Fernanda, 110
  Jose A., 220
  Santiago, 221

Guzman, Eugenio, 224
  Juan Andres, 151

Hadden, Henry, 153
  Jackson, 153
  John, 153
  William, 153
Haley, Allen, 51
  Charles, 51
  James, 231
  John, 51, 212
  John R., 211
  Mark, 51
  Mary, 211
  Mary Ann, 51
  R. B., 51
  Richard, 51, 210
  Richard, Sen., 211
  Sharper, 236
  Thomas, 51, 211
Hall, A. J., 223
  Burges, 155
  Burgess G., 51
  Elisha, 18, 153, 197
  G. B. heirs, 13
  Harvay, 51
  Isaac, 189
  J. C., 153
  James, 30
  James Jr., 153
  Jemima, 18
  John, 39, 153
  Joseph, 153, 196
  Julietta, 12
  Luke, 230
  Nancy, 22
  R. G., 204
  Robert, 201
  Thos Jeff, 22
  Warren D., 12
  Winneford, 30
Ham, Cauaohas K., 51
Hambleton, Frances, 209
Hamey, Louisa, 13
Hamilton, Fanny, 37
  Francis, 37
  Josiah F., 37
  Thomas, 64
Hammer, Rosalie, 30
Hammond, George, 5
Hamner, Rolalie, 51
Hampton, Abraham, 222
  Adam, 156
  Andrew, 156
  John, 200

Index 259

Lawrence G., 51
Margaret, 200
William, 200
Hancock, Edwin, 52
Haney, 12
  James, 195
Hanks, Isabella, 155
  John, 200
  S. G., 232
  Samuel G., 51
  Wyatt, 155
Hansome, Aaron, 156, 200
Hanson, David, 39
  Thomas, 39, 153
Harbour, G. W., 237
  George W., 153
  James M., 155, 237
Hardin, A. B., 153
  B. W., 153
  Caroline, 37
  Franklin, 153, 233
  Jerusha, 153, 195
  Thomas, 203
  William, 37, 153
Hardiman, Eliza, 190
  Henry, 230
  Thomas, 222
Hardison, John, 51
Hardwick, Nathan, 51
Hardy, 7
  John, 232
  Margaret, 12
  William, 12
Hargis, James, 235
Harkins, William, 52
Harmon, David, 153
  John, 194, 235
Harper, Clayton, 153, 194
  Henry, 52
  Isaac D., 205
Harrell, Ezekiel, 207
Harrington, Arrabella, 24
  J. W., 234
  Moses, 237
Harris, Abner, 153
  Andrew, 233
  David, 14, 206
  Enoch, 155
  Isaac, 7, 155
  James, 52, 223
  John, 38
  John R., 191
  Martha, 7
  Wiley, 155
  William, 183

William P., 31
Harrison, Almond, 52
  Ambrose, 222
  D. C., 237
  Elenor, 211
  Henry, 13
  Jonas, 52
  Joseph D., 24
  Rachael F., 24
Hart, Bridget, 213
  John, 213
  Patrick, 236
Harter, Henry, 32
Hartwell, Steven, 205
Hartz, Xaime, 121
Harvey, Susan, 192
Haskins, Francis J., 18
  William, 5
Hatch, Harlem, 27
  Mary, 27
  Pamelia, 12
  Sylvanus, 12, 153
Haven, Eben, 68, 189, 231
Hawkins, John, 5
  Thomas, 218
Hayes, Thomas, 222
Haynie, John A., 183
Hays, Coleman, 38
Hazel, Seth, 52
Hazlett, Samuel, 183
Heard, America, 41
  William, 40
  William H., 5
Hearst, George, 234
  Lewis, 18, 153
Heath, Richard, 65
Hedy, Elizabeth, 155
  S. E., 155
  W., 155
Helm, Thos P., 22
Hemphill, Washington, 237
Henderson, C., 153
  Chs, 198
Hendrez, Pedro, 155, 156
Hendrick, Henry, 52
  Obideah, 52
Hendricks, Edwin, 155
  Thos D., 155
Henon, Juan Igenin, 188
Henry, John, 66
  Thornton, 235
Hensen, Elizabeth, 37
Hensley, 44
  Betsey, 16
  Charles, 214

Elizth, 214
Harman, 16, 214
  Jackson, 214
  John M., 21
  Johnson, 11, 218
  Mary, 21
  Sarah, 11
  William, 11, 153
Henson, David, 156
Heradio, Justo, 229
Hernandez, Antonio, 100, 220
  Bernal, 110
  Candido, 155
  Crecencio, 109, 238
  Dolores, 231
  Encarnacion, 107
  Eugenio, 89
  Feliciana, 106
  Franca, 103
  Franco, 106
  Geraldo, 156
  Gertrudis, 106
  Gregorio, 106, 184
  Isidro, 224
  Jeraido, 83
  Jesus, 186, 221
  Jose', 107
  Jose' Antonio, 156
  Jose' J., 217
  Jose' Ma, 109, 155
  Juan, 94
  Juan Antonio, 156, 183
  Juan Franca, 94
  Manuel, 94, 106, 155, 184
  Manuel Sr., 222
  Maria Francisco, 156
  Ma Juliana, 83, 156
  Nepomucena, 80
  Nicolosa, 104
  Santiago, 238
  Timoteo, 155
  Vicente, 155
Heron, Wm, 195
Herrera see Errera
  Anto, 83, 156, 238
  Benito, 221
  Blas, 156, 221
  Francisco, 106, 155, 220
  Guadalupe, 155
  Hilario, 156
  Ignacio, 186
  Jose', 99
  Manl, 82

Manuel de, 122
Ma Gertrudis, 82
Miguel, 120
Pedro, 155
Placido, 228
Rafael, 82, 155
Roman, 82
Torivio, 99, 155
Victor, 83, 156
Hesmite, Guiliam, 127
Hibbens, John, 153
Hickman, Asa, 156
Edmond, 230
Hickoke, Horatio H., 9
Highland, Joseph, 187
Highsmith, Abijah, 17
Debora, 17
Samuel, 66, 183
William, 219
Hill, Moses, 155
William, 70
Hilyard, Henry, 223
Hillyard, Jacob, 218
Hinch, Leah Anne, 24
Samuel, 24
Hinds, Gerren, 65
James, 64, 190
Hines, Albert, 52
Allen, 52
Davis, 205
Elbort, 204
J. A., 236
Mathew T., 42
Ransom, 205
William, 52
William Jr., 236
Hinkson, John, 22
Hinojosa, Cipriano, 232
Jose' Ma, 236
Refugio, 236
Hiroms, Nancy W., 12
Samuel C., 12
Hislop, James, 39
Hixon, John B., 52
Hobson, Henry H., 52
Hodge, Alexander, 13, 153
Alexr E., 14, 153
Archie, 14
Charlotte, 14
James, 37
John, 15
Polley, 15
William, 153, 230
Hodges, Robert, 10
Susan, 10

Hoffman, Andrew, 205
Hogan, Edwd, 35
Hannah, 35
Hoit, Saml, 30
Holden, Mastin, 23
Holdridge, Asa, 20
Holdy, Joses, 52
Holland, Francis, 155, 200
James, 17, 202
Tapley, 155, 200
Hollingsworth, James, 38
Holloway, Caleb, 52
Daniel, 52
John, 206
Lewis, 52, 208
Simpson, 52, 207
Holmes, Asahel C., 43
Henry, 234
Samuel, 52
Stephen, 211
Holt, Benjamin, 53
Thomas C., 205
Holtham, John G., 29
Homes, Bryant, 201
Hone, Heni, 121
Quiton, 121
Hope, Adolphus, 15, 153
Prosper, 15, 153
Richard, 153
Hopkins, 43
Eldridge, 201
Frances, 200
James E., 53, 156
Richard M., 156, 201
William H. H., 201
Hornsby, Joseph, 183
Malcolm M., 182
Reuben, 29, 183
Sarah, 29
W. W., 155
Hortis, Maria Luisa, 99
Timotea, 99
Horton, Alexander, 155
H. P., 155
Susanna, 209
Hotchkiss, Anne, 29
Augt, 29
House, George, 53
Isaac, 13, 65
Joseph, 37
Joseph Junr., 191
Kizia, 13
John P., 153
Mary, 37
Sally, 53

William, 69
Howard, Hartwell, 53
Jackson, 182
Mordecai, 155
Howe, Joseph, 53
Hubbell, John, 7
Hubbs, Eliza, 24
Levina, 24
Hubert, Frances, 28, 53
M., 28
Mathew, 53, 152, 195
Hudson, John, 156
Obadiah, 21
Huff, John, 153, 199
William P., 230
Hufman, David, 52
Hughart, Edward, 73, 156
Hughes, Benjamin F., 6
J. W., 6
James, 73
Hughson, James, 197
Huizar, Anto, 112, 221
Carlos, 155
Domingo, 112
Franca, 112
Gravicias, 112
Jose' Francisco, 155
Lasaro, 112
Pablo, 112
Seferino, 155
Humphres, George, 211
John, 156
Squire, 210
Humphrey, Lawrence, 192
Humphreys, James, 195
William, 211
Hundley, Jas C., 209
Hunt, Rhody, 39
William R., 39
Hunter, Ely, 153
Nancy, 13
Robert H., 153
T. W., 225
Thomas J., 230
William, 13
William W., 5
Huron, Vivian, 221
Husham, Thomas, 42
Hutchins, John, 218
Hutcheson, Mary, 17
Nathaniel, 17

Iiams, John, 190, 232
Ilaniz, Prudencio, 157

Index   261

Iles, Nancy, 35
    Perry B., 35
Inglish see English
Ingram, Elijah, 157
    Ira, 30
    John, 156, 188
    Seth, 156
Irion, Jas H., 204
    Joseph, 206
Irons, Edward, 212
Irvine, James T. P., 53
    Josephus S., 157, 210
    R. Boyd, 208
    William A., 53
    W. D., 157
Irving, Wm D., 205
Isaacs, Eliza, 191
    George, 157
    Henry, 234
    Samuel, 192
    William, 23, 156, 157
Ives, Amasa, 19

Jack, Laura H., 30
    Wm H., 30
Jackson, Cato, 230
    E. D., 237
    Elish, 13
    Emory, 204
    Henry, 225
    Hugh, 156, 195
    Isaac, 14, 22, 156, 157, 224
    Jacob, 231
    James, 225
    John, 218, 225, 234
    Samantha, 14
    Stepney, 218
    Thomas, 66
    Tillah, 156
    Tilly, 22
    Wm., 224
Jacobs, Wade, 219
    William, 53
Jaime, Antonio, 157
    Felipe, 185
    Ma, 138
    Maria Josefa, 157
Jaimes, Anta, 91
    Jose', 220
James, A. J., 33
    Milburn, 223
    Jarrel, 201
    Phineas, 66
    Thomas, 156, 157

Jamieson, Isaac, 28
    Margaret, 28
    Thomas, 234
Janes, Henry S., 200
    John E., 201
    Massack H., 201
Janey, James, 153
Jaques, Adelina, 23
    Benjn F., 23
Jefferson, J. R., 31
Jenkins, 6
    Frank, 225
    John H., 219
Jerez, Berabas, 228
Jerina, Ma de, 103
Jerrell, Major, 225
Jermain, Saml, 157
Jesus, Colesto, 157
Jett, Absalom, 193
    James, 156
    John, 193, 194
    Sarah, 194
    Stephen, 194
Jewell, Benjamin, 42
    Winney, 53
Jimenes, Juan, 220
    Manuel, 228
Jinkins, Edward, 17, 182
    Sarah, 17
Johan, Joan Ferdan, 203
Johns, Wm, 156, 195, 197
Johnson, Abraham, 203
    Alva R., 53, 210
    Chas, 199
    Chs. S. P., 34
    Ennin, 222
    Francis W., 17
    Franklin, 218
    Henry, 218, 231
    Hugh B., 156
    Jackson, 223
    John, 53, 156
    Joseph, 35
    William, 157
Jones, Allen C., 156
    Benjamin A., 4
    Crawford, 53
    Emily, 157
    Everett, 204
    Frederick, 204
    Gabriel, 225
    Geo W., 157
    Henry, 156
    Ira D., 204
    James, 207

John, 5, 28, 68, 156, 199
Jno Brown, 157
John H., 42, 157
Kelton, 156
Levi B., 38
Lewis, 53
Mary, 28
Milly, 42
Myers F., 5
Nancy, 199
Norris H., 207
Oliver, 60
Phinneas, 27
Richard S., 4
Sarah, 38
Silas, 42
Stephen 23, 197
Susannah, 23
William, 156
Jordan, William, 53, 156
Jowers, John, 207
Juanseca, Franco, 92
    Refugia, 92
    Ygnacio, 92
Juares, Juan Nepomuceno, 157
    Maria Marcia, 92
Juarez, Nicolas, 228
Jurada, Juan R., 227

Kalier, Juan T., 121
Kean, Jas E., 225
Kegans, James, 16
    John, 219
    Nancy, 16
Keith, John W., 225
Kellen, Levi, 53
Keller, Anne, 15
    Francis, 15
    Francis G., 26, 53, 191
    John, 14
    Levina, 26, 53
    Lucinda, 53
Kelly, William, 157
Kelser, Geo., 230
Kemp, Caleb, 25, 157, 197
    Charlotte, 44
    Jonathan, 44, 157
Kennedy, Margaret, 27, 53
    Rhody, 25
    Sarah, 18
Kennelly, Jane, 39
    Samuel, 39
Kennerly, Everton, 157
Kenney, Louisiana, 19

Kent, Andrew, 67, 189
   Joseph, 73
Kerlew, John, 190
Kerley, John, 7
Kerr, James, 75, 157
   Santiago, 75
Kiggins, James, 158
   John, 157
   Nancy, 158
   Washington, 158
Kilgore, Hugh, 16, 190
Killen, Levi, 28
Kimball, George, 30
   George C., 71
Kimble, Elena, 119
   Prudence, 214
Kimbro, Samuel, 53
Kincaid, John, 31
Kincheloe, Augustus, 157, 198
Kinchelow, Lewis, 157
Kincheloe, Mary, 198
King, Carson, 230
   Jas H., 212
   John G., 24, 64
   Jno S., 207
   Pamelia, 24
   William, 54, 212
Kindead, John, 54
Kinley, Thomas H., 54
Kinman, Carey, 35
   Samuel, 35
Kinnard, A. D. Senr, 157
   A. D. Jr., 157
   Michael, 157
   William, 157
Kinne, Louisiana, 157
Kinyon, Alfred, 214
Kinzy, Peter, 44
   Sarah, 44
Kirkham, S., 157
Kistler, Frederick, 74
Kitchens, Preston, 202
Klonne, Henry, 42
Knap, Asa, 207
Kneeland, David, 29, 54
   Silence, 29
Knight & White, 6, 45
Knight, James, 157, 195
Kornegay, David S., 157
Kuykendall, Abner, 46
   Adam, 157
   Barzilla, 158
   Elizabeth, 182
   Gibson, 158

   Jas, 182
   James W., 231
   John, 157
   Joseph, 157
   Rob$\underline{t}$, 44, 236
   Rob$\underline{t}$ H., 157
   Thornton P., 16, 157
   William, 157, 188

Labadie, N. D., 158, 194
Labaume see Baume
Labaume, Baberio, 115
   Gertrudis, 80
   Jose' Benigno, 115
   M$\underline{a}$ Constancia, 115
   Maria Ursina, 115
   Pedro, 115
   Jose', 80
   D$\underline{a}$ Vitorina, 80
Lacey, William D., 37
   M. K., 204
   W$\underline{m}$ Y., 217
Lafuente, Jose', 97
   M$\underline{a}$, 97
   Pedro, 97
Lagow, David, 208
Lake, John W., 204
Lakey, Joel, 6
   William, 208
Lamb, Alexander, 192
Lambert, Uleses, 230
Lampier, P. M., 234
Landin, Cruz, 158
Landrum, John, 20, 158
   Letitia, 158
   Lettuce, 28
   Mary, 20
   Nancy, 20
   William, 20, 158
   Zacariah, 28
Lang, Edward, 9
   Jackson D., 207
   W$\underline{m}$ E., 208
Langabilla, Francico, 87
Lani, Alfred, 158
Lanier, Benjamin, 158
Lankford, Asa, 211
   Benjamin, 159
   Eleanor, 159
   Garrett M., 54
Lara, Guillermo, 112
   M$\underline{a}$ Eugenia, 82
   M$\underline{a}$ de Jesus, 82
Larrison, Allen, 14
   Thomas, 159

Larkin, Baker, 182
   Peter, 209
Larvana, Clementas, 224
Laso, Dolor de, 94
   Jose', 94
   M$\underline{a}$ Luisa, 85
Lasoya, Juan, 220
Lasso, Charles, 231
Latham, John, 54, 203
   John Jr., 211
   John Sen., 212
   King, 203
   Lewis, 210
   R. H., 237
   Susan, 213
Laughlin, William, 33
Laurence, Jos, 196
   Preston T., 206
Lavigena, Jose' Palmora, 159
Law, Ross, 54
Lawlor, Joseph P., 74
Lawrence, Adam, 22, 158
   David, 22
   Jenny, 22
   John, 30
   Sam$\underline{l}$, 22, 158
Lawson, Josiah D., 159
Lazarin, Antonio, 236
   Fran$\underline{co}$, 115
   Jose', 119
   Jose' Ant$\underline{o}$, 115
   Jose' Eugenio, 115
   Jose' Guadalupe, 119
   Juan M$\underline{a}$, 115
   Julian, 159
   Julio, 119
   Maria Cassida, 119
   Maria de la Luz E., 119
   Maria Estefana, 119
   Maria Teodora, 115
   Marselina, 119
Lazo, Antonio, 159
   Chapita, 158
   Xavier, 158
Leach, William, 73
Leal, Antonio, 222, 238
   D$\underline{a}$ Consolacion, 80
   Concepcion, 90, 110
   D. Crecencio, 81
   Fran$\underline{ca}$, 110
   Francisco, 90, 159
   Geronimo, 90
   Herinomo, 222
   Jeronomo, 158
   Jose' Angel, 189

Index   263

Jose' Antonio, 159
Jose' Esperidion, 110
Jose' Maria, 90, 158
Josefa, 159
Josepa, 87
Juan Andres, 87
Juana, 80, 87
Juana Isidora, 158
Manuel, 158
Maria, 87
Maria del Carmel, 90
Maria Ignacia, 158
Ma Josefa, 110
Ma de Jesus, 80, 81, 159
Mariana, 101
Melchor, 110, 158
Petra, 81
Plaval, 90
Vicente, 80
Leander, Antonio Sr., 231
  Raphael, 231
Lee, Abner, 35, 214
  Hiram, 18, 159
  Isaac, 4, 18, 235
  Patsey, 18
  Rensalleer W., 5
  Thomas, 209
  Wm L., 204
Leftwich, Jesse, 26, 54
  Sarah, 26, 54
Leiba, Ma Gertrudis Gil, 159
Leila, Jose' Maria Gil, 185
Leon, Anto de, 105
  Benita de, 111
  Carmel de, 110
  Donato, 130
  Franco de, 110, 158
  Josefa de, 105, 110
  Juan de, 81, 111, 217, 220
  Juana de, 185
  Ma Josefa, 179
  Mariana de, 105
  Pablo, 130
  Refugio de, 110
  Semon de, 105
  Teresa de, 111
  Tomas de, 111, 112
  Ygno de, 105
Lerma, Santiago, 100
Lerna, Blas de, 109
Leroy, Wm, 209
Leruia, Cayetano, 184
Lesassier, Eliza, 11
  Luke, 11

Lester, Josiah, 26
  Solita, 26
Letcher, Stephen G., 39
Levins, James, 159
  Jas Jr., 159
  John, 202
  Joseph, 159
  Nicholas, 159
Lewis, A. A., 206
  Elizabeth, 210
  Franklin, 18, 158
  Frederic, 194
  Gabriel, 223
  Geo W., 159
  Harman, 191
  Harold, 218
  Henry Senr., 232
  Henry K., 28, 190
  James, 158
  John L., 54
  Louis, 222
  Nathl, 23, 219
  Robert, 182
  Thomas, 193, 223
  William, 43
  William Sen., 158
  William Junr., 192
Leyva, Maria Guadalupe, 117
Lial, Angel, 217
  Geronimo, 98
  Jose' Ma, 98
Lick, John Sr., 201
Lidstrand, Ludowick, 159
Lightfoot, John W., 158
  Wilson T., 158
Ligon, Jose', 227
  Juan, 227
Lilly, Abraham, 218
Linche, Juan Bautista, 120
  Pedro, 120
  Teresa, 120
  Tomas, 120
Lindley, James N., 159
  Joseph, 54, 158
Lindsey, Benj., 207
  Charles, 54
  D. A., 233
  James, 26, 54
  Micagah, 54
  Pennington, 54
  Thos., 54
Linn, Charles, 159, 213
  Edward, 159, 213
  Isaac W., 206
  J. J., 159

John J., 158, 213
Linney, Henry, 29
  Hugh, 54
  Michael, 233
Linnville, Aaron, 159
Lion, Maria Jesus de, 124
Lione, Maria Anta, 125
Lionor, Mari Juana, 119
Lipkins, Joshua G., 223
  Levi, 222
Lippincott, Elizabeth E., 188
Little, Edith, 12
  John, 10, 204, 211
  John W., 12
  Winniford, 10
Littleton, White, 207
  Willis, 222
Litton, John, 158
Livas, Petra, 103
Livingston, Nelson, 218
  Pickins, 218
  Spencer, 218
Llino, Ma, 129
Lloyd, Benage, 201
  Hiram, 201
  William M., 55, 159
Loa, Anastacia, 80
  Demetria, 80
  Felipe, 80
  Juana, 80
  Romalda, 80
Lock, John, 55
Lockhart, Andrew, 71, 189
  Byrd, 63, 64, 75
  Byrd B., 65, 189
  Charles, 65, 158, 189
  Charles S., 219
  Conicy, 31
  George Washington, 70
  John, 189
  John B., 71
  Samuel, 31, 55, 69, 159
  Washington, 70
  William B., 74
  Winey, 55
Lockridge, Alsey, 30, 55
  Nicholas, 30, 55
  Reuben, 237
Logan, John, 39
Logins, Wm, 218
Lombraña, Antonio, 106, 159, 221
  Juan, 106
Loned, Juan, 89
  Tomas, 89

Long, Fred, 230
Longaville, Francois, 159
Longordia, Francisco, 202
Longoria, Felipe, 104
　Josefa, 104
　Juan, 125
　Maria Carmen, 125
　Maria Getrudes, 125
　Maria Trinidad, 87
　Nopomocena, 234
Looney, Jos K., 19
Lopez, Alexandra, 100
　Atanacio, 126
　Barbara, 106
　Bentina, 229
　Francisco, 186
　Gregorio, 126
　Guadalupe, 227
　Jose' Elauterio, 119
　Jose' Felis, 126
　Jose' Leonicio, 125
　Jose' Ma, 229
　Juan, 126
　Juana, 111
　Manuel, 100, 184
　Maria Antonia, 96
　Marselino, 99
　Martin, 226
　Pedro, 126, 228
　Teresa, 81
　Tomas, 227
Lorance, S., 224
Lorenzo, Jose' Justo, 122
Losano, Antonio, 231
Losova, Da Alejandra, 81
　Antonia, 186
　Concepcion, 159, 183
　Domingo, 96, 221
　Isabel, 84, 159
　Juan, 79
　Juana, 79
　Maria Anta, 118
　Toribio, 158
Louis, Frederick, 158
　Henry, 41
　James C., 223
　John M., 223
　Sarah, 41
　W. F., 223
Lout, Alfred, 212
　Bailey, 237
　John, 237
　Martin V., 206
Love, David W., 205
　John G., 159

Nancy, 14
Samuel, 14
Lovejoy, Caroline, 31
　Perkins, 31
Loving, James L., 22
Lowe, Eliz, 204
　Garret, 35
　Isaac, 55, 159, 206
　Isaac H., 206
　Jesse, 159
　Joel, 159
Lowen, Francis, 35
Lowery, Even, 211
　John, 55
Loya, Alcaria, 228
　Franca de, 97
　Julian, 97
　Loquario, 228
　Ma de, 97
　Narcia, 229
Lozolla, Blas, 126
Lucas, Wm, 218
Lucero, Elatario, 228
　Panfilo, 228
　Santos, 228
　Vicento, 228
Lucker, Dennis, 223
Lujan, Jesus, 229
Lujaro, Jose', 229
Lujan, Martin, 229
Lumpkin, Richd C, 208
Luna, Gregorio, 235
　Jose' Felipe de, 106
　Jose' Gregorio de, 128
　Jose' Matias de, 128
　Juan Jose' de, 127
　Maria Barbara de, 127
　Perfecta, 81
Lusere, Torinio, 229
Lynch, Benj F., 159
　F., 158
　James, 158
　N., 158
　Nancy, 17
　Nicholas, 17
　Stephen, 55
　William, 190
Lyons, W. F., 230

McAdams, John D., 205
McBride, Edward, 209
McCain, James, 23
　Sarah, 23
McCallister, M.D., 233
McCarley, Celia, 40
　Samuel, 40

McCaslen, Thomas, 38
McCausland, Mark, 26
McCelay, Hugh, 202
McCelvey, James, 57, 210
　Jesse, 57, 210
　Susannah, 57, 211
McClaren, John, 31, 57
McClure, Abraham O., 69
　Bartholmew D., 26, 70
　Sarah Anne, 26
McConnell, Elizabeth, 41
McCormick, A., 161
　Arthur, 190
　Mrs. Arthur, 190
　Michael, 161, 190
McCoy, Alexander, 15, 160
　Daniel, 74
　Green, 161
　James, 19, 160
　Jesse, 64
　John, 64, 65, 66, 190, 222
　Joseph, 66, 69, 74, 231
　Matilda, 19
　Prospect, 161
　R. C., 231
　Samuel, 69
　Thomas, 160
McCrabb, John, 69
McCrery, Cyreny, 56
McCroskey, John, 160
McCulloch, Alexander, 23
　Mariam, 23
McCullough, Jas A., 161
　Samuel, 223
McDaniel, Benj, 160
　James, 161
　Lydia, 42
　Winston S., 41
McDavid, Dortrick, 210
　John, 209
McDevitt, John, 161
McDonald, Catherine, 25
　Daniel, 5, 27, 33
　Donald, 163
　Hannah, 33
　Hugh, 5, 25
　Hugh Senior, 5
　Hugh Jr., 27
　James C., 218
　Mary, 27
　Mary Ann, 27
　William, 160
McDonough, Wm, 208
McDowell, Mills, 41, 200

McElroy, Betsey, 35
  Howard, 34
  Wm, 208
McFaddin, Andrew, 211
  Baley, 211
  J. F., 235
  James, 160
  Jonathan, 56, 210
  Samuel, 56, 210
  Wm, 193, 203
  Wm Jr., 160, 193
McFarland, Robert, 232
  Thos S., 206
  William, 192, 201
McFarlane, Dugald, 27, 160
  Eliza, 27
  Martha, 18
  William, 18
McGahea, James, 161
McGale, Charles, 230
McGaley, James, 161
McGary, Isaac, 10, 160
McGee, Joseph, 192
McGeorge, Joseph, 9
McGinness, John, 163
McGloin, Patrick, 213
McGrew, John, 212
McGuffie, John, 193
McGuffin, John F., 160, 200
McHenry, Andrew, 207
McHenry, John, 35, 160
McIntire, Margaret, 25, 160
  Robert, 160
  William, 25, 160
McIntyre, Elizabeth, 56
  Thomas, 57
McKean, John, 163
McKelvy, Hezekiah, 57
McKerley, Samuel, 191
McKey, Charles, 203
  Nancy, 203
McKim, Charles, 163, 205
  James, 163, 203
  William, 163
McKinney, 44
  Ashley, 161
  Blackly, 161
  Collin, 161
  Daniel, 161, 201
  G. Y., 161
  Hiram C., 161
  Jas, 57, 161
  Wm, 161
  Wm C., 57
  Younger S., 161

McKinstry, George B., 9
McLain, James, 208
McLaren, John, 57
McLaughlin, Charles, 19
  James, 40
  Laughlin, 20
  Wm, 161
McLean, Hannah, 163
  James, 57, 233
McManus, W. S., 225
McMillen, Samuel, 218
McMullen, Chas, 209
  Joseph, 209
McNautt, John B., 183
McNeal, Anthony, 223
  Daniel, 192
McNeil, Pleasant D., 223
McNeily, Elizabeth, 18
  Jesse B., 18
McNutt, Elizabeth, 161
  Nicholas, 160
McQueen, T., 5
  Thomas, 42
McRe, John, 208
McRoss, Ervin, 221
McVay, Polly, 57

Macaria, Ma, 113
Machel, Samuel B., 126
Maden, Isaac, 37
Madregol, Felipe, 55
Mahan, Timothy, 55
Mahuna, John, 7
Maiden, Isaac, 160
Maise, Tomas, 228
Malcolm, William, 42
Maldonado, Juan, 95, 162
  Ynacia, 95
Maloas, Maria Ginovesa, 92
Malone, W. T., 55
Malvin, Johnson, 208
  Richd, 208
Man, Jno, 212
Managhan, George F., 66
Mancha, Agapo, 164
  Alifonso, 85
  Antonio, 31, 163
  Benino, 164
  Felicia, 188
  Jose' Franco, 43
  Malina, 43
  Ma Anta, 85
  Pablo, 85, 162
  Sebastian, 127
  Tomas, 162

Manchaca, Antonio, 219
  Concepcion, 187
  Nasario, 184
Manchagua, Santa, 98
Mandiola, Francisco, 189
Mandosa, Louis, 189
Manent, G., 30
  Gabriel, 55
  J., 31
  Jacque, 55
Manifee, Agnes, 40
  Thomas, 5, 41
  William, 5
  William C., 40
Mangilla, Mariano, 232
Manna, Robert, 208
Manning, Noel, 208
Mansolo, Anastacio, 75, 81
  Clemente, 79
  Maria Manla, 81
  Pablo, 81
Manson, Reubin, 206
Mantolvo, Manuel, 224
Manuel, Edward, 236
Manzolo, Dolores, 129
  Juan Bautista, 122
  Jose' Maria, 120
  Maria Josefa, 120
  Melchor, 122
  Trenidad, 120
Maquedagnel, Juan, 126
Maragte, Lucy, 211
Maria, Lopez Jose', 199
Marlin, John, 203
Marquez, Madalino, 226
  Polito, 227
  Siriaca, 226
Marshall, Elias, 182
  Eliza, 45
  Hugh L., 160
  John, 26
  John Senr., 160
  John Jr., 160
  John L., 44
  Joseph, 160
  Leah, 26
  Samuel, 160
Martin, Elizabeth, 28, 55
  Gabriel, 161
  Geo, 230
  Henry, 55, 163
  J. C., 195
  James, 160, 195
  John, 160
  Joshua W., 37

Josiah C., 160
Laurence, 24
Philip, 200
Robert, 33
Tolliver, 28, 55
Martinas, A. D., 212
Martinez, Anavato, 164, 221
  Anicolo, 84
  Aniseto, 220
  Bruno, 88, 161
  Candelaria, 109
  Cesario, 163
  Concepcion, 104, 186
  Dionicio, 83
  Dolores, 102, 128
  Domingo Servantes, 128
  Doreteo, 238
  Faustina Ayala, 128
  Feliciana, 103
  Ferman, 103, 162, 220
  Gabriel, 186, 187, 221
  Gerarda, 84
  Gertrudis, 103
  Graviel, 81, 84
  Gregoria, 163
  Gregorio, 109
  Guadalupe, 162
  Ilario, 238
  Isidro, 238
  Jesusa, 79, 81, 85, 106
  Jose', 101
  Jose' Agapito, 128
  Jose' Andres, 128
  Jose' Lorenzo, 128
  Jose' Ma, 84, 85, 99, 128, 187
  Jose' Maria Sen., 162
  Jose' Maria Jr., 162
  Josefa, 100, 163
  Juan, 103, 106, 128, 164, 222
  Juan Jose', 125, 163
  Juana, 163
  Lugarda, 101, 164
  Luisa, 81
  Manl, 103, 107, 162, 187, 220
  Manuel the Elder, 164
  Ma Alvina, 82
  Ma Anta, 106
  Mari Candelaria, 128
  Maria de Jesus, 82
  Ma del Carmel, 106
  Maria Dolores, 85, 164
  Ma Getrudes, 113
  Ma Josefa, 101
  Ma Paula, 85
  Ma Rafaela, 81
  Marian, 109
  Nicolas, 162
  Pedro, 103, 163
  Refugia, 163
  Sencion, 107
  Tomasa, 81
  Trenidad, 106, 186
  Ursula, 85
  Ylario, 220
Marujo, Benito, 226
  Victor, 229
Mask, Jas V., 209
  Jno, 209
Mason, J. W., 42
  James, 55, 163
  James Y., 55
  John, 55
  John S., 208
  Malinda, 42
  Robert, 160
  William, 163
Masters, Henry, 159
  Jacob Sen., 160
  Jacob Jun., 160
  Lawrence, 208
  Ned, 233
Mata, Andreas, 222
  Lino, 238
  Miguel, 162
Matthews, John, 39
  Robert, 24
  S. S., 206
  William A., 65
  Wm H., 229
Maxamillian, John Sen., 163
  John Junr., 163, 203
May, Morris, 55
Mayes, Betty, 35
  Francis S., 35
  Nancy, 211
  Squire, 161
  Thos H., 33
  Wm D., 29
Mayfield, Alfred, 56
Mayo, John W., 26, 56
  Nancy, 211
Medina, Jesus, 228, 229
  Juan Jose' 123, 229
  Ma Getrudes, 113
  Ma Guadalupe, 125
  Maria Teresa, 125
  Maria Ynes, 81
  Pedro, 125
Medro, Batiste, 162
Meltin, Elial, 121
Melton, Elizsabeth, 56, 163
  William, 56
Mencha, Jose' Francisco, 163
Menchaca, Anto, 101, 118, 161
  C---, 89
  Carmel, 88, 164
  Crestina, 108
  Franco, 89
  Gertrudis, 79, 101, 162
  Honor, 88
  Jose', 88, 106, 130
  Jose' Francisco, 213
  Jose' Ma, 110, 161
  Josefa, 102
  Juaquin, 102
  Juaquina, 101
  Leonor, 162
  Manl, 83, 94, 100, 162
  Ma, 94
  Mari Anta, 129
  Mari Concepcion, 118
  Ma de Jesus, 93, 101
  Ma de los Santos, 164
  Maria Rafaela, 118
  Ma Seledina, 101
  Martin, 130
  Rafael, 164
  Ramon, 162, 221
  Refugio, 88
  Serafina, 109, 164
Mendes, Catarino, 128
  Ignacio, 231
  Nicolas, 162
  Vicente, 163
Menefee, Frances, 171
  George, 160
  John S., 161
  Quin M., 229
  Thomas, 160
Mercer, Eli, 19
  Levi, 188
  Nancy, 19
Merchant, Edward A., 56, 210
Mermea, Andres, 126
Merry, Thomas, 237
Mersed, Maria de la, 120
Mesa, Maria Ignacia, 164
Messenhama, Jacob, 56
  John, 56
Metcalf, Alfred, 31

Index   267

Michel, Blas Ramon, 121
  Mari Matilda, 121
  Vicenta, 121
Michem, Antonia, 130
  Jose', 130
  Juan Bautista, 130
  Maria, 130
  Maria Calorina, 130
  Manuel, 130
Micoless, Miguel, 21
Middleton, J. F., 56
  Samuel P., 70, 161
Milam, Jefferson, 161
Milburn, Allen T., 36
Miles, Edwd, 197
  James, 37
  Sarah, 37, 160
Milhome, Francis, 162
Miller, Andrew, 12, 213
  Celia, 12
  Edmund R., 12
  Hannah, 17
  James B., 9
  Jeremiah, 222
  John, 232
  John R., 161
  Joseph, 17, 219
  Lucinda, 13
  Ruth, 160
  Samuel, 161
  Sam R., 236
  Saml S., 161
  Simon, 13
  Thomas R., 71
Millican, A. A., 161
  Barry, 223
  Elizabeth, 25
  Elliot M., 25
  John, 214
  John H., 161
  William, 161
  William T., 213
Millo, Maria Tomaza, 120
Mills, David G., 74
  Robert, 7, 70
Milton, Eliel, 160
Mirales, Felipe, 224
  Getrudis, 101
Mirales, Teodora, 106
Miranda, Agustina, 89
  Franco, 97
  Macedonia, 99, 238
  Maria Malena, 184
Mitchal, A. J., 205
  Eli, 231

Elizabeth, 56
Jn W., 14
Reuben, 161
Thos S., 163
Modesta, Maria, 120
Mojaras, Remijio, 220
Molino, Carlos, 189
  Jose' Maria, 162
Monett, Narcissa, 56
Money, John H., 37
Monfarar, Carmel, 93
  Manl, 93
  Manuela, 93
  Remijio, 93
Monfaras, Anto, 107
  Jose' Ma, 84
Monjares, Manuel, 164
Monroe, Daniel, 37, 160
  John, 208
  Peter, 208
  Sally, 37
  Wm T., 208
Montalvo, Franca, 105
  Juan Manuel, 162
  Manl, 110
  Manuela, 97
  Simon, 162
Montes, Alejo, 102
  Anta, 110
  Anto, 102
  Carmel, 102
  Crescencio, 184
  Fiodora, 94
  Jose', 106, 162, 163
  Jose' Ma, 102, 111, 235
  Juan, 102
  Juana, 87
  Juanita, 102
  Ma Leonarda, 96
  Telesforo, 228
Montgomery, Andw, 34
  Burrell, 238
  Edley, 160
  John, 163, 199
  Wm, 37, 163, 199
Montolla, Anastacio, 87
  Antonia, 87
  Dolores, 87
  Jusefa, 94
  Lusiano, 92
  Martin, 87, 238
  Pomneseno, 87
  Ylaliario, 87
Montoya, Feliciana, 107
  Helario, 238
  Juan J., 227

Nepomuceno, 162
Montoya, Ysidra, 85
Moon, D.S.D., 56
Mooney, James, 206
  Richard, 56
Moore, David L., 208
  Daniel T.D., 163
  Elisha, 20, 199
  Elisa W., 56
  Francis, 19
  Henry, 56
  James, 10, 160
  James Walker, 35
  Jane, 20, 192
  John, 30, 56, 163
  Jno H., 6, 229
  John W., 11
  Louis c., 24
  Luke, 190
  Matilda, 35
  Nancy, 23
  Nathaniel, 41
  Nathl B., 207
  Olive, 10
  Rebecca, 41
  Saml T., 208
  Sarah, 20
  Thomas, 23
  William, 160
  Wm B., 229
Mora, Emedia, 235
  Estevan, 127
  Eulogio, 127
  Franco, 129
  Jose' Anestacio, 130
  Jose' de los Santos, 127
  Jose' Maria, 130
  Jose' Sefrana, 162
  Juan, 115, 127
  Maria Eduvijen, 130
  Maria Elena, 130
  Maria Luiza, 127
  Marian, 120
  Mariano, 120
  Maria Masedonia, 122
  Mauricio, 127
Moraida, Biscorte, 90
  Jose' Ma, 90, 162, 163
  Santos, 90
Moral, Martina del, 164
Morales, Andres, 130
  Corones, 91
  Francisco Flores, 162
  Francisco R., 219
  Grutiudis, 91

Gualupe, 91
Jose' Maria, 91
Jose' Miguel, 130
Jose' R., 162
Ma Encarnacion, 130
Maria de Jesus, 95
Martina, 91
Miguel, 95
Rafael, 108
Trinida, 91
Morfit, Pedro, 121
Morgan, Celia, 36
   Henry, 56
   James, 36
   Richard, 213
Morin, Jose', 125
Moring, Charles, 207
Morris, Bethel, 73
   Cathrine, 31
   Delila, 190
   J. D., 17, 183
   John, 33, 74
   Lee, 161
   Levi, 230
   Nancy, 33
   Richard, 31
   Robert, 161
   Silas M., 68
   Spencer, 65
   William B., 218
Morrison, Edmund, 56
   Stephen B., 68
   William, 160, 197
Morrow, Thos., 160, 161
Morse, Eliza, 27
   Henry, 27
   Matthew, 200
   Willie, 207
Morton, Alexr H., 5, 29
   James, 209
   Elenor, 29
   John, 161
   John S., 160
   Peter, 209
Morvan, Jose' Romalda, 127
   Manuela, 127
   Ma Josefa, 127
Moseley, Robert J., 27, 44
   S. J., 27
   Socrates S., 56
   Susan Ann, 44
Moss, Elihu, 72
   Matthew, 24, 182, 234
   Samuel, 206
   Silas, 207

Mourhouse, Seymour, 206
Mumford, David, 161
Munguia, John B., 232
Munguio, Manuel, 189
Muñis, Dorateo, 220
Muños, Anselmo, 91
   Eugenio, 79, 164
   Franco, 79
   Jose' Maria, 79
   Juan Jose', 85
   Ma Rosa, 79
   Ponciano, 79
Munson, Anne B., 10
   Henry W., 10
   M. B., 161
   William, 10
Murchison, John, 217
   Martin, 160
Murfy, Isaac, 201
Murphee, Wm, 19
Murphy, James, 40
   Willis, 163
Murray, Bartlett, 161
   Rice F., 11
Murvoir, Pierre, 210
Musquiz, Ana Ma, 107
   Camilio, 95
   Felipe, 89
   Jose' Maria, 119
   Juan, 123
   Ramon, 95
   Ramos, 95
Myrick, E. P., 14
   Niema, 14

Nabseta, Jucepa, 88
Nabarsete, Petra, 100
Nabner, George, 222
Nail, Elizabeth, 211
Najar, Guadalupe, 185
Nall, Barkley, 201
   John, 164, 201
   John H., 201
   Martin G., 164
Nancaro, Maria Bifida, 118
Nantz, Albert, 235
Nash, Coleman, 190
   Hannah, 164, 190
   Ira, 66
   Prudence, 214
Nava, Doroteo, 83
   Gasinto, 109
   Jose' Adnres, 83
   Ma del Carmel, 83
Navarrer, Mariana, 82

Navarrete, Luz, 101, 183
Navarro, Angl, 105
   Agela, 105
   Anto, 105
   Barnardo, 238
   Cecilia, 105
   Desedoro, 164
   Eugenio, 185
   Gertrudis, 105
   Jose' Angl, 105
   Jose' Antonio, 105, 219
   Josefa, 98, 105
   Luciano, 105
   Ma del Carmel, 105
   Nepomuceno, 164, 165
   Nepusera, 222
   Nicolas, 164
   Sension, 92
Neal, William F., 190
Neato, Jose', 164
Neely, John M., 203
Neill, A. C., 223
   George J., 164
   George T., 225
   John A., 65, 164
   Robert E., 217
Nelson, James, 188
   Joshua, 28, 57
Ness, David, 165
Nevaro, Lorenzia, 164
New, William, 19, 165
Newell, David, 209
   J. D., 230
   Samuel W., 205
Newman, Felix, 164, 196
   Jonathan, 13, 165
   Joseph A., 226
   Polley, 13
   William, 188
Newsom, Tom, 223
Newton, Jacob, 208
   John, 208
Nians, James Sr., 238
Nicholas, 44
   Robert, 205
Nichols, Fanny, 42
   John, 42
   William, 57
Nicholson, Mary Anne, 27
   Roderick, 5, 27
   Stephen, 164
Niebes, Ma, 115
Niesta, Jose' Bernardino, 164
Nieto, Andres, 165
   Juana de Dios, 110, 186

Index   269

Nieves, Ma Guadalupe, 126
Nixon, Fanny, 42
Noble, Benjamin, 165
　　E. M., 225
　　Fanny, 12
　　John, 209
　　John W., 12
Noll, M. G., 232
Nocaro, Maria Bifida, 124
Noris, Franco Sarapio, 128
　　Jose' Guillermo, 128
　　Jose' Agustin, 118
　　Jose' Santiago, 128
　　Juan, 128
　　Maria Clara, 118
　　Maria Juliana, 118, 128
　　Maria Presela R., 118
　　Nate Niel, 118
　　Nateniel Feliciano, 118
　　Tomas, 128
Norman, Nancy, 200
Norris, J. C., 236
　　John, 57, 235
　　Samuel, 212
　　Sarah H., 57
　　Thomas, 57
Northcross, James, 30, 57
Northrop, Orvill, 206
Norton, James, 27, 57, 164
Nugent, John, 164
　　Quintius Cincinnatus, 57
Nuñes, Gabriel Martines, 187
　　Juan Jose', 228
　　Ma Josefa, 83, 164
　　Manl, 108
　　Nepomuceno, 164
Nyro, James R., 202

Obidia, Guadalupe Bit., 118
　　Mariana, 118
　　Mari del Carmel, 118
Oban, Thomas, 57
Oca, Alejo Montes de, 221
　　John Anto Montes de, 220
　　Manuela Montes de, 98
Ocon, Dolores, 83
　　Encarnaction, 83
　　Jose' Maria, 222
　　Ma, 84
Ochoa, Ignacio de, 232
　　Pacifico, 232
Oden, Alexander, 6
Odle, Benjamin, 57

Odon, Sam, 234
Ogden, Abraham, 202
Ogoda, Jose' Antonio, 94
Oldivas, Florensia, 92
Olgin, Ambrosia, 228
　　Anacleto, 229
　　Andreas, 228
　　Antiqui, 228
　　Apolonio, 227
　　Calistro, 227
　　Filipe, 227
　　Gregorio, 229
　　Manl, 104
　　Regina, 228
Olibaria, Dolores, 95
Olibarri, Plasido, 165, 221
　　Teresa, 93
　　Jose', 183
Oliber, Juana, 125
Olivar, Casimero, 165
　　Polonia, 106
Olivares, Jose', 188
Olivarez, Albino, 228
Oliver, John, 66
Oliveravi, Pablo, 217
Oment, Washington, 165
Ontero, Jose', 79
Oporto, Victoriana, 228
Orivalin, Maria Antonia, 95
Ormsbee, Samuel B., 24
Ornos, Josefa, 102
Orr, George, 197
　　Thomas, 165
Orsment, Washington, 57
Ortega, Desidora, 79, 165
　　Fecundo, 79, 165
　　Perfecto, 228
Ortiz, Dionicio, 110
　　Dolores, 87
　　Gregorio, 227
　　Jesus, 165, 187
　　Jose', 103, 165
　　Jose' Maria, 187
　　Juan, 110, 165
　　Juana, 103
　　Monico, 220
　　Pablo, 165, 186
　　Perfecto, 228
　　Victoria, 109
　　Ygnacio, 81
Osborn, Benjn, 14
　　Claiborn, 219
Osburn, Charles, 165
　　John L., 165
　　Nathaniel, 188

　　Thomas, 165, 198
Osgood, James, 201
Otelo, Matias, 165
Otona, Alvina, 90
Owen, Christina, 29, 58
　　John, 29, 58, 190
Owins, J., 165
Owens, Mary, 22
Owns, Mary, 165, 190
Oxtolan, Ana Maria, 80

Pace heirs, 30
　　Albert Gallatin, 58
　　Dempsey, 166
　　Dempsey Council, 58
　　Gideon, 58, 166
　　Isaac F., 167
　　J. F., 205
　　James R., 166
　　James Robert, 58
　　John, 167
　　Mary Ann Elizabeth, 58
　　Patsey Jones, 58
　　Wesley Walker, 58
　　William, 58, 203
　　William Carrol, 58
Pacheco, Antonio, 83, 166
　　Bitoriano, 105
　　Doroteo, 80
　　Franco, 83
　　Jose', 83, 166
　　Luciana, 83
　　Luciano, 167
　　Policarpia, 167
　　Wesceslao, 83, 166
Padia, Leandro, 229
Padilla, Antonio, 217
　　Antona, 110
　　Bautsa, 79
　　Decidenia, 81
　　Florentino, 227
　　Franco, 109
　　Gabriel, 166
　　Hilario, 229
　　Jose', 102, 103, 167
　　Josefa, 79, 109
　　Juana, 102
　　Maria Antonia, 184
　　Nicolas, 226
　　Rafael, 102, 166, 226
Padron, Gertrudis, 102
Page, J. W., 166
　　Samuel Harrison, 236
　　William, 70

Paiz, Antonio, 227
  Gregorio, 226
  Martin, 228
Palacio, Juan, 112
Palanco, Felix, 227
Palbado, Candida Rosa, 116
  Juan, 131
  Maria Bitorina, 116
  Maria Luiza, 116
  Ma Norin, 116
Palmer, Jerry, 237
  Silas, 193
Panky, Widow, 6
  James, 13, 43
  Mary, 43
  Mary Ann, 13, 166
Pantalion, Bernardo, 126
  Juana, 112
  Moriel, 126
  Olibe, 126
Parada, Trinidad, 228
Parker, Jesse, 165
  Matthew, 167, 206
  Richd V., 209
  Sarah, 15
  Willis, 206
Parmer, Johnson Junior, 58
Parra, Jose' Ventura, 189
Parron, Wm E., 208
Parrott, Elizabeth, 188
Parson, King, 233
Partin, John, 10
  John C., 58
  Nancy, 10
Passing, James, 208
Patillo, George A., 165
  James H., 194
  Leroy, 235
Patrick, George M., 35
  James B., 70
Patterson, G. H., 58
  John, 58
  Lewis Y., 207
Payne, John C., 58, 210, 237
Peyton, Alex G., 166
  Edmund, 234
  J. C., 166
  Jonathan C., 198
  William, 58
Peace, Hiram, 194
Pearce, Rufus, 207
Pearson, J. H., 166
Pechea, Miguel, 106, 185
Pechi, Miguel, 217
Peck, Abraham, 33

Ancil C., 167
Pedrasa, Victor, 187
Pedraso, Martias, 227
Pebles, Pamelia, 9
  Robert, 9, 226
Peebles, S. W., 31
Peña, Ana Petra de la, 83, 184
  Franco Javier de, 120
  Jacinto, 166
  Juana, 89
  Jusefa, 96
  Luis, 118
  Ma de Jesus de la, 84
  Manuela de, 105
Pendergrass, Sarah, 166
Peneda, Jose' Maria, 166
Penn, Eli, 204
  Granville, 230
Pentecost, Geo W. Jr., 165
  Geo S., 165
Pepin, V., 31
  Victor, 58
Pereida, Maria d. Pilar, 166
  Thomas, 185
Peres, Ambrosio, 94
  Anta, 94
  Antonio, 88, 166, 227
  Carlos, 88
  Catarina, 94
  Concepcion, 98
  Concesion, 92
  Disodora, 87
  Domingo, 98, 167
  Gertrudis, 98
  Gregorio, 166
  Franco, 98, 125, 166
  Francisco elder, 166
  Franca, 109
  Ignasio, 95
  Jesus, 95, 220, 238
  Jeusa, 94
  Jose' 1st, 228
  Jose', 88
  Jose' Anto, 98, 167, 238
  Jose' Eugenio, 118
  Jose' Lino, 94
  Jose' Ma, 94, 125
  Jose' Maria Mart., 187
  Jose' Ygnacio, 96
  Juan, 125
  Juana, 106
  Jusefa, 96
  Leandra, 92
  Malena, 167

  Manuel, 166
  Maria, 92
  Ma Anta, 98
  Ma de Jesus, 98
  Maria Jesusita de, 166
  Ma Franco, 84
  Maria Josefa, 125
  Ma Juliana, 125
  Maria Luisa, 92
  Maria Trenidad, 125
  Policarpa, 88
  Rafela, 94
  Regina, 85
  Rosalia, 99, 167
  Rosaria, 95
  Rosario, 220
  Salome, 84
  Seguro, 96
  Senovia, 81
  Tomas, 218
  Trenidad, 96, 98
  Valentine, 166
Perezda, Pedro, 236
Perkins, James, 58
  John, 218
  Leonora, 21
  William, 21
Perry, Burrel, 34
  Daniel, 36
  Edward, 213
  Eliza, 36
  Elizabeth, 36
  Emily M., 29
  James, 36, 73, 165
  James F., 29
  Jane, 34
  Polly, 165
Peterson, Elijah, 207
  John, 9, 167
Pettus, Eduardo, 74, 75
  Freeman, 74
  John F., 167
  Saml O., 167
  William, 75
Peveyhouse, James, 14
  Mary, 14
Pharr, Augustus, 222
  Samuel, 15
Philips, Isham B., 167
  Jarvis, 205
  James R., 6, 25
  Nathaniel, 205
Phinney, Andrew L., 31
Piarote, Victoriano, 226
Pickens, Charles, 208

Index 271

Pierce, Demis Maria, 24
Pierson, John H., 200
   W. M., 234
Piertecha, 166
Pilgrim, Thomas J., 10
Pineda, David, 123
   Jose', 123
   Jose' Ma, 104
   Maria Dorotea, 122
Pirote, Esteban, 226, 229
Pitts, Obadiah, 38
   Polly, 38
Planes, Juana Maria, 167
Pleasants, G. W., 230
Plummer, Kemp, 230
Poaso, Jose' Olivie, 121
   Juan Barnardino, 121
   Silvestre, 120
Podilla, Francica, 95
Poleto, Ma Cosiana, 126
Polito, Gorge, 126
Poleto, Jose' Benigno, 126
Polk, Chesterfield, 223
Polvadore, John, 58
   Joseph S., 211
Polveda, Joseph, 233
Ponces, Getrudis, 90
Ponton, 45
   Andrew, 73, 165
   Isabella, 165
   Wm., 165
Pool, B. B., 34
   G., 204
   John C., 165
   Martin, 219
   Sarah, 34
   W. M., 234
Pope, Caesar, 208
Porras, Ma Caledonia de, 167
Porter, Alexander, 68
   B. A., 32
   Edward, 223
   Isiah, 223
   James G., 204
Potter, John, 200
   Steven, 205
Powe, A., 204
Powell, Elizabeth, 12
   Joseph, 40
   Sam, 234
   Thos, 17
Prado, Apolima, 95
   Jose' Anselmo, 122
   Juan, 235
   Juan Nepomuceno, 122

Maria Antoa, 122
Maria Faustina, 122
   Martin, 122
Pragedis, Vitoriana, 106
Prater, Richard, 230
Prather, Freeman, 167
Pre, Auselmo, 185
Prelles, Salvador de los, 96
Prentiss, George P., 205
Prese, Jose' Anto, 206
Price, James, 40
   Margaret, 40
   Robert, 232
Pride, William, 5
Pridonso, Madalena, 123
Priestly, Philander, 72
Procell, Atruis, 58
Prosela, Felipe S., 113
   Franco, 113
   Gertrude, 58
   Jose' Antonio L., 129
   Jose' de Jesus, 129
   Jose' Maria, 129
   Jose' Policarpio, 129
   Luis, 123
   Mari Anta, 130
   Maria del Pilar, 129
   Maria Remigia, 113
   Maria Telesforo, 121
   Maria Trenidad, 120
   Ma Vicenta, 115, 129
Provencio, Andreas, 227
   Blas, 227
Prudencio, Marcelo, 227
Pruett, Beasly, 166, 196
   Elisha, 166
   Jacob, 167
   Jesse, 165, 166, 194
   Levi, 165
   Martin, 165
Pruvencio, Manuel, 227
Pry, Peter B., 166
Pryor, Charles, 232
   Thomas Jefferson, 13
Puabla, Luis, 224
Puarie, Juan Bautista, 118
   Juana, 118
   Maria, 128
   Maria Lusaya, 118
Puaso, Favasina, 119
Pugh, Spencer A., 42
   Susan, 42
Pulido, Encarnacion, 83
   Maria Encarnacion, 166
Purdue, James, 209

Purnell, Chas S., 208
   Wm S., 208

Qualls, Anderson, 219
Quese, Roberto, 130
Quevedo, Guillermo, 167
Quinn, Patrick, 213
Quiñones, Agator, 85
   Antonio, 85
   Ma Dorotea, 85
Quinto, Manl, 96
Quirk, Henry, 212
   Henry M., 58
   Wm., 206

Raba, Jesusa, 89
   Manuel, 89
   Maria Rosa, 89
   Martin, 89
Rabb, John, 235
   Thomas, 188
   Ulysses, 230
Ragsdale, C. C., 230
   Wm., 168
Raimond, Samuel, 58
Rains, E., 210
Raines, Emory, 238
Rainules, Juana, 102
Ramirez, Amciti, 224
   Anta, 92
   Eduardo, 103, 168
   Gertrudis, 97
   Juan Lazaro, 189
   Locario, 170
   Magdalena, 109
   Ma Anta, 109
Ramon, Antonio, 189, 224
   Canuta, 100
   Carmel, 106, 186
   Concepcion, 101
   Dolores, 118
   Jose' Ma, 104
   Juaquin, 101
   Ma Canuta, 170
   Ma Guadalupe, 122
   Martin, 101
   Rosario, 101, 169
   Refugio, 101
   Teresa, 101
Ramos, Carmel, 80
   Clestonia, 95
   Galupe, 92
   Isidro, 186
   Maria Luisa, 170
   Vicente, 168, 169

Ramsey, Ralph, 222
Randen, Anderson, 230
　John, 169
Raney, John, 58
　Nancy, 58
Rankin, James, 29
　James Jr., 58
　James M., 169, 196
　N. B., 226
　Sarah, 28
　T. B., 235
　Thos B., 168
　William, 29, 59
　Wm Junr., 191
　Wm M., 28, 168
Raper, Daniel, 168
Rariden, Thomas M., 204
Ratliff, John J., 233
Ratliffe, William, 226
Rawls, Benj, 198
　George, 168, 198
Ray, Allen S., 209
　Andrew, 39
　Elizabeth, 200
　Margaret, 16
　Robert, 16, 169
Raydon, John, 59
Reaves, Green, 59
Rechur, Estevan, 122
　Maria Franca, 122
　Guadalupe, 122
Recio, Josefa, 102
Rector, Claiborne, 40, 167
　Joseph, 5
　Pendleton, 40
Recuedo, Ed--ige, 96
Redonda, Maria Josipa, 87
Reed, Elsey, 198
　Ely, 168
　Martha, 40
　Martin T., 207
　Thomas J., 40
Reeder, Benjn C., 24
　Mary, 24
　Mary Ann, 168, 197
Rees, Joseph, 22
　Margaret, 22
Reese, Charles K., 34
Reeve, James R., 204
Rendon, Joaquin, 169
Renfro, David, 59, 205
　Isaac, 59, 169
　Martha, 206
Resendos, Juan, 101
Reyes, Anestacia, 112

Anto de los, 80
Damasio de los, 168, 219
Enriques de los, 104
Franca de los, 80
Jose' de los, 170
Juan Jose' de los, 80
Maria de Jesus de los, 80
Reynolds, A. C., 39
　Harriet, 39
Rhodes, James Junr., 203
　Richard, 202
Rians, James, 169
Rice, Claiborn, 207
　Clinton, 59
　Clinton A., 167
　John R., 233
　Joseph, 59, 169
　Lemuel, 167
　Levi M., 200
　Peter, 218
　Robert, 218
Richards, Francis, 169
　Jacob, 206
　Jesse, 44
　Stephen, 235
Richardson, Andrew, 192
　Benjamin, 191
　G. F., 36
　Geo F., 169
　Lemuel, 206
　Lewis, 202
　William, 192, 235
Richeson, Edwin, 71
Richey, J. S., 204
Richie, Joseph, 191
Richmond, John R., 205
　Truman, 205
Rigby, Benjamin, 23, 167
　Cathrine, 23
Riggs, Pleasant B., 35
Rio, Anto del, 109
　Encarnacion del, 91
　Manuel del, 109
　Maria Anta del, 80
　Ygno del, 109
　Ygnacia del, 91
Rion, James, 34
Rios, Anestacio de los, 98
　Concepcion de los, 98
　Hermengilda, 93
　Jose' Ma, 92
　Raphael, 169, 213
Risa, Luisa, 105
　Ma de la Merse, 105
Ritchie, Archibald, 194

Ritchey, Hiram, 193
　Uel, 167
　William, 167, 193
Rivas, Anto, 93
　Celletano, 108, 186, 220
　E., 219
　Eduardo, 108, 186
　Franco, 102, 108
　Jose', 108, 168, 187, 220
　Jose' Luis, 102
　Juan Manuel, 101, 168, 185
　Ma de Jesus, 93
　Maria Juana, 119
　Rafael, 96
Rivera, Maria, 112
　Matilde, 170
Rivers, Antonio, 167
　Tom, 230
　Wm M., 199
Roark, Leo, 167, 188
Robas, Juan, 128
Robbins, Cinthia, 167
　Early, 169
　John, 169
　Joshua, 168
　Lucy, 169
　Mary, 169
　Nat., 169
　Rebecca, 168
　Thomas, 169
Roberds, Richard, 204
Robert, Josias, 169
　William, 169
Roberto, Buillermo, 123
Roberts, Abraham, 9, 191
　Alfred, 218
　Charles, 169
　Elisha, 12, 206
　F. G., 237
　Geo H., 169
　James, 197
　John F., 235
　Luke, 202
　Lysurgus S., 217
　Noel, 59
　Patsey, 12
　Redding, 168
　William, 167
Robertson, Geo W., 169
Robinson, Andrew Jr., 21, 168
　Geo W., 167, 234
　George, 168
　James, 168, 169, 196

Index 273

Jeremiah S., 59
Jeremiah J., 26
Jesse, 66, 187, 233
Joel, 192
John B., 192
Mary, 21
Oscar, 168, 196
S. W., 168
Thomas, 205
William, 9, 168, 169
Roble, Maria Ygnacia, 112, 170
Josefa, 81
Roblo, Jose' Nepomuceno, 123
Maria, 123
Maria Teresa, 123
Maria Tranquilo, 123
Pedro, 123
Rocha, Benito, 184
Rodila, Benito, 226
Rodes, James, 201
Rodrigues, Agustin, 85
Ambrozio, 93, 168
Andres, 85
Andrella, 87
Anto, 83, 107, 169, 187, 220
Antonia, 84, 91, 104, 107
Concision, 87
Crescencio, 184, 217
Encarnacion, 109
Formosa, 104
Franco, 107
Getrudis, 91, 185
Gil, 170
Jesus, 97
Jose', 169
Jose' Anto, 120
Jose' Gil, 82
Jose' Graviel, 84
Jose' de Jesus, 120
Jose' Ma, 93, 110
Jose' Maria Anta, 93
Josefa, 87, 103, 104
Juan, 97, 107, 110, 186, 219
Juana, 100, 186
Juan M., 238
Juan Manl, 107
Justo, 169
Margaricio, 185
Margarita, 110
Maria, 90, 185

Ma Antonio, 170
Maria de la Cruz, 120
Maria Gabriela, 87
Ma de Jesus, 97
Maria Ynacia, 87
Mauricio, 98
Petra, 87
Refugio, 110
Regina, 110
Rufino, 168
Rufius, 221
S., 222
Santos, 186
Simona de la, 97
Teodoro, 80
Ynes, 97
Roe, John, 74
Rogas, Maria Celeste, 116
Rogers, Elizabeth, 210
J. Y., 232
James, 167, 209
Polly Anne, 39
Raleigh, 39, 167
Robert, 167
Samuel, 5
Rohus, Mary, 203
Rojo, Ma del Pilar, 89
Ma Concepn, 89
Rolen, Catarina, 93
Francisco, 168
Rollins, Wm., 233
Romaldo, Jose', 127
Romano, Domasio, 111
Josefa, 111
Mariano, 185
Romero, Candelario, 112
Estevan, 112
Franco, 112
Gertrudis, 104
Julio, 186
Luis, 112, 183
Maria de Jesus, 112
Melchora, 112
Nicholas, 229
Pilar, 112
Teresa, 112
Rondonda, Maria Luisa, 87
Roof, John Eberhard, 200
Rosales, Encarnacion, 84
Franco, 123
Ylaria, 107
Rosas, Anta, 107
Jose' Ma, 103, 168
Rose, John E., 59
Ross, James T., 230

John, 170
Rosseau, 7
Francis, 203
Mosea, 169
Moses, 16
Roubdoux, Nelson, 203
Rovet, Licurges P., 121
Rovinson, Jose', 115
Jose' Santiago, 118
Maria Elena, 118
Moses, 118
Rowark, Jackson, 169
Rowson, K., 204
Roxo, Jose' M., 238
Royall, Anne R., 14
R. R., 7
Richd R., 5, 14
Rubio, Cristobal, 168
Ramon, 169
Ruda, Anglestina, 107
Ruddle, Archibald, 169
Ruiz, Antonio, 238
Bernardino, 112, 170
Concepn, 84
Dolores, 110
Eduvije, 100
Esmerigildo, 112, 168
Fernando, 169
Franco, 100, 112, 186, 221
Francisco Antonio, 168
Gertrudis, 105
Guadalupe, 105
Jose', 100, 238
Jose' Anto, 100
Jose' Maria, 112
Josefa, 105
Lino, 112
Ma Luisa, 100
Ma Paubla, 126
Ma Sinforosa, 100
Ygnacio, 112
Rumsey, Joseph, 225
Runnels, Johnson, 59
Russel, Luisiana, 20
Reuben R., 20
Wm J., 24
Ruta, Juan, 189
Rutia, Nepomucena, 107
Ramon, 107
Ruvio, Franco, 99
Ryan, Polly, 191
Ryon, William, 168

Saballes, Julio, 127
Saco, Anamaria Rosa, 119
   Juana Bautista, 119
   Maria Rosa, 119
   Maria Teresa, 119
   Michael, 200
   Miguel, 119
St. Clair, Duncan, 193
St. John, William, 73
Sais, Anto, 100
   Franco, 107
   Jose' Anto, 99
   Jose' Maria, 171
   Ma Josefa, 99
   Polonia, 100
   Pedro, 99
   Vicenta, 100
Salanveda, Jose' Alameda, 83
   Jose' Franco, 83
   Maria Rita, 83
   Santos, 83
Salasar, Anto, 109
   Francisca, 94
   Jorge Franco, 82
   Jose' Basilio, 82
   Jose' Joaquin, 82
   Maria Luisa, 94
   Ma Trinidad, 82
   Mariano, 110
   Refugio, 220
Salas, Fermin, 236
   Franco de, 80
   Justo, 236
   Valentine, 224
Salinas, Anto, 106
   Antonia, 87
   Franco, 92
   Francisca, 110, 189
   Francisco, 224
   Gertruds, 90, 97
   Jose' Antonio, 187
   Jose' Ma, 97
   Levcadio, 224
   Locadio, 236
   Luis, 107
   Margil, 106, 224
   Manuel, 92, 238
   Melchor, 224
   Pablo, 88
   Trenidad, 107
Salusar, Ehinis, 231
Sambrano, Anastacia, 110
   Anto, 110
   Benicia, 105
   Casiana, 105
   Concepcion, 105
   Jose', 108
   Jose' Ma, 110
   Juan, 108
   Melchora, 105
   Petra, 103
   Susana, 105
Sampier, Joseph, 199
   Monroe, 199
Sana, Silvestus, 172
Sanches, Antonio, 109, 172
   Antonio Gomez, 171
   Barvara, 91, 172
   Bentura, 125
   Candido, 119
   Cuñados Nep., 118
   Davi, 122
   Encarnacion, 103
   Gertrudis, 96
   Hosa Fancisco, 59
   Jose', 91
   Jose' Anto, 118, 127
   Jose' Damacio, 127
   Jose' Ignacio, 127
   Jose' Maria, 127, 171
   Juan, 221
   Juan Jose', 118, 185
   Juana Francisca, 97, 172
   Julian, 127
   Lucas, 221
   Luis, 127
   Manuel Bictorio, 122
   Manuela, 109
   Marcos, 109
   Ma Antonio, 127
   Ma Concpcion, 85, 127
   Maria Dolores, 117
   Maria Elena, 128
   Ma Feliciana, 118
   Maria Gertrudis, 187
   Ma Gregoria, 124
   Mari Jordana, 127
   Maria Josefa, 122
   Ma Manuela, 115
   Ma Mersed, 115
   Maria Olaya, 118
   Ma Ygna, 99
   Mariano, 126
   Migl, 101
   Nicholas, 221
   Pedro, 126
   Segunda, 102
   Simon, 126
   Tomas, 227
   Trinidad, 171
Sandefur, Elizabeth, 20
   M., 20
   M. D., 172
Sanders, Charity, 206
   Stephen F., 71
Sandobal, Beriana, 111, 172
   Carlos, 91, 221
   Fernando, 91
   Ma Josefa, 84
   Miguel, 80
   Petra, 91
   Salome, 80
   Ygnacio, 222
San Germain, Jas., 196
San Pierre, J., 37
   Joseph, 7
   Margaret, 37
Santa Cruz, Guillermo, 119
   Juan, 119
   Maria Benancia, 119
   Maria C., 127
Santos see Stos
Santos, Antonio de los, 87
   Barvara de los, 91
   Fernando de los, 87
   Guadalupe de los, 92, 171, 172
   Jose', 59, 210
   Jose' G. de los, 91
   Josepa de los, 85
   Margarita de los, 87
   Maria Anta de los, 126
   Maria Getrudis, 94
   Maria Manuela de los, 95
   Maria Paubla de los, 87
   Rafael de los, 91
   Teresa de los, 82
Sapp, Billy, 235
Sargent, Frederick, 205
   Ralph, 205
   Thomas, 205
Sartuche, Guadalupe, 111
   Jose' Candelario, 115
   Rosalia, 111
   Ygnacio, 115
Saucedo, D. Anto, 92
   Lorenso, 221
   Maria, 90
   Trinidad, 89
   Vizente, 99
   Ynez, 107
Saul, Chas., 212
   James B., 204
   Jno, 196
   Melissa M., 15

Index   275

Rachel, 192
Thos S., 14
Savage, Mary, 25
  Emelius, 25, 172
Savala, Manl, 94
  Santiago, 94
Sawey, James, 233
Sawlsbury, John R., 192
Sawyer, Jane, 172, 190
  Samuel, 190
Say, P., 190
Scanlon, Michael, 32
Scarbrough, Paul, 171
Scates, W. B., 225
Scath, Geo W., 233
Schrier, James, 20, 172
  Sarah, 20
Schritchfield, Henry, 59
Schutte, John A., 38
Scott, 4
  Andrew, 171
  David, 170, 219
  Henry, 10
  James W., 170
  John, 171, 172, 198
  John H., 33
  Jonathan, 68, 171, 199
  Jonathan P., 219
  Levy P., 171
  Noah, 170
  Patrick, 10, 171
  Patsey, 10
  Rozelia, 172, 196
  Simpson, 170
  T. W., 204
  Timothy, 219
  William, 42, 199
Seal, Solomon, 67
Seale, W., 41
Seana, Franca, 107
Seeligson, Edward, 231
Seely, Sarah, 75
Seguia, Antonio, 232
Seguin, Angela, 97
  Anto, 222
  Antonia, 92
  Carmel, 97
  Erasmo, 89, 92
  John N., 184
  Juan Angl, 92
  Juan Nepno, 92
  Manl, 100
  Ma Josefa, 93
  Da Ma Leonides, 89
  Mariano, 97

Teresa, 92
Ysabel, 100
Ysidra, 102
Segura, Antonio, 95
  Ma Antonia, 172
Sehaznaca, Ma del Pilar, 125
Self, Jacob E., 170, 196
  Taylor B., 170, 195
Selinas, Pablo, 171
  Pedro, 172
Selines, Maria Catalina, 186
Selkirk, William, 171
Selkriggs, David, 12
Selva, Maria Josefa, 171
Semboaner, Luis, 229
Sembranon, Nipomeseno, 229
Sentehfield, Henry, 59
Sepeda, A., 220
Sepulbeda, Jose' Anto, 117
  Jose' Esiquio, 117
  Jose' Seg., 117
  Maria Anta, 117
  Maria Juana, 117
  Mari Bernabe, 117
  Mari Torivia, 117
Sepulvera, Jose' D., 227
Seraes, Naravio, 189
Serda, Adanto se la, 81
  Barbara de la, 101
  Dolores de la, 81
  Getrudes de la, 92
  Guadalupe de la, 81
  Ma Getrudes de la, 127
  Maria Manuela de la, 129
  Nemesio de la, 92
  Nicolasa de la, 81
  Pedro de la, 83
  Refugio de la, 83
Serna, Blas, 221
  Mariano, 221
Serra, Jesus, 109
Serrano, Estevan, 186
Servantes, Agapito, 220
  Feliciano, 104
  Ginomena, 91
  Guadalupe, 111
  Juana, 80
  Ma de, 104
  Nepomucena, 80
Sessum, Ellis, 213
  Michael, 171
Sewell, John C., 205
  William H., 59
Sexton, William, 28, 59

Shadoin, Thomas, 44
Shamar, Jose' Miguel, 116
  Jose' Ysidro, 116
  Ma Francisca, 116
  Ma Yasenta, 116
Shannon, Catherene, 41
  Charlotte, 38
  J. M., 235
  Jacob, 41, 170, 199
  John, 38
  Simon, 237
  M. W., 235
  Margaret, 39, 170
  Owen, 39
Shaw, Hugh B., 200, 201
  James, 73
  John, 25, 214
  Jones, 172, 196
  Polly, 25
  William Jur., 201
Shelby, David, 218
Shepherd, William, 59
Sheridan, John, 172
  Lucinda, 172
  William N., 232
Shipman, Daniel, 190, 237
  Edward, 30, 170
  J. R., 230
  Jas R., 172
  John M., 170
  Moses G., 172
Shropshier, H., 171
  Harrison, 171, 198
Shropshire, Hicks, 198
Shupe, Samuel, 65, 172, 191
Sidic, Antonio, 172
  John B., 172
  Peter, 172
Sierra, Antonio, 219
  Noverto, 172
Sills, Wilson W., 193
Silva, Matias, 102, 171
Simen, Carlos H., 126
Simes, Candelaria, 130
Sims, Bartlett, 171
  James, 172
Simmons, Hannah, 167, 193, 194
Simons, John, 172
Simpson, Gains, 207
Sinclair, William, 59
Singleton, Ira, 205
  James W., 191
  Jefferson, 21
Spyars, 191

Wesley, 21
Sirala, Margarita, 172
Sisnera, Ramon, 227
Skinner, James H., 29
Slaughter, George, 59
　Samuel, 59
Slaydon, Arthur, 171
　John, 171, 192
Sleight, John L., 44, 213
Slingland, William, 172
Small, Emeline, 59
　James, 10, 59, 182
　Rhody, 59
Smally, Andrew, 170
Smelzer, John, 223
Smith, 7
　Alona, 42
　Archibald, 60, 211
　Bryan, 233
　Charles S., 45
　Daniel, 42
　Darkay, 12
　Deaf, 186
　Elizabeth, 30, 31
　Felix, 207
　George, 233
　George W., 192, 225
　Henry, 31
　James, 29
　James B., 170
　James N., 5, 11
　John, 30, 35, 203
　John D., 171
　John R., 231
　John W., 60
　Joseph, 40, 60
　Luther, 170
　Major, 172
　Margaret, 44
　Mary, 5, 29, 60
　Menan, 60
　Monair, 210
　Lancelot, 60
　Nancy, 211
　Narcissa, 45
　Nelson, 12
　Nimrod, 60
　Noel, 219
　Osborne, 232
　Philip, 172
　Phinneas, 36, 44
　R. B., 225
　R. H., 236
　Reuben H., 207
　Richd, 44

Robert, 65
Saml C., 203
Sarah, 30, 60
Sarah Anne, 11
Silas, 170
Sophia, 36
Stephen, 64, 172
William, 30, 60, 170, 172, 211
William D., 193
Wm H., 194, 214
Wm M., 172, 196
Willie, 170
Wily B. D., 32
Smithwick, Noah, 31, 60, 171
Smither, L., 30
Smothers, Archibald, 170
　John, 72
Snyder, John, 208
Soleto, Franca, 108
Soliñe, Maria Catarina, 123
Soliz, Bentara, 234
　Caliste de Jesus, 19
　Fermin, 110
　Fernando, 235
　Jose' Anto, 125
　Jose' Dolores, 125
　Jose' Fernando, 125
　Juan Jose', 112
　Maria Anta, 125
　Maria Pioquinta, 125
Somers, W. W., 172
Sosa, Brigida de, 92
　Felis, 95
　Gillermo, 95
　Jose' de, 92
　Juan Jose', 95
　Manuel, 171
　Margarita de, 92
　Maria Francisca, 171
Sotelo, Baltasar, 87, 172
　Hipoleto, 187
　Ignacia, 217
　Juan Esteban, 87
　Maria, 87
Soto, Andres, 185
　Dolores, 123
　Franco, 125
　Jose', 104
　Jose' Ma, 125
　Ma Encarnacion de, 117
　Maria Getrudes, 122
　Maria Josefa de, 120
　Maria Manuela, 121
　Pabla, 104

Sowell, John, 68
　Jno T., 209
　Lewis D., 68
　M., 209
　William A., 67
Soza, Julian, 238
Spade, Ado, 218
Sparks, Aaron, 207
　Betsey, 44
　Matthew, 44
Spears, 4
　Andrew, 206
　Robt, 33
Spence, William, 25, 199
Spencer, Nancy, 170
Spilman, James H., 172, 190
Spinks, B. M., 196
Spinosa, Ygnacio, 91
Splane, Peyton R., 13
Spriggs, Alexander, 218
Stack, Florence, 10
Staffen, Geo, 230
Stafford, Adam, 18, 171
　Elizabeth, 25
　Leroy, 25
Stallings, Jacob, 60
Standeford, Elizabeth, 34
　Jacob, 171
　James, 34, 183
　James W., 219
　Sarah, 34
Stanley, Betsey, 35
　Willis, 35
Stapp, Darwin M., 68, 171
　Elijah, 69, 171
　William P., 68, 171
Starks, Moses, 207
Stearn, John W., 206
Stephen, Elias, 207
Stephens, A., 234
　Amos, 60
　H. W., 234
　James, 15
　Jas R., 171
　Mary, 15
Stephenson, Amelia, 9
　Dimanes, 34
　Elisha, 170, 194, 225
　George, 193
　Gilbert, 193
　James, 9, 34, 193
　John, 193
　John Sr., 193
　Lydia, 193
　Thomas B., 170

Sterrett, A. B., 60
  Martha, 60
Stevens, Jacob, 14, 172
  James, 214
  James R., 214
  John M. Jr., 171
  Nancy, 14
  S. M., 233
  T., 44
  Thomas, 171
Steward heirs, 43
  C. B., 34, 170
  Cassia, 183
  Cassy heirs, 15
  Charlton, 234
  J. R., 223
  Jackson P., 205
  Jacob, 230
  James, 183
  John, 193, 231
  John W., 172
Stibbens, Benj, 205
Stiddum, Samuel, 172
Stiles, William, 170
Stinnett, Claiborne, 64, 170
Stockman, Catharine, 212
Stockton, Epps G., 206
Stockman, Henry T., 212
  Peter, 60, 210
Stoddard, David, 31, 60
Stokes, John, 203
Stone, Wm J., 206
Story, Benjamin, 205
  E., 212
  Jack, 223
  Rachael, 210
Stos see Santos
Stos, Concepn de los, 82
  Josefa de los, 108
  Juana Ma de los, 82
  Ma de los, 85
  Ma Gertrudis de los, 79
  Ma Ynes de los, 83
  Nicolas de los, 82
Stout, Henry, 201
  James, 201
  William, 60
Strang, Samuel, 170
Strange, James, 172
  John, 60
Stratton, David, 207
Strickland, Amos, 210, 212
  Benj, 212
  David, 202, 210
  David C., 188

Henry G., 203
Ira, 33
John, 202
Joseph, 202
Mary, 210
Samuel, 60, 212
Stringer, H. B., 34
Strode, William, 74
Stuart, James, 28
  Zillah Anne, 28
Stubblefield, Thos, 170, 195
Suares, Ma Apolian, 126
Sullivan, Dennis, 25
  Eunice, 27
  John, 27
Summers, Henry, 204
Suniga, Maraguita, 171
Sutherland, Frances, 11
  George, 5, 6, 11, 171
  John, 5
  Susan, 27
  Walter, 46
  Wm., 27
Sutton, James, 207
  Phillip, 207
  Polk, 233
Swail, Amy, 170, 194
Swearingen, Elmeleck, 42
Swift, Margaret, 192
  Rich M., 182
Sythe, Francis, 172

Talbott, John, 7
  Susanna, 7
  Williston P., 61
Tannehill, J. C., 30
  Jane, 30, 61
  Jesse C., 61, 173
Tanner, Daniel, 204
  Edward, 173
  John, 212
  James R., 173
Tapia, Dolores, 82
  Eugenio, 82
  Francisco, 226
  Josefa, 82
  Manl, 82
  Merced, 82
  Merel, 109
  Pilar, 82
  Polonio, 82
  Ramon, 82
  Rosa, 82
Tapp, Charles, 183
Targenton, Burton, 173

Tarin, Amicacio, 229
  Joaquin, 220
  Juan Maria, 174
  Macario, 220
  Manuel, 173
  Vicente, 173
Tate, Elijah, 66
Taylor, Anson, 174, 196
  Creed, 174, 234
  Felix, 67, 188
  Henry, 237
  Hepzibeth, 69, 174
  Isaac, 201
  James, 42
  Jane, 173, 195
  John, 205, 217
  John B., 19
  John D., 6
  John W., 192
  Joshua, 174
  Josiah, 69, 174
  Levi, 38, 174
  Owin, 61
  Margaret, 199
  Mary, 19
  P. B., 226
  Rachael, 42
  Robert Jr., 35
  Spicy, 192
  Tom, 230
  Truman, 205
  William, 174, 234
  Wm H., 27, 61, 70
Teal, Edward, 61
  Edward J. 174
  Henry, 174
  John, 173
  Peter, 65
  Richard S., 173
Tebosha, Marshack, 203
Tecie, Batis, 125
  Lenor, 131
Tega, Maria Selestina, 128
Tejeda, Bentura, 116
  Iginio, 183
  Jinio, 238
  Manuel, 184
  Ma Getrudes, 116
  Maria Paula, 187
  Mariano, 186
  Pedro, 222
  Vicente, 183
Telles, Francisco, 228
  Jose', 226
  Jose' Ma, 226

Manuel, 226
Marcial, 226
Marcos, 227
Pablo, 227
Rafel, 227
Ricardo, 226
Santos, 227
Tennell, George, 32
  George C., 226
  Sally, 32
Tevis, Andrew, 173
  G. W., 194
  George W., 173
  Nancy, 173, 193
Texeda, Clemente, 173
  Gavino, 80
  Jose', 173
  Juan Jose', 80
  Juan Ygo, 80
  Mariano, 80
  Paula, 80
  Pedro, 80
  Sebastian, 174
  Ventura, 174
Texas, A. J., 233
  Daniel, 230
  Egay, 230
  Harry, 230
Thaya, Michl, 206
Thomas, Benj, 220
  J. Francis, 206
  Jackson, 174
  Shadrac D., 174
  Theophilus, 174
  William, 222
Thombison, Thomas, 203
Thompson, 6
  Alexander, 21, 200
  Alph, 230
  Asena, 21
  Charles, 173, 211
  Daniel, 202, 208
  H. L., 219
  H. W., 230
  Hendrick, 217
  Henry, 223
  Hiram, 211
  Hiram M., 173
  Isham, 173
  James, 13, 64
  Jas M., 173
  Jesse, 173, 230
  John, 173
  Joseph E., 191
  Samuel, 61

Thomas, 21, 173, 174
  W., 225, 230
  W. W. W., 42
  Wm, 174, 196, 230
Thornburgh, Alex. C., 61
Thorpe, Henry, 5
Tier, Mary, 195
  Polly, 173, 195
Tierwester, Henry, 24, 190
Tigerina, Jose' Manuel, 175
  Jusefa, 94
Tilton, Charles, 196
Tinnin, Caleb, 174
  J., 174
Tinsley, J. T., 223
  Nathl, 207
Tipps, Thos, 206
Toar, Maria Bibiana, 122
Toban, Joan Ferrian, 174
Tomas, Emele Margarita, 123
  Guiare, 123
  Maria Luaye, 123
Tomlinson, Teresa, 61
  Thos S., 209
  Wm S., 209
Ton, Fros, 126
  Jose' Eduardo, 126
  Ma Susana, 126
Tone, Thomas J., 173
Tong, John B., 173
Tony, William C., 223
Toole, Martin, 188
Topa, Ma Concepcion, 129
Toran, Jerry, 225
Toro, Cipriano del, 174
  Diego del, 104
  Guadalupe del, 174
  Jesus del, 82
  Joaquin del, 183
  Margarita del, 102, 111, 174
  Martin del, 79
  Mateo del, 174
  D. Pedro del, 79
Torres, Anamaria, 124
  Antonia, 102, 182
  Casme, 224
  Guadalupe, 95, 174
  Jose' Andres, 124
  Jose' Julian, 124
  Jose' Nasario, 124
  Manuel de, 81
  Maria Anta, 90
  Maria Carmel, 123
  Ma Josefa, 97

Ma Josefa de, 123
Ma Lucia, 83, 173
Patricio de, 123
Pero, 226
Pilar, 90
Toscana, Getrudis, 94
  Ma Rosalia, 127
Totan, Mari Modesta, 124
  Remi, 124
Toulson, Thomas, 7
Tovar, Juan, 122
  Juan Ferman, 120
  Juana, 128
  Maria de los Ang, 119
  Maria Ocasia, 120
  Maria Teresa, 122
  Refugio, 92
Townsend, Jacob, 193
  Maria, 32
  Nathl, 32
Trabiero, Andres, 89
  Francisco, 89
  Ynacio, 89
Trammell, Burk, 41, 174
  James, 21, 174
Tratiero, Justo, 99
Travieso, Jose' Ig. E., 224
  Juana, 79
  Jusefa, 91
  Maria de Jesus, 91
Treat, Chauncey, 22
  George H., 231
  Mary, 22
Treviño, Brigida, 108
  Concepcion, 99
  Damian, 111
  Franco, 99
  Jose', 174
  Jose' de Jesus, 99
  Jose' M., 224
  Juana, 107
  Lorenzo, 238
  Ma del Carmen, 125
  Maria Dorotea J., 185
  Ma de Jesus, 99, 108, 174
  Maria Juanita, 186
  Mariano, 220
  Polinaria, 99
  Ramon, 99, 174
  Teresa, 88
  Ygnacio, 224
Trew, Demion, 204
Trudo, Margaret, 173, 213

Index   279

Truegas, Estevan, 83
  Melchora, 83
Trujillo, Bernard, 229
  Tinisted, 226
Truworthy, Thos T., 206
Tullus, Nancy, 199
Tumlinson, Absalom T., 217
  Andrew, 66
  David C., 73
  George, 190
  James Jr., 72
  John, 40
  John J., 67
  Joseph, 70, 225
  Laura, 40
  Littleton F., 73
  Peter, 173
  William P., 213
Turner, Edmond, 208
  Elizabeth, 173
  Winslow, 4, 64, 66, 174
Tuscano, Santiago, 174
Tutt, Clement, 61, 212
Tyler, Daniel, 173
  Edward, 174
Tyres, James, 207

Ulali, Ma, 126
Umstead, Francis, 223
Urban, Joseph, 42
Ureña, Franca, 92
  Jose' de Jesus, 91
  Jose' Ma, 91
  Teresa, 106
Urest, Jose' A. de la G, 224
Uron, Esteban, 221
Uriegas, Juan Manl, 102, 175
  Ramona, 175
  Ugenia, 102
  Xabiel, 102
Urrutia, Encarnacion, 175
  Jose' Maria, 175
  Juan Anto, 175
  Maria Rosa, 175
  Vicente, 175
Urtiaga, Alexandro, 227
Utilaga, Jesusa, 104
  Ma, 104

Vaca, Ana Maria, 187
Valdes, Bitoriana, 107
  Felipa, 103
  Franco, 80
  Geronimo, 175
  Jose' Antonio, 175

Jose' M., 220
Juan, 220
Valentine, Joseph, 212
Valverde, Anselmo, 175
  Luciano, 175
Van, Mason, 61
  Mason M., 210
  Odee, 234
  William, 212
Vandewier, Anne, 24
  Cornelius H., 24
Vandiver, C. H., 175
Vandom, Isaac, 175
Vandorn, Isaac, 198
Vansickle, Elias, 236
Varcinas, Andres, 175
  Trinidad, 175
Varias, Martias, 189
Vargues, Juan Antonio, 224
Varmor, Jose' Ignacio, 189
Varon, Anastatio, 188
Varron, Auginio, 189
Vasques, Antonio, 188
  Dolores, 103
  Incarnacion, 188
  Jesus, 222
  Juan, 175
  Leonarda, 103
  Rafael, 184
Vaughn, Charles, 235
  Steven, 218
  Theo, 228
Vecerra, Anta, 102
  Jose' Ma, 102
  Paula, 102
Veeder, Lewis L., 24
Vela, Maria Romona, 187
  Peter, 232
  Raphael, 225
  Sebastian, 83, 176
Velard, Lewis, 200
Velasco, Juan Jose', 175
Venavides, Feliciana, 101
Veramende see Beremende
Veramende, M. A., 219
  Marco Anthony, 175
Vess, Jonathan, 16, 175
Vidal, Alexandro, 80
  Gerusa, 99
  Ma Juana, 82
  Lonjino, 89
  Mariano, 189, 238
Villagran, Gabriel, 175
Villalpando, Ma de Jesus, 85
  Ma Josefa, 85

Ma Lina, 85
Ma Ufemia de, 85
Pablo, 85, 175
Villanueva, Candelario, 175
Villareal, Estavan, 184
  Gabriel, 220
  Gregorio, 232
  Jose' Ma, 131
Villegas, Jesusa Perez, 175
  Ma Guadalupe, 99
  Miguel, 189
  Tomas, 99
Vince, Allen, 175
  John T., 36, 175
  Richard, 175
  Susan, 34
  Wm, 175
Vincent, Henry, 202
Vizar, Seferino, 221
Vueno, Juana, 112
  Manl, 112
  Maugricia, 112

Waldrope, Wiley, 61
Walker, Danl, 176
  Henry T., 32
  Jacob, 40, 178
  John, 201
  John C., 176
  John M., 177, 237
  Leonard, 207
  Mary, 40
  Nancy, 214
  Prudence, 32
  Sarah Anne, 40
  Tandy, 39
  Tandy H., 176
  Wm., 214
Walkins, Alfred, 209
Wallace, Caleb, 176
  James, 13, 178
  J. W. E., 35, 177
  Patsey, 13
Wallis, E.H.R., 176, 194
Walless, Wm., 176, 195
Walters, John B., 19, 177
Walthington, 205
Walton, Moses, 235
Ward, J. J., 236
  James, 177
  James J. Senr., 177
  James J., 177
  Joseph J., 200, 202
  Russel, 69, 177
  Wm B., 177
  Wm C., 177

Ware, Hardy, 61, 178, 234
  Mary, 176
Warren, Daniel, 178
  Jesse, 205
  Lewis, 178
  Nehemiah, 205
  W. G., 234
Washington, Jacob, 233
Waters, William, 188
Watkins, Lewis, 232
Watson, London, 222
Watts, Hiram, 191
  John, 196
  Solomon, 232
  Thos, 192
Webb, Charles, 176
  Green, 43
  Isham G., 176
  Stephen, 218
Webber, John F., 19, 177, 232
Welch, C. P., 176, 196
  Chas C., 61
Weldon, Isaac, 67, 182
Wells, H. B., 219
  Martin, 20, 183
  Martin J., 177
  Sarah, 20
  Weyman F., 177
Welsh, Gross, 26, 61
  Henry P., 61
Wentworth, Tobias, 72
West, Claiborn, 193
  Gade, 61, 192
  Larkin N., 231
Westnor, Christian, 178
Wharton, Sarah Anne, 61
  William H., 61
Wheaton, Elizabeth, 36
  Joel, 36
Whetstone, Anderson, 211
  Edwd, 208
  Peter, 211
  Silas, 208
Whittaker, Alex, 178
  Nancy, 26
  Nathaniel, 194
  Peter, 176
  William, 26
Whitcher, N., 176
White, 6
  Anne, 33
  Archibald S., 28, 61, 178
  Benjamin, 5, 61, 178
  Bethis, 38

Dudley J., 38
Elizabeth, 62, 178
G. L., 204
George, 191
Henry, 191
J., 56
J. T., 225
J. Walter, 223
James G., 177
James T., 176, 194
Jesse, 5, 11, 190
John, 195
John M., 177
Littleton, 207
Lucy, 197
Margaret, 28
Martin D., 178
Mary, 11
Matthew G., 197
Nancy, 20
Peter, 20, 177
Peter L., 198
Reuben, 191
Samuel A., 62, 177
Saml W., 203
W. B., 18
Walter C., 60
Wm., 197
William F., 204
Wm M., 177
Whitehead, Edward P., 177, 190
  N., 178
  Nichs, 21
  Sidney, 36
Whiteside, 44
  Elisha, 214
  Elizabeth, 13
  George W., 214
  Henry, 62
  James, 60
  John, 13
  John J., 176
Whiting, Elizabeth, 196
  Saml, 177
Whitlock, Mary, 176, 194
  Robert, 176, 233
Whitson, Benjamin, 177
Wickson, Asa, 20, 176
  Barna, 177
  Barnabas, 20
  Byrum, 66
  Cyrus, 176
  Dryun, 176
  Eli, 176

Hutrah, 20
Wiggins, Harbor L., 62
  Norris, 223
Wightman, B., 177
  Elias R., 176
  John, 177
  Margaret, 22
Wilbarger, Josiah, 17, 177
  Margarette, 17
Wilcox, Charles, 176, 177, 195, 225
  James, 177
Willey, Burt, 223
Wiley, John, 178, 213
  William, 178, 213
Wilkason, David, 210
Wilkerson, David, 62
Wilkins, Jane, 176, 197
Willett, Andrew, 178
Williams, A. M., 224
  Absalom, 176
  Allan B., 72
  Augustus, 41
  Cary W., 207
  Christopher, 72
  Christopher C., 214
  David, 234
  Edmund, 231
  Ezekiel, 67
  George W., 177, 198
  Harry, 223
  Henry, 171
  Hezekiah, 176
  James, 62
  Job, 10
  John, 4, 11, 176, 177, 213
  Johnson, 204
  Malkijah, 71, 177
  Moses, 229
  N. B., 177, 198
  Nancy, 10
  Neal, 233
  Parker, 62
  R. H., 177
  Rebecca, 11
  Richard, 62
  Robert H., 197
  Samuel, 73
  Solomon, 223
  Stephen Senr., 192
  Stephen Junr., 192
  T. J. 176, 196
  Thomas, 191
  Thomas Sen., 176
  Thos J., 15, 176

Tilmon, 209
W. M., 206
William, 62, 176, 223
William A., 62
Williamson, J. W., 177
John W., 45
Mary T., 31
R. M., 177
Robt M., 11
William, 31
Willis, Arthur, 62
Wills, Roben, 231
Willson, James B., 192
Robt H., 208
Wilson, Abram, 232
George W., 176
Jane, 33
Jesse, 33
John, 235
Robt, 23
William, 177
William K., 21, 232
Wimbley, James, 202
Winfree, A.B.J., 176, 194
A. E., 192
J. F., 176
Jacob F., 195
Sarah, 192
Wingfield, H., 176
Henry, 176
Jane, 176
Matilda, 176
Winn, James, 176
Win, John, 62
Winston, Anthony, 4, 11
Isaac, 4
Joel W., 4
Milton, 4
Sally Anne, 11
William, 4
William O., 4
Winter, Thacker, 5
Wiseman, G. C., 231
Robt, 196
Witmore, Alexander O., 202
Geo C., 177
Witt, Hughes, 28
Wood, James F., 67
Joseph, 178, 200
Martha, 8
Prissa, 203
Reuben D., 8
William R., 177
Woodruff, Zachy, 209
Woods, Isabelle, 17

James B., 196
Jasper, 201
Leander, 15, 188
Montraville, 17
Norman, 27, 176
Zadock, 176, 188
Woodward, Alvin, 177, 198
Nancy, 18
Sandford, 18
Woodworth, Jonathan, 35, 62
Woody, Samuel, 37, 182
Wooldridge, Gibson, 4
Wootan, N. D., 233
Wooten, Moses, 62, 210
Wootton, Greenville T., 178
Wootton, Thos J., 178
Worrell, Wm., 207
Wright, Adam, 202
Alexander, 192
Alexander W., 202
Anne, 27
Buford, 177
Felix, 176, 182
Francis G., 177
Geo W., 177, 202
Henry Q., 27
James, 5
John, 192, 235
Ralph, 58, 198
Sherrod, 192
Travis G., 202
Wm F., 177
Wroe, Nancy, 25
William, 25
Wyatt, C. C., 34
Wyres, Robert, 62

Xaime, Jose', 100
Josefa, 100
Marcos, 100
Ximenes see J and Z
Ximenes, Alexandro, 108
Anto, 98
Franco, 98, 107, 238
Casiano, 108, 178
Catarina, 99
Gil, 108
Jose', 98, 178
Jose' Ma, 108
Josefa, 100, 106, 178
Juan, 108
Margarita, 185
Maria Jesus, 184
Maria Josefa, 81

Maria Trenidad, 99
Ma Yfinea, 108
Manl, 93
Melchor, 98, 238
Pabla, 84
Ponceano, 108, 178
Sinforiana, 108
Trenidad, 99

Yancey, Abner, 219
Yates, Phillip, 205
Ybarra, Carlos, 100
Ybarbo see Barbo
Ybarbo, Anastacio, 115
Antonio, 179
Balentin, 120
Benigno, 115
Candelario, 88
Candraises, 179
Concepcion, 117
Damacio, 131
Domingo, 128
Gregorio, 129, 178
Jesus, 178, 179
Jose', 116
Jose' Antonio, 179
Jose' Anto de Jesus, 116
Jose' Acario, 129
Jose' de Jesus, 129
Jose' Desiderio, 115
Jose' Franco, 116
Jose' Lauriano, 128
Jose' Leonicio, 116
Jose' Maria, 129
Jose' Ygnacio, 115
Juan, 129, 235
Juan Antonio, 115, 128
Juan Bautista, 117, 128
Juan Benigno, 179
Juan de Jesus, 121
Juan Jose', 128, 129
Leonardo, 115
Luciana, 179
Luciano, 121
Lucien, 235
Manuel, 129
Manuel M., 179
Manl Marian, 115
Manuel Onoje, 121
Marcimiliano, 115
Maria, 128
Maria Alejandra, 128
Maria Anta, 117
Maria Barbara, 128
Maria Brijida, 129

Maria Canuta, 121
Maria Carmel, 115
Maria de la Luz, 128
Maria Dorotea, 128
Maria Encarnacion, 115
Maria Estefania, 128
Maria Gregoria, 115
Maria Josefa, 121
Maria Mariana, 115
Maria Petra, 115, 116
Maria Rafaela, 121
Maria Telesforo, 120
Maria Teresa, 115
Maria Tomasa, 115
Mari Feliciana, 121
Martin, 116, 179
Martina, 129
M<u>a</u> Tiburcia, 128
Maximilian, 178
Miguel, 179
Pedro, 121
Ramigeo, 121, 178
Trenidad, 123
Vicente Ysiderio, 116
Yeamins, Asa, 27, 178
Daniel, 26
Elias, 178
Erastus, 178
Jerusha, 27
Joseph, 26, 178
Yearly, Isaac, 232
Yendo, Miguel, 238

Yglesias, Dionisio, 179
Yndo, Miguel, 179
Ynojosa, Bentura, 178
Yocum, Thomas D., 193
Yone, Alen C., 121
   Charles, 121
   Clarese, 121
   Dilete, 121
   Mateo, 121
   Mimes, 121
   Santiago, 121
   Terice, 121
York, James A., 178
   John, 8, 60, 179
   Jonathan, 226
   Thomas, 178
   Zutitia, 8
Young, Horatio, 204
   Jesse, 200
   Michael, 33
   Rachael, 33
Ysur, Eusevio, 117
   Maria Agli, 117
   Maria Crisantos, 117
Yturri, Blasade, 104

Zalazar, Antonio, 187
Zambrano, JuanAndres, 179
Zamora, Margarita, 101
   Mariana, 101
Zapata, Manuela, 106
Zepeda, Bizenta, 110

   Catarina, 99, 179
   Concepcion, 100
   Jose' Miguel, 84
   Josefa, 111
   Juan Fran<u>co</u>, 110
   Juan Jose', 84
   Man<u>l</u>, 84, 110, 184, 238
   Maria del Carmel, 84
   Mariana, 110
   Rosalia, 110
   Vicente, 179
Zerda, Nemecio Andres, 179
   Pedro de la, 179
Ziegler, Edmund, 209
Ziekanski, John D., 20
Zimenes, Gil, 238
Zorlosols, Polonio, 229
Zotelo, Ypolito, 93
Zoto, Bisente, 99
   Fran<u>co</u> Man<u>l</u>, 99
   Juan, 99
   Man<u>l</u>, 110
   Maria Pabla, 179
   M<u>a</u> del Rosario, 93
   Miguel, 189
Zuber, Abraha<u>m</u>, 179
   W<u>m</u> P., 179
Zumwalt, Abraham, 70
   Adam, 71, 189
   Adam 2d, 72
Zunega, Jose', 179
   Maria Candida, 186

www.ingramcontent.com/pod-product-compliance
Lightning Source LLC
Chambersburg PA
CBHW051117160426
43195CB00014B/2247